THE AMBIVALENT CONSUMER

THE AMBIVALENT CONSUMER

Questioning Consumption in East Asia and the West

EDITED BY

Sheldon Garon and Patricia L. Maclachlan

CORNELL UNIVERSITY PRESS
ITHACA AND LONDON

Copyright © 2006 by Cornell University

All rights reserved. Except for brief quotations in a review, this book, or parts thereof, must not be reproduced in any form without permission in writing from the publisher. For information, address Cornell University Press, Sage House, 512 East State Street, Ithaca, New York 14850.

First published 2006 by Cornell University Press
First printing, Cornell Paperbacks, 2006

Printed in the United States of America

Library of Congress Cataloging-in-Publication Data

The ambivalent consumer : questioning consumption in East Asia and the West / edited by Sheldon Garon and Patricia L. Maclachlan.
p. cm.
Includes bibliographical references and index.
ISBN-13: 978-0-8014-4487-6 (cloth : alk. paper)
ISBN-10: 0-8014-4487-X (cloth : alk. paper)
ISBN-13: 978-0-8014-7302-9 (pbk : alk. paper)
ISBN-10: 0-8014-7302-0 (pbk : alk. paper)
1. Consumption (Economics) 2. Consumption (Economics)—East Asia. I. Garon, Sheldon M. II. Maclachlan, Patricia L.
HB820.A45 2006
339.4′7—dc22

2006007160

Cornell University Press strives to use environmentally responsible suppliers and materials to the fullest extent possible in the publishing of its books. Such materials include vegetable-based, low-VOC inks and acid-free papers that are recycled, totally chlorine-free, or partly composed of nonwood fibers. For further information, visit our website at www.cornellpress.cornell.edu.

Cloth printing 10 9 8 7 6 5 4 3 2 1
Paperback printing 10 9 8 7 6 5 4 3 2 1

CONTENTS

ACKNOWLEDGMENTS

This volume took shape over the course of two "Writers' Workshops," the first in April 2003 at the Arden Homestead in Harriman, New York, and the second at the International House of Japan in Tokyo. These highly stimulating meetings would not have been possible without the generous support of the CGP-SSRC Seminar Series, which is funded by the Japan Foundation Center for Global Partnership and administered by the staff of the Abe Fellowship Program at the Social Science Research Council in New York and Tokyo. In addition, Sheldon Garon and Sven Steinmo received Abe Fellowships in support of the research presented in their respective chapters.

We would like to thank several individuals who assisted us at various stages of this project. We are grateful to the SSRC's Ellen Perecman and Asia Sherman and to Takuya Toda for planning the New York and Tokyo meetings, respectively. We also thank Okazaki Ryoko and Masunaga Rei of the Bank of Japan and Sophia University's Linda Grove for their valuable contributions as discussants at the Tokyo workshop. We are indebted to Frank Baldwin from the SSRC's Tokyo office; his professionalism and friendship have been instrumental in bringing this volume to fruition.

Princeton University's Molly Loberg performed admirably as our rapporteur. Along with Rena Lauer, she provided invaluable support in the preparation of the manuscript. We also thank Cornell University Press, especially Roger Haydon, and the two anonymous reviewers for helping us hone our arguments.

Working on this project has been a privilege and a pleasure, thanks to the outstanding contributions of our authors. We deeply appreciate their hard work, high standards, and illuminating insights into the dynamics of contemporary consumption.

Finally, a note on language. Following East Asian practice, Japanese, Korean, and Chinese surnames precede given names, excepting those East Asians whose English-language works have been cited.

NOTES ON CONTRIBUTORS

TAKATSUGU AKAISHI is associate professor in the department of economics at Nagasaki University.

LIZABETH COHEN is the Howard Mumford Jones Professor of American Studies in the department of history and the American civilization program at Harvard University.

DEBORAH S. DAVIS is professor of sociology at Yale University.

SHELDON GARON is professor of history and East Asian studies at Princeton University.

ANDREW GORDON is the Lee and Juliet Folger Fund Professor of History at Harvard University.

CHARLES YUJI HORIOKA is professor of economics at the Institute of Social and Economic Research at Osaka University.

PATRICIA L. MACLACHLAN is associate professor of Asian studies and government at the University of Texas at Austin.

LAURA C. NELSON is assistant professor of anthropology at California State University, East Bay.

TAKAO NISHIMURA is professor of consumer studies in the department of education and human science, Yokohama National University.

JORDAN SAND is associate professor of Japanese history and culture at Georgetown University.

SVEN STEINMO is professor of political science at the University of Colorado at Boulder.

FRANK TRENTMANN is senior lecturer in history at Birkbeck College at the University of London and director of Britain's Cultures of Consumption research program (funded by the Economic and Social Research Council and the Arts and Humanities Research Council).

SHUNYA YOSHIMI is professor at the Institute of Socio-Information and Communication Studies at Tokyo University.

THE AMBIVALENT CONSUMER

INTRODUCTION

SHELDON GARON AND PATRICIA L. MACLACHLAN

In 1930, Sigmund Freud published his famous polemic, *Das Unbehagen in der Kultur.* The book would later be translated as *Civilization and Its Discontents,* though Dr. Freud himself had proposed the English title "Man's Discomfort in Civilization." The thesis was blunt but memorable: "What we call our civilization is largely responsible for our misery . . . we should be much happier if we gave it up and returned to primitive conditions." Freud granted the seductive quality of civilization (*Kultur*), particularly its recent advances in science and technology. People, he grudged, do feel some "positive gain in pleasure" through modern medicine or telephoning one's child who lives hundreds of miles away. Yet such advances do not "make them feel happier," protested Freud: "What good to us is a long life if it is difficult and barren of joys, and it is so full of misery that we can only welcome death as a deliverer?"[1]

Freud bitterly rejected civilization itself. At the turn of the twentieth-first century, others likewise assert that human advances have generated serious "discontents," yet they do not repudiate the advances per se. That has been the message of several books entitled *Globalization and Its Discontents,* most notably the 2002 bestseller by the World Bank's former chief economist, Joseph Stiglitz. To Stiglitz, the "discontents" issue from the failure of globalization to bring promised benefits to much of the developing world. Blame for this failure, he argues, lies not with closer integration of national economies—at base a good thing—but rather with the imposition of the

[1] Sigmund Freud, *Civilization and Its Discontents,* trans. and ed. James Strachey (New York: W. W. Norton, 1961), 5–6, 33, 34–35.

America-centered "free market mantra," which has robbed nations of the sovereign right to adopt developmental strategies that would safeguard and improve the lives of their people.[2] As witnessed by recent protests and resistance in the third world and the first world alike, American-style globalization has hardly been welcomed by all, and its discontents have surfaced as political and economic problems that cannot be ignored.

Similarly, this volume analyzes the discontents, ambivalence, and dilemmas aroused by the global spread of another "American" phenomenon—that of mass consumption or consumer culture. To be sure, few people in the world are opposed to something as pleasurable as consumption. Proffering human happiness in the ever-increasing supply of affordable goods and services, consumer culture is far more attractive than Freud's "civilization," which the psychoanalyst blamed for *repressing* human desires. Indeed, it has become an article of faith in American culture that the greater good of society is best measured by the consumer's right to buy things at the cheapest price. As one "Yale-educated" employee of Wal-Mart recently asked, are the critics of the company's labor practices "prepared to tell the American people that they can no longer have a $7 polo shirt?" Every week, "millions of Americans find something they need or want at a Wal-Mart store, at a price that *empowers* them to buy it."[3] Consumption, in short, occupies a prominent place in the economic and cultural landscape of the United States today.

Yet as the following chapters reveal, large numbers of people—even entire societies—remain openly ambivalent about American-led global trends that privilege the consumer and consumption. In contemporary South Korea, writes Laura C. Nelson, "no act of consumption is innocent." While Koreans have steadily increased their levels of consumption over the past two decades, they continually question each other about everyday consumer choices. Does a particular purchase constitute "excessive consumption" or morally "appropriate consumption"? Have consumers patriotically favored Korean products or succumbed to foreign "luxuries"? Have they impeded their family's and nation's development by spending too much and saving too little? In neighboring Japan, decades of thrift campaigns have likewise deepened popular anxieties about high-level consumption while encouraging greater saving. Americans remain mystified that Japanese households would have chosen to economize over the past fifteen years, rather than spend freely and thereby jump-start their economy. In these societies and elsewhere, the ambivalent consumer regularly ponders

[2] Joseph E. Stiglitz, *Globalization and Its Discontents* (New York: W. W. Norton, 2002), 16; see also Saskia Sassen, *Globalization and Its Discontents* (New York: New Press, 1998) and Roger Burbach et al., *Globalization and Its Discontents: The Rise of Postmodern Socialisms* (London: Pluto Press, 1996).

[3] Emphasis added. Neylan McBaine, Letter to the Editor, *New York Times,* August 1, 2004, sec. 4, p. 10.

the tradeoffs between individual consumption and other needs such as saving, investment, social services, and a clean and safe environment.

By profiling the discontents and dilemmas surrounding mass consumption, we illuminate some of the key problems in the globalization of consumer culture. A growing body of scholarship tells the story of "consumer revolutions" in various parts of the globe. New products abound; people increase their spending; the masses come to participate in the purchase of goods and services. Much of this work focuses on the rise of "consumer societies" in the United States, Britain and, to a lesser extent, Western Europe.[4] These studies also highlight the simultaneity of the American, British, and West German consumer revolutions following World War II. Although Europeans initially resisted mass consumption in the decades before 1945, "the most significant conquest of the twentieth century may well have been the triumph of American consumer society over Europe's bourgeois civilization," writes Victoria De Grazia.[5] Likewise, historians increasingly argue that the Japanese embraced the American-style promotion of domestic consumption as a key to economic growth during the 1950s.[6] As for China and other rapidly developing Asian economies, American observers are fond of predicting that Asian consumers will invariably follow their western counterparts in abandoning thrift and reveling in credit-card purchases.[7]

This volume questions the assumption that all consumer revolutions are fundamentally alike or are converging toward the endpoint of the American model. We provide a more open-ended analysis of the globalization of consumerism, examining how a variety of nations have been both attracted and repelled by the phenomenon of rising consumption. To investigate ambivalence and dilemmas in consumer cultures, we offer a comparative perspective that may strike readers as unconventional. Comparative volumes on consumption are generally dominated by essays on the United States, Britain, and Western Europe. American consumer society necessarily serves as the reference point against which other cases are measured. In this volume, although several chapters discuss issues of consumption in Europe and the United States, the great majority deal—comparatively or

[4] See Victoria de Grazia, ed., *The Sex of Things: Gender and Consumption in Historical Perspective* (Berkeley: University of California Press, 1996); Martin Daunton and Matthew Hilton, eds., *The Politics of Consumption: Material Culture and Citizenship in Europe and America* (Oxford: Berg, 2001); and Susan Strasser, Charles McGovern, and Matthias Judt, eds., *Getting and Spending: European and American Consumer Societies in the Twentieth Century* (Cambridge: Cambridge University Press, 1998).

[5] Victoria de Grazia, *Irresistible Empire: America's Advance through Twentieth-Century Europe* (Cambridge: Belknap Press of Harvard University Press, 2005), jacket.

[6] Simon Partner, *Assembled in Japan: Electrical Goods and the Making of the Japanese Consumer* (Berkeley: University of California Press), 3.

[7] See, for instance, Walter Russell Mead, "The Real Asian Miracle; Asia Devalued," *New York Times Magazine,* May 31, 1998, 38.

solely—with Japan and other Asian societies. Japan thus serves as the comparative base from which we study consumer cultures globally.

Our focus on Japan provides a fresh way of examining ambivalence toward consumerism throughout the world. Japan has long embodied the tensions of a modern consumer society. Since the 1920s its densely populated cities have been home to a vibrant culture of department stores, mass entertainment, and one of the most highly developed advertising industries on earth. As the world's second largest economy, Japan today conjures up images of expensively attired consumers with insatiable appetites for the latest in gadgetry. At the same time, Japanese policies and culture manifest profound ambivalence toward consumption when it seems to threaten notions of morality, thrift, community, and national production. During the postwar era, the Japanese people emerged as the exemplar of a thrifty nation, saving some 23 percent of disposable income by the mid-1970s.

Just as America provided the model for consumer revolutions, Japan has generated transnational discourses on consumption and saving that have shaped debates in other countries. One thinks back to the "trade wars" of the 1980s and early 1990s, when rival approaches to consumption lay at the heart of U.S.-Japanese tensions. The U.S. government demanded that the Japanese stop "oversaving" and instead stimulate consumer demand. Japanese leaders shot back with a condemnation of the United States for having lost its equilibrium in an orgy of consumption. The most effective way for the U.S. government to reduce its massive fiscal deficits, the Japanese insisted, was to curb the American people's "excessive consumption" by aggressively promoting saving and severely restricting credit cards.[8] Indeed, critics of the U.S. economy at the time advocated adoption of a "Japanese model" that would raise household savings and invest the capital in American industries.[9] In the rest of Asia, the Japanese experience has significantly influenced the developmental strategies of the region's rapidly growing economies over the past four decades. Unable or unwilling to foment an American "consumer revolution," several Asian leaders sought instead to replicate postwar Japan's "economic miracle" by promoting saving and investment while restraining consumption (Garon, chap. 7).

The comparative study of the Japanese case also prompts a scholarly reassessment of the role of discontents and dilemmas in other advanced consumer cultures. It is tempting to explain Japanese or Korean anxieties simply in terms of cultural differences with "the West." Yet many European nations exhibit remarkably similar ambivalences toward consumption. Germans are famous for local regulations that close many stores at 2 p.m. on Saturday and all of Sunday. To the bewilderment of American observ-

[8] *Yomiuri shinbun,* October 28, 1990, 11.

[9] Beginning with Chalmers Johnson, *MITI and the Japanese Miracle: The Growth of Industrial Policy, 1925–1975* (Stanford: Stanford University Press, 1982), 313.

ers, they forego extra sales in favor of giving shopkeepers time to be with their families.[10] Moreover, few continental European polities display unqualified enthusiasm for the American-style expansion of consumption based on consumer debt, particularly credit cards. On the contrary, European governments—and now the European Union—have moved aggressively to prevent "overindebtedness" among their peoples, believing it to be a major source of poverty. In Belgium, a model for the EU's measures, regulations require that the names of all legally defined "overindebted" individuals be reported to a bureau of the central bank, which then activates an array of social services to help consolidate the individual's debts and stabilize the household.[11] And in an issue that unites globalization's and consumer culture's discontents, notes Patricia L. Maclachlan (chap. 10), large numbers of consumers in Europe and Japan, motivated by political and cultural anxieties that go well beyond safety considerations, oppose the sale of genetically modified (GM) foods. Nor should we assume that Europeans consume as much as Americans. As Charles Yuji Horioka demonstrates, the Germans, Italians, and French more closely resemble the historically frugal Japanese in their saving rates and consumption levels than they do the free-spending Americans. This is not to say that European or East Asian polities are hostile to the expansion of consumption. In these countries, too, national leaders, economists, and laymen generally agree that consumption is a driving force behind the health and prosperity of the national economy. Nonetheless, many societies have been willing to adopt measures that may constrain consumption in the interests of higher priorities. Sven Steinmo and Takatsugu Akaishi describe one such choice in the case of Sweden's high consumption taxes, which Social Democratic governments instituted to help finance the welfare state.

The Asian and European cases further encourage scholars to take a closer look at consumer culture's discontents within contemporary American society. America, too, has had a long history of ambivalence toward consumption and debt. The much-read Benjamin Franklin warned against ruinous extravagances, and moral reformers—most potently in the case of Prohibition—campaigned to eliminate allegedly wasteful and sinful consumption. While transplanted European intellectuals of the Frankfurt School critiqued mass consumption at the theoretical level, jeremiads such as John Kenneth Galbraith's *The Affluent Society* (1958) and Vance Packard's *The Hidden Persuaders* (1957) found broad audiences. In *The Waste Makers* (1960), Packard castigated "consumerism" and the accompanying

[10] *New York Times,* February 26, 2002, sec. C, p. 5.

[11] Gianni Betti, Neil Dourmashkin, Maria Cristina Rossi, Vijay Verma, and Yaping Yin, "Study of the Problem of Consumer Indebtedness: Statistical Aspects," Final Report, Commission of the European Communities, Directorate-General for Health and Consumer Protection (London: ORC Macro, 2001), 5, 43; and National Bank of Belgium, Central Office of Credits to Private Individuals, http://www.nbb.be/Sg/En/Produits/publication/4370e.htm.

marketing strategies that "would make Americans in large numbers into voracious, wasteful, compulsive consumers."[12] These critiques appear, in retrospect, little more than rearguard actions against the unparalleled development of mass consumption in the United States following World War II. To an extent not seen in the rest of the world, as Lizabeth Cohen describes in chapter 2, Americans embraced consumption as the ultimate objective of politics, economics, and society.[13] And yet the discomforts remain close to the surface. In contrast to East Asian and Western European citizens, rarely does the ambivalent American consumer join others in political resistance to consumerism—confined for the most part to subcultures of environmentalists, labor opponents of free-trade agreements, or organizers of "Buy Nothing Days." Nonetheless, discontents fester among the millions of Americans who currently struggle with staggering levels of consumer debt.[14] One need only look at the proliferation of debt-counseling services, self-help groups, and personal finance books—many of which are associated with the growing force of evangelical Christianity.[15] Although an in-depth study of American consumer culture is beyond the scope of this volume, our comparative analysis may advance the rigorous discussion of not only the triumph of consumerism in the United States but also the persistence of ambivalence toward it.

Thanks to generous funding by the Social Science Research Council and the Japan Foundation's Center for Global Partnership, we were able to bring together leading scholars of Japan, the United States, Europe, South Korea, and China. In two lively workshops, the contributors took advantage of the unusual opportunity to exchange thoughts across national, regional, and disciplinary divides in ways that enhance the comparative potential of this project. Our authors include historians, political scientists, cultural studies specialists, an economist, an anthropologist, and a sociologist. Trained in economics and education, Takao Nishimura offers the unusual perspective of a practitioner, having worked with the Japanese government to develop programs of financial education for consumers. Our respective methodologies and disciplines, we believe, permit a more integrated and multifaceted analysis of consumer cultures in the modern world.

[12] Vance Packard, *The Waste Makers* (New York: David McKay, 1960), 24–25. See also Max Horkheimer and Theodor W. Adorno, *Dialectic of Enlightenment,* trans. John Cumming (New York: Seabury Press, 1972).

[13] See also Gary Cross, *An All-Consuming Century: Why Commercialism Won in Modern America* (New York: Columbia University Press, 2000), 11–13.

[14] Teresa A. Sullivan, Elizabeth Warren, and Jay Lawrence Westbrook, *The Fragile Middle Class: Americans in Debt* (New Haven: Yale University Press, 2000).

[15] See, for example, Larry Burkett, *Debt-Free Living: How to Get Out of Debt (And Stay Out)* (Chicago: Moody, 2000). The book aims to "equip individuals with sound biblical principles and solid practical advice" (back cover).

Situating Consumption and the Consumer

Scholars tend to study consumption in isolation from other behaviors, ideologies, and identities. Not so long ago, historians approached the last hundred years as the story of unparalleled violence or the development of industrial society. Now, two historians of Germany observe, it is the consumer who has "emerged as the most readily recognized subject of twentieth-century history, the allure of mobility and abundance replacing the fascination with firepower."[16] Contemporary American discourse goes one step further. The consumer is not only the subject but also the "sovereign." From economics to politics, the *public* good is increasingly measured by the degree to which the *individual* consumer receives choice, the lowest price, and perfect information.

This volume moves beyond conventional American definitions of the consumer as a self-interested economic actor. Embracing a more dynamic, multifaceted conceptualization, the chapters reinsert consumers into their evolving societies, polities, and cultures. Like all human beings, consumers have juggled multiple and often contending identities. How they navigate among these identities has varied across time and space. We begin appropriately with Frank Trentmann's historical essay, which cautions us against reading the current American understanding of "the consumer" onto anyone who has purchased goods and services over the last three hundred years. Until recent decades, those whom we today call "consumers" rarely identified themselves as self-interested, acquisitive consumers but rather as patriots, producers, socially minded citizens, or watchdogs against the wasteful use of resources. In a recent book, Patricia L. Maclachlan similarly explores the consumer's multiple identities in the Japanese context while offering new ways of envisioning the consumer elsewhere. Sensitive to the negative connotations of selfishness and "waste" in the Japanese word for consumption (*shōhi*), consumers there constructed an identity that moved beyond the act of purchasing to embrace some of the interests of producers and national citizens. To the surprise of American economists and trade negotiators, Japanese consumers have often made common cause with producers and government to keep foreign products out of the domestic market and to protect the livelihoods of workers, farmers, and shopkeepers.[17] As Steven Vogel notes, these alliances may defy American conceptualizations of consumer rationality, but they make good sense when measured against the economic and political contingencies of the

[16] Konrad H. Jarausch and Michael Geyer, *Shattered Past: Reconstructing German Histories* (Princeton: Princeton University Press, 2003), 269.

[17] Patricia L. Maclachlan, *Consumer Politics in Postwar Japan: The Institutional Boundaries of Citizen Activism* (New York: Columbia University Press, 2002), 78–82.

Japanese context.[18] Contributors to this volume broaden our understandings of the consumer and consumption, notably in relation to the following phenomena:

Citizenship. Several chapters describe the emergence of "citizen-consumers." The empowerment of consumers has been an important element in democratization in many modern societies. Like workers before them, consumers have struggled to find a collective voice and to secure the rights to be informed, to be protected, and to participate in decision-making. Deborah S. Davis reports on this contest in contemporary China, where the Communist party-state strives to maintain a political monopoly while explicitly encouraging mass consumption and the massive privatization of property. Taking advantage of newly granted legal rights, homeowners have experimented with consumer representation by organizing homeowners' committees. These committees, Davis argues, represent a deepening of consumer consciousness among Chinese citizens, not to mention a potential challenge to political authority.

In other chapters, we see consumers taking an expansive view of citizenship that goes well beyond their self-interests as consumers. Japanese and British consumer advocates have put considerable pressure on their governments to maintain the safety of food for all citizens, with Japanese activists further opposing the import of genetically modified (GM) foods on the grounds that it endangers the livelihoods of their fellow citizens, the farmers (Maclachlan, chap. 10). In Europe and the United States a century ago, consumer groups similarly encouraged people to shop in a socially responsible manner that improved the welfare of workers and shop employees (Trentmann, chap. 1). In early postwar America too, government, business, and labor explicitly promoted mass consumption to advance democratic citizenship and an egalitarian society. The consumer had the "civic responsibility" to create well-paying manufacturing jobs and improve the living standards of all Americans (Cohen, chap. 2). Consumers have also identified themselves as global citizens when boycotting the products of sweatshop labor, purchasing "fair trade" commodities, or supporting free trade to stimulate job growth in poorer nations.[19]

Production and the National Economy. This volume also analyzes the complex ways in which the consumer interacts with production and the modern nation-state. During the nineteenth century and the first half of the twentieth century, states and societies generally subordinated domestic consumption to production in their visions of the national economy. Neo-

[18] Steven K. Vogel, "When Interests are Not Preferences: The Cautionary Tale of Japanese Consumers," *Comparative Politics* 31 (January 1999): 187–207.

[19] See also Patricia L. Maclachlan and Frank Trentmann, "Civilising Markets: Traditions of Consumer Politics in Twentieth-Century Britain, Japan, and the United States," in *Markets in Historical Contexts: Ideas and Politics in the Modern World,* ed. Mark Bevir and Frank Trentmann (Cambridge: Cambridge University Press, 2004), 170–201.

mercantilist thinking dominated in continental Europe and Japan, where governments protected domestic producers and favored exporters. Moreover, with democratization, the political clout of producers—businesses, farmers, and workers—overpowered the inchoate interests of "consumers." The two world wars reinforced official perceptions of personal consumption as inversely related to the national priorities of fighting inflation and financing wars. During and immediately after World War I, from Germany and Britain to Japan, the term *consumption* gained wide currency in the context of persuading "the consumer" to economize, not to spend.[20]

Following World War II as well, British governments admonished citizens to defer consumption for the sake of investment in British production, jobs, and Cold War defense. In the words of Labour's Chancellor of the Exchequer Stafford Cripps, "If we consume too many of the goods which we produce ourselves, we cannot export them; and if, in the process, we force up our costs and so our prices, we shall lose our export markets."[21] Or as Winston Churchill stated in 1951: "The defence programme requires a diversion of goods and services from the consumer—that is *from* you and me—to the national needs—that is *for* you and me."[22] As global consumer markets expanded in the postwar years, Japan, South Korea, and other Asian economies went further to privilege export-led development over the growth of domestic consumption.

Conversely, societies and states have often *promoted* consumption—not simply for individual betterment but also to stimulate national production and employment. The relationship between consumption and production varies considerably in our cases, across space and time. American consumers of the 1950s related their purchases to creating good jobs for their countrymen. Yet as imports increasingly vied with domestic manufactures, the link between the American consumer and the American producer weakened to the point that policymakers have become preoccupied with raising the level of aggregate consumption regardless of where the goods are produced. The American "citizen consumer" who once considered the general good has given way to the self-interested "purchaser consumer," who simply buys things.[23]

[20] See chapter 1. See also Sheldon Garon, "Fashioning a Culture of Diligence and Thrift: Savings and Frugality Campaigns in Japan, 1900–1931," in *Japan's Competing Modernities: Issues in Culture and Democracy*, ed. Sharon A. Minichiello (Honolulu: University of Hawai'i Press, 1998), 319.

[21] "The Economic Debate: The Danger of Inflation," *National Savings* 7, no. 2 (1949): 15, NSC 3/14, Public Record Office, London.

[22] "Lend Strength to Britain: The National Savings Campaign for 1951–1952," pamphlet to Local Committees, 1951; "Special Campaigns: Lend Strength to Britain Campaign, 1950–1952," NSC 7/183, Public Record Office, London.

[23] Lizabeth Cohen, *A Consumers' Republic: The Politics of Mass Consumption in Postwar America* (New York: Knopf, 2003), 8–9, 18–19.

Other industrial societies have been more selective in encouraging consumer spending, invariably promoting the consumption of their own manufactures. Ludwig Erhard, the acclaimed architect of West Germany's consumer-led growth, exhorted consumers to contribute to the country's industrial recovery by retaining their "German" sensitivity to the "good taste" and "quality" of goods made in West Germany.[24] During the 1950s and 1960s, Germans generally preferred these higher-priced "quality" goods over cheaper imported products[25] In what Nelson calls "consumer nationalism," East Asian consumers have been particularly influenced by government, business, and media campaigns to buy "national products." As in West Germany, Japanese consumption became bound up with a national pride in the technological sophistication of goods "Proudly Made in Japan," writes Shunya Yoshimi in chapter 3. In contemporary China, too, the leaders have channeled popular consumption toward the purchase of cars and other durables produced domestically (using high tariffs, for example, to induce foreign manufacturers to set up joint ventures in China).[26]

Saving and Consumer Credit. This volume is distinctive in the many chapters that relate consumption to other aspects of economic behavior, particularly saving. The qualities of saving and thrift rarely figure in the rapidly growing body of literature on consumer culture. When they do, they generally appear as older practices that had to be overcome before mass consumption could occur.[27] However, in both daily life and the macro-economy, saving and consumption are intimately related. In postwar Japan and recently in China, households steadily expanded their consumption levels while saving more of their disposable incomes (Garon, chap. 7; Davis, chap. 12). Several European nations also maintain relatively high saving rates and moderate levels of consumption (Horioka, chap. 5). Saving and spending, moreover, coexist with decisions to invest and borrow, as Andrew Gordon describes in his historical analysis of installment buying and the sewing machine (chap. 6). Even the high-saving Japanese, he reveals, have readily availed themselves of consumer credit, accumulating massive levels of consumer debt on a par with the United States since the late 1980s.

There is no one resolution to these apparent paradoxes, but the chapters suggest new ways of relating consumption to saving. Taken together, they critique the common conflation of mass consumption with modernity, and saving and economizing with the traditional past. In actuality, the modern histories of consumption and saving have been intertwined over

[24] Quoted in Erica Carter, *How German is She? Postwar West German Reconstruction and the Consuming Woman* (Ann Arbor: University of Michigan Press, 1997), 40. See also 19–20, 165.

[25] Jarausch and Geyer, *Shattered Past,* 285.

[26] *New York Times,* June 8, 2004, sec. W, p. 1.

[27] For example, Carter, *How German is She?* 232. See also 3, 55–59.

the past two centuries. The growth of surplus income and new consumer choices prompted households to "rationalize" their spending while planning for the future. The prudent consumers Trentmann describes in European societies reappear in the chapters on East and Southeast Asia. These people consume, of course, but to remain solvent, they also strive to eliminate "waste." In twentieth-century Japan and more recently in other Asian economies, the impetus both to increase and to restrain consumption often flowed from the same modern movements to introduce science, rationality, and financial discipline to daily life. Changes in gender roles cemented the close association between spending and thrift, as Japanese and South Korean women became primarily identified as modern "housewives" responsible for improving the family's consumer life while maximizing its savings.

The Discontents

Societies rarely oppose improvements in consumption, nor do they criticize "appropriate" consumption. However, precisely because consumption does not occur in isolation, ambivalence toward consumer culture often surfaces when people believe that consumption has become "excessive"—that is, when it threatens a culturally understood "balance" with morality, citizenship, production, saving, or the environment. Although the cases here are inflected by different histories, values, and relations to world markets, the chapters reveal several common threads in the structure of these discontents.

The Fear of Moral Decay. Criticism of avarice and praise for frugality have been cornerstones of an array of religions and beliefs, from Christianity to Confucianism and Buddhism. In modern times, these discontents manifested themselves in the widespread preoccupation with creating self-disciplined individuals who would not depend on the community or state. In the nineteenth-century western world and Japan, the independent person was one who eschewed unnecessary purchases, avoided debt, saved money, and abstained from self-destructive and socially harmful consumption (alcohol, tobacco, or narcotics). Samuel Smiles, the Victorian writer whose bestseller *Self-Help* (1859) was as influential in Japan as it was in the West, declared extravagance to be the "pervading sin of modern society." When "people live in a style beyond their means," the moral consequences follow in bankruptcies and "in criminal courts, where businessmen are so often convicted of dishonesty and fraud."[28] Such modern reformulations of traditional beliefs have proven to be very enduring. In the United States, too, observes one historian, the media has long covered the ever-increas-

[28] Samuel Smiles, *Thrift* (London: J. Murray, 1875), 252.

ing levels of consumer debt as a morality play, in which America declines into "a nation of bankrupts . . . and pleasure-seeking hedonists."[29] In places like contemporary South Korea, as Nelson vividly depicts, moralistic attacks on "excessive consumption" routinely affect consumer behavior.

In other instances, as Jordan Sand reminds us, ambivalence may take the form of a moral angst about consumer culture, rather than resistance to consumption per se. His chapter 4 examines the widespread uneasiness (*fuan*) with mass marketing and real-estate speculation in the Japan of the 1980s. Consumers and cultural critics longed for the Tokyo of bygone eras, when values of hard work, simple living, and community seemingly reigned. Ironically, he concludes, this yearning itself became commodified as a "nostalgic consumerism."

The Erosion of Collective Interests and Exacerbation of Social Inequality. Many societies have been troubled by the self-serving individualism inherent in consumerism. Personal consumption has appeared to divert resources from the monumental projects of war and postwar recovery. Urging cutbacks in spending, Britain's Chancellor of the Exchequer in 1949 called on citizens to "renounce and to denounce that easy-going get-rich-quick attitude to life."[30] Proponents of the welfare state have been wary of building an affluent, equitable society on the basis of empowered consumers. They have instead sought to "socialize" consumption among citizens by providing substantial universal services—education, health, and welfare—financed by high levels of taxation (Akaishi and Steinmo, chap. 9). In Japan and other Asian countries, nationalist leaders have commonly characterized excessive consumption as "self-indulgent" behavior that saps the nation's ability to generate domestic savings and capital and thereby achieve independence from foreign creditors (Garon, chap. 7; Nelson, chap. 8).

Then there are the pervasive anxieties that rampant consumption results in greater social inequality. Although its postwar champions in the United States insisted that mass consumption would *advance* equality and citizenship, Europeans and Asians have more commonly spotlighted the adverse social effects of consumer culture. Western Europe's postwar left wing and intelligentsia feared that consumption would weaken social solidarity and widen the gap between the haves and the have-nots. The early postwar Labour Party in Great Britain championed austerity policies not only to generate national savings but also to defuse the social tensions resulting from conspicuous consumption by the rich.[31] Half a world away,

[29] Lendal Calder, *Financing the American Dream: A Cultural History of Consumer Credit* (Princeton: Princeton University Press, 1999), 293–94.

[30] Stafford Cripps, in "The Economic Debate: The Danger of Inflation," 15.

[31] Jaraush and Geyer, *Shattered Past,* 302–3. On Britain, see Susan Cooper, "Snoek Piquante," in *Age of Austerity,* Michael Sissons and Philip French (London: Hodder and Stoughton, 1963), 33–54.

postwar Japanese governments often regarded the needs of individual consumers as impediments to their rather successful efforts to lessen socioeconomic inequality, including rural-urban inequality. Indeed, much of Japanese "welfare" has taken the form of granting protection and subsidies to millions of small farmers and petty retailers and wholesalers, whose tiny plots and unwieldy distribution systems keep consumer prices high (Akaishi and Steinmo, chap. 9). Moreover, in Japan as elsewhere in the world, consumers and political leaders worry about the effects of mass consumption on the cohesiveness of local communities. Japanese consumer advocates strongly supported the (now defunct) Large Scale Retail Store Law, which authorized the government to restrict the size of new stores that threatened a neighborhood's small retailers.[32] Similarly, South Koreans today continue to voice anxieties that consumer affluence has sparked class envy and eroded feelings of national unity (Nelson, chap. 8).

Anxieties about Environmental Degradation. In keeping with their evolving identity as "citizens," consumers pay increasing attention to the effects of consumption on the natural environment. In countries like Britain and Japan, consumer cooperative movements have long sought to harmonize consumer and environmental concerns. As they extol the virtues of consumer rights, these movements have also championed consumption patterns that contribute to "sustainable development." Recently, consumers in Europe and Japan have voiced opposition to farming practices that pose potential risks to local ecosystems, and they are "buying organic" in greater and greater numbers (Maclachlan, chap. 10). The consumer's preoccupation with environmentalism points to a holistic approach to consumption that defies neoliberal economic arguments, in which consumers are economic animals with short-term horizons.

Americanization and Its Many Discontents. This may be the most potent set of discontents today—at least in the rest of the world, where most people eagerly embrace consumption while coding *excessive* consumption as "American." Americans are hardly blameless in this formulation. From the early postwar era to the present, the U.S. government and business interests have aggressively marketed consumer culture as an integral part of the "American Way of Life" (Cohen, chap. 2; Yoshimi, chap. 3). The reaction to American-style consumer culture appears in many forms. The French in the 1950s became famous for their anti-American diatribes. Jean-Marie Domenach put it bluntly: "This almost unlimited capacity to acquire and to consume is the fundamental characteristic of the American model."[33] The American model of the consumer society, observes one historian, seemed to threaten France's independence, its civilized tastes, and the na-

[32] Maclachlan, *Consumer Politics*, 82, 271 n10.

[33] "Le modèle américain," *Esprit* (September 1960): 1368, quoted in Richard F. Kuisel, *Seducing the French: The Dilemma of Americanization* (Berkeley: University of California Press), 111.

tion's conceptions of "a balanced economy and traditional ways of production, selling, saving, and spending."[34] More recently, many societies—European and Asian—struggle to constrain what they regard as the American-led globalization of credit cards and GM foods.

In Asia, "America" often serves as a metaphorical siren song against which a balanced economy must seal its ears if it is to avoid dashing itself on the shoals of extreme consumerism. To be sure, in the early stages of Japan's high economic growth, policymakers and manufacturers explicitly promoted American lifestyles in stimulating the mass consumption of electrical appliances (Yoshimi, chap. 3). However, since the late 1970s, when the surging Japanese economy reached the point of becoming an American-style consumer culture, the media and politicians repeatedly warned the Japanese against catching the "American disease." Symptoms almost always include wasteful, hedonistic consumption. As depicted by Japan's top savings-promotion official in 1987, America is the cautionary tale of "excessive consumption resulting from the use of credit cards," where millions of households are up to their necks in consumer debt and where the "Puritan ethic of thrift" has rapidly declined.[35] In Japan, as Nishimura writes, one antidote to excessive debt has been the recent expansion of consumer education programs designed to prevent indebtedness or to help consumers cope with it. In South Korea "frugality campaigns" attempted to shield schoolchildren from foreign magazines lest they develop American consumer habits (Nelson, chap. 8). And in Singapore and Malaysia, the discourse of "Asian Values" contrasts Asian thrift with the degenerate materialism of Americans (Garon, chap. 7).

An All-Consuming Globalization?

Although the chapters in this volume examine the recent past and the present, they necessarily offer visions of the future that may interest policymakers, businesses, and consumer groups. Taken together, they challenge widely held assumptions that global consumer culture is overwhelming local difference, transforming nations into loose collections of acquisitive, self-interested consumers. Some aspects of globalization, as Davis and Nishimura observe, encourage East Asians to become informed, empowered, and socially minded consumers. Their essays make the important point that the world has been guided by more than one American model of "consumerism." When other nations look at the United States, they see not simply the unbridled consumption depicted in Packard's *The Waste*

[34] Kuisel, *Seducing the French,* 17

[35] Toyama Shigeru, *Nihonjin no kinben, chochikukan* [Japanese sense of diligence and thrift] (Tokyo: Tōyō keizai shinpōsha, 1987), 163–64.

Makers, but also the consumer activism unleashed by President John F. Kennedy's "Consumer Bill of Rights."[36] The Japanese consumer movement, for example, continues to be inspired by "Citizen Nader" while eschewing many of the practices of American-style consumption.

Above all, the chapters describe the ongoing interaction of local differences with the American-led global consumer culture. Gordon presents Japanese practices of consumer credit that surprisingly resemble the American model, while observing that decades of political deals and inculcated consumer behavior have retarded the rise of a full-blown "credit card nation."[37] Maclachlan notes the emergence of Japanese and European consumer activism against the perceived American invasion of GM foods. Moreover, in Asia, as Garon and Nelson argue, the globalization of consumer culture must also contend with the persistence of historically constructed discourses of frugality, thrift, social cohesiveness, and national or regional exceptionalism. At the same time, we are impressed by how differently the three largest East Asian polities have balanced global and local forces in recent years. Anxious about unemployment and their aging society, Japanese leaders and households have been the most reluctant to embrace American-style consumption. In China, ironically, the Communist leadership exuberantly promotes consumer spending, even as it seeks to contain consumer activism. South Korea falls somewhere in the middle, a veritable battleground between globalization and the nation. In just a few short years since the 1997 financial crisis, Korean policymakers have shifted from frugality campaigns to American policies of stimulating spending and credit card usage and finally, in 2003–2004, to a profound soul-searching as millions of households sank into credit-card debt and growth sputtered. At present, Korean officials are disinclined to return to the days of the frugality campaigns, while remaining acutely aware of the social costs of transforming their people into an Americanized credit card nation. The dilemmas facing East Asia remind us that although consumers are exposed to ever more powerful transnational currents, consumer cultures remain significantly shaped by local histories, politics, and institutions.

[36] In a speech to Congress in 1962, Kennedy articulated an informal policy consisting of the consumer's rights to safety, to choice, to know, and to be heard.

[37] A reference to Robert D. Manning, *Credit Card Nation: The Consequences of America's Addiction to Credit* (New York: Basic Books, 2000).

PART I

CULTURES OF CONSUMPTION

The ambivalence people feel toward mass consumption reflects the existence in the modern world not of one culture of consumption, but of many. All too often we view other times and places through the lens of present-day America, ascribing one-size-fits-all meanings to such concepts as "the consumer," "consumer society," and "consumer culture." Beginning with eighteenth-century Europe and ending with the prosperous Japan of the 1980s, the four chapters in part I examine key developments in the global evolution of consumer cultures. But rather than tell a simple story of how "western" consumer-centered culture spread to the rest of the world, they highlight the ways in which local cultural and political circumstances have shaped a variety of understandings of consumption and the consumer.

For the purposes of this volume, Frank Trentmann's chapter may be read as a history of the origins of the consumer as a central agent in the political economies of Europe and the United States. Although early modern societies in East Asia experienced their own upsurges in consumption, western formulations of the consumer profoundly influenced thinking in modern Japan, China, and Korea—indeed, the terms for *consumption* and *consumer* in each language did not appear until the early twentieth century, initially in translations of western tracts. At the same time, Trentmann reminds us that even in the West, societies have by no means agreed on the place of the consumer and consumption. Seldom in his survey of the nineteenth and early twentieth centuries does he find the current American image of the consumer as an autonomous individual who pursues his or her desires and stimulates the economy by purchasing goods and services. Germans and French were reluctant to envision a universal "consumer" whose interests would stand above those of nation or class, while liberal Britons promoted a socially responsible consumer who was more citizen than purchaser. Trentmann confines his analysis to the years before post–World War II affluence, yet the ambiguities and ambivalence that he describes resonate today in attitudes toward consumption in Europe as well as in Asia.

Lizabeth Cohen continues the story by examining the particular circumstances that gave rise to postwar America's explicitly consumer-centered culture, which itself became an export model for the rest of the world. In its earliest years following the shared sacrifices of World War II, this "Consumers' Republic" too had to justify itself in a culture still ambivalent about the self-interested, hedonistic aspects of consumption. Accordingly, its American apostles promoted a multidimensional citizen-consumer whose spending would improve the lives of American workers, thereby advancing equality and democracy. In reality, concludes Cohen, suburban housing and shopping centers often widened social gaps and eroded the sense of community, while the consumer increasingly became a mere purchaser of goods oblivious to whether they were made at home or abroad. Although Americans rarely spoke about social consequences of mass consumption, Europeans and Asians remained ambivalent about this American model, which seemingly raised living standards and drove the economy—at the expense of social cohesion.

Despite varying degrees of ambivalence, all of the postwar industrial societies ended up stimulating consumer demand to further economic growth. Nevertheless, as Shunya Yoshimi suggests in his chapter on Japan, the emerging cultures of consumption were not simply made in America. To be sure, urban Japanese directly encountered America's servicemen and popular culture during and shortly after the Allied Occupation (1945–52), and many came to admire America's rich consumer life. Yet when Japan reached the stage of mass consumption around 1960, the new consumer culture represented itself as proudly "Japanese." It revolved not around Coca-Cola and blue jeans but rather home appliances produced domestically and marketed nationalistically as the products of Japan's distinctive technological prowess and even imperial tradition. Moreover, much more than in Trentmann's Britain or Cohen's America, where the gendered role of the consumer remained ambiguous, postwar Japan's consumer culture clearly defined the consumer as the rational "Japanese" housewife (a point made elsewhere in this volume).

In the final chapter of part I, Jordan Sand dissects the widespread ambivalence toward Japan's mature consumer culture at the highpoint of the nation's economic success during the 1980s. This uneasiness, he notes, was decidedly "postmodern"—detached from a genuine historical awareness of the past—and it took the form of a nostalgic consumption of eras predating the nation's consumer revolution. Unlike Yoshimi's exuberant consumers of 1960, Sand's ambivalent consumers made little effort to distinguish "Japanese" consumer culture from its American variant. Instead they decried the rise of a deracinated, global consumer culture that had robbed Tokyo of its traditional vitality and "Asian-ness." Sand raises some important issues for this volume: To what extent should ambivalence about consumerism be interpreted primarily as a form of cultural expression—a discomfort or angst with the general conditions of modernity? And under what circumstances has ambivalence prompted political and economic responses, such as consumer nationalism, saving, regulation of credit, and anti-GM food movements?

1

THE EVOLUTION OF THE CONSUMER

Meanings, Identities, and Political Synapses Before the Age of Affluence

FRANK TRENTMANN

Consumers have been elusive characters. The sociologist Claus Offe has stressed that consumers do not form a "clearly delimitable and organizable complex of individuals. Rather they constitute an abstract category that defines certain aspects of the social actions of almost all individuals. Everyone and at the same time no one is a 'consumer.'"[1] This chapter takes this sociological observation in a historical direction and asks how and when this category evolved and why at certain historical moments (but not others) some groups (but not others) managed to arrive at a distinct sense of themselves as consumers.

"Consumption" has become widely recognized as a central or even dominant dimension in many societies—"the vanguard of history."[2] Donald Quataert has even presented modernity as marked by the "ascendancy of the consumer over the producer."[3] But who is this consumer? Three approaches dominate. The first pictures the consumer as representing a universal economic category. The second treats consumers simply as the

For their helpful comments, I am grateful to the editors, Mark Bevir, John Brewer, James Livesey, John Styles, Vanessa Taylor, and Donald Winch, and my colleagues in the Cultures of Consumption program. I also thank the Economic and Social Research Council and the Arts and Humanities Research Council (UK) for their generous research grant (L143341003). A longer discussion appears in John Brewer and Frank Trentmann, eds., *Consuming Cultures: Global Perspectives* (Oxford: Berg, forthcoming).

[1] Claus Offe, *Contradictions of the Welfare State* (Cambridge: MIT Press, 1984), 228.

[2] Daniel Miller, "Consumption as the Vanguard of History," in *Acknowledging Consumption,* ed. Daniel Miller (London: Routledge, 1995), 1–57.

[3] Donald Quataert, ed., *Consumption Studies and the History of the Ottoman Empire, 1550–1922* (Albany: State University of New York Press, 2000), 1.

natural product of a commodity culture that expanded from the eighteenth century. A third, more recent approach sees the "active consumer" as the product of contemporary social transformations. These approaches share an essentialist, under-historicized view of the consumer. Whether conceived as free (neoliberal economics), manipulated (Frankfurt School), or discursively constructed (postmodernism), consumers are taken as given.

Yet, if consumption is a universal aspect of human culture, it is also a disparate form of social practice that has been tied to a multitude of self- and collective identities. To describe purchasers or users as consumers in different settings might be convenient shorthand. But it does not *explain* how, when, where, and which actors began to conceive of themselves or others as consumers. This chapter offers a new, historicized narrative. Instead of drawing a straight line from market and commodity to consumer, or presenting a narrative of global convergence or Americanization, it argues for the uneven and contested evolution of the consumer, highlighting the role of agency and political conflict that energized the consumer in some societies in the nineteenth and early twentieth centuries—but not in others.

The configuration of consumers required political synapses, that is, political traditions and languages through which actors were able to connect material experiences to a sense of belonging, to interests and entitlements. We shall examine the contribution of these political synapses in two conjunctures in which the political status of "necessaries" became pivotal in the course of the nineteenth century. The first was the battle over accountability, access, and representation in nineteenth-century Britain that turned groups of users into articulate, organized, and increasingly demanding "water consumers." The second was global: rising economic nationalism, imperial tension, and a growing concern about the survival of national culture in an age of advancing globalization at the turn of the twentieth century. It was the synapses of political traditions, rather than just state power or material interests, that determined whether this mobilization of consumption led to a stronger vision of consumers (free trade Britain), was diluted by prior collective traditions of producers (Imperial Germany), or became a means for fostering alternative identities, such as the patriotic citizen (Republican China). World War I and the interwar years saw the consolidation of different traditions of consumers, a process shaped from within civil society (as much as by state or business) through discourses of ethics and citizenship (rather than neoclassical economics) and around questions of the social and political values guiding consumption (rather than simply affluence or an unreflective pursuit of commodities).

This genealogy of the consumer raises questions about the periodization of conventional narratives of consumer society and their teleological model of convergence around American "consumerism." Other chapters in this volume challenge the widely held view of the American model as a normal endpoint of development for modern societies. It isn't helpful, argues this chapter, to envision some ideal-typical American model of affluence as the starting point for critical inquiry. We unfold here instead an alternative genealogy of the consumer that points to contingency and diversity and to the centrality of political tradition, civil society, and ethics, through which agents have discovered themselves as active consumers.

"Consumer Revolution"? The Limited Formation of Consumer Identity in Eighteenth- and Early Nineteenth-Century Europe and America

The rich historiography on the "consumer revolution" of the early modern transatlantic world is a natural starting point in our search for the consumer. If viewing the upsurge in consumption as a uniquely "western" phenomenon has become debatable,[4] there can be little doubt that the commercial world of goods expanded quantitatively and qualitatively in an unprecedented fashion. By the mid-eighteenth century there was one shop for every forty-two people in Britain.[5] The working classes bought virtually all their food through markets and worked longer hours to enable them to buy more goods.[6] Exotic articles like tea, coffee, and tobacco had become "mass consumer" goods reaching more than 25 percent of the population in Britain and the American colonies. The consumption of cultural artifacts and services transformed the subjectivity of the middling sort and its cult of civility and sensibility.[7] In the very year that Adam Smith laid down the famous dictum that "consumption is the sole end of all production,"[8] American colonists declared their independence after a struggle that had begun with a series of nonconsumption protests. In Europe, the old century ended and the new began with a spate of bread and flour riots.

It is against this background that many commentators have argued for the rise of the consumer. The American Revolution, T. H. Breen has ar-

[4] Kenneth Pomeranz, *The Great Divergence: China, Europe, and the Making of the Modern World Economy* (Princeton: Princeton University Press, 2000).

[5] Carole Shammas, *The Pre-Industrial Consumer in England and America* (Oxford, Clarendon Press, 1990), 111, 145ff., 224ff.

[6] Hans-Joachim Voth, "Work and the Sirens of Consumption in Eighteenth-Century London," in *The Active Consumer: Novelty and Surprise in Consumer Choice*, ed. Marina Bianchi (London: Routledge, 1998), 143–73.

[7] See John Brewer, *Pleasures of the Imagination: English Culture in the Eighteenth Century* (New York: Farrar Straus Giroux, 1997) and Amanda Vickery, *The Gentleman's Daughter: Women's Lives in Georgian England* (New Haven: Yale University Press, 1998).

[8] Adam Smith, *The Wealth of Nations* (1776), book IV, ch. 8, ed. Edwin Cannan (Chicago: University of Chicago Press, 1904), 2:159.

gued, grew out of a consumer revolution. The boycotts of tea and other commodities were "rituals of non-consumption" through which political independence was discovered: "No previous rebellion had organized itself so centrally around the consumer."[9] The problem with Breen's argument is that it rests on an essentialist ascription of the consumer deduced from a shared material culture rather than from the colonists' self-understanding. Organizers of boycotts rallied their fellow "countrymen," "honest industrious patriot[s]," "freemen," or "Americans." The language of "consumers" was almost never used. The principal group identity invoked by John Dickinson in his influential *Late Regulations* was that of "the reputable freeholder," while it was "our merchants and the lower ranks of people" who were immiserated by the stamp duty. America was turning into a nation of debtors who needed to learn "strict frugality and industry, [so] we may render ourselves more independent of the merchants."[10] American colonists had two choices: they could supply more manufactures of their own or they could reduce imports by practicing what is today called "slow consumption," that is keep foreign manufactures longer in use. Far from unleashing "the consumer" on the world of politics, the American Revolution impeded its arrival: it was a battle between frugal patriots and Empire. Republicanism advertised an organic nationhood in which the imperative of home production and self-sufficiency muffled any sense of the independent existence, rights, or identities of consumers.

In eighteenth-century Europe and America, meanings and practices of consumption remained embedded in older social identities defined by craft, land, trade, and production.[11] The consumer makes an occasional appearance as a synonym for purchaser, as in Daniel Defoe's writings at the beginning of the eighteenth century or Emmanuel Joseph Sieyès's *Qu'est-ce que le tiers état?* towards its end,[12] but these rare references carried little weight in relation to collective interests endowed with recognized social or constitutional meanings. Defoe, who in 1728 compared the "large, populous, rich, fruitful" state of England and its "large, luxurious, vain and expensive . . . way of living" to the austere Dutch, limited his reference to "the consumer" to discussions of the value paid to a retailer.[13] Even after the

[9] T. H. Breen, "Narrative of Commercial Life: Consumption, Ideology, and Community on the Eve of the American Revolution," *William and Mary Quarterly* 50, no. 3 (July 1993): 471–501, quotation 486.

[10] [John Dickinson], *The Late Regulations Respecting the British Colonies on the Continent of America Considered* (London, 1766).

[11] Michael Sonenscher, *Work and Wages: Natural Law, Politics, and the Eighteenth-Century French Trades* (Cambridge: Cambridge University Press, 1989) and Jamie Bronstein, "Land Reform and Political Traditions in Nineteenth-Century Britain and the United States," in *Critiques of Capital in Modern Britain and America: Transatlantic Exchanges,* ed. Mark Bevir and Frank Trentmann (London: Palgrave, 2002), 26–48.

[12] Emmanuel Joseph Sieyès, *Qu'est-ce que le tiers état?* (Paris, 1789).

[13] Daniel Defoe, *A Plan of the English Commerce* (1728; repr. Oxford: Blackwell, 1928), 144, 154.

French Revolution, when deputies in Restoration France considered consumers' interests, it was only to render them insignificant compared to people's social station and the larger national interests represented by land, production, and trade.[14]

The many battles over basic provision and "just price" in food riots or complaints against corrupt traders in eighteenth- and early nineteenth-century Europe developed equally without a notion of the consumer. In France, food rioters were generally "the people," "'the poor' and 'workers,'" "petits laboureurs," or "women of the people."[15] Britons complaining about fraudulent weights and measures invoked the "good of the public" or "the poor people."[16] As late as the 1840s, Germans referred to the "lamentation of the people," "the public," or "rabble." Where they disaggregated these identities, it was by profession (e.g., clothmakers) or by age and gender ("old people, boys, apprentices, fellows, girls and old women").[17]

In early socialist thought, social categories of emancipation centered on the independent farmer and the independent artisan (versus the wage "slave"). Consumption was subordinate to the primacy of productive welfare: good consumption was collective consumption.[18] There was little room for the consumer as a separate identity in the increasingly masculine productivist language of independence and community[19] or in gendered notions of women's domestic sphere unsullied by the market. Women's boycotts against slave goods thus invoked a sympathetic femininity with its "'purely human' sympathy unpolluted by commercial desires."[20]

Where social groups embraced the expanding world of goods and where thinkers came to defend the public benefits from luxury, they did so by viewing consumption through cultural value systems and intellectual

[14] David Todd, "Before Free Trade: Commercial Discourse and Politics in Early Nineteenth Century France," in *Worlds of Political Economy,* ed. Martin Daunton and Frank Trentmann (London: Palgrave, 2004), 54–57.

[15] Cynthia A. Bouton, *The Flour War: Gender, Class, and Community in Late Ancien Regime French Society* (University Park: Pennsylvania State University Press, 1993), 83–85, 109.

[16] Avril D. Leadley, "Some Villains of the Eighteenth-Century Market Place," in *Outside the Law: Studies in Crime and Order 1650–1850,* ed. John Rule (Exeter: University of Exeter, 1982), 27.

[17] Manfred Gailus, *Strasse und Brot: Sozialer Protest in den deutschen Staaten unter besonderer Berücksichtigung Preussens, 1847–1849* (Göttingen: V&R, 1990), 220, 242, 246, 255, 266–74.

[18] See Noel Thompson, "Social Opulence, Private Asceticism: Ideas of Consumption in Early Socialist Thought," in *The Politics of Consumption: Material Culture and Citizenship in Europe and America,* ed. Martin Daunton and Matthew Hilton (Oxford: Berg, 2001), 51–68.

[19] Gareth Stedman Jones, "Rethinking Chartism," in *Languages of Class: Studies in English Working Class History, 1832–1982* (Cambridge: Cambridge University Press, 1983) and Gregory Claeys, "The Origins of the Rights of Labor: Republicanism, Commerce, and the Construction of Modern Social Theory in Britain, 1796–1805," *Journal of Modern History* 66, no. 2 (June 1994): 249–90.

[20] Kate Davies, "A Moral Purchase: Femininity, Commerce, and Abolition, 1788–1792," in *Women, Writing and the Public Sphere, 1700–1830,* ed. Elizabeth Eger and Charlotte Grant (Cambridge: Cambridge University Press, 2001), 150.

traditions that did not yet turn on the model of a consumer society. New cultures of consumption were first domesticated in the Dutch Golden Age, as luxury was turned inwards, toward home and body.[21] They then underwent a more public transvaluation as Scottish Enlightenment thinkers identified the social benefits of personal pleasures and self-interest. The appreciation of luxury must not be confused with consumer identity. Consumption as a public good was embedded in a vision of commercial society—not consumer society. Adam Smith used the consumer to illustrate technical aspects of the economy, such as the tax burden of mercantilism or the distribution of goods, and stressed that "in the mercantile system the interest of the consumer is almost constantly sacrificed to that of the producer."[22] For society and culture, however, the focus was firmly on commerce and merchants. "Where luxury nourishes commerce and industry," David Hume emphasized, "the peasants, by a proper cultivation of the land, become rich and independent: while the tradesmen and merchants acquire a share of the property, and draw authority and consideration to that middling rank of men, who are the best and firmest basis of public liberty."[23] Consumption was managed through a commercial society that elevated a specific social strata—the middling sort—rather than a universal consumer.

Will the Real Consumer Please Stand Up?

The conceptual evolution of "the consumer" before the middle of the nineteenth century, then, was limited, carrying little significance for social and political identities. Isolated instances of the consumer as a wasteful shopper can be traced back to the sixteenth century.[24] Well into the nineteenth century, however, the "consumer" mainly appeared with reference to particular physical or metaphysical processes of use and destruction. Consumers were individuals who used up energy resources or basic utilities (water, gas, coal, electricity)[25] or who were affected by particular consumption taxes, such as excise duties. German statutes for tobacco "consumption-factories," for example, regulated the prices. Traders and shopkeepers could charge "the consumer and common man."[26] Next to

[21] Jan de Vries, "Luxury in the Dutch Golden Age in Theory and Practice," in *Luxury in the Eighteenth Century: Debates, Desires, and Delectable Goods,* ed. Maxine Berg and Elizabeth Eger (Basingstoke: Palgrave, 2003), 41–56.

[22] Smith, *Wealth of Nations,* book IV, ch. 8, 2:159.

[23] David Hume, *Essays Moral, Political, and Literary* (1742; London: Oxford University Press, 1963), 284.

[24] See, for example, Angell Daye, *The English Secretorie* (London, 1586), 225.

[25] *The Coal Traders and Consumers Case* (London, [1692?]); Lawrence Duckworth, *The Consumer's Handbook of the Law relating to Gas, Water, and Electric Lighting* (London, 1903).

[26] *Preiss-Satzung, Nach welcher die aus denen Churfuerstl. Taback-Consumptions-Factorien zur Abnahm vorgelegte Sorten von denen Handels-Leuthen und craemeren hinwiderumben an den Consumenten und gemeinen Mann in Minuto abzugeben seynd* (1745).

this, an older use survived of referring to consumers in the metaphysical sense of devourers, likening them to time and death, "the two consumers of the whole world."[27]

If there were growing references to the "consumer" among economic writers, however, its socioeconomic status remained ambiguous and controversial well into the early twentieth century.[28] The late twentieth century saw a popular association between liberalism and the consumer that has all but eliminated our awareness of the disagreements among nineteenth-century liberal political economists about the place of consumers in economic theory and public policy. At one end of the spectrum stood J. B. Say, who included the "reproductive consumption" of goods in factories in a special section on consumption.[29] At the other end was J. S. Mill, who denied that consumption was a worthy subject for the science of political economy and associated such a view with the dangerous idea of underconsumption.[30]

Taxation was a crucial point of contact among economic knowledge, social mobilization, and the discursive broadening of the concept of the consumer, especially in nineteenth-century Britain. Debates about free trade and empire inserted "the consumer" into an expanding range of political relationships and material goods. Thus consumers of West Indian sugar made their case against slavery and duties in 1828.[31] The novelist James Fenimore Cooper in 1847 referred to "true free trade," meaning no taxation or restrictions whatsoever, not even free ports, since "the consumer" would still have to pay "customary impositions."[32]

Debates about who paid import duties helped solidify the persona of the consumer, and this in turn could result in an antinomy between social groups—"the producer and the consumer."[33] Yet this was not the inevitable outcome: the consumer had not yet narrowed to mean the private end user. Victorians spoke of the "consumer" as the "occupier" who bore the tax on the value of the house. In 1913, accounts of the London taxicab drivers' strike still used "consumers" to refer to users of petrol, not passengers.[34] The feminist socialist Teresa Billington-Greig's concern for the consumer expressed her belief in the union between consumption and

[27] Samuell Rowlands, *A Terrible Battell Betweene the Two Consumers of the Whole World: Time, and Death* (London, 1606).

[28] See Hans Mayer, "*Konsumtion,*" in *Handwoerterbuch der Staatswissenschaften,* 4th ed. (Jena: Gustav Fischer, 1923), 5:867–74.

[29] Jean Baptiste Say, *Traité d'économie politique* (Paris, 1814), III, ch. 2.

[30] John Stuart Mill, *Essays on Some Unsettled Questions of Political Economy* (London: J. W. Parker, 1844), 132.

[31] *The Consumers of West India Sugar* (London, 1828).

[32] James Fenimore Cooper, *The Crater, or, Vulcan's Peak* (New York: Burgess, Stringer, 1847), 123.

[33] See *Justitia, the Queen, and the Constitution, the Producer and the Consumer, or Protection, What Is It, and Where to Put It* (London, 1851). Note that Grimm's *Woerterbuch,* vol. 12 (1886), still did not have an entry on *Verbraucher* or *Konsument.*

[34] *The Times* (London), January 2, 1913, 8.

production.[35] In the free trade campaign, "the consumer" served as an organic category of the nation uniting the interests of shoppers with those of industrial consumers who imported raw materials.[36]

If it is problematic to draw a straight line from commodity culture to the consumer, it is similarly questionable to presume a correlation between the consumer and developments in "neoclassical" economics with its emphasis on rational utility-maximizing individuals. The marginalist revolution in the 1870s and 1880s would come to shape twentieth-century economics and marketing, but it was far from dominating the discourse of the consumer at the time. It was frequently outside or on the margins of market-oriented liberal economics that the discovery of the consumer took place in the late nineteenth century. In Germany, it was national economists like Wilhelm Roscher and Karl Oldenberg who saw a maturing consumer as an integral part in the cultivation of "strong people and strong nations" dominating others.[37] In the United States, the progressive Simon Patten saw selfish individuals as atavistic survivors of a past age of scarcity, which would give way to the socialized generosity of an age of abundance.[38] In Britain, the radical John Atkinson Hobson invoked a "citizen-consumer" whose material acts and desires would increasingly be informed by civic values.[39] And in France, the cooperator Charles Gide focused on collective action among consumers to advance the interests of society.[40] For all their differences, consumers were here mobilized for their civic and collective characteristics, not some inherent economic individualism.

From User to Consumer: The Victorian Battle over Water

The growing attention to the consumer in different intellectual traditions in the late nineteenth century did not occur in a vacuum but followed from a discursive and sociopolitical strengthening of the consumer as a category of identity, social praxis, and persona with legal and political rights. At the same time, the politics of taxation and consumer mobilization were not au-

[35] Teresa Billington-Greig, *The Consumer in Revolt* (London: Stephen Swift, 1912).

[36] Frank Trentmann, "National Identity and Consumer Politics: Free Trade and Tariff Reform," in *The Political Economy of British Historical Experience, 1688–1914,* ed. Patrick O'Brien and Donald Winch (Oxford: Oxford University Press, 2002), 236.

[37] Karl Oldenberg, "Die Konsumtion," in *Grundriss der Sozialökonomie* (Tübingen, 1914), 2:123.

[38] Simon N. Patten, *The Consumption of Wealth* (Philadelphia: University of Pennsylvania, 1889).

[39] Michael Freeden, ed., *Reappraising J. A. Hobson: Humanism and Welfare* (London: Unwin Hyman, 1990); Frank Trentmann, "Commerce, Civil Society, and the 'Citizen-Consumer,'" in *Paradoxes of Civil Society: New Perspectives on Modern German and British History,* ed. Frank Trentmann (New York: Berghahn, 2000), 312–15.

[40] Charles Gide, *Cours d'économie politique,* trans. as *Political Economy* by William Smart and Constance H. M. Archibald (London: Harrap, 1914).

tonomous social processes but were shaped in part by inherited traditions. Consumer cooperatives spread from the 1840s across Europe but did not automatically create a collective identity of consumers. German cooperatives significantly called themselves "consumption associations" (*Konsumvereine*), not "consumer associations" (*Konsumentenvereine*); consumption here was object, not identity, and it remained centered in production and class—as in the big consumption, building, and savings' association "*Produktion*" in Hamburg Altona.[41] In France, the centrality of labor in political discourse delayed the arrival of a distinct consumer identity until the 1880s; cooperative consumption was a medium for strengthening a brotherhood of workers.[42]

More than anywhere else, it was in Victorian England that the ideological barriers to collective identity and action were overcome and that the political synapses of the consumer politics sprang into action. Commercial traditions left more discursive openings for the formation of collective consumer identities than did traditions that privileged production or the land. Let us now examine the emergence of the consumer as a more distinct social actor and public voice in two crucial historical settings—first, in local political battles over access and control of water in Victorian London; and second, in a more global-local conjuncture in which anxieties over trade energized consumption as a question of national identity and citizenship around the turn of the twentieth century.

The conflict between users and natural monopolies in Victorian Britain produced a seminal link between material needs and collective consciousness and action. This early synapse of consumer politics was initially fused by propertied and commercial users through notions of access, public accountability, and representative government, rather than choice or universal consumer democracy. For a utility like gas, those who defended their interests as "consumers" were almost exclusively merchants, shopkeepers, and industrialists. The consumer was mobilized in a battle against monopoly for cheaper and safer service, with the goal of making companies accountable to their consumers in a way analogous to parliamentary government.[43] In short, the consumer acquired shape through a model of citizenship: accountability via representation went hand in hand with consumer protection in the form of lower and stable prices.

[41] Michael Prinz, *Brot und Dividende: Konsumvereine in Deutschland und England vor 1914* (Göttingen: Vandenhoeck and Ruprecht, 1996), 235ff.; and Peter Gurney, *Co-operative Culture and the Politics of Consumption in England, 1870–1930* (Manchester: Manchester University Press, 1996).

[42] Ellen Furlough, *Consumer Cooperation in France: The Politics of Consumption, 1834–1930* (Ithaca: Cornell University Press, 1991).

[43] See *Are the Citizens of London to have Better Gas, and More of It, for Less Money? A Dialogue between (C. P.) Mr. Charles Pearson and (G. C.) a Gas Consumer of the City* (London, 1849) and Martin Daunton, "The Material Politics of Natural Monopoly," in *Politics of Consumption,* ed. Daunton and Hilton, 69–88.

Water was the single most fiercely contested good in nineteenth-century London politics and the site of a widening social identity of consumers.[44] Water users became articulate consumers whose growing self-confidence sparked an infrastructure of consumer defense leagues and consumer boycotts. By the 1880s, the social category of consumers had widened from propertied rate-paying private and commercial users to include the public more generally. Water carried a high cultural capital as "the first necessary of life," a significance reinforced by the politics of public health in the early Victorian period.[45] While local councils after midcentury were required to provide a clean and adequate supply of water, the supply in London and many other cities remained in the hands of private monopolies.[46] Water was paid for through rates, a local tax on property. In the eyes of local government, water companies, and taxpayers, "consumers" were rate-payers—that is, property owners, owner-occupiers, and tenants above a certain rent who paid their rates directly. Consumers were not just anyone using water (women, children, and poorer tenants were initially not included). It was this more privileged section that first agitated as consumers for greater accountability and representative powers. It was in the pressure cooker of increasing rates and rising norms of personal comfort and hygiene—water closets and bathtubs were subject to additional water rates—that the consumer found its voice. In 1882–83, the barrister Archibald Dobbs brought a successful legal challenge to the water companies' rating policy on his modest home. He became the hero of the "rate-paying public" and began a crusade to secure the same advantage for "every water consumer in London."[47] A network of Water Consumers' Defense Leagues sprang up all over London. They set up advice bureaus, circulated posters with "Instructions to Consumers," organized boycotts, and provided legal support for aggrieved consumers.[48]

At first, consumer rights remained tied to property rights as the basis of citizenship and representation. Dobbs charged that the water companies had led an "invasion of the property of water consumers . . . a confiscation of the statutory rights of ratepayers."[49] Without a system of regulation, however, the battle over rights, rates, and accountability quickly developed

[44] See Frank Trentmann and Vanessa Taylor, "From Users to Consumers: Water Politics in Nineteenth-Century London," in *The Making of the Consumer: Knowledge, Power, and Identity in the Modern World,* ed. Trentmann (Oxford: Berg, 2006).

[45] Christopher Hamlin, *Public Health and Social Justice in the Age of Chadwick: Britain, 1800–54* (Cambridge: Cambridge University Press, 1998).

[46] See Robert Millward, "The Political Economy of Urban Utilities," in *The Cambridge Urban History of Britain, III: 1840–1950,* ed. Martin Daunton (Cambridge: Cambridge University Press, 2000).

[47] *The Times,* December 20, 1883, 6.

[48] The National Archives [TNA], MH 29/6, Clapham, Stockwell and South Lambeth Water Consumers Defence Association, January 1884.

[49] *The Times,* May 7, 1884, 5.

into a contestation of the nature of the "consumer" and the rights and responsibilities that came with a legal entitlement to an "adequate" supply of water for "domestic use." Commercial users in the city tried to mobilize these categories in their battle for lower rates. The water companies sought to block the consolidation of consumer interest, but in the process they gave the "consumer" even greater currency through a massive countercampaign that blamed irresponsible and "wasteful consumers" for the water shortages, dirt, and increased prices experienced by honest consumers.[50]

In the expanding political culture of late Victorian Britain, rate-payer activism expanded the social universe and public imagery of the consumer. The mobilization of the consumer reached its peak during the "water famines" of the mid-1890s. Mobilization could be spontaneous, triggered by the experience of scarcity against a backdrop of rising norms and consumption practices assisted by better and more constant supply and fueled by a distrust of monopoly communicated through a broadly liberal tradition of freedom. For all its ebbs and flows, consumer activism was not the matter of an instant—a bubble that would burst when pricked because of the amorphous nature of consumers' interests. The contestation of water left behind an enriched sense and symbolism of the consumer as representing the public interest. In the early nineteenth century, the debate between supporters and critics of the private water companies invoked the "rate-paying public" or the "health of the public."[51] By the late nineteenth century, a shared language of the consumer began to be invoked by householders as well as users more generally, from affluent property owners in Belgravia to mechanics in rental accommodation in the East End.

The formative history of the consumer in local water politics in Britain is important because it was marked by features not conventionally associated with "consumer society." Water combined a popular sense of a "necessary" with the civilizing properties of bodily comfort and hygiene. As a scarce good that was easily lost or exhausted, it raised questions of waste, not abundance. Water was not sold and bought on the market but provided by private monopolies; nor was the price determined by the volume of consumption. Users turned into consumers protesting about conditions of supply as well as price, and demanding civic rights and public control—not individual choice in the marketplace. Consumers, in short, acquired their voice in an arena of consumption that lay outside the widening universe of commodity culture.

[50] TNA, MH 29/5, "Notice to Consumers and Sanitary Authorities," East London Waterworks Company, August 2, 1883.

[51] See John Wright, *The Dolphin: or, Grand Junction Nuisance* (London: 1827), 8; and William Matthews, *Hydraulia: An Historical and Descriptive Account of the Water Works of London* (London: Simpkin, Marshall, 1835), 332–33.

Consumption, International Trade, and National Power

Trade and imperial rivalries added a more intense national and global dynamic to such local and particular mobilizations of the consumer, particularly starting in the 1890s. Against the background of an increasingly global circulation of food and commodities and a shifting balance between town and country, consumption became a contested site in debates about agricultural and trade policy, social reform, racial strength, and the relationship between citizenship and nationhood. The agitation over free trade in Britain, protectionism in Germany, and alien commodities in China can be seen as part of this global conjuncture. The degree to which consumer identities were mobilized in these debates, however, differed according to traditions of citizenship and social and national solidarities. Whereas the consumer became a firmly established political and social voice in Britain before World War I, that voice remained underdeveloped in Imperial Germany and was stillborn in the Chinese case of commodity nationalism.

It was the popular politics of free trade that firmly established the consumer as an identity and actor in Britain, especially in the Edwardian campaigns (1903–10).[52] References to the consumer had been not altogether absent from the earlier anti–corn law movement or debates about the public exhibition of commodities,[53] but they had played a marginal, descriptive role that never acquired the broader, inclusive normative appeal of "the people" nor the status of the merchant spreading the civilizing "douceur" of commerce. Popular editions of Frédéric Bastiat's *Sophismes économiques* went some way in disseminating an image of consumers as humanity.[54] Yet it was Edwardian politics that made "the consumer" an altogether more active, ubiquitous character. Between the elections of January and December 1910, one free trade body alone organized 6,000 public meetings, magic-lantern lectures, and traveling exhibits, offering lessons on the adverse effects of an import duty on consumers. The Women's Cooperative Guild invoked the civic rights and contributions of their members as consumers.

Consumption was a gendered subject, but, as evidence of the male propertied gas and water consumers indicates, this did not mean that the identity of the consumer was necessarily female. Debates concerned the moral properties and civic status of male as well as female consumers.[55] In addi-

[52] See Trentmann, "National Identity and Consumer Politics."

[53] See, for example, *Speeches on the Questions of Public Policy by Richard Cobden,* 3d ed. (London: Macmillan, 1908).

[54] Frédéric Bastiat, *Sophismes économiques* (Paris, 1846), 49.

[55] Lynda Nead, *Victorian Babylon: People, Streets, and Images in Nineteenth-Century London* (New Haven: Yale University Press, 2000) and Christopher Breward, *The Hidden Consumer: Masculinities, Fashion, and City Life 1860–1914* (Manchester: Manchester University Press, 1999).

Figure 1.1. *The Male Consumer Source: Free Trade Union,* leaflet no. 328, November 24, 1909, Bristol University Archive, DM 669.

tion to posters appealing to female shoppers, the Free Trade Union also depicted the male middle-class consumer standing in front of a shop window featuring leather goods at higher prices under tariff reform (see figure 1.1).

The strength of free trade rested partly on its ability to incorporate older and newer images of the consumer. Free traders moved beyond a fixation on necessities (the cheap loaf) to a broader display of goods, ranging from basic foodstuffs to branded goods and clothing for different social groups. At the same time, discussions about how duties were paid by the "home consumer" rather than the foreigner grouped all Britons together. Free trade businessmen emphasized that industries were consumers too. In contrast to the earlier, more bounded tradition of the consumer, with its persona of the propertied rate-payer and its emphasis on specific utilities, the consumer had become an integral part of society.

There was nothing inevitable about the coming together of this synapse of consumer politics. Mass movements and debates about the standard of living and trade regulation occurred in many societies at the time without producing an equally strong identity or discourse of the consumer. In Imperial Germany, a public agitation about price increases fueled opposition to agricultural protection. Milk wars, butter boycotts, and protests against expensive meat between 1905 and 1912 articulated a new sense of entitlement among blue- and white-collar workers and parts of the middle class. Yet political parties were slow to adopt a unifying language of the consumer. Contemporaries bemoaned the "pure consumer point of view" of the lower middle classes. Even national-liberal advocates for this group separated salaried employees ("first of all consumers") from the rest of the middle classes rather than stressing shared, public interests.[56] The consumer was a sectional interest, far from representing the nation, let alone humanity. From Britain, France, and America, consumer leagues spread to Imperial Germany. But here too, a more inclusive identity of the consumer remained underdeveloped. The emphasis was on developing socially responsible habits of consumption among middle-class "consumers" to improve the social conditions of "workers."[57] Tellingly, the German housewives' association remained skeptical of the category of the consumer and presented itself as a corporate organization of women in charge of managing and preparing goods as much as purchasing them.[58]

In China, consumption moved to the center of popular politics in the context of weak state power and militant patriotism. From 1900 until 1931, there was a steady series of campaigns for the recovery of sovereign rights, directed first against Russia and the United States and later Japan. These involved anti-imperialist boycotts and exhibits promoting the use of national products. In a state that had lost the power to control imports, the regulation of consumption became a substitute for state sovereignty. For bodies like the National Products Preservation Association, as Karl Gerth has recently shown, "material culture such as fabrics and clothing styles played a direct role in connecting individuals to the nation: individual bodies were key sites of a national symbology and hence for the construction of modern Chinese nationalism as such."[59] In Groups of Ten for National Salvation, members pledged their lives to forego the consumption of all imports. Economic nationalism was promoted by students and shopkeepers as well as producers who used boycotts to increase their market share.[60]

[56] Albrecht Patzig, 1905, cited in Christoph Nonn, *Verbraucherprotest und Parteiensystem im Wilhelminischen Deutschland* (Düsseldorf: Droste, 1996), 76, 78.

[57] Elisabeth von Knebel-Doeberitz, "Die Aufgabe und Pflicht der Frau als Konsument," in *Hefte der Freien Kirchlich-Sozialen Konferenz,* no. 40 (Berlin, 1907), 41.

[58] Beatrice Strauß, *Die Konsumtionswirtschaft* (Borna-Leipzig: Robert Noske, 1929), 59–62.

[59] Karl Gerth, *China Made: Consumer Culture and the Creation of the Nation* (Cambridge: Harvard University Press, 2003), 118. Thanks to Karl Gerth for additional discussion.

[60] Sherman Cochran, *Big Business in China: Sino-Foreign Rivalry in the Cigarette Industry, 1890–1930* (Cambridge: Harvard University Press, 1980), 68–77.

Governments elsewhere in the interwar years also introduced marketing and cultural initiatives to boost the purchase of home or imperial products, but these were dwarfed by the scale of the Chinese movement; Hangzhou's West Lake Exhibition had eighteen million visitors in 1929.[61] The wise consumption of national products was seen as a duty of all citizens fighting for national survival, but especially of women. The "determined use of national products" raised her status in the household to the equivalent of a battlefield commander asked to "kill the enemy for the country," as organizers of the Women's National Products Year of 1934 put it.[62] Building a strong Chinese nation required more conscious habits of consumption, but the subject addressed was not the consumer, but the "citizen," "compatriot," "the Chinese People," or "the masses."[63]

The contrasting forms in which consumption was politicized point to the contingent and diverse trajectories of the consumer in modernity. Commodity culture played an increasingly important part in all three societies in this earlier period of globalization, but it was negotiated through different social and political traditions that mapped consumption practices onto different social identities. One favorable condition for the creation of a consumer identity, these cases suggest, was the comparatively early erosion of rival social identities based on estates, work, or corporation. By the late nineteenth century, workers in Britain and America had largely accepted the reality of wage labor and given up earlier ideals of artisanal, corporate, or republican independence.[64] In this indirect way, the early commercialization of society created elbow room for the consumer. In Britain, free trade created a more inclusive, universal sense of consumers with a stake in society and polity. Where corporate, producer, and landed identities remained stronger and were seen as commensurate with the national interest, by contrast, the space for the consumer was more limited. In Germany, it was not until after the defeat of Nazism that the consumer became an attractive cultural vehicle of national refashioning.[65] Early twentieth-century Japan, Korea, and India offer different variations on this theme (see Garon, chap. 7; Gordon, chap. 6; and Nelson, chap. 8).[66] In Korea, national product promotion campaigns sought to instill a new sense of moral and national self-sufficiency to overcome Japa-

[61] Compared to the record 70,833 people who visited the Empire Marketing Board's pavilion at the Cardiff Empire Exhibition in 1928. Stephen Constantine, "Bringing the Empire Alive," in *Imperialism and Popular Culture* ed. John M. MacKenzie (Manchester: Manchester University Press, 1986), 207.

[62] Gerth, *China Made,* 296.

[63] Gerth, *China Made,* 103, 105, 139, 175, 239, 253.

[64] Lawrence B. Glickman, *A Living Wage: American Workers and the Making of Consumer Society* (Ithaca: Cornell University Press, 1997).

[65] Erica Carter, *How German is She? Postwar West German Reconstruction and the Consuming Woman* (Ann Arbor: University of Michigan Press, 1997).

[66] Lisa N. Trivedi, "Visually Mapping the 'Nation': Swadishi Politics in Nationalist India, 1920–1930," *Journal of Asian Studies* 62, no. 1 (February 2003): 11–41.

nese colonial domination. In a strong state like Japan, too, consumption remained culturally ambivalent and contested: even as urban Japanese were expanding their consumption habits and using new forms of consumer credit, the state and social movements attacked the consumption of imported goods as leading to moral and national dependence. It was the saver in Japan who was mobilized as the pillar of economic and military strength in contrast to Britain, a similarly export-oriented economy, where a liberal tradition linked the national interest with urban and industrial consumers' interest in an open economy. In India, the campaign to promote *khadi* (homespun cotton cloth) turned to indigenous craft and consumption practices for moral and sexual cleansing to create conscious nationals; here was an extreme version of self-sufficiency that rejected the modernity of commodity culture as such and prescribed less consumption altogether. Whereas free traders and proponents of international cooperation projected the consumer as an internationalist link between societies, the politicization of consumption in nationalist traditions favored identities of citizens in territorially bounded states.

Attention to social and political traditions suggests that the degree of commodification might account less for the strength of the consumer in the modern period than conventionally thought. The campaigns over water and gas provision indicate that the formation of consumers need not take place in commercial market settings. Paradoxically, too, it was free traders' ambivalence toward consumerism that provided the "citizen-consumer" with public legitimacy. The initial focus on necessaries and taxed goods was crucial in the British case because, in the liberal tradition of the tax-paying citizen, it allowed the construction of an organic public interest around taxpayers. Radical and progressive traditions were subsequently able to build on this liberal foundation, presenting the House of Commons as a virtual representation of all consumers and invoking the civic, community-oriented outlook of a citizen-consumer. Politics, of course, was not immune from the expanding world of consumption, which through new commercial spaces like the department store facilitated the entry of middle-class women into public spaces.[67] At the same time, the identity of the consumer in political culture remained largely distinct from commercial culture. Consumers here were citizens with a social conscience and with supposedly limited needs, not the *flâneur* or *flâneuse* exploring infinite desires, nor the utility-maximizing individual of economic theory. The consumer in Britain was thus largely able to withstand the charge, so overwhelming on the European continent and in Asia, of being a selfish, unpatriotic individual whose obsessions with universal cheapness eroded the collective good. Instead of picturing a natural synergy among the con-

[67] Erika Diane Rappaport, *Shopping for Pleasure: Women in the Making of London's West End* (Princeton: Princeton University Press, 2000).

sumer, individualism, and liberal economics, it is vital to retrieve this earlier moment of an association among civil society, citizenship, and the consumer. Next to the citizen-consumer in the free trade mindset, we can also think here of the consumer leagues that sprang up in America and continental Europe in the 1890s, with their emphasis on the social responsibility of consumers to shop wisely. These leagues strove to improve the welfare of workers and small traders by refraining from shopping after 8 p.m., by paying in cash, by planning ahead, and by taming the impulse to buy shoddy, fashionable goods made by exploited labor.[68] The identity of consumers and the mentalities and responsibilities ascribed to them here are worlds apart from the universe of hedonism, unlimited choice, or the city as twenty-four-hour mall.

Social Ethics and Political Empowerment: Consumers between State and Civil Society

The populist consummation of the consumer happened in World War I, driven forward by the state as well as civil society. Scarcities and inflation produced consumer boycotts and demands for representation. Equally significant, state planning led to state-sponsored recognition and institutionalization, as in the war committees of consumer interests set up in Germany in December 1914.[69] Subjects graduated from the war with an elementary education of themselves as consumers and citizens. Within the state, rationalization and campaigns for thrift highlighted the vital economic role of consumers in national survival.

The war thus placed new social, ethical, and political responsibilities on the consumer, even or especially in producer-oriented national traditions. Consumers were identified as vital, if compliant, partners in the state's project of a more rational and equitable allocation of resources. "Consumption," the German planner and industrialist Walther Rathenau argued, "was not a private affair but an affair of the community, the state, ethics and humanity."[70] Citizens needed to overcome their "crazy hunger for commodities," which he held responsible for misallocating natural resources. Overcoming waste through a mixture of consumption taxes and

[68] Kathryn K. Sklar, "The Consumers' White Label Campaign of the National Consumers' League, 1898–1918," in *Getting and Spending: European and American Consumer Societies in the Twentieth Century*, ed. Susan Strasser, Charles McGovern, and Matthias Judt (Cambridge: Cambridge University Press, 1998), 17–35 and Marie-Emmanuelle Chessel, "Women and the Ethics of Consumption in France at the Turn of the Twentieth Century," in *Making of the Consumer*, ed. Trentmann.

[69] Robert Schloesser, *Konsumentenkammern* (Cologne: Verlags- und Versicherungsgesellschaft des Reichsverbandes deutscher Konsumvereine, 1916).

[70] Walther Rathenau, *Von Kommenden Dingen* (Berlin: Fischer, 1917), 39, 90, 131ff.

import controls would create more conscientious consumers and a more productive nation that, in turn, would allow for state-funded social welfare and higher forms of cultural consumption.

For organized consumers, too, the suffering and responsibilities placed on them during wartime led to a new focus on the state. The demand for consumer councils and the attacks on profiteering corporations and middlemen were its political articulation. The demand for state controls to provide consumers with a stable supply of commodities was its policy implication.[71] In Britain, consumers now advocated secure provision and regulation instead of cheapness and freedom of trade.

The maturing of the consumer during and after World War I was inextricably tied to the development of welfare policies, the development of "social citizenship," and the state's challenge to civil society. The consumer was increasingly only an individual citizen or private end user. The earlier inclusion of commercial or collective users became rare (though still traceable in Weimar corporatism). State planning projected socioeconomic rights onto a universal private consumer. Britain's Harold Macmillan, for example, advocated a minimum standard of life to all households "whether the consumer is in or out of work," as part of economic reconstruction.[72] At the local level, the British Council for Art and Industry urged education authorities in 1936 to remember, "even where it conflicts with a strict economy . . . that they are educating the future consumer; and may be setting a standard for industry in the next generation."[73] At the global level, internationalists expected consumers to play a key role in the program of "economic appeasement" and international peace by absorbing excess production.[74]

To some liberals, consumers became the last defense against totalitarianism. In the United States, Horace Kallen argued in 1936 that human beings were born consumers and only became producers under coercion. To preserve humanity it was necessary to develop the full personality of consumers, for their "cultural spirit, their personal disposition, their social attack, their economic method must oppose themselves in unmistakable contrast to those of the *duces, Führers,* and *commissars* of the Fascist, Nazi and Communist cults as well as those of the captains of industry and fi-

[71] Frank Trentmann, "Bread, Milk and Democracy: Consumption and Citizenship in Twentieth-Century Britain," in *Politics of Consumption,* ed. Daunton and Hilton, 129–63; Christoph Nonn, "Vom Konsumentenprotest zum Konsens," in *Konsumpolitik: Die Regulierung des Privaten Verbrauchs im 20. Jahrhundert,* ed. Hartmut Berghoff (Göttingen: Vandenhoeck & Ruprecht, 1999), 30ff.

[72] Harold Macmillan, *The Middle Way: A Study of the Problem of Economic and Social Progress in a Free and Democratic Society* (London: Macmillan, 1938).

[73] *The Times,* December 24, 1936, 9.

[74] *Final Report of the Mixed Committee of the League of Nations on the Relation of Nutrition to Health, Agriculture, and Economic Policy,* League of Nations, Document No. A-13. 1937. II. A.

nance of the capitalist economy."[75] Here was an ethical conception of the trinity of consumption, freedom, and American leadership before it mutated into the material visions of mass consumption that became an American export staple during the Cold War (see Cohen, chap. 2).[76]

The unprecedented attention to the consumer in questions of citizenship and economic policy was part of a larger social and cultural trend that associated the consumer with an increasingly ambitious and diversified field of practices, goods, and services. Already in the late nineteenth century, France's Charles Gide expanded the scope to include "houses, gardens, money, furniture, curios."[77] The consumer's interest moved beyond food, gas, and water, though this did not automatically point to consumerism. Gide urged recycling, for example, and imagined an ideal state of consumption where goods never wore out; in the United States, Patten looked toward a wiser use of natural resources. The consumer interest expanded in class and practice, encompassing health, housing, leisure, and collective forms of consumption. Cooperatives in France spoke of "consumers of health" in the 1920s and included free holidays for children and families as "consumer" activities; consumers had become bourgeois and petit bourgeois as well as workers and farmers.[78] By 1936, the British Institute of Adult Education was investigating "the Consumer's View of Adult Education."[79] In the United States, college and secondary school courses on consumption included medical care and the purchases of services, automobiles, and electrical appliances, as well as food and clothing.[80] Within the federal government, the Consumers' Division identified housing as a critical issue for "John Public—the consumer."[81] The enrichment of the social body and practice of the consumer, then, was well under way by the time John Maynard Keynes in his *General Theory* (1936) accorded the consumer a central role in the creation of wealth and full employment.

The growing attention to the consumer in society, culture, and political economy in the interwar years, however, was not all positive. As subsequent chapters illustrate, "consumer" and "consumption" remained ambivalent or even troubling categories in many Asian societies. In Europe and the

[75] Horace M. Kallen, *The Decline and Rise of the Consumer: A Philosophy of Consumer Coöperation* (New York: D. Appleton-Century, 1936), 14–15, 94.

[76] See also Lizabeth Cohen, *A Consumers' Republic: The Politics of Mass Consumption in Postwar America* (New York: Knopf, 2003) and Sheryl Kroen, "Aufstieg des Kundenbürgers?", *Der Lange Weg in den Überfluss: Anfänge und Entwicklung der Konsumgesellschaft seit der Vormoderne,* ed. Michael Prinz (Paderhorn: Ferdinand Schöningh, 2003) 554–64.

[77] Gide, *Political Economy,* 700–701.

[78] Furlough, *Consumer Cooperation in France,* 275ff.

[79] W. E. Williams and A. E. Heath, *Learn to Live: The Consumer's View of Adult Education* (London: Methuen, 1936).

[80] Henry Harap, "Survey of Twenty-Eight Courses in Consumption," *School Review* (September 1937): 497–507.

[81] *The Consumer,* no. 3 (November 15, 1935): 11.

United States, too, the liberal upgrading of the consumer worked in tandem with progressive debates about the civic nature and limits of consumers. The father of Keynesianism was deeply critical about the kind of mass consumer society with which his theory became associated. Abundance, Keynes hoped, would eventually be enjoyed by people who "cultivate into a fuller perfection, the art of life itself and do not sell themselves for the means of life" and recognize the "love of money" as a "somewhat disgusting morbidity."[82] Other progressives began to ask how the growing emphasis on choice and demand could be reconciled with the universal principles of citizenship or the ethics informing social solidarities. Two divergent responses deserve attention here.

In one response, "social citizenship" began to question the organic union of the "citizen-consumer" imagined by radicals. The British Fabian Beatrice Webb argued that democratization had meant that "the nation comes very near to becoming . . . an Association of consumers." Governments carried out "the common will of the citizens," from carrying their letters and providing news and entertainment to supplying medical care and high culture.[83] Webb had long appreciated the consumer cooperatives' contribution to a democratic culture of self-government. The question was how far the consumerization of the political system could advance before it undermined a shared sense of citizenship, rights, and obligations. Social citizenship rested on different premises from that of consumer representation. It involved the enforcement of universal services (schools, health), and it required compulsory taxation to fund these services irrespective of a person's use. Membership was fixed, not optional. Citizenship provided members of a community with a sense of belonging. To Webb, then, a welfare state deflated rather than inflated the consumer as a political subject; it would draw new boundaries between citizens and consumers in an effort to protect the state from the threatening expansion of consumers and consumer representation in society.

The New Deal created a very different political synapse of citizen-consumers from earlier traditions, combining an economic model of growth through increased purchasing power with a democratic model of mobilizing consumers as citizens supported by the state. Whereas in free trade the public identity of the consumer was anchored in a basic range of goods, the New Deal expanded it to cover everything from food quality to inefficient machines and corporate structure. After the Depression the economic power of consumers became a vehicle for a public project of safeguarding the general good, in competition with the more individualist commercial project of the "purchaser consumer" that came to dominate

[82] John Maynard Keynes, "Economic Possibilities for Our Grandchildren" (1930), in *Essays in Persuasion* (London: Macmillan, 1984), 328–29.

[83] Beatrice Webb, *The Discovery of the Consumer* (London: Ernest Benn, 1928), 4–5.

after World War II (see Cohen, chap. 2). Historians have paid attention to the rise of consumer rights and activism and the new state support of the "citizen consumer" via local consumer committees.[84] A second strand of scholarship has traced the more technocratic concept of the rational consumer through organizations like Consumers' Research.[85] Here I want to tease out briefly an ethical dimension that informed this public accreditation of individual purchasing.

The development of the rational consumer had as much to do with an ethical conception of how individual consumers made their decisions as with material interests or an institutional critique of corporations. For the burgeoning home economics and consumer education movement, ethics and choice were symbiotic. Established in 1899, the American Home Economics Association had 12,000 members by the 1930s. Colleges, secondary schools, and women's clubs carried an ever-increasing number of courses and study guides. One author of key texts was Hazel Kyrk, the influential home economist at the University of Chicago.[86] For Kyrk the goal was to teach the consumer to "consult his individual need, to form his own judgements, to desire for himself and to respect in others a creative, experimental attitude toward the various means that are offered him for the enhancement of his health and comfort, or the enrichment of his experience." "Wise consumption choices" were linked to greater mental stimulation and sociability as well as to matters of personal comfort and safety. Kyrk distinguished between a "consumer" and a "buyer." Importantly, these were not rival social models but stages in the individual practice of consumption. The first was concerned with the evaluation of choices and the setting of standards, the latter with efficient purchasing decisions. The "buyer" was about the "technology of consumption": exercising choice, saving money and time, and securing a fair price necessary to keep labor and capital fully employed. The "consumer" was about cultivating tastes and forming new concepts of need. Choice concerned "questions of motives, of values, of ends."[87]

[84] Meg Jacobs, "'How About Some Meat?': The Office of Price Administration, Consumption Politics, and State Building from the Bottom Up, 1941–1946," *Journal of American History* 84, no. 3 (December 1997): 910–41.

[85] Lawrence B. Glickman, "The Strike in the Temple of Consumption: Consumer Activism and Twentieth-century American Political Culture," *Journal of American History* 88, no. 1 (June 2001): 99–128; Christopher Beauchamp, "Getting Your Money's Worth: American Models for the Remaking of the Consumer Interest in Britain, 1930s-1960s," in *Critiques of Capital*, ed. Bevir and Trentmann, 127–50 and Matthew Hilton, "The Fable of the Sheep, or, Private Virtues, Public Vices: The Consumer Revolution of the Twentieth Century," *Past and Present* 176, no. 1 (August 2002): 229ff.

[86] Frances W. Inenfeldt, "Teaching Consumer Buying in the Secondary School," *Journal of Home Economics* 26, no. 5 (1934): 280 and Marjorie East, *Home Economics: Past, Present, and Future* (Boston: Allyn and Bacon, 1980), 48.

[87] Hazel Kyrk, *Economic Problems of the Family* (New York: Harper and Brothers, 1933), 393, 396, also chs. 5, 19, 22, 23.

Kyrk's work reflects how broad and interdisciplinary the intellectual sources behind the consumer remained in the interwar years. In her critique of the utility-maximizing individual in neoclassical economics, Kyrk drew on philosophy, social and functional psychology, and, in particular, John Dewey's philosophy of knowledge through practice. Dewey was a key influence on many consumer advocates. Through the League for Independent Political Action (est. 1929) he stressed the affinities between consumer and citizen. Empowering consumers needed to begin with reflections on higher values and new ideals and purposes. Freedom of choice would let individuals develop higher social and personal ethics. By the 1930s, questions of value, the position of the consumer in society, and educational theory were as familiar in consumer education as labeling, quality, and price. A culture of thrift was being eroded, but instead of being swamped by a culture of materialist individualism, choice was also being channeled into a social ethics of consumption.

Conclusion

Taking the consumer seriously as a historical actor and category raises larger questions about the standard interpretations of modern "consumer society." Most interpreters of "consumer revolutions" and commodity culture have instinctively relied on an essentialist category of the consumer. While this may yield insights into goods, symbols, their distribution, and their economic consequences, it reveals far less about the self-identification and ascription of the actors themselves. To follow the consumer as an evolving category of knowledge and identity, we must jettison the instinctive assumption that any user of commercial commodities and services is naturally a consumer. This assumption says more about us than about past actors. Indeed, it is a result of the historical evolution of the consumer, not its explanation. The consumer, like "class," "citizen," or "nation," is no natural or universal category but rather the product of historical identity formations in which actors through available traditions make sense of the relationship between material culture and collective identity.

Importantly, the birth and maturing of the consumer is principally a nineteenth- and early twentieth-century story. It sits uneasily between the early modern consumer revolutions—with their emphasis on exotic goods, luxury, and a cult of sensibility—and the mid–twentieth-century stories of mass consumption or consumer society—with their fixation on affluence, advertising, mass-produced durables, and visions and dystopias of consumerism. The material culture of consumption and the political culture of the consumer did not map onto each other neatly. In Britain, utilities and taxed necessaries were the consumer's domain—not the growing number of commercially traded goods and services. Taxpayers, especially propertied male householders and commercial users of utilities, were the first to speak up as consumers. Property was a vital ingredient in the consumer's initial self-definition. The mobilization of the consumer in mid- to late Victorian Britain reveals the centrality of political synapses, in this case the liberal and radical traditions through which material relations were connected to collective identities and a sense of rights and accountability. Cooperatives added a popular dimension to the expanding social universe of consumers, but the continued importance of commercial consumers cautions us against seeing the evolution of the consumer as a simple story of democratization. Equally, it puts into question the dominant tendency in the social sciences to turn first to business, liberal economics, advertising, and states to account for the rise of the consumer.[88] These agencies, indeed, came to compete for the consumer's soul and money, but it was actors in civil society who first breathed life into this identity in Europe and America by mobilizing as consumer defense leagues, shopping leagues, free trade groups, and consumer education movements.

Modernity created different openings for consumers in different political and cultural spaces, depending on the role of nation, state, traditions of citizenship, and social identities. There is no universal history of the consumer, just as there is no essentialist consumer. The prominence of the consumer as citizen in Edwardian Britain was a particular developmental stage in the genealogy of the consumer in a liberal radical tradition. In societies with corporate traditions and nation- or producer-oriented discourses of citizenship, like Imperial Germany, the consumer was more marginal and more easily seen as a special interest. In societies where the control of consumption became a means of overcoming weak statehood, as in China, or of promoting economic modernization, as in Japan, the consumer did not emerge as an actor and identity because national consumption became the responsibility of patriotic citizens. Modern liberal traditions (though not republicanism) allow for an easier development of consumer identity because of a less territorially or corporately bounded sense of citizenship. In societies like early twentieth-century Japan, users or purchasers found it difficult to imagine themselves and agitate as consumers, preoccupied instead with the imperative of strengthening themselves as a nation (*kokumin*). The resulting identity of producer and patriot—more than the negative cultural connotations of consumption (*shōhi*, referring to extinction and waste)—explain the historical weakness of Japanese consumer identity. After all, it was around the waste of finite resources that consumers found a voice in nineteenth-century Britain—

[88] Raymond Williams, *Keywords: A Vocabulary of Culture and Society* (London: Fontana, 1983), 78–79; Theodor W. Adorno and Max Horkheimer, *Dialectic of Enlightenment* (London: Verso Editions, 1979); and Stuart Ewen, *Captains of Consciousness: Advertising and the Social Roots of the Consumer Culture* (New York: McGraw-Hill, 1976).

and continued to do so in the late twentieth century in pursuit of sustainable consumption.

The genealogy of the consumer is not a linear story, nor does it converge. To be sure, we observe in the early twentieth century an expansion of the social body and of the set of practices (including social services) appropriated by consumers that foreshadows the controversial inflation of the consumer in recent neoliberal public policy. Citizenship and consumption became more frequently linked, but actors in different settings created different configurations working within different social and political traditions. Viewing the evolution of the consumer from multiple positions opens up some constructive perspectives for current debates over the place of consumers. Much of the debate in Europe, America, and Asia has become stuck around the civic costs or benefits of neoliberal consumerism. Supporters present the introduction of market-style rational consumers in public services as a way of empowering citizens and democratizing public institutions as well as of creating choice and efficiency. Critics warn that consumerism will unravel the sources and solidarities of citizenship themselves. It is tempting to see the twentieth century as a fall from grace of an earlier, more civic-minded age of consumers eroded by the power of profit, markets, and individualism.

The modern genealogy of the consumer suggests a more cyclical and contingent story. There is no zero-sum game between market and politics. Starting the comparison between past and present in the middle of the nineteenth century, for example, would reveal the importance of a small group of propertied men whose self-interest fused with a sense of public accountability in very limited spheres of consumption. Their agitation contrasts with a much larger spectrum of social movements that today speak out on a vast range of consumer interests, from nutrition to the environment, from choice to media regulation. Starting the story in Britain before World War I would highlight a dominant consumer interest much more committed to freedom of trade than the current landscape of consumer movements. Similarly, in the United States of the interwar period, freedom of choice would appear to be part of a social ethics of civic consumption—not necessarily selfish or hedonistic consumerism. Starting the story elsewhere, however—say, in early twentieth-century China and Japan—might suggest not the fall but the recent rise of active consumers willing to speak out as such. A multicentered understanding of the genealogy of the consumer not only sheds doubt about a U.S.-centered story of convergence but also offers a more realistic view about the potential synapses between consumption and citizenship so often ignored by western critics of consumerism.

2

THE CONSUMERS' REPUBLIC

An American Model for the World?

LIZABETH COHEN

In the years following World War II, the United States developed what I elsewhere have called a "Consumers' Republic."[1] By this I mean the emergence of an ideological consensus shared by diverse interests in American society and supported by a consistent set of policies, regardless of political regimes in the White House and in Congress. This consensus held that an economy and society built around mass consumption would deliver not only great prosperity but also more democracy and equality.

In our quest to think comparatively and transnationally about spending and saving, this chapter delineates the American model of an economy, culture, and polity built around mass consumption. The model reigned domestically after World War II—and was projected to the rest of the world as "the American way." The American example consisted both of an idealization of the Consumers' Republic and the more complex reality that resulted from its embrace, which often diverged from what was expected. I will conclude with a brief examination of how American leaders in government and business promoted this model abroad, particularly in Western Europe and Japan, from the late 1940s through the 1960s. I also offer a preliminary assessment of the extent to which it was adopted. As other chapters further illustrate, different national settings, I argue, produced variations on the American model—variations that in turn underscore the ambivalence many societies feel toward consumption and the dilemmas they face when trying to balance American principles against the values

[1] This analysis is more fully developed in Lizabeth Cohen, *A Consumers' Republic: The Politics of Mass Consumption in Postwar America* (New York: Alfred A. Knopf, 2003).

and objectives of their own specific historical, political-cultural, and economic contexts. Nonetheless, the Consumers' Republic figured centrally in postwar debates in the non-Communist world over how to create the "good society." It was the main topic of conversation, even when it created more contention than conviviality between America and her allies.

Promoting Mass Consumption

The United States came out of World War II deeply determined to prolong and enhance the economic recovery brought on by the war, lest the crippling depression of the 1930s return. During wartime, a mass-production war machine, operating at full throttle to produce materiel for battle, had already provided many new jobs and filled many empty pockets and bank accounts. Ensuring a prosperous peacetime society would require making new kinds of products and selling them to different kinds of markets. Although military production would persist and, indeed, expand greatly with the Cold War, its critical partner in delivering prosperity was the mass consumer market. A wide range of economic interests and players, including stridently anti–New Deal businessmen, moderate and liberal capitalists, labor and its allies on the left, and government officials all came to endorse the centrality of mass consumption to a successful reconversion from war to peace. In some ways, this was the same Keynesian scheme that the New Dealers had seized upon to pull them out of the Great Depression in the late 1930s. But the experience of war had turned promising strategy into proven reality. Factory assembly lines newly renovated with Uncle Sam's dollars stood, awaiting conversion from building tanks and munitions for battle to producing cars and appliances for sale to consumers.

If encouraging a mass consumer economy seemed to make good economic sense for the nation, it still required extensive efforts to get Americans to cooperate. Certainly, there was tremendous pent-up demand for goods, housing, and almost everything else after a decade and a half of wrenching depression and war, but consumers were also cautious about spending the savings and war bonds that they had gladly accumulated while consumption was restricted on the home front. Hence, during the war and with great fervor after it, businesses, labor unions, government agencies, the mass media, advertisers, and many other purveyors of the new postwar order conveyed the message that mass consumption was not a personal indulgence. Rather, it was a civic responsibility designed to improve the living standards of all Americans. Expanding consumer demand had become a critical part of a prosperity-producing cycle that fueled greater production, thereby creating more well-paying jobs and, in turn, more affluent consumers who stoked the economy with their purchases.

For its promoters, this mass consumption–driven economy held out the promise of political as well as economic democracy. Reconversion after World War II raised the hopes of Americans of many political persuasions and social positions that not only a more prosperous but also a more equitable and democratic American society would finally be possible in the middle of the twentieth century due to the enormous (and war-proven) capacities of mass production and mass consumption. As more Americans lived better and on a more equal footing with their neighbors, the dream of an egalitarian America seemed in reach. Politicians never tired of tying America's political and economic superiority over the Soviet Union to its more democratic distribution of goods. In 1959, at the American Trade Exhibition in Moscow, Vice President Richard Nixon went so far as to tell the Russian people that all the homes, televisions, and radios owned by Americans had brought Americans closer than the Soviets to the Marxist ideal of a classless society.[2]

Thus, in this new postwar order, the good customer devoted to "more, newer, and better" was in fact the good citizen, responsible for making the United States a more desirable place for all its people. As *Bride Magazine* told the acquisitive readers of its handbook for newlyweds, when you buy "the dozens of things you never bought or even thought of before, . . . you are helping to build greater security for the industries of this country. . . . [W]hat you buy and how you buy it is very vital in your new life—and to our whole American way of living."[3] Wherever one looked in the aftermath of war, one found a vision of postwar America in which the general good was best served not by frugality or even moderation but by individuals pursuing personal wants in a flourishing mass consumption marketplace.

Private consumption and public benefit, it was widely argued, went hand in hand. And what made this strategy all the more attractive was the way it promised a socially progressive end of social equality without requiring a politically progressive means of redistributing existing wealth. Rather, it was argued, an ever-growing economy built around the twin dynamics of increased productivity and mass purchasing power would expand the overall pie without reducing the size of any of the portions. When President Truman challenged Americans in 1950 to "achieve a far better standard of living for every industrious family" within a decade, he characteristically reassured them that "raising the standards of our poorest families will not be at the expense of anybody else. We will all benefit from doing it, for the incomes of the rest of us will rise at the same time."[4]

It is important to recognize that both labor and business shared this confidence that expanding purchasing power would benefit all Americans. In

[2] Quoted in Thomas Hine, *Populuxe* (New York: Alfred A. Knopf, 1987), 129.

[3] *Bride Magazine* quotation from Brett Harvey, *The Fifties: A Women's Oral History* (New York: HarperCollins, 1993), 110.

[4] "Address in Pendleton, Oregon," May 10, 1950, *Public Papers of Harry S. Truman, 1950* (Washington, DC: U.S. Government Printing Office, 1951), 362.

an era when a dynamic manufacturing sector still flourished within the United States, where new and better-paying jobs could easily be traced to high levels of consumption in the society, that was not surprising. As early as 1944, the Congress of Industrial Organizations (CIO) proclaimed that "our economy feeds and grows on purchasing power as a baby does on milk. . . . The CIO knows that the baby will sicken if he does not have milk, that the whole community will suffer if purchasing power is not maintained." The leader of the other major labor organization, the American Federation of Labor (AFL), concurred: "Without adequate purchasing power in the form of wages we cannot get full postwar employment. Yes, we have the machinery to build all of the automobiles, all of the radios, washing machines and such things; we have the workers to build all of the houses that we could possibly use. But we will not make those things unless there is purchasing power available to buy them."[5] As the postwar era progressed, alternative voices within the labor movement, many of them Communist, were silenced by the repressive Taft-Hartley Act and McCarthyism more generally. With these radical challengers within unions muzzled, the major measure of democracy and equality within America became the extent to which workers shared in the trappings of the American middle-class lifestyle. Organized labor proceeded to elaborate a political stance where high consumption by its members provided the best route to a more egalitarian society. Cost-of-living adjustments (COLAs) pegging wages to consumer prices were just one of the demands labor commonly made to tie workers' fortunes to a strategy of maximizing purchasing power.

New housing provided the bedrock of the postwar mass consumption economy, both through turning "home" into an expensive commodity for purchase by many more consumers than ever before and by stimulating demand for related commodities. As today, the purchase of a new single-family home almost always obligated buyers to acquire new household appliances and furnishings and, if the house was in the suburbs, as over 80 percent were, at least one car. The scale of new residential construction following World War II was unprecedented. And it was made possible by a mixed economy of private enterprise bolstered by government subsidy. Veterans' benefits under the 1944 G.I. Bill granted mortgage guarantees with low interest rates and no down payments directly to home buyers, while buyers benefited indirectly when the Federal Housing Administration (FHA) gave loan insurance to lenders and developers building the homes they sought to purchase. The federal government assisted as well by granting mortgage interest deductions on income taxes (a mass tax since World War II) and constructing highways to rural areas that overnight were being transformed into vast suburban tract developments.

[5] "Unemployment and Social Security," *Economic Outlook* 5 (November 1944): 6; "Wage Freeze Is Assailed," *American Federationist* 51 (December 1944): 6–7.

This promotion of private market solutions to boost the mass consumption economy—even if heavily subsidized by the federal government—turned a dire social need for shelter into an economic boom. The groundwork had been laid during wartime, when consumers across the economic spectrum were encouraged to imagine "home" as a newly built single-family detached house for purchase in the suburbs, not a rented residence in a multiple dwelling in the city. One of every four homes standing in the United States in 1960 went up in the 1950s. As a result of this explosion in house construction, by the same year 62 percent of Americans could claim that they owned their own homes, in contrast to only 44 percent as recently as 1940—the biggest jump in homeownership rates ever recorded. Home building became so central a component of postwar prosperity, in fact, that beginning in 1959, the United States Census Bureau began calculating "housing starts" on a monthly basis as a key indicator of the economy's vitality.[6]

A Segmented Consumer Society

The greater democracy and equality expected to accompany the flourishing of private real estate markets in the Consumers' Republic proved illusive, however. The passage of time revealed that certain kinds of metropolitan locales as well as particular social groups benefited over others. The massive construction of single-family, privately owned, detached homes was intended to solve the enormous postwar housing crunch and to fuel the economy, but it also increasingly privileged suburbs over cities. As millions of Americans concluded that it was cheaper and more desirable to own rather than rent, they left older, often deteriorating housing in urban neighborhoods for the new suburban communities favored by the VA and FHA loan programs and reinforced by the lending policies of private banks. Between 1947 and 1953 alone, the suburban population increased by 43 percent, in contrast to a general population increase of only 11 percent. Over the course of the 1950s, in the twenty largest metropoli-

[6] Pearce C. Kelley, *Consumer Economics* (Homewood, IL: Richard D. Irwin, 1953), 464–67; Harold Vatter, "The Inheritance of the Preceding Decades," Department of Commerce, "We the Americans . . . Our Homes," and President's Committee on Urban Housing, "A Decent Home," all in *History of the U.S. Economy since World War II*, ed. John F. Walker and Harold G. Vatter (Armonk, NY: M. E. Sharpe, 1996), 21–23, 235–37, 358–62; United States Bureau of Labor Statistics, Department of Labor, *How American Buying Habits Change* (Washington, DC: United States Government Printing Office, 1959), 74–75; Thomas A. Bailey, David M. Kennedy, and Lizabeth Cohen, *The American Pageant*, 11th ed. (Boston: Houghton Mifflin, 1998), 927; Kathryn Murphy, *New Housing and Its Materials, 1940–56, Bulletin No. 1231* (Washington, DC: United States Department of Labor, Bureau of Labor Statistics, 1958), 2; United States Department of Commerce, Bureau of the Census, *Construction Reports—Housing Starts, C-20 Supplement*, 1972, 68. Prior to 1959, housing starts were estimated on a monthly basis and calculated on an annual basis by the Bureau of Labor Statistics, suggesting that the interest was as much in employment opportunities as in construction activity.

tan areas, cities would grow by only 0.1 percent, their suburbs by an explosive 45 percent. By 1965, a majority of Americans would make their homes in suburbs rather than cities. Today, typical American metropolitan areas range in the proportion of their central city population from the 20 percent of Boston to the 30 percent of New York, making them overwhelmingly suburban.[7]

The home ownership at the heart of the Consumers' Republic did more than expand the numbers and enhance the status of suburbanites over urbanites. Through their greater access to home mortgages, credit, and tax advantages, men benefited over women, whites over blacks, and middle-class Americans over working-class ones. Men, for example, secured low VA mortgages—and the additional credit that home ownership made available—as a result of their veteran status in World War II and the Korean War, while women generally did not. White Americans more easily qualified for mortgages, including those dispensed through the G.I. Bill, which worked through existing—and consistently discriminatory—banking institutions, and they more readily found suburban houses to buy than African Americans could. And while some working-class Americans did move to the suburbs, increasingly they tended to settle in "cops and firemen" suburban towns quite distinct from the places successful professionals and entrepreneurs lived. Studies of Levittown, Long Island, in 1950 and 1960 documented a shift away from the mixed-class suburb to a more exclusively working- and lower middle-class one as white-collar residents moved out of Levittown to more affluent communities nearby.[8] Even when factories moved out of cities into suburban areas, welcomed by communities eager for their property tax dollars, often their workers could not live there because such towns were often unwilling to rezone to make neighboring housing affordable.

The class sorting that took place in Levittown was indicative of a metropolitan landscape where whole communities were increasingly being stratified along class and racial lines. As home, particularly a new one, in the Consumers' Republic became a commodity to be traded up rather than an emotional investment in a traditional neighborhood or church parish, "property values" became the new mantra. Of course, people still chose the towns they lived in, but increasingly they selected among internally homogeneous suburban communities occupying different rungs in a hierarchy of property values. Communities of new homes could easily be pegged. In the early 1960s in the new middle-class suburb of Parsippany–Troy Hills in Morris County, New Jersey, the annual income required to

[7] Jon C. Teaford, *The Twentieth-Century American City: Problem, Promise, and Reality* (Baltimore: Johns Hopkins University Press, 1986), 98; "Cities and Suburbs: A Harvard Magazine Roundtable," *Harvard Magazine* (January-February 2000):54.

[8] William S. Dobriner, "Social Change in Levittown," in *Class in Suburbia,* ed. Dobriner (Englewood Cliffs, NJ: Prentice-Hall, Inc., 1963), 85–126.

buy and maintain a typical newly built home was estimated at $12,000. At the time, policemen and firemen in Northern New Jersey earned about $8,000 a year, while only 17 percent of all Newark families—and only 9 percent of nonwhite families—earned over $9,000. Moreover, local zoning regulations that enforced plot and house size and prohibited multiple dwellings in suburban towns contributed to the sorting out of prospective buyers by social class and, implicitly, by race.

Along with house prices, a community's racial profile further positioned it on the ladder of prestige. Many suburban whites left cities with growing African-American populations, reflecting the linked trends of white flight and the massive black migration north and west after World War II. These whites felt that only an all-white community would ensure the safety of their investment, often their entire life savings, and they did everything within their means to restrict the access of blacks to real estate. What one cynical Newark public official in 1962 labeled "segregurbia" flourished, he said, because "the free enterprise system lurking in many American hearts has provided more moves to all-white suburbs than the billion words of love have promoted the spiritual advantages of economic and integrated city living."[9] When William and Daisy Myers, the first black family to buy a house in Levittown, Pennsylvania, tried to move in in 1957, one of their neighbors who joined the violent protests against them conveyed to a *Life* magazine reporter how important property values were to people whose major asset was their home: "He's probably a nice guy, but every time I look at him I see $2,000 drop off the value of my house."[10]

The increasing segmentation of suburbia by class and race fueled even more damaging social inequality because of Americans' traditional devotion to home rule as a critical pillar of democracy.[11] With the advent of suburbanization, this conviction only intensified in the postwar period—despite the common assumption by ordinary Americans as well as scholars that the federal level was the principal site of governmental action in the post–World War II era. As a result of postwar Americans' loyalty to localism, the quality of crucial services soon varied much more than they had when more people lived within the larger units of cross-class and interracial cities. Education, for example, widely recognized as the best ticket to success in postwar America, became captive to the inequalities of the new metropolitan landscape, since local communities substantially paid for their own schools through local property taxes. The wealthier the community, the more it had to spend, and the greater the prospect of its chil-

[9] Daniel S. Anthony, "Some Psychological Implications of Integration," The Brookings Institution Committee on Problems of the American Community, Newark, New Jersey, February 23, 1962, Daniel S. Anthony Papers, Newark Public Library, New Jersey Room, Box 3, pp. 9, 12.

[10] "Integration Troubles Beset Northern Town," *Life,* September 2, 1957, 43–46.

[11] This discussion of "localism" is drawn from Cohen, *A Consumers' Republic,* 227–51.

dren receiving the kind of education that led to prestigious colleges, graduate degrees, and well-paying jobs. (This inequality has in fact led to intense battles in state supreme courts throughout the nation—everywhere from New Hampshire and Vermont to Texas and New Jersey—over equalizing school spending across communities in a state.)

By putting its faith in the potential of the private mass consumption marketplace to deliver opportunity to all—rather than in expanding publicly funded rental housing or adopting policies that redistributed wealth—the Consumers' Republic contributed to growing inequality and fragmentation, both spatially and structurally. Residential suburbanization, which engineered a social landscape that would serve property values over broad human needs, was one major factor in postwar America that led to Americans sharing less and less common physical space and civic culture.

The stratification of the residential metropolis in postwar America was accompanied by the similar segmentation, commercialization, and privatization of public space in what previously had been the urban downtown. Initially, most postwar suburban home developers made little effort to provide for residents' commercial needs. Rather, new suburbanites were expected to fend for themselves by driving to the existing "market towns," which often offered the only commerce for miles, or by returning to the closest major city to shop. By the mid-1950s, however, a new market structure—the regional shopping center—emerged to service this suburbanized, mass consumption–oriented society. Although it had precedents in the branch department stores and prototypical shopping centers constructed during the interwar period in outlying city neighborhoods and in older suburban communities, the new regional shopping center existed on a much larger scale. In the absence or inadequacy of existing town centers, the postwar shopping center offered commercial developers a unique opportunity to reimagine community life with their private projects at its heart. What developed was a vision and soon a reality of suburban living in which the center of community life became a site devoted to mass consumption. What was promoted as public space was in fact privately owned and geared to maximizing profits.[12]

The typical shopping center was strategically located at the intersection of major highways or along the busiest thoroughfares, with patrons commonly living more than a half-hour's drive away. Customers would usually come by car, park in the abundant lots provided, and then proceed by foot. Most shopping centers had two or three department stores serving as anchors, surrounded by fifty to seventy-five smaller stores. In the early years, when shopping centers were establishing their legitimacy as community centers, it was not unusual for them to house services such as post offices, banks, meeting and exhibit spaces, theaters, and even churches. Moreover,

[12] For more on the regional shopping center, see Cohen, *A Consumers' Republic*, ch. 6.

in selling themselves as improvements on the chaos, inefficiency, and ugliness of downtowns, shopping centers boasted that their centralized administrations determined the perfect mix and scientific placement of stores. Greater shopper pleasure and storeowner profitability inevitably followed, they bragged.

When developers and store owners set out to make the shopping center a more perfect downtown, they explicitly aimed to exclude from this community space unwanted social groups such as vagrants, racial minorities, political activists, and poor people. They did so through a combination of marketing and policing. Location alone helped, for the suburbs where shopping centers developed were overwhelming white and middle-class, and they were not easily reached by more diverse urban dwellers. Although buses served some shopping centers, only a tiny proportion of patrons arrived that way, and bus routes were carefully planned to transport not low-income consumers from cities but non-driving customers—particularly women—from neighboring suburbs. Moreover, as developers sought sites close to the affluent populations to which they catered, their presence augmented the prosperity of host communities, exacerbating the already unequal distribution of economic resources in metropolitan areas. Not only did a suburban municipality with a shopping center find that its residential property values increased by proximity to stores, but the presence of major commercial development greatly enhanced its tax base and, in turn, its core services like schools.

Shopping centers also excluded unwanted elements through explicit market segmentation. To be sure, individual department stores in city centers had long targeted particular markets defined by class and race, some selling to "the carriage trade" at the upper end and others to the bargain hunters at the bottom. Yet shopping centers applied market segmentation on the scale of a full downtown. Almost all aimed at middle-income customers or above, and over time they more and more targeted differentiated publics, minimizing the opportunities for social mixing that had occurred on the city street if not on any particular retail shop floor.

Whereas at first developers sought to legitimize the new shopping centers by arguing for their centrality to commerce and community, they gradually discovered that those two commitments could be in conflict. When antiwar protesters or striking employees noisily took their causes to the mall, it became clear that the rights of free speech and free assembly were not always good for business and, indeed, conflicted with the rights of private property owners—the shopping centers—to control entry to their land. Beginning in the 1960s, American courts all the way up to the Supreme Court struggled with the political consequences of developers having moved public life off the street into the privately owned shopping center. The ultimate outcome was that the United States Supreme Court in 1980 ruled definitively that the First Amendment of the U.S. Constitution did not guarantee free access to shopping centers, leaving it to the states to decide whether or not their own constitutions did. Only in six states have state supreme courts protected citizens' rights in privately owned shopping centers, and even in some of those states free speech and assembly have been limited.

Meanwhile, shopping centers began to reconsider the desirable balance between commerce and community in what had become the major sites where suburbanites congregated. In time, they retreated from housing public services and, whenever possible, banned or aggressively discouraged "undesirables" such as loitering young people, striking employees, leafletting and signature-collecting political activists, and individuals whose appearances were deemed menacing.

The shopping centers of the 1950s and 1960s also contributed to a new calibration of consumer authority in the household between men and women that in many respects limited women's power over the family purse. In some ways, the physical space of shopping centers was designed for women shoppers, ranging from the extra-wide parking spots for new female drivers to interiors with stroller ramps, babysitting services, and special lockers for ladies' wraps. "I wouldn't know how to design for a man," admitted Jack Follet of John Graham, Inc., a firm that built many shopping centers. But for all the attention that shopping centers lavished on women, they did little to enhance women's social and economic power. Rather, as mass consumption became more central to the health of the economy and the success of a household, shopping centers and the stores within them celebrated the family as a consumer unit and paid increasing attention to men as chief breadwinner. Women may have orchestrated their families' shopping, but marketing research documented that other family members, particularly decision-making husbands, increasingly accompanied them on buying expeditions. As the manager of a toy store in Shoppers' World in Framingham, Massachusetts, explained it in 1953, "It's a curious thing about a shopping center. Most of our daytime shoppers are women, who are just looking around. It's hard to sell to them during the day but if they're at all interested, they'll be back at night—with their husbands. That's when we do the real business."[13]

Men's increased involvement in family purchasing was also reinforced by the huge expansion of credit that shopping centers encouraged. Credit cards and other forms of credit became the legal tender of mall purchasing. Until the passage of equal credit legislation in the 1970s, the growing importance of credit deepened men's oversight of their wives and daughters, as male names and credit ratings were required for women's own access. Finally, shopping centers put limits on women's independence as workers, not just consumers, as suburban stores came to depend on part-

[13] Quotations from Cohen, *A Consumers' Republic,* 278, 279–80.

time female sales help who lived nearby, and to whom they offered low pay and few benefits. Not only did suburban housewives provide cheap and flexible labor, but their hiring also helped branch department stores undermine the retail clerks unions that had successfully organized the main stores downtown.

Urban policies have, moreover, magnified the segmentation, commercialization, and privatization of public space in postwar America. Confronted by population decline, the flight of retail trade, and the public's fear for its safety on increasingly unfamiliar urban streets, city leaders tried to beat the suburbs at their own game—by modeling the renovation of urban public space on the suburban model. Over the last half-century, few American cities have avoided the "mallification" of downtown, as urban leaders established pedestrian malls, festival marketplaces closed to transportation, and enclosed shopping centers entered through parking garages. For those shoppers and workers who still venture downtown, the city increasingly resembles the suburban mall, offering them, in their private cars, direct access to privately owned and policed, usually commercial, spaces; they can even access stores and offices without setting a foot onto a city street. As a Catholic priest and community activist described downtown Newark in 1997, "Prime office space is that with garage parking, and they are all built like fortresses, with their lobbies up on the second floor and retail space in atriums and courts. . . . It's not very pedestrian-friendly and inviting. The result is you have two cities downtown: the one in and around the offices, and the one on the streets where the people are."[14]

Urban downtowns thus have mimicked the suburbs' increasing privatization of public space—blurring the lines between what is public and private, what is civic and commercial—and infringing on civil rights. For example, a Starbucks coffee shop recently opened in the public library of a New England city, modeled after the increasingly ubiquitous café-bookstores like Borders and Barnes and Noble. As its vice president had promised, by opening a new Starbucks franchise every forty hours, "we are the third place in your community."[15] The proliferation of private cell phones makes public telephones fewer in number and higher in cost. Self-taxing private improvement districts perform more and more of the work that public agencies once did—cleaning, policing, and upgrading neighborhoods—and they do so free of the municipal oversight and public accountability that protects the rights of all citizens in those spaces. As celebrated recent cases in New York reveal, the guardians of public space are seeking the same rights to exclude that private property owners already enjoy, with Amtrak executives seeking to eject homeless people from Penn Station and the mayor of New York trying to bar protesters from the steps

[14] "In Riot's Shadow, a City Stumbles On," *New York Times*, July 14, 1997.
[15] Tracy Challenger, "Agora Coalition, Network Member Update," February 8, 2000.

of City Hall.[16] More and more Americans—estimated at one in six—now live under the private police protection and private services of gated or other kinds of association-managed communities, such as condominiums or cooperatives.

Despite initial commitments to selling to the "mass," ironically this postwar economy and society—ostensibly built on "mass consumption"—rapidly produced more economic and social stratification. The segmentation of metropolitan America was only reinforced by marketing and advertising, which simultaneously discovered the greater profits to be made in segmenting the market into distinctive sub-markets based on gender, class, age, race, ethnicity, and lifestyle. The Consumers' Republic was founded in the 1940s and 1950s on the conviction that mass markets offered endless potential for growth—that the "janitor's appetite for a sirloin steak is as profitable as the banker's," in the language of Chester Bowles, one of its influential designers. But by the late 1950s, advertisers, marketers, and manufacturers began to worry that mass markets would soon be saturated as more and more Americans bought a house, car, refrigerator, and washing machine.[17]

In 1956, marketing expert Wendell Smith, past president of the American Marketing Association and director of marketing research for Radio Corporation of America (RCA), proposed an alluring alternative to mass marketing that over the next ten years would revolutionize the field: market segmentation.[18] Companies increasingly adopted the strategy of dividing mass markets into smaller market segments defined by distinctive orientations and tastes, each to be sold different products or even the same product packaged and marketed in totally different ways. Two years later Pierre Martineau, a University of Chicago–trained sociologist and marketing director of the *Chicago Tribune,* elaborated the concept by arguing that a member of a market segment defined by social class or other criteria is "profoundly different in his mode of thinking and way of handling the world. . . . Where he buys and what he buys will differ not by economics but in symbolic value."[19] Together Smith and Martineau launched a new axiom of marketing, to be applied to cigarettes or refrigerators: homogeneity of buyers within a segmented market, heterogeneity between segmented markets.

[16] "Amtrak Is Ordered Not to Eject the Homeless from Penn Station," *New York Times,* February 22, 1995; "Can Amtrak Be a Censor?" *Washington Post,* February 22, 1995; "Judge Strikes Down Rule Limiting Protesters on City Hall Steps in New York," *New York Times,* April 7, 2000.

[17] Chester Bowles, "Why OPA Will Stand Pat on Price Control," *Printers' Ink,* October 12, 1945, 149.

[18] Wendell R. Smith, "Product Differentiation and Market Segmentation as Alternative Marketing Strategies," *Journal of Marketing* 21 (July 1956): 7.

[19] Pierre Martineau, "Social Classes and Spending Behavior," *Journal of Marketing* 23 (October 1958): 122–23.

The complexity of this change is too extensive for thorough examination here. Suffice it to say, as market segmentation exacerbated the divisions between social groups, it reinforced the fragmentation created by residential communities and commercial centers. And when politicians and campaign managers began to apply the techniques of market segmentation to the political sphere beginning in the 1960s, the shift from mass to segment took on larger political significance. Politicians targeted voters with distinctive messages aimed at their political interests, construed very narrowly. The voters, much like the segmented buyers of goods who sought the best match for their distinctive tastes and desires with what was available in the commercial marketplace, similarly came to expect the political marketplace—consisting of candidates, government agencies, and political action committees (PACs)—to respond to their particular needs and interests. In multiple arenas, then, Americans were propelled away from the common ground of the mass toward the divided, and often unequal, territories of population fragments. This process accentuated everything that made them different from each other, undermining any broad-based political agenda designed to serve the public good.

The application of market segmentation to politics beginning in the 1960s was part of a larger tendency in the Consumers' Republic to let the techniques and standards of the private marketplace define success in more and more spheres of American life. As the test of value increasingly became market viability, even the notion of public government itself was put at risk. Take, for example, the Clinton-Gore National Performance Review Report, which aimed at "reinventing government." Entitled *From Red Tape to Results: Creating a Government That Works Better and Costs Less,* the 1993 document drew its inspiration from the private transaction of retailer and customer: "Effective, entrepreneurial governments insist on customer satisfaction. They listen carefully to their customers—using surveys, focus groups, and the like. They restructure their basic operations to meet customers' needs. And they use market dynamics such as competition and customer service to create incentives that drive their employees to put customers first."[20]

During the last half-century, Americans' confidence that an economy and culture built around mass consumption could best deliver greater democracy and equality led the nation from the Consumers' Republic to what I call the "consumerization of the republic." Advocates first for the postwar suburb, then for the city, and increasingly for the nation itself all came to judge the success of the public realm much like other purchased goods, by the personal benefit that individual citizen-consumers derived from it. When Americans in the twenty-first century ask of the public do-

[20] *From Red Tape to Results: Creating a Government That Works Better and Costs Less* (Washington, DC: United States Government Printing Office, 1993), 6.

main "Am I getting my money's worth?" rather than "What's best for America?" they speak in an idiom that evolved out of the perhaps initially naive but ultimately misguided conviction of the Consumers' Republic that dynamic private markets could deliver democracy and prosperity to one and all. By the late twentieth century, moreover, American affluence itself became defined more by what consumers could buy than by the availability of well-paying jobs that made it possible for the mass of workers to be full citizen-participants in the Consumers' Republic. As inexpensive goods manufactured "off-shore" replaced domestically made items, the interdependence of production and consumption at the heart of the Consumers' Republic in the 1950s and 1960s unraveled. At the same time, the promise of a more egalitarian America gave way to growing inequalities of wealth.

Exporting the American Model

Even as the full realization of the lofty ideals of the Consumers' Republic eluded many Americans, the United States exported this model in the hope that mass consumer markets would deliver greater prosperity, democracy, and equality to other nations in its sphere of influence during the Cold War era. The most explicit effort to extend the reach of the formula of the Consumers' Republic was the Marshall Plan in Western Europe. In the late 1940s and early 1950s, the U.S. government committed to reconstruct economically and politically the war-ravaged European nations as a bulwark against the spread of Soviet communism. European historian Sheryl Kroen has been investigating both the way Marshall Plan officials linked consumerism and citizenship in their prescriptions for postwar recovery and the relative receptiveness of Germany, France, and Britain to that message. She argues that a combination of preexisting, in many cases prewar, political cultures and prevailing postwar political orientations dictated how each nation responded.[21]

The vision of what I have called the Consumers' Republic lay at the heart of the Marshall Plan's message, asserts Kroen. Its creators argued that greater national prosperity, rooted in and popularly experienced through higher levels of private consumption, would ensure the uncontested dominance of American-style capitalist democracy. Rising productivity, higher wages, lower prices, and the importation of American-made goods all promised to provide Europeans with the economic and political benefits of the "American way of life." Americans feared that persistent economic

[21] Sheryl Kroen, "A Political History of the Consumer," *Historical Journal* 47, no. 3 (September 2004): 709–36. Other helpful discussions of the Marshall Plan's consumer orientation can be found in Irwin M. Wall, *The United States and the Making of Postwar France, 1945–1954* (Cambridge: Cambridge University Press, 1991) and Richard Kuisel, *Seducing the French: The Dilemma of Americanization* (Berkeley: University of California Press, 1993).

hardship and the failure to reform prewar social structures to create more widespread opportunity would breed communism. Instruction came on many fronts, from the high-level advice given by officials of the Economic Cooperation Administration (ECA) charged with implementing the Marshall Plan, to the hundreds of "missions" organized for Europeans to observe firsthand how the American model actually worked, and to the popular fantasies fueled by widely disseminated Hollywood movies and the more explicit American propaganda efforts like the traveling exhibition "The True Face of the United States." This exhibition, which made its way around France in 1952, explicitly encouraged the French to imagine a rosier future of shorter working hours and greater earnings that still made possible the ownership of new consumer durables. For example, displays proclaimed that one of six Americans owned a television, that 822 hours of work bought an American worker a car, and that there were 300 cars for every thousand inhabitants in the United States (in contrast to the 2,290 hours of labor required and only 15 cars per thousand in the Soviet Union). It took 144 working hours for an American to earn the money for a washing machine, and so on down the shopping list to clothing and butter. Thanks to all these consumer opportunities, the exhibition concluded, "the American worker knows that he receives an equitable part of the wealth he creates."[22]

Western Europeans responded in varied ways to this American call to rebuild postwar economies and polities around the expansion of consumer purchasing power and to turn citizens into consumers whose affluence would then mark the success of capitalist democracy. Western Germans offered the strongest support, explains Kroen. In Britain, the "fair shares"–oriented Labour Party was more resistant, fearing that mass consumption would prove socially divisive, though their reticence later allowed the Conservatives to ride to power on the popular rejection of austerity. The French emerged as the staunchest opponents of the American vision, fearing that a greater commitment to mass consumption might accentuate, not reduce, social inequality.

Where nations fell on the spectrum depended on their prior attraction to alternative ideologies—such as support for a European-style welfare state that granted greater importance to the power of government or long-established traditions of consumer cooperatives—as well as current polit-

[22] Photographs from "The Real Face of the United States" exhibition provided to me by Sheryl Kroen from Archives nationales, F60ter 394; she described the exhibition in a lecture, "The Magic of Things: The Marshall Plan, the Cold War and the Making of Consumer Democracy," Cambridge, England, March 2003. The exhibit is also discussed in Kuisel, *Seducing the French,* 76–77. Less ideologically, the American businessmen who served as the Marshall Plan's overseers hoped that the embrace of this message might also help break down French protectionism and expand the market for American-made goods; see Wall, *The United States and the Making of Postwar France,* 113–14.

ical realities. In Germany, where defeat in World War II had delegitimized prewar precedents, the architect of the German economic miracle, Economics Minister Ludwig Erhard, celebrated the convergence of citizen and consumer and the importance of free markets to Germany's success with democracy. As West Germans became "a free nation of consumers," he promised in 1950, not only would they achieve prosperity but also the fulfillment of their "demand that [its] social product . . . should be employed for its own ends, for the ends of human and social welfare."[23] In France, by contrast, ordinary French people's loyalty to the republican state as a protector of equality and liberty, strong support for the Communist Party and Communist unions, and entrenched anti-Americanism combined to undermine support for the consumerist solution set out in the Marshall Plan until late in the 1950s and the 1960s. Even then a more mass consumer–centered economic strategy coexisted with a still vigorous social welfare state and the Fifth Republic's Gaullist brand of anti-Americanism.

Across the globe, at the other edge of the United States' anti-Soviet sphere of influence, the postwar experience of Japan offers another example of a complex response to the American model of the Consumers' Republic. In the immediate postwar era, despite the U.S.-dominated occupation of Japan (1945–52), both the Japanese government and American officials emphasized the revival of basic industry—not the production of consumer durables—as the critical first step to economic recovery after the devastation of the war. To fund that recovery, Japanese policymakers maintained their prewar and wartime commitment to viewing civilian savings as a critical source of investment capital for economic growth. In fact, Japan's leaders employed language strikingly parallel to that used by the framers of the Consumers' Republic in linking individual and national interest, but the message here was the opposite: frugality, not spending, was the route to prosperity for household and nation alike. One should economize, save, and invest in order to fuel "revival of the realm." Producing for export, not stimulating internal demand, was considered the linchpin of a prosperous postwar economy.[24]

By the mid-1950s, however, many Japanese government bureaucrats and business leaders began to recognize the important lessons to be learned from the American model and a more Keynesian conception of a

[23] Ludwig Erhard, *The Economics of Success,* trans. J. A. Arengo-Jones and D. J. S. Thomson (London: Thames and Hudson, 1963), 80, quoted in Erica Carter, *How German Is She? Postwar German Reconstruction and the Consuming Woman* (Ann Arbor: University of Michigan Press, 1997), 26. See Carter for a discussion of the centrality of consumption and consumers to visions of Germany's postwar success as an economy and a democracy. Also see Konrad H. Jarausch and Michael Geyer, *Shattering Past: Reconstructing German Histories* (Princeton: Princeton University Press, 2003).

[24] Sheldon Garon, "Luxury is the Enemy: Mobilizing Savings and Popularizing Thrift in Wartime Japan," *Journal of Japanese Studies* 26, no. 1 (Winter 2000): 41–78, quotation 74; Andrew Gordon, "Managing the Japanese Household: The New Life Movement in Postwar Japan," *Social Politics* 4, no. 2 (Summer 1997): 245–83.

demand economy. Greater consumer purchasing power would stimulate production, while also raising the Japanese standard of living. Economic Planning Agency economist Gotō Yonosuke, for example, was inspired by a visit to the United States in 1956. Authoring the agency's white papers in 1956 and 1957, Gotō argued that economic growth depended on the nurturing of an American-style middle class that had the purchasing power to expand domestic markets.[25] Electrical manufacturers like Matsushita, meanwhile, worked to create new domestic markets for their products.[26] Private consumption became increasingly important to Japan's postwar economic miracle as consumers were encouraged to acquire the latest in large consumer durables. The Ikeda administration's "Income Doubling Plan" of 1960 codified the importance of consumption to Japan's economic growth, promising to double average household incomes within the next decade in order to create a true mass market.[27]

But even with this greater orientation to private consumption, the Japanese retained a more critical role for the government as regulator and stabilizer than in the more laissez-faire American version of the Consumers' Republic. Moreover, Japanese households never abandoned saving as extensively as the Americans, constraining consumption whenever the economy faltered (see Horioka, chap. 5, and Garon, chap. 7).[28] Nonetheless, the Japanese did mirror some key aspects of the Consumers' Republic, both in its ideal of linking democracy to expanded purchasing power and in its more disappointing reality. For example, as private markets were increasingly entrusted with solving land and housing shortages in the densely populated nation, they exacerbated economic inequality between those who owned valuable property and those who did not, much in the same way that their American counterparts did. The reliance of postwar Japan's electrical goods industry on cheap (often female) labor, moreover, belied the more equitable promises of the Consumers' Republic.[29]

[25] Scott O'Bryan, "Gotō Yonosuke, Statistical Knowledge and the Idea of Consumption in Post-World War II Japan," paper delivered at the Annual Meeting of the Association for Asian Studies, March 29, 2003, New York, in possession of the author, and "Growth Solutions: Economic Knowledge and Problems of Capitalism in Postwar Japan, 1945–1960," Ph.D. dissertation, Columbia University, 2000.

[26] Simon Partner, *Assembled in Japan: Electrical Goods and the Making of the Japanese Consumer* (Berkeley: University of California Press, 1999).

[27] Laura Hein, "Growth Versus Success: Japan's Economic Policy in Historical Perspective" and Marilyn Ivy, "Formations of Mass Culture," in *Postwar Japan as History,* ed. Andrew Gordon (Berkeley: University of California Press, 1993), 114–15, 247–51.

[28] Hein, "Growth Versus Success," 104, 106. The Japanese retreated from consumption during the oil shock of 1973–74 and the slump of the 1990s. The continued Japanese economic crisis has been met by stagnant consumer spending and, most recently, by a sharp and uncharacteristic drop in the saving rate (by half, to 6.9 percent of income) between 1990 and 2001, as Japanese have used their savings to maintain their lifestyles. See Ken Belson, "Japan Builds a Recovery on the Boom or Bust of Exports," *New York Times,* December 1, 2003.

[29] Partner, *Assembled in Japan,* 188–89, 231; Hein, "Growth Versus Success," 101, and Koji Taira, "Dialectics of Economic Growth, National Power, and Distributive Struggles," in *Postwar Japan as History,* ed. Gordon, 185.

Just as the impact of the Consumers' Republic in the United States differed substantially from the democratizing ambitions of its promoters, so too did the extent of its adoption abroad vary. Together with its current political orientation, a nation's prior experience—such as the French preference for a strong state or Japan's history of aggressive savings campaigns—shaped how the Consumers' Republic was understood and embraced. Because national cultures assigned distinctive consumer roles to men and women, the gender dynamics of the mass consumption economy particularly differed. Whereas men gained consumer authority in postwar America at the expense of women, housewives in post-1945 Japan and South Korea achieved unprecedented control of household finances, even as the purchasing of consumer durables grew (see Garon, chap. 7; Gordon, chap. 6; and Nelson, chap. 8). Furthermore, the American model often played into existing tensions between different camps over how their nation should be rebuilt. When societies perceived that model of modernism as endangering valued aspects of traditional culture, as seen in the French commitment to the vitality of "centre ville" or the Japanese loyalty to small, independent retailers, the embrace of American-style mass consumption provoked considerable opposition.[30]

But even if the Consumers' Republic provided no automatic blueprint for the postwar "free world," as the United States and its allies often chose to call themselves, it provided a powerful vision for the desirability of widespread economic prosperity and participatory democracy. Moreover, much as that linkage set a new, ambitious standard for a postwar society's success, it can now provide historians with a useful gauge of the extent to which the postwar years—now viewed nostalgically as a golden age—often failed to measure up.

[30] This opposition continued through the twentieth century into the twenty-first, with the French for a long time resisting MacDonald's and more recently Starbucks, and the Japanese famously opposing the opening of Toys 'R' Us stores.

3

CONSUMING AMERICA, PRODUCING JAPAN

SHUNYA YOSHIMI
TRANSLATED BY DAVID BUIST

It is often said that postwar Japanese popular culture is basically "American." In other words, American influence has been decisive for the development of cultural consumption in everyday life in postwar Japan. But the issue here is in the very concept of "America" in the historical context of postwar Japan and East Asia. Clearly there are many cases in everyday practices, especially consuming practices, in which we can find an American influence (see Cohen, chap. 2). For example, since the 1950s the ideal of postwar Japanese home life flowed explicitly from the model of the American way of life. People wanted to buy all kinds of home electric appliances and live in American-style suburban houses. In the field of design and advertising, American influences were more evident. American films and TV dramas were quite popular, particularly during the 1950s. So we might say that postwar Japanese consumer culture emerged from the overwhelming American influence beginning in the late 1940s. However, by the mid-1960s Japanese no longer recognized these influences as specifically American. Already in the late 1950s, the symbolic products of the American way of life, such as the TV, the refrigerator, and the washing machine, had come to be viewed nationalistically, as symbols of the Japanese imperial house. Beginning in the 1960s, American TV drama series were eclipsed by domestically produced Japanese "home drama" series. In addition, many new household products were given traditional-sounding Japanese names. Rather than openly question Americanization (as the French did), Japanese came to regard the postwar American influence as essentially Japanese in origin.

This chapter examines the complex influence of "America" on postwar

Japanese society by looking at two particular cases. First, I analyze the American influence on Japanese urban space from the time of the Occupation of Japan (1945–52) through the 1950s and the way that this influence has been remembered (or rather, not remembered). The second case relates to the introduction of the American way of life into the Japanese domestic sphere in the 1950s and 1960s. Besides considering the process through which these influences worked, I discuss how they have been represented in popular memory and consciousness. The analysis of both cases is only a first step toward more comprehensive research. It nevertheless helps to illuminate the complexity of what we tend simplistically to call "the American influence." This influence is not merely a matter of cultural contact, it is part of a dynamic process of identity formation mediated by a sense of desire and prohibition related to the representation and appropriation of the "Other."

"Americanism" in Interwar Japan

Cultural Americanization in Japan had, of course, begun much earlier. In the late 1920s, middle-class inhabitants of large urban areas such as Tokyo and Osaka became captivated by Hollywood films, consumer goods, and the American lifestyle. In his book *Amerika* (1929), Murobuse Takanobu wrote: "Where could you find a Japan not Americanized? How could Japan exist without America? And where could we go to escape Americanization? I dare to declare that America has become the world; Japan is nothing but America today." America, he continued, had exported its civilization not only to Latin America, Japan, China, and India, but also to England, Germany, France, even Communist Russia, and the historical center of civilization, Rome; the world was entering the age of America; America would dominate not only the dollar (i.e., economy) but also the world civilization based on the dollar.[1] In retrospect, Murobuse's argument comes across as a crude statement of the cultural imperialism thesis, filled with illogical leaps and exaggerations. Yet it is noteworthy that Japanese were extensively discussing the phenomenon of Americanization as early as the 1920s.

From the late 1920s to the 1930s, Japanese monthly magazines often grouped together several articles on America by prominent writers. For example, Nii Itaru wrote in 1929 that the world was entering an age in which the colors, smells, and sounds of nations were rapidly melting together, and Americanism pervaded this "cocktail age." As Nii observed, Japanese young people were fascinated with jazz, and they willingly imitated the hairstyles, makeup, and dress of the Hollywood movies that had begun to

[1] Murobuse Takanobu, *Amerika: sono keizai to bunmei* [America: Economy and civilization] (Tokyo: Senshinsha, 1929), 4.

flood Japan. In the urban lifestyle of the day, it had become fashionable to work in an American-style building, watch a baseball game, go driving on Sunday afternoon, or spend the evening going dancing or to the cinema. Nii noted the relationship between the vogue of Americanism in lifestyle and the vogue of Russianism in social thought. In Japan, "a man who adheres to Russian ideology often prefers American tastes, and the 'modern boy' who maintains an American lifestyle also knows much about socialism." In Japan, these two tendencies were not contradictory, they were concurrent.[2]

Ōya Sōichi seized upon another aspect of the current Americanism that had spread in large cities like Osaka in the form of "modern life." In his words, "Osaka is Japan's America." Japanese modernization from the late nineteenth century had been led by the governmental elite in Tokyo and had persistently followed the model of the major European nations: Britain, France, and Germany. As a result, Tokyo became an urban center full of western imitations. During this period, "America was seen as a colony of Anglo-Saxon origin, and Russia as a developing country extending over Asia." But these cultural geopolitics drastically changed after World War I, observed Ōya. From this upheaval emerged two types of twentieth-century culture: Russian and American. In particular, "America, with its enormous capital and Hollywood films' propagandistic capacity among other things, is sweeping over Europe, its cultural motherland now exhausted by war, and also over Asian countries, even over the whole world." Ōya then compared this cultural condition of Europe with that of Tokyo after the Great Kanto Earthquake of 1923. Because the culture of Tokyo had developed by imitating European countries, he argued, the Tokyo copy would also likely degenerate now that the original had lost its vitality. It was Osaka—not Tokyo—whose influence would dominate and sweep over the rest of the country, insisted Ōya, deeming Osaka's vibrant culture to be popular American culture.[3]

Osaka's preeminence in modern life proved short-lived. From the 1930s, Ginza in Tokyo became the exemplary center where Americanism flourished in prewar and postwar Japan alike. During the Meiji period (1868–1912), Ginza, which the government designed as a model of westernization, had been a clear imitation of the western-style main street of Victorian London and also resembled streets in the British colonies. Later, a French vogue strongly influenced the taste of the elite and the bourgeoisie, who gathered in Ginza to frequent a number of newly established French-style cafés. Starting out in Ginza, Japan's largest cosmetics com-

[2] Nii Itaru, "Amerikanizumu to Roshianizumu no kōryū" [Rise of Americanism and Russianism], *Chūō kōron* 44, no. 6 (June 1929): 63–66.

[3] Ōya Sōichi, "Ōsaka wa Nihon no Beikoku da" [Osaka is Japan's America], *Ōya Sōichi zenshū*, vol. 2 (Tokyo: Sōyōsha, 1980–82), 152–55.

pany, named Shiseido, propelled this taste in things French to the cultural forefront. However, during the 1930s, American consumer culture rapidly overwhelmed British and French styles. As Andō Kōsei wrote in 1931:

> It is Americanism that dominates Ginza today. If you look at pedestrians on the sidewalks, you find at once that their styles and behaviors are completely imitated from American movies. . . . The majority of restaurants in Ginza do not serve French dinner with wine, but American lunch with beer. You can hear American jazz in every cafe. . . . Instead of French taste, Ginza is filled with the Americanism of big capital, speed, and the movies. Today, most Japanese want to understand the world only through America.[4]

It is this Ginza of Americanism, not the Meiji period's Ginza of westernization, that became the dominant center of Japanese consumer culture from the 1930s to the 1960s. By the 1960s, more than 500 shopping streets all around Japan were named "Ginza" to emphasize their modern image.[5]

The flourishing Americanism in large Japanese cities after the late 1920s did not merely import American culture, it remade it. Although "America" was often said to have swept over Japanese popular culture, the latter was not reduced to dependency on American mass cultural products but strove instead to naturalize and reinvent them. Already in 1943, in the midst of the war against America, Shimizu Ikutarō pointed out that the prevailing Americanism in contemporary Japan was not the same thing as the original Americanism as found in the United States. According to his sociological perspective, when detached fragments of American culture were imported into Japan, it was impossible for them to keep their original functions, because the functions of culture always depended on context. In particular, he argued, cultural elements related to leisure and consumption predominated in Japan, while Americanism originally meant the basic philosophy that knitted together all aspects of American life and culture. In Japan, most patterns of modern leisure and consumption after the mid-1920s were dubbed "Americanism." Moreover, Japan's Americanism was strongly related to private, domestic life, whereas the original usage expressed American public consciousness.[6]

In a sense, the private character of Japanese Americanism derived from structural changes in Americanism itself during the 1920s. As many sociological studies, including Robert and Helen Lynd's *Middletown* (1929) and

[4] Andō Kōsei, *Ginza saiken* [A detailed look at Ginza] (Tokyo: Chūō kōronsha, 1977), 29–30.

[5] Hattori Keijirō, "Ginza, soshite Ginzanizeeshon" [Ginza, therefore Ginzanization], *Toshi mondai* 67, no. 5 (May 1976): 63–80.

[6] Shimizu Ikutarō, "Teki toshite no Amerikanizumu" [Americanism as enemy], *Chūō kōron* 58, no. 4 (April 1943): 82–85.

Frederic Allen's *Only Yesterday* (1931) describe, mass consumption swept over American life in the 1920s. Through this process, Americanism in the United States became more and more associated with the private life of mass consumption. The advertising industry expanded, and commodities such as the automobile, the radio, and household electric appliances became the symbolic elements of Americanism. The movement of "Seikatsu Kaizen" (daily life improvement) exemplified the growing relationship between American consumer life and Japanese Americanism in the 1920s (see Garon, chap. 7). The movement's leading proponent, Morimoto Kōkichi, had studied consumer economics at Johns Hopkins University. His concept of "cultural life" was strongly influenced by the image of private life among the American middle class. He established an association in Tokyo for "cultural life" with the aim of propagating rational knowledge of life among housewives, using as its model correspondence education, which was popular in the United States at the time. Although Morimoto's movement did not succeed, similar ideas of "cultural life" continued to influence the popular image of "modern life."[7]

The Unconscious Occupation of Tokyo's Urban Spaces

The process of widespread Americanization can be dated to the late 1940s. The postwar era marked the beginning of the process whereby the concept of America, which had initially entered the everyday consciousness of Japanese urban dwellers before World War II, expanded to all of Japan. For instance, only one month after Japan's unconditional surrender on August 15, 1945, an English conversation guide book, *Nichibei Eikaiwa techō* (Japanese-American English Conversation Booklet), became a bestseller with over four million copies in circulation. In 1947, NHK (Japan Broadcasting Corporation) began broadcasting a radio program, "Amerika Tayori" (Letter from America), consisting of current affairs reports from Washington. This program, too, became very popular. In 1949, the morning edition of the *Asahi* newspaper began carrying the comic strip "Blondie," a lighthearted illustration of American lifestyles and prosperity. "Blondie" continued to enjoy wide popularity right up to 1951, when she was replaced by her Japanese counterpart, "Sazae-san." Although the scenes portrayed in "Blondie" did not directly feature electric appliances and automobiles, postwar Japanese read the symbols of "American prosperity" into the cartoon strip.[8] In 1950, the *Asahi* newspaper sponsored an "American Expo-

[7] See also Jordan Sand, *House and Home in Modern Japan: Architecture, Domestic Space, and Bourgeois Culture, 1880–1930* (Cambridge: Harvard University Asia Center, 2003).

[8] Iwamoto Shigeki, *Sengo Amerikanizeeshon no genfūkei* [The original landscape of Americanization] (Tokyo: Haabesutosha, 2002), 43–62.

sition" in the outskirts of Osaka. The exposition proved to be far more popular than expected. Large crowds came to see the exhibits, which included a "White House Hall" (recounting American history from the Mayflower to Roosevelt), a main exhibition hall with displays of American prosperity, a television hall, and panoramas providing a virtual scenic tour of America with pictures of New York skyscrapers, the Statue of Liberty, and the Golden Gate Bridge.[9]

However, the complexity of the postwar Japanese encounter with America cannot be understood simply as an extension of the prewar Americanization. Needless to say, from 1945 to 1952, America took the form of the army of occupation, a singularly powerful and directly present "Other." As John Dower demonstrates, U.S. domination was not entirely one-way, and it did not always achieve the intended effect.[10] Nevertheless, from the perspective of the occupied Japanese, America presented itself as an overwhelming source of authority, against which it was difficult to mount any challenge. America represented more than the image of new lifestyles and culture—it had become an ever-present force intervening in people's daily lives. The Americans consciously engineered change, of course, through censorship and various cultural policies. Other important changes occurred, without any conscious design, through the interaction of occupier and occupied.

Indeed, the army of occupation itself became an integral part of the cultural scenery of postwar Japan. When one considers the realm of unintentional change, America seems less a "prohibiting" presence than a "seducing" presence in the everyday consciousness of the times. As an illustration, let us consider the link between U.S. military bases and postwar popular music. Many young popular Japanese singers began their careers entertaining American troops on the bases and in recreation facilities. Life there existed largely in isolation from the surrounding Japanese society, and working conditions were relatively good. At the age of six, Itō Yukari began singing on American bases from her father's back. Eri Chiemi first sang to American soldiers while in the fourth grade of primary school. Matsuo Kazuko took the stage at Kita Fuji Base when she was fifteen. Meanwhile, Mori Mitsuko made a living touring bases, singing the jazz she had learned. Several hundred musicians used to gather daily at the northern Marunouchi exit of Tokyo Station, where they were "auctioned off" as band players in front of American military trucks. From this developed the postwar system of talent recruitment by brokers, which later dominated mass entertainment in the age of television.[11] Numerous powerful cultural

[9] Hirai Tsunejirō, *Amerika hakurankai* [American exposition] (Tokyo: Asahi Shinbunsha, 1950).

[10] John W. Dower, *Embracing Defeat: Japan in the Wake of World War II* (New York: Norton, 1999).

[11] Kuwabara Inetoshi, "Shinchūgun to sengo geinō" [The occupation army and postwar performing arts], in *Bessatsu shinpyō sengo Nihon geinōshi* (Tokyo: Shinpyōsha, 1981), 48–54.

influences—jazz, fashion, sexual culture—spread out from the American bases and took root in Japan from the early days of the Occupation.

However, the linkage between popular culture and U.S. bases in postwar Japan cannot simply be reduced to American influence. Although direct connections with the occupying power enabled many aspects of popular culture to regain their footing after the war, popular culture itself rhetorically negated this connection. As the Occupation drew to a close, Japanese popular culture attempted to forget its links with the occupier. Underground images associated with the Occupation, such as the "black market" and the ubiquitous unlicensed prostitutes known as "pan-pan girls," faded to the margins. As the violent America of the Occupation receded, "America" instead became a model of lifestyle consumption.

The link between these two aspects of America is highly complex, one worth exploring at the level of urban space. Japanese people related to America in very different ways. At one extreme was the direct encounter with the violence of the bases in such places as Okinawa, Tachikawa, and Yokosuka. At the other extreme lay the hidden relation with America in the centers of consumer culture, notably Roppongi, Harajuku, and Ginza. The public today does not typically associate these latter districts with the American military. Nevertheless, these areas became special places for Japanese youth after the war in part because of their relation to American military facilities that once existed within them.

Before the war, Roppongi had been a "soldiers' town." Numerous military facilities were concentrated there, including those of the territorial army, Konoe Division, and Kenpeitai (military police). American bombers devastated the area during the war, and the U.S. forces inherited the remaining facilities after the surrender. Military headquarters, barracks, and housing for military personnel came to be located there. Since these facilities were not returned to Japan until around 1960, Roppongi remained in the shadow of the American military throughout the 1950s. Unlike Yokota, Tachikawa, and Yokosuka, however, Roppongi lacked an air base or large concentrations of troops. There was therefore little sense of America as "the source of violence" there. Japanese young people flocked to the area, becoming known as the *Roppongi-zoku* (Roppongi tribe). TV personalities, rockabilly singers, and their associates gathered in Roppongi, as the district developed its present image as a place for fashionable and colonial-style night life.

Likewise, the development of Harajuku into a "young people's town" cannot be explained without reference to Washington Heights, once a residential facility for American officers. The construction of the Heights began immediately after the end of the war. It was fully equipped with a hospital, school, fire station, church, department store, theatre, tennis courts, and golf course. Washington Heights thus became a symbol of American affluence, appearing suddenly like a mirage amid the surrounding burnt-out ruins, barracks, and underground markets. In the

1950s, shops catering to officers' families, such as Kiddy Land and Oriental Bazaar, lined the streets. It was in this new townscape that the Central Apartments was built. Known as the most luxurious residence in Tokyo, the facility stood as a symbol of the district. In the words of Kobayashi Nobuhiko, who lived in Harajuku in the early 1960s, those who lived in this building mostly worked for trading companies or in other occupations connected with the American military; they were "people who were above the clouds to 'ordinary Japs.'"[12] At that time, Harajuku still seemed off-limits, a place largely reserved for the American military. Eventually the American military presence diminished, and the residents of the Central Apartments changed from personnel connected with the American military to people working in trend-setting professions, such as cameramen, designers, and copywriters.

Meanwhile, in the Ginza district of Tokyo during the Occupation,

> the main buildings were requisitioned for use as occupation army facilities. . . . Stars and stripes were seen fluttering all over the area, giving an impression just like that of an American town. There was great activity around the PX set up in Matsuya Department Store, since it was frequented by officers and troops from all branches of the Allied forces. War orphans thronged around the entrance selling things or offering their services as shoeshine boys.[13]

Even before the war, Ginza had projected an air of Americanism, but during the Occupation it "Americanized" in the more direct sense of becoming a foreign concession. Even the streets acquired names invoking a colonial landscape, such as "New Broadway," "X Avenue," "Embassy Street," "St. Peter's Street," "Poker Street," and "Hold Up Avenue." Nor was the American-style naming of streets restricted to Ginza. The occupation forces called the main roads radiating outwards from the imperial palace "avenues," while the roads running in irregular circles around the center were called "streets." The "avenues" were labeled A to Z in a clockwise order, and names were given to the sixty or so streets. The official names were used mostly for functional purposes, but in Ginza, where the central command headquarters was located, the Japanese public also used some of the American names.[14]

References to the Ginza district in popular songs of the time give some indication of the heavy presence of the occupation army, combined with

[12] Kobayashi Nobuhiko, *Shisetsu Tōkyō hanjōki* [My Tokyo history] (Tokyo: Chūō kōronsha, 1984), 41–44.

[13] Harada Hiroshi, *MP Jeep kara mita senryōka no Tōkyō* [Occupied Tokyo as seen from an MP's Jeep] (Tokyo: Sōshisha, 1994), 176.

[14] Fukushima Jūrō, *G. H. Q. Tōkyō senryō chizu* [Maps of the allied occupation in Tokyo] (Yūshōdō shuppan, 1987), 10–13.

sexual images of the ruined and burnt-out city. For example, the 1946 hit song "Tokyo Flower Girl" represented the contemporary landscape of Ginza as follows:

> Jazz is playing, the lamplight shadow of the hall
> Buy my flowers, buy my flowers
> An American soldier in a chic sweater
> A sweet fragrance chases after his shadow.[15]

Given the strict censorship by the Occupation's Civil Censorship Detachment, it is somewhat strange that such a song should have been performed, drawing so direct a connection between the Ginza and American soldiers. Later songs tended to make these references more obliquely. The 1949 hit, "Ginza Cancan Girl," goes like this:

> That girl is cute, that cancan girl
> Wearing a red blouse and sandals
> Waiting for someone on a street corner of Ginza
> Looking at the time, grinning nervously
> This is the Ginza Cancan Girl.[16]

In 1951, a song called "Tokyo Shoeshine Boy" came out with these lyrics:

> That girl in red shoes
> Today still walking the Ginza
> With presents of chocolate
> Chewing gum and castella.[17]

Historical discontinuities have obscured the memory of how places once occupied by American military facilities became centers for the consumer culture of youth. I have mentioned the appearance of the "Roppongi tribe" beginning in the late 1950s and the curious changes in the lyrics of songs about Ginza. In addition, the "Western Carnival" was held in 1957 at the Nissei Theatre in Ginza, starring Yamashita Keijiro, Hirao Masaaki, and Mickey Curtis. This spectacle achieved enormous popularity and, along with the influence of Elvis Presley, spurred the fashion for rockabilly. However, by this time the connection with the occupation forces was

[15] Komota Nobuo et al., *Nihon ryūkōkashi* [History of Japan's hit songs] (Tokyo: Shakai shisōsha, 1970), 345. "Tōkyo no hana uri musume" composed by Uehara Gento, lyrics by Sasa Shisei.

[16] Komota, *Nihon ryūkōkashi,* 355. "Ginza kankan musume" composed by Hattori Ryōichi, lyrics by Saeki Takao.

[17] Komota, *Nihon ryūkōkashi,* 364. "Tōkyō shūshain bōi" composed by Sano Suki, lyrics by Ida Seiichi.

no longer obvious. Whereas Japanese musicians in the 1940s had polished their skills playing for American soldiers, the musical trends of the 1960s were supported by an audience of Japanese youth. Already at the beginning of the 1950s, as the American military pulled out of the Japanese mainland, the Japanese jazz bands that had played for the troops were leaving the bases and starting to play with Japanese singers instead. At that time, there were as many as 150 jazz bands in Tokyo, and more than 3,000 band players.[18] Eri Chiemi and Yukimura Izumi both debuted with jazz numbers. Together with Misora Hibari, these two singers attained stardom as part of the same trend. It was against this background that the TV entertainment world took shape, around the beginning of the 1960s. By this time, popular culture's link with America had become indirect.

America Fragments: Between "Desire" and "Oblivion"

The period of the late 1950s and the 1960s, which saw the development of the youth culture described above, was also a time of intense struggle over the military bases. This began in 1953 with protests against the U.S. Army's test-firing range in Ishikawa. The first anti-base movement in Tokyo occurred that same year with a large rally of residents opposed to the Setagaya Base. In 1955, protests erupted over the enlargement of the American military air base in Tachikawa in the outskirts of Tokyo. In October 1956, farmers, trade unionists, and students staged a sit-in to prevent surveying of the land. They clashed with police, resulting in around a thousand casualties. At roughly the same time, large protests took place in Okinawa in response to the repeated rapes and killings of Okinawan women by American soldiers and an occupation policy generally at odds with residents' wishes.

Thus, in the Japan of the late 1950s, two Americas emerged. On the one hand, there was America the object of consumption, manifesting itself in material goods and media images. This America had gradually shed its associations with military violence, despite having been started on American bases and in military recreation facilities. There was also America the violent, the object of the anti-base protests. These images reflected different aspects of the same America. A relation with U.S. military bases lay behind the formation of the fashionable postwar images of all the places mentioned above. To this extent, it is possible to trace a continuous cultural geopolitical horizon from Ginza, Roppongi, and Harajuku, on the one hand, to Yokosuka and Okinawa, on the other.

Nevertheless, as Japan entered the era of high economic growth in the late 1950s, a fault line opened up between the two Americas of Japanese

[18] Komota, *Nihon ryūkōkashi,* 143.

perception. The America embodied in such places as Ginza, Roppongi, and Harajuku and the America of Yokosuka and Okinawa came to be seen as completely different things. The Japanese now understood the consumerist America entirely at the level of consumer culture, as if it had existed from the very beginning. However, in the case of the violent America, Japanese erased the cultural dimension, focusing their overwhelming attention on the problems of pollution, violence, and prostitution emanating from the bases.

This differentiation of the two Americas was reflected in and reinforced by the division in roles between the Japanese mainland and Okinawa. We see one remarkable expression of this in the currency exchange-rate policy. In the mainland, the rate was fixed at one dollar to 360 yen in accordance with the "Dodge Line" of 1949, the plan to solve Japan's economic problems formulated by Detroit businessman Joseph M. Dodge. The United States deliberately undervalued the yen to spur economic recovery by encouraging exports. In Okinawa, by contrast, the U.S. government's main goal was not economic recovery but the establishment of a stable environment for the construction of military bases. Local labor, construction companies, and service industries were mobilized to build the bases. The money thus earned was used to import goods and was recycled into the local economy. To encourage imports, United States set the exchange rate at 120 "B-yen" to the dollar. The sharp difference in exchange rates between the mainland and Okinawa led to the development of very different economic structures. In the mainland, an export-led growth economy developed, while in Okinawa the economy became heavily dependent on the bases. These were two sides of the same coin. The policy adopted in Okinawa encouraged the development of a subordinate economic structure with a weak manufacturing sector and an inordinately large tertiary sector centered on trading imports. On the mainland, export industries grew steadily, nurturing the formation of a mass consumer society.[19]

The separation of the mainland from Okinawa clearly reflected the great change in U.S. policy toward Asia that occurred around 1947. With the beginning of the Cold War, the focus shifted from the earlier goal of democratization and the decentralization of power to a policy designed to make Japan into the leading member of the western bloc in Asia. This policy turnaround became permanent after the Chinese Revolution of 1949. Japan would have been far less important to American policy if there had still been a pro-American government in mainland China to block the southward spread of Soviet power. However, with the formation of a Communist government in China, Japan ended up becoming the cornerstone

[19] Makino Hirotaka, *Saikō Okinawa keizai* [Rethinking the Okinawan economy] (Naha: Okinawa taimususha, 1996); Minamura Takeichi, *Sengo Nihon no keisei to hatten* [Formation and development of postwar Japan] (Tokyo: Nihon keizai hyōronsha, 1995).

of America's Asia policy. It became necessary to construct Japan as a military bulwark against communism in East Asia, requiring the stabilization of the Japanese economy as the center for economic growth in the region. In the absence of any immediate prospect for the expansion of economic relations between Japan and China, George F. Kennan had already advised the Truman administration to revive the Japanese economy by linking it to the markets of Southeast Asia. This plan was tantamount to establishing a new "East Asian Co-Prosperity Sphere" under the aegis of the American military. However, U.S. policymakers recognized that such a co-prosperity sphere could not by itself transform Japan into the center of anticommunism in Asia. It would also be necessary to reduce Japan's military burden to avoid any drag on its economic recovery. To solve this dilemma, the United States placed the military burden primarily on Okinawa, while permitting the Japanese mainland to concentrate on economic growth.

As a result of this strategy, U.S. military facilities became less visible in the urban areas of the Japanese mainland after the 1960s. This was in stark contrast to the situation in Okinawa, where the worsening situation in Indochina made the presence of the bases more prominent. In 1953, there were 733 American military facilities located in mainland Japan, covering a total land area of about 1000 square kilometers. These facilities were found in every region of the country; they included 44 air bases, 79 training ranges, 30 naval port facilities, 220 barracks, and 51 residential complexes. The U.S. military presence was thus a fact of daily life visible to anyone. However, this presence gradually diminished over the late 1950s and 1960s. By 1968, mainland Japan was home to only 7 U.S. air bases, 16 training ranges, 9 port facilities, 4 barracks, and 17 residential complexes. The number of U.S. troops on the mainland also decreased from 260,000 in 1952 to 150,000 in 1955, then down to 77,000 in 1957 and 46,000 in 1960. The greatest reductions affected land forces, as the emphasis of the American military presence shifted to the navy and air force. By the end of the 1960s, there were just a few facilities left in the Tokyo area, including the bases at Yokota, Tachikawa, Yokosuka, and Zama. The presence of American military personnel ceased to be a central part of people's everyday lives.[20]

So it was that the image of America in mainland Japan came to be divorced from the experience and memory of direct encounters with the bases and their associated violence, in contrast to the situation in other parts of East Asia—namely Okinawa, South Korea, and Taiwan. America had been sanitized as an image consumed through the media, and it extended its seductive power uniformly among the whole population. In the

[20] *Nihon no Beigun kichi* [U.S. bases in Japan], *Shisō no kagaku* 160 (October 1968), special issue. See also *Shutoken no naka no Beigun kichi* [U.S. bases in the Tokyo area], *Asahi journal*, June 29, 1969.

late 1940s and early 1950s, America had held very different meanings for different groups of Japanese. For some people, America represented a liberator, while for others it was a conqueror. America was simultaneously an object of desire and a source of fear. It represented both wealth and decadence. There were many different Americas, depending on the variables of class, generation, gender, region, and individual circumstances. This was because America was no mere image but a reality encountered in everyday life. Popular notions of "America" were shaped by individuals' direct experience of particular American soldiers, systems, or changes.

However, starting in the late 1950s, America in the role of occupier ceased to be part of most people's everyday experience, as it was now confined to the few regions still hosting bases. For most Japanese, America had been distilled into a consumerist image possessing even greater power than before to win people's hearts. This can be illustrated by the depictions of America in advertising. Until the early 1950s, Japanese had invoked the word *America* simply as a model to be followed. But starting in the late 1950s, advertisers presented Japanese families performing the "American lifestyle"—especially housewives—as the ideals worthy of emulation. America also became associated with the pop culture of Japanese youth. So long as America was simply presented as the ideal, the meanings people attributed to it could be diverse. However, just as America ceased to be a matter of direct and concrete daily experience, its image became inscribed in the identities of Japanese people. As America became less direct, more mediated, and increasingly confined to images, it conversely became more interiorized and profound in people's consciousness and identity.

Home Electrification, or the Domestic Agency of the Housewife

Along with the shift in geopolitical structures in the late 1950s came a change in the image of America in the eyes of many Japanese people. America was no longer the ever-present and all-powerful "Other" but instead an object of everyday consumption and a symbol of wealth located far away. This is not to deny that America had already become an object of consumption from the time of the Occupation. However, not until the late 1950s could the image of America as an object of consumer desire be separated from the immediate reality of America as the agent of domination and violence. With the demilitarization of the Japanese mainland—especially the Tokyo area—and the shift of the military burden to Okinawa, South Korea, and Taiwan, postwar Japanese rediscovered America as a model of consumption. They restructured their own identity and desires through the mediation of their gaze on America as the "Other." I have already described the process through which this occurred on the level of urban space. In the 1950s and the 1960s, America mediated a similar process of restructuring everyday practice and desire in the domestic sphere.

The image politics surrounding domestic electrification vividly illustrates the relation between the gendered restructuring of agency in the household and the image of America. The ever-present image of home electric technology that would become popular after the 1950s did not appear immediately after the war. The words *kaden* (home electric appliance) and *katei denka* (home electrification) were not used before the middle of the 1950s, when home electrification first emerged as a prominent popular image separate from the prewar lifestyle improvement movement. In 1955, the popular newsweekly *Shūkan Asahi* took note of the rapid spread of home electronics in the landmark article, "Washing Machines and Refrigerators: The Coming of the Home Electrical Age." The article categorized households into seven "classes" measured by the degree of their electrification. At the bottom of the scale were homes that used only electric lighting. Next came homes that supplemented electric lighting with radios and electric irons. Above that were households with electric heaters and toasters. The next class possessed electric mixers, fans, and telephones. Households in the third class from the top owned washing machines, and the second class further possessed refrigerators. The top class owned televisions and vacuum cleaners.[21]

Beginning in the mid-1950s, Japanese articulated the symbolic changes in the images of home electric appliances in the expression "Sanshu no Jingi" (three sacred treasures). This widely invoked phrase explicitly referred to the washing machine, the refrigerator, and the black-and-white TV. Although these electric appliances were quite expensive for an ordinary family at that time, they rapidly entered Japanese homes. In 1955, 4 percent of households reportedly possessed washing machines and the percentages for television and refrigerator ownership were both less than 1 percent. By 1960, 45 percent of Japanese homes had washing machines, 54 percent had TVs, and 15 percent had refrigerators. By the 1970s, the figures for all of these appliances exceeded 90 percent. In the late 1960s, a new set of "three sacred treasures" emerged: car, air conditioner, and color television.[22]

Opinion is divided as to when and by whom the expression "three sacred treasures" was first used, but there can be no doubt that the phrase coincided with the naming of the economic boom beginning in 1955 as the "Jinmu Boom" (after Japan's first mythological emperor) and the next boom in the 1960s as the "Izanagi Boom" (also the name of a mythologi-

[21] "Sentakuki to reizōko: katei-denka jidai kuru" [Washing machines and refrigerators: The coming age of home electrification], *Shūkan Asahi* 60, no. 35 (August 21, 1955): 3–11.

[22] Yamada Seigo, *Kaden konjaku monogatari* [Tales of the days of home electric appliances] (Tokyo: Sanseidō, 1983).

cal figure). At the time, it became fashionable to talk about the economy in terms of Japanese mythological antiquity—a vogue reinforced by nationalistic discourses. What is important is the mythical meaning conveyed by the expression. The original "three sacred treasures" consisted of the imperial sword, the jewel, and the mirror. They served as national symbols for authenticating the position of the emperor as the ruler of the Japanese archipelago, and they were much emphasized during the formation of the modern nation-state. However, since the late 1950s this expression has referred to the private sphere. It has been invoked as a symbol for authenticating the identity of the individual household as a "modern family." The axis of discourses, one might argue, centered on household electric appliances throughout the high-growth period.

Here I want to examine the changing history of the image of electric appliances in prewar and postwar Japan, focusing on Matsushita Electric. One of the major electric appliance companies, Matsushita played the leading role in the industry throughout the period of high economic growth. In developing its advertising strategy, Matsushita also dominated in promoting images of the electric appliance industry at least until the 1970s. The company popularized the notion of life with electric appliances, a life surrounded by washing machines, refrigerators, and televisions. Already in the prewar period, Matsushita had become renowned for its advertisements of radio sets. In the wake of rapid improvements in radio reception technology, Matsushita completed a prototype of a radio in 1931. At the time Matsushita began aggressively advertising its products, notably by means of large posters and full-page magazine advertisements.

Many of those prewar advertisements focused on young women in a manner reminiscent of the image of the "*moga*" (modern girl), presenting the radio as a symbol of the fashionable style of urban modernism. The radio was closely associated with city life but not yet connected with "home electrification." In that era's urban modernism, men were positioned as the producers or players of music, while women were situated as the consumers who listened to the music. These depictions did not change during the second half of the 1930s, and young women remained the target of such advertising.

Such gendered appeals typified not only the ads of Matsushita and other electric appliance manufacturers but also advertising in general during the prewar period. The advertisements portrayed "modern girls" as having a special tie to "modern" products. They suggest a metaphorical relationship that unites the modernity of the products with the modernity of young urban women. When prewar advertisements for electric appliances featured women, the women appeared as symbols of the modernity of the products, but they were not yet portrayed as "housewives"—the users of electric appliances in the home. Even in an advertisement for battery-operated lamps that clearly refers to the "kitchen" and the "family economy," the woman portrayed resembles a movie star more than a housewife.[23] These images of young modern women continued into the postwar period, as seen in Matsushita's advertisements in the late 1940s. The female models conveyed images of movie stars and the modernity of products, not the image of housewives. At the same time, the postwar ads drew more on the image of America as the embodiment of affluence. In a 1949 advertisement for Japan Columbia Records, the popular singer Kasagi Shizuko—best known for her gyrating renditions of boogie-woogie—exuberantly promoted American life. In 1951, an advertisement for inter-office phones had a catchy copy that urged consumers to "speed up the delivery of instructions and communications in an American way." Matsushita also employed a radio commercial advertisement that proclaimed the coming of "two radios to a home as clearly expressing America." In particular, Matsushita's advertisements in 1951 highlighted American-Japanese differences in the use of household electric appliances: "In America, cooking, laundry, cleaning . . . are all done by electricity; in Japan, only ten percent of the population have radios, and the introduction of household electric appliances has a long way to go." While the image of women in the advertisements of the postwar period retained the image of the *moga,* housewives began to appear as the agents promoting the strategy of home electrification and the development of an American way of life.[24]

It was not only Matsushita that connected the American way of life to the consumption of multiple electric appliances. Sanyo Electric also employed the movie star Kogure Michiyo as "Mrs. Sanyo," promoting the connection between the use of household electric appliances and the adoption of an American way of life. In an advertisement for washing machines in 1954, Sanyo proudly announced that its product was the "agitator type, the most popular in America and Europe." The following year, its ad showed Kogure surrounded by numerous electric appliances, evoking the lifestyle image of a housewife in an American home. In those days most Japanese could only dream about such things. In another Matsushita ad, refrigerators, washing machines, mixers, radios, TV sets, electric fans, electric rice cookers, electric irons, and vacuum cleaners enveloped the smiling Takamine Hideko, a famous movie star. "Madame smiles as she buys the products one by one," stated the copy.[25] Indeed, this was the ideal image of the new home life: the housewife stood at the center as myriad household electric appliances orbited about her.

By the end of the 1950s, the dominant image of home electric appliances had changed from the "agent of rationalization" to the "the house-

[23] Takeoka Ryōichi and Ozaki Kazusaburō, *Matsushita denki senden 70 nenshi* [70–year history of Matsushita Electric advertisements] (Tokyo: Matsushita denki sangyō, 1988), 47–48.

[24] Takeoka, *Matsushita denki senden,* 72.

[25] Yamakawa Hiroji, ed., *Shōwa kōkoku 60 nenshi* [Sixty-year history of Shōwa-era advertisements] (Tokyo: Kōdansha, 1987), 252.

wife's good partner." Advertisements published in *Shufu no Tomo,* the most popular women's magazine of the postwar period, illustrate this transformation. Until 1956, even when a housewife appeared as the main figure, ads emphasized only the acceleration and "rational" management of housework. A Denso ad in 1955 went so far as to claim that its machine washed better than "Mama." Similarly, the following year Toshiba proclaimed the "automation age in the household," portraying home electric appliances as furthering the process of rationalization—in which the role of housewife might come to be unnecessary. However, in 1957 advertisements began to present the washing machine as the housewife's best partner. Matsushita that year marketed its machines as having been designed from the housewife's viewpoint. A Toshiba ad in 1959 cast a housewife as the director of her house giving orders to a washing machine.

In the images equating the introduction of electric appliances with Americanization, the housewife was not depicted simply as the recipient of a life with electric appliances. Instead, ads projected her as an agent who would promote and manage such a lifestyle. Constructing the housewife as the agent of power, ads for household electric appliances boldly claimed that "introducing electric appliances is the same thing as democratization." Relating the theme of democratization to the necessity of bringing electric appliances into the home, a 1959 ad made this point most emphatically: "In Article 25 of the Japanese Constitution, there is a phrase declaring that 'The people of Japan have the right to enjoy a healthy and cultural life.' One of the things that people wish to realize is the possession of electric appliances in the home." This advertisement suggested the possibility of achieving "democratization" by bringing electric appliances into the home. The ad also appealed to housewives to become agents in this process, enticing them to "look around yourself and create a life plan to make your life more convenient and fun."[26] The advertisements of this period unequivocally positioned the housewife as the subject who utilized all the available household technologies.

National Subjectivity under the Gaze of America

In the late 1950s to the 1960s, Japanese electric appliance manufacturers presented consumers with an image of the American way of life, in households using electric appliances at an advanced level. They also projected the housewife as the agent who would introduce this lifestyle. Alongside these tendencies, another demonstration of agency appeared in the electric appliance advertisements of the early 1960s and gradually formed the main theme of the advertisements for home electric appliances. In 1960,

[26] Takeoka, *Matsushita denki senden,* 110, also 112.

an ad for a Sony portable TV clearly revealed the new approach, declaring, "We have one more instance of Nippon's pride!"[27] This advertisement instructed Japanese consumers that Japanese technology had become highly recognized in the "world's eye."

Other electric appliance manufacturers vigorously appealed to the same techno-nationalistic sentiments in their advertising during the 1960s.[28] In the case of Sanyo, the following copy appeared in 1961: "A small piece of metal surprised doctors all over the world." A 1962 Matsushita ad asserted: "Proudly made in Japan." We see similar messages in the marketing of a variety of products, including automobiles and precision tools. What permeates all of these ads are the somewhat conflicting claims that the "world" is taking note of "Japanese technology," while "Japanese technology" prospers due to its "uniqueness." The "severe and earnest scrutiny of the world" was said to be on Japan, which was receiving "awards for technology" in the "eyes of the world."[29]

By the late 1960s, many ads proclaimed Japan's "world leadership" in technology to be an expression of Japanese culture. When Matsushita advertised in 1966 for the "artificial intelligence" color TV, it highlighted the television's ability to search out "Japanese color." The advertisement quoted a Japanese painter:

> In the world of art, I feel there are excellent mechanisms in the West and refined sentiments in Japan. The Japanese nation absorbed the mechanisms of the West and digested them to produce something more advanced based on its own delicate sentiments. The dehumanized mechanisms of the West came to Japan and evolved into something suited to the warmth of human skin. This thing is the National [Matsushita] color television set.

Asserting the connection between Japaneseness and technological orientation, numerous ads insisted that only a Japanese color television could express "Japanese color."[30]

As elaborated in the advertisements of the late 1960s, Japanese electric technologies were closely related not only to Japanese "native" color but also the country's artisanal traditions and nature—embodied in delicate craftsmanship as well as in a "native" and "authentic" sense of Japanese beauty. One interesting marketing strategy employed by electric appliance companies was to give their products names evocative of "native" elements of traditional Japanese culture. The first domestic appliance product overtly displaying this nativistic labeling and design tendency was a stereo

[27] Yamakawa, *Shōwa kōkoku,* 283.

[28] On techno-nationalism, see Richard J. Samuels, *"Rich Nation, Strong Army": National Security and the Technological Transformation of Japan* (Ithaca: Cornell University Press, 1996).

[29] Takeoka, *Matsushita denki senden,* 119–20.

[30] Takeoka, *Matsushita denki senden,* 144–45.

launched in April 1965 by Matsushita under the name Utage ("banquet," from an ancient imperial chronicle). The company's ad declared that the "beauty of the lustrous wood grain" and also the design emphasizing horizontal lines represented "the new direction in stereo design." It was sold as a new item of furniture in which "traditional Japanese beauty and modern sensibility are harmonized." That autumn Matsushita introduced other products in the same series: stereos named Asuka (site of the imperial court, 645–710) and Ushio (also related to the ancient imperial myth). These models displayed the "beauty of Japanese design." The same idea was behind the November 1965 launch of the Saga television set, named after an ancient emperor. This was offered to consumers "in order that you might quietly enjoy television as a familiar part of life" and remained a leading feature of Matsushita's TV product line into the 1970s. Many appliance manufacturers adopted the same basic strategy of emphasizing "Japanese style" in their products in the mid-1960s. For example, at the about the same time as the launch of Matsushita's Saga, Sanyo brought out a television set bearing the very name of the country, the Nippon. This product claimed to take its design themes from the architectural principles of "*Azekurazukuri*, said to be the pinnacle achievement of ancient Japanese architecture." The advertising copy explained that the product was "diligently assembled from carefully selected fine wood with the extensive use of handcrafting, and finished off using the unique Japanese technique of *sukashi-nuri*." These products by Matsushita and Sanyo were perhaps the earliest television sets to explicitly promote the theme of Japanese style. Similarly, in the latter half of the 1960s many other manufacturers, including Toshiba and Mitsubishi, would introduce televisions that resembled pieces of "high-class Japanese furniture." This boom soon spread to other household products, such as washing machines, refrigerators, air conditioners, even vacuum cleaners. Appliances in all these categories came to be sold under product names evocative of Japanese "tradition" and "nature." Matsushita brought out a range of three refrigerator models whose wood-grain exteriors were designed to blend in with the surrounding furniture: the teak-finish Kiso, the rosewood-finish Yoshino, and the walnut-finish Michinoku. The names evoked, respectively, the exquisite wood from the historic Kiso valley, the Emperor Go-Daigo's stronghold, and a famous imperial province. In contrast to the continued use of foreign names for the constantly changing automobile models—Bluebird, Skylark, Corolla, Crown—"Japanese-style" marketing images dominated the field of domestic appliances in the 1960s.

It is noteworthy that such image politics developed some time before Japanese electronic technology attained its reputation in the West. In the 1970s and especially in the 1980s, Japanese electronic manufacturers massively exported the products of their technologies in world markets. However, in the 1960s, they were still eagerly importing the more advanced know-how of the American electronics industry. Although Matsushita's first full-page advertisement appeared in an American popular magazine in 1964, the company only developed a fully active advertising strategy in the United States and Europe in the 1970s, when it began to promote its image under the Panasonic and Technics brand names. In the 1960s, western consumers still looked upon Japanese electric appliances as having the low quality of products manufactured in a developing country.

In his book *Made in Japan* (1986), Morita Akio, the president of Sony, describes his company's determined efforts to improve the image of Japanese products in America and Europe. In the 1950s, Morita frequently visited the United States and Europe to promote Sony products. He recalls the overseas image of Japanese technology:

> Quality Japanese consumer goods were virtually unknown before the war. The image of anything marked "Made in Japan" that had been shipped abroad before the war was very low. Most people in the United States and Europe, I learned, associated Japan with paper umbrellas, kimonos, toys, and cheap trinkets. In choosing our name we did not purposely try to hide our national identity—after all, international rules require you to state the country of origin on your product—but we certainly did not want to emphasize it and run the risk of being rejected before we could demonstrate the quality of our products. But I must confess that in the early days we printed the line "Made in Japan" as small as possible, once too small for U.S. Customs, which made us make it bigger on one product.[31]

In short, foreign consumers did not necessarily share their Japanese counterparts' image of Japanese products as possessing high-tech features and traditional aesthetics. On the contrary, their image until the early 1960s was that of second-rate products of low quality. Nevertheless, the world would later embrace the "techno-nationalist" image of Japanese electric appliances that took hold among Japanese at this time. Before the image of "Japanese high-tech" had been established abroad, it was first received at home as something that postwar Japanese people shared. Furthermore, this self-image was mediated by an internalized consciousness of the Other's gaze. It was enabled by the recognition in the "eyes of the world," which in effect meant the "eyes of America." From the 1960s on, postwar Japanese society reconstructed itself according to a techno-nationalist image under the gaze of the Other. Rather than simply "rediscovering" its essential cultural distinctiveness and aesthetic traditions, Japan invented them.

[31] Akio Morita et al., *Made in Japan* (New York: Dutton, 1986), 85.

Conclusion

This chapter demonstrates how a particular geopolitical context enabled the everyday practice of "consuming America" from the period of the Occupation up to the era of high economic growth. I have also examined the process by which gendered and nationalized postwar social agents were structured through consuming America. Two types of postwar agents emerged in the mid-1950s and the 1960s as a result of the introduction of American lifestyle patterns centered on home electric appliances. The housewife emerged as the agent managing the household, while the engineer developed in society as the bearer of technological excellence. Advertising in the 1960s promoted both of these images of Japanese technological power—the image of the exceptional skills of Japanese engineers mixed with the image of the active agency of the housewife in the domestic sphere. These two images of agency—or subjectivity—are structurally linked in the historical context of postwar Japan. Gender differentiation lies at the core of this link. The housewife's subjectivity was assigned to "consumption," while the engineer's subjectivity apparently functioned within the sphere of "production." However, both of these aspects—"consumption" and "production"—were socially constructed in the process of consuming America. Furthermore, the image of home electric appliances symbolized in the "three sacred treasures" lay at the heart of this consumption.

In the first half of this chapter, I considered how the practice of consuming America was enabled by the historical context and by a particular process of forgetting or disconnecting history. Throughout the postwar era, America served as an indispensable point of reference for the Japanese people's own process of reconstructing their identity. This process of identity formation under the American gaze occurred not only in the field of military and political affairs but also in the area of culture. During the Occupation, however, America was more than just an imaginary Other for Japan. America at that time was an immediately present, all-encompassing Other holding the Japanese people in a trance while overpowering them by physical force. Japan's direct relation with this American Other during the Occupation was inevitably complicated and fraught with ambivalent feelings. While America penetrated deeply into people's daily lives, it also constituted an object of furious resistance and hatred, just as it does to this day in Okinawa. On the mainland, by contrast, this ambivalence faded as Japan was drawn into the Cold War division of roles: the military burden was concentrated on Okinawa, South Korea, and Taiwan, while Japan enjoyed economic growth and prosperity. Since the end of the 1950s, the American military presence largely disappeared from view in mainland Japan, especially in the Tokyo area. America thus ceased to be an immediately present and directly perceived Other. It was from this time that the everyday practice of consuming America began.

This "consumption of America" and the process of gendered identity formation mediated by it therefore contained an inherent structural element of historical discontinuity and forgetting. As illustrated by the case of the urban environment in Tokyo, Japanese popular culture and consumption patterns from the 1970s embodied many continuities with those of the Occupation period, and even with those of the earlier prewar and wartime eras of imperialism and militarism. Nonetheless, since the 1960s, the relation between mainland Japan and America has become an indirect one. As the reality of "consuming America" became widespread, these aspects of continuity with the Occupation have gradually faded from people's memories. Having initially been a product of the Occupation, the practice of consuming America was enhanced by the removal of the dimension of violence. The turning point in this history occurred in the 1950s. Although I have illustrated this process by examining urban space and household appliances, this story could also be told by examining other cases, such as cinema, popular songs, and various genres of entertainment, fashion, and youth subcultures.

4
THE AMBIVALENCE OF THE NEW BREED
Nostalgic Consumerism in 1980s and 1990s Japan

JORDAN SAND

Consumers, Critics, and the Bubble

This essay examines connections between youth consumption habits and critical responses to consumer society that emerged in Tokyo during the 1980s and took new forms in the 1990s. To illuminate the cultural constellation of late twentieth-century Japanese consumerism, I have adopted an approach that is more synthetic than analytic, noting family affinities between various contemporaneous trends without plumbing the full depths of possible meaning in each. The family of related trends here runs from "ethnic" food and dress to retro-chic, to slumming, to historical preservation, to critical theory. Broadly, these trends all fall under the rubric of nostalgia. Nostalgia presents a problem of special interest in connection to the themes of this volume since it is at once an expression of ambivalence about modern life—and therefore potentially a reaction against consumerism—and at the same time the underlying sensibility of a set of consumer tastes.

Nostalgia in its original sense means homesickness, a longing to return to the security of a place of origin one has left. In affluent, mobile societies like that of late twentieth-century Japan (as well as the United States), however, individual life histories often involve multiple "homes." The wealth of images and stories related to home and homelessness in both traditional and modern media further make it difficult to dissociate our personal feelings about actual homes we have left from idealized notions of home in common circulation. Increasingly, images of the homes we have lost fuse with popular and mass-mediated images to form a utopian composite that exists only in the mind. This unmooring of feelings about the past from actual experience is one of the key points of departure for theories of postmodern culture. Frederic Jameson, for example, has written of a "nostalgia mode" in contemporary culture that replaces true historical awareness with a pastiche of images "cannibalized" from the past.[1] Jean Baudrillard asserts that an ahistorical code of commodities as signs and signs as commodities has so completely encompassed contemporary society that the possibility of other forms of mental experience—authentic memory of a world before consumerism, for example—has been irrevocably erased. Advertising, he claims, has created a new language of arbitrary juxtaposition rather than logical signification that severs consumers' apprehension of the world from any grounding in lived reality.[2] These scholars and many others share the assumption that the casual, seemingly haphazard, use of cultural references to the past in marketing reflects consumers' loss of genuine historical awareness and the advent of a superficial relationship to the past that treats historicity as just another infinitely exchangeable commodity.

The congeries of trends in Tokyo that I will describe bespeaks a free-floating nostalgia that can attach itself to many places and times. In this sense, it conforms readily with the perspective of postmodern cultural critique, as several scholars of Japan have noted.[3] Yet although the objects of late twentieth-century Japanese nostalgia were various, they reflected a certain consistent sensibility that valued notions of rootedness and community; preferred low-tech, small, and intimate spaces; and sought to mark out territory outside the dominance of the state, capitalism, or global culture centered in the West. In examining these trends, I do not intend to show that Japanese consumers in fact had any more profound historical awareness than Jameson's postmodern characterization would suggest—only that their nostalgia was part of a more generalized condition of ambivalence about capitalist modernity in Japan—an ambivalence in which "postmodern" consumers, social critics, and mass marketers, as well as historians, cartoonists, and a host of other players all partook.

There is no easy place at which one can pinpoint the beginning of consumerism as a cultural problem (see Trentmann, chap. 1). Capitalism tirelessly generates new forms, and critics invent theories in response. The confrontation between consumer capitalism and mass culture critique is

[1] Frederic Jameson, *Postmodernism or, the Cultural Logic of Late Capitalism* (Durham: Duke University Press, 1991), 17–21.

[2] See "Simulacra and Simulations," in *Jean Baudrillard: Selected Writings*, ed. Mark Poster (Stanford: Stanford University Press, 1988), 166–84; Mark Poster, *The Mode of Information: Poststructuralism and Social Context* (Chicago: University of Chicago Press, 1990), 56–68.

[3] Marilyn Ivy, *Discourses of the Vanishing: Modernity, Phantasm, Japan* (Chicago: University of Chicago Press, 1995), 48–65; Koichi Iwabuchi, *Recentering Globalization: Popular Culture and Japanese Transnationalism* (Durham: Duke University Press, 2002), 173–81.

thus an endless cat-and-mouse game in which the capitalists always have the upper hand. When signs become commodities—when advertising speedily appropriates any new image or idea to have surfaced in public discourse, that is—every act of resistance will always be commodifiable. A theory of consumer society, if it proves useful, will be as useful to marketers as to Marxists. In 1980s Japan, the capitalists and the critics were not far apart intellectually, and they enjoyed a common audience.

From 1985 to 1990, Japan experienced a speculative bubble of unprecedented proportions. Tokyo real estate prices reached the highest levels of any in world history.[4] Much of the subject matter discussed here emerged in these years, so it relates closely to the economic changes wrought by the Japanese bubble. The economy, however, had already moved into a new phase in the late 1970s, with large consequences for the social and physical structure of Tokyo. Internal surpluses in the late 1970s encouraged Japanese manufacturers to invest overseas. Pressure from the United States to curtail exports provided another push to move operations offshore. Meanwhile, the weight of manufacturing within Japan was shifting toward micro-technology. By 1982, two Japanese firms were among the top five semiconductor manufacturers in the world. By 1986, Japanese firms held the top three positions.[5] These shifts in manufacturing meant that heavy industry became a less visible part of the domestic urban landscape and that many more Tokyoites were donning suits and "office-lady" uniforms to commute to their bright new office blocks. They commuted through the enormous rail and retail complexes at the stations of Ikebukuro, Shinjuku, and Shibuya on the west side of the city, where they now encountered dense clusters of department stores and tall commercial buildings, each containing dozens of restaurants, bars, or boutiques, their façades covered with electric signage and moving-image billboards. In short, Tokyo, whose name had been synonymous with industrial pollution in 1970, had become, for many, the archetype of the postindustrial city.[6]

The target of both marketers and critics in these years was a new generation of consumers who had been born in the 1960s. Raised in prosperity, distant from both the horrors of World War II and the struggle to rise out of defeat and poverty that followed it, Japan's new youth were politically disengaged, distinguishing themselves from their elders instead by lifestyle choices. More fundamentally, they distinguished themselves by choosing to place lifestyle above work, a difference of values with their

[4] Christopher Wood, *The Bubble Economy: The Japanese Economic Collapse* (London: Sidgwick and Jackson, 1992).

[5] Tsuru Shigeto, *Japan's Capitalism: Creative Defeat and Beyond* (Cambridge: Cambridge University Press, 1993), 181–85, 192–99.

[6] For descriptions of two of these west-Tokyo hubs, see Roman Cybriwsky, *Tokyo: The Changing Profile of an Urban Giant* (Boston: G. K. Hall, 1991), 156–70.

workaholic parents that seemed so profound that they were dubbed *shinjinrui,* "the New Breed."[7]

Influential Japanese disagreed profoundly in their evaluations of this new phase of consumer society. Economists and policymakers in the late 1980s predicted the dire impact the New Breed would have on the Japanese economic miracle. Social critics were torn between enthusiasm and angst. Since the failure of the student movements at the end of the 1960s, intellectuals on the left had developed a bleak view of what they called Japan's "managed society" (*kanri shakai*) and of the passive consumerism that seemed to have infected it.[8] On the positive side in the eyes of these critics, here was a generation of young professionals prepared to poke Japan, Inc. in the eye by refusing to sacrifice for nation and company. On the negative side, all that the new youth knew how to do was consume.

Perhaps more telling of the changes wealth had brought to the cultural climate, a new position emerged on the right that optimistically dismissed concerns about both managed consumerism and the decay of the Japanese work ethic. In widely discussed writings on what he called "soft individualism," literary critic Yamazaki Masakazu claimed that prosperity had liberated the nation from its feudal past. Thanks to Japan's transition from production-led industrial society to consumption-led postindustrialism, Japanese were at last free subjects, he asserted, defining themselves through consumption, while capitalism was their servant, compelled to deliver ever new opportunities for their pleasure. Turning Baudrillard on his head, Yamazaki claimed that the new individual, freed from the fetters of community tradition, found genuine life satisfaction in selecting among subtly differentiated commodities.[9] Baudrillard and Yamazaki were frequently cited in Japan in the 1980s, in both high-brow and popular media.

Tokyo Disneyland opened in 1983. Around the same time, critics of the managed society began to note what they perceived to be the progressive Disneyfication of Tokyo itself, particularly in Shibuya, the most recent of the commercial districts that had grown up around the commuter train hubs on the western side of the city. If Shibuya was Disneyland, then the equivalent of the Walt Disney Company was the Seibu-Saison Group, whose first Parco building, an agglomeration of boutiques in the guise of a single store, opened there in 1973. The mouseketeers of Shibuya, or sim-

[7] Literally translated, "the new human species." Chikushi Tetsuya, editor of the *Asahi Journal,* claims to have coined the word, and he certainly had a major role in popularizing it, although it appeared earlier in the marketing journal *Across.* Chikushi Tetsuya, "Young People as a New Human Race," *Japan Quarterly* 33, no. 3 (July-September 1986): 291–94; Akurosu henshūshitsu, *Shinjinrui ga yuku: kansei sabetsu shakai e mukete* [Onward march the new breed: Toward a society of sensual distinctions] (Tokyo: PARCO shuppankyoku, 1985).

[8] Marilyn Ivy, "Formations of Mass Culture," in *Postwar Japan as History,* ed. Andrew Gordon (Berkeley: University of California Press, 1993), 239–58.

[9] Yamazaki Masakazu, *Yawarakai kojinshugi no tanjō* [Birth of soft individualism] (Tokyo: Chūō kōronsha, 1984), 144–79.

ply its Disney tourists, were the hedonistic new youth in their teens and early twenties who turned out there in the hundreds of thousands every weekend.[10]

Writing of Tokyo Disneyland as the archetype for 1980s Japanese urbanism, sociologist Shunya Yoshimi (who also contributes to this volume) pointed out at the end of the decade that marketing had come to be a question of manipulating urban space; the city itself was now an advertising medium. Parco, Yoshimi observed, had reshaped Shibuya into a theatrical space, a single encompassing advertisement, and a fantasy land.[11] As a spatial typology, Disney represented for critics like Yoshimi more than simply fantasy and commercialism. As Yoshimi noted, Disneyland operates through a strategy of immersion: the park is so constructed as to render it impossible for visitors either to see outside or to view the entire park at once. In this way, visitors are always enveloped, so that the "magic" of Disney can work on them continuously, without giving them an opportunity to relativize it or detach themselves. In addition, there are no mirrors in attractions (unlike in the classic funhouse), so that park visitors never have the chance to see and reflect on their own pleasure-absorbed—some would say infantilized—selves. The Disneyfication thesis thus proposed that more than merely commodifying the products of culture, the sophisticated new retail giants were transforming the space of the city itself into a colossal enclosed amusement park with no outside and no possibility for critical subjectivity.[12]

Critique: Searching for Gaps in the Consumer Society

The dilemma of Disneyfication was connected to the last phase of a process of globalization of the Japanese city or its loss of local identity: the transformation of Tokyo into a "world city." Municipal and national politicians regarded "world city" status as a goal to be achieved. Suzuki Shunichi, governor of Tokyo from 1979 to 1995, chose the phrase "World City Tokyo" as

[10] The figure of 250,000 on an average Sunday is from Cybriwsky, *Tokyo: The Changing Profile of an Urban Giant,* 166–67.

[11] Yoshimi Shun'ya, "Yūenchi no yūtopia" [Theme park utopia], *Sekai* 528 (June 1989): 293–306.

[12] This critique of late twentieth-century urbanism and Disney has been developed by numerous critics in the West as well. Baudrillard was probably the critic of Disneyfication most cited in the 1980s. One classic early source, although not dealing with Disney, is Guy Debord, *The Society of the Spectacle* (1967), trans. Donald Nicholson-Smith (New York: Zone Books, 1994). See also E. C. Relph, *Place and Placelessness* (London: Pion, 1976) and the essays in *Variations on a Theme Park: The New American City and the End of Public Space,* ed. Michael Sorkin (New York: Noonday Press, 1992). The film *The Truman Show* (1998), made in the United States by Australian director Peter Weir, portrays the nightmare of a Disneyfied world in literal fashion.

a slogan of what he called the "Tokyo Renaissance."[13] Critics invoked it in more ominous tones, emphasizing the contradictions of Japan's position in the capitalist world system while noting that as Tokyo became a world city, all that was not "efficient" from the point of view of capitalism would be callously discarded.[14]

It was under these inauspicious circumstances that Tokyo citizens mobilized for the first time to preserve historic buildings threatened with demolition. Since much of the city had been destroyed by an earthquake in 1923 and again by American firebombing in 1945, Tokyo retained only small pockets of building stock more than fifty years old. Faced with the overwhelming power of real estate developers in the bubble economy, local preservationists saw things in tragic terms, sensing that the few remaining physical traces of the city's past would almost certainly be lost.

The sense of loss was shared by critics of Disneyfication and the managed society. They recalled the open lots and alleyways of Tokyo childhoods before the high economic growth of the 1960s as what was commonly called an "originary landscape" (*genfūkei*).[15] In the 1980s, this lost Tokyo landscape of the recent past had a specific iconography, repeated in television, comics, and other popular media: narrow alleys paved with irregularly spaced stepping stones, overgrown empty lots, walls and fences built of wooden boards, and woods of mixed untended foliage (*zōkibayashi*)—all the marks of what at one time would have been called "underdevelopment."[16] By the late 1960s, urban planning and new construction had largely consigned this landscape to the past. Yet its imagery remained canonical. Yoshimi, who was himself of the New Breed generation, asserted that, having grown up in a middle-class neighborhood in the prosperous 1960s, he belonged to a generation that "possessed no originary landscape."[17]

[13] Mikako Iwatake, "The Tokyo Renaissance: Constructing a Postmodern Identity in Contemporary Japan," Ph.D. dissertation, University of Pennsylvania, 1993. For an analysis of the entwined political rhetoric of internationalism and localism during these years outside Tokyo, see Jennifer Robertson, "It Takes a Village: Internationalization and Nostalgia in Postwar Japan," in *Mirror of Modernity: Invented Traditions of Modern Japan,* ed. Stephen Vlastos (Berkeley: University of California Press, 1998), 110–29.

[14] See, for example, Inoue Jun'ichi et al., *Tōkyō: sekai toshika e no kōzu* [Tokyo: Restructuring toward the global city] (Tokyo: Aoki shoten, 1990), 92–98.

[15] The term may have come from architecture critic Kawazoe Noboru's book *Tōkyō no genfūkei: toshi to den'en to no kōryū* [Tokyo's originary landscape: The city's contact with the country] (Tokyo: NHK bukkusu, 1971).

[16] For a colorful description of this iconography, see Yomota Inuhiko, "Shaauddo wa doko e itta ka: shōnen manga ni okeru 'harappa'" [Where did Sherwood go? Open lots in children's comics], in *Rojō kansatsugaku nyūmon* [Primer in street observation studies], ed. Akasegawa Genpei, Fujimori Terunobu, and Minami Shinbō (Chikuma shobō, 1986), 290–307. Yomota also notes the anachronism of the empty lot in the Kubo Kiriko cartoon reproduced here in Figure 4.2. In 2005, the same lost townscape of open lots and concrete pipes was reproduced in a popular outdoor exhibition at the Edo-Tokyo Open-Air Architectural Museum.

[17] Yoshimi, *Toshi no doramaturugii: Tōkyō, sakariba no shakaishi* [Dramaturgy of the city: A social history of gathering places in Tokyo] (Tokyo: Kōbundō, 1987), 352.

In addition to expressing the loss of a low-tech urban lifeworld, Yoshimi's observation that his generation lacked an "originary landscape" rang true at the time because it related to another fact of Japan's social transformation during the economic boom: the end of urban migration. Before the 1970s, most people in Tokyo came from elsewhere. The majority of Tokyo youth had shared the experience of leaving behind a home in the provinces to make their way in the capital. Between 1970 and 1980, the number of young people who migrated to Tokyo in search of work after high school or junior high school fell by more than half. A survey of fifteen- to twenty-four-year-olds living in the central wards of Tokyo in 1981 found that 74 percent of them had been born in Tokyo.[18] Unlike earlier generations, then, most New Breed youth had direct experience only of the developed and prosperous city and its suburbs—a place critics characterized as devoid of local culture or memory.

For people disturbed by the loss of Tokyo's local identity to global capitalism, the city's precursor Edo (capital of the Tokugawa shogun, 1603–1868) presented a more distant and complete utopian antithesis to the present, the city before its opening to world markets, the world they had lost. Nostalgia for Edo (which was not itself new) together with a new interest in urban studies fueled the growth of a field known as Edo studies, subsequently Edo-Tokyo studies. A team led by architecture and urban historian Jinnai Hidenobu, a leading figure in Edo-Tokyo studies, conducted extensive surveys of land patterns, waterways, and architectural forms, revealing that despite repeated destruction in the twentieth century, Edo still lived on in isolated pockets of the modern city or in subtle patterns hidden in its fabric.[19] With the support of the city government, Edo-Tokyoologists ultimately succeeded in memorializing the everyday spaces of the premodern city inside the walls of the mammoth, high-tech Edo-Tokyo Museum.[20]

In its popular versions, rediscovery of the spatial forms of the old city clustered around two things: Tokyo's "Asian-ness" (a common phrase, suggesting its unplanned and chaotic character) and its intimate spaces. Jinnai and his students championed the virtues of the city's Asian-ness in a special issue of the journal *Process Architecture* called "Ethnic Tokyo."[21] Architects Kurokawa Kishō and Maki Fumihiko had earlier written of the city's many alleys as the locus of a distinct urban culture. The Japanese alley was a native counterpart to the piazza and the public square in the West,

[18] Sōgō kinkyū kaihatsu kikō, ed., *Wakamono to toshi* [Youth and the city] (Tokyo: Gakuyō shobō, 1983), 16–17.

[19] See Jinnai Hidenobu, *Tokyo: A Spatial Anthropology*, trans. Kimiko Nishimura (1985; repr. Berkeley: University of California Press, 1995).

[20] Jordan Sand, "Monumentalizing the Everyday: The Edo-Tokyo Museum," *Critical Asian Studies* 33, no. 3 (Fall 2001): 351–78.

[21] Jinnai Hidenobu et al., "*Tōkyō esunikku densetsu* (Ethnic Tokyo)," *Process Architecture* 72 (July 1988), special issue.

an urban space to which Japanese were peculiarly disposed, Kurokawa claimed.[22] These ideas suddenly enjoyed greater prominence in the media, as journalists and urban specialists came to see the city's intimate spaces as fragile and disappearing. The alleyways of the working-class city, long a favorite setting for popular literature and storytelling, now acquired new significance as an asylum from modern forms of control, urban management, and city building.

Edo-Tokyo scholarship and its many popular manifestations fed a generalized nostalgia for the old downtown districts collectively known as *shitamachi.* Yet popularization created a new theater of conflict, as local residents and activists resisted the incursion of outsiders attracted to their neighborhoods as objects of nostalgia. In 1986, municipal offices in the *shitamachi* wards played to the nostalgic mood by advertising officially sponsored events with posters featuring images and graphic styles from the 1920s. Around the same time, large numbers of outsiders began attending *shitamachi* shrine festivals that traditionally had been celebrated locally. Television stations and magazines began doing features on minor historical sites, old shops, traditional crafts, and other local attractions in these former backwaters.[23] A preservationist community group that published the local magazine *Yanesen* in one of the better-preserved—which is to say more forgotten—downtown neighborhoods succeeded in drawing attention from the national media, including repeated segments on morning television news programs. Eager to draw supporters but anxious that publicity might have adverse effects on the community, *Yanesen*'s editors viewed contact with larger media as a Faustian bargain (see figure 4.1).[24]

Opposition to scrap-and-build redevelopment took other, less conventional forms as well. A group of artists and scholars calling themselves the Street Observation Studies Society (*Rojō Kansatsu Gakkai*) formed in 1986 with the stated purpose of searching out "deviations" or "gaps" (*zure*) in the urban fabric: improbable juxtapositions, anomalies of scale, failures of functionality, or functional objects that possessed what they termed an "expressive excess."[25] The group embarked on a series of urban wandering expeditions, photographing and labeling odd discoveries and visual puns, which they referred to, in ironic reference to the real estate trade, as "properties" (*bukken*). Beneath its surface of wit and irony, the Street Observa-

[22] Matsuba Kazukiyo, *Tōkyō posuto modan* [Tokyo postmodern] (Tokyo: Sanseidō, 1985), 172–73. See also Kurokawa Kishō, *Michi no kenchiku* [Architecture of streets] (Tokyo: Maruzen, 1983); Maki Fumihiko et al., *Miegakure suru toshi* [Elusive city] (Tokyo: Kajima shuppankai, 1980).

[23] Theodore Bestor, "The Shitamachi Revival," *Transactions of the Asiatic Society of Japan,* 4th series, vol. 5 (1990): 71–86.

[24] Mori Mayumi, *Yanesen no bōken* [Yanesen adventure] (Tokyo: Chikuma shobō, 2002).

[25] Fujimori Terunobu, "Rojō kansatsu no hata no moto ni" [Under the banner of street observation], in *Rojō kansatsugaku nyūmon,* ed. Akasegawa, Fujimori, and Minami (Tokyo: Chikuma shobō, 1986), 17.

Figure 4.1. Alley and rowhouses in the district favored by the editors of *Yanesen* magazine. Photo by the author.

tionists' work too was tinged with a sense of tragedy, since their interests tended strongly toward the ephemeral and the self-built and highlighted the fragility of the vernacular city. Spokesman Fujimori Terunobu also linked the search for "gaps" to a battle with mass consumer society—or "the consumption empire," as he proclaimed it in the group's manifesto, which bristled with military metaphors. "This empire," he wrote,

> has for a long while limited its territory to the inside of shops . . . but recently they have revealed a territorial ambition for the streets we have occupied by custom since the time of our ancestors, and have steadily accumulated weapons for an invasion. . . . They have developed strategies to commodify the entire town, and in some places have already succeeded in their river-fording operation.[26]

Fujimori raised this alarm not simply against the proliferation of consumption opportunities in Shibuya and the other huge shopping districts of western Tokyo but also against the new approach of the Seibu group and other marketing organizations, which were using their own street obser-

[26] Fujimori, "Rojō kansatsu no hata," 9–10.

vation techniques to penetrate more deeply into the psychology of the consumer masses. Two marketing research offices, one associated with Seibu, the other with the advertising agency Hakuhōdō, had begun charting street fashions and conducting spot interviews in Shibuya in 1981. Drawing on the ideas of urban sociologists, they compiled studies of mental maps and public group behavior, which retailers then used in deciding shop location and displays.[27] To Fujimori and the Street Observationists, it seemed that neither the public space of the streets nor the act of walking in them was safe from the manipulation of consumer capitalism.

Commodifying the Gaps

Yet even these critiques and acts of resistance were commodifiable—and commodified. Marilyn Ivy has noted the symbiosis between urban critics and marketers in their readings of the new consumer's hedonism.[28] The influences cut both ways. Some sociologists wrote about Japan's new consumerism in ways that accorded well with the interests of marketing, and they contributed to Seibu/Parco's mythic status as cultural catalyst. From the other end, Seibu chairman Tsutsumi Seiji, a former student radical, wrote theoretical critiques of consumer society, quoting Baudrillard and Bataille.[29]

Seibu Group marketing and critical discourse intersected most visibly in the pages of *Across*, the company's monthly trend-watching magazine, which began publication in 1980. Writing at a level of abstraction well above the ordinary concerns of retailing, *Across* staff writers attempted to read trends in the mass psychology of the Japanese public concerning everything from child-rearing to world politics. Their writing in the late 1980s frequently emphasized signs of anxiety and of decadence. Special features were organized around themes such as "The Collapse of Old Myths," "The Fin de Siècle," and "The Anxiety of the Present Age."[30] The authors of these features refrained from the moralist pronouncements of the more strident social critics, but they viewed Japanese society in similar terms. Their own countercultural tastes may have determined much of the magazine's content. But the repeated themes of cultural critique must also have met with their employers' approval to persist. Whatever relationship the magazine's characterizations actually bore to the dominant sentiments among Japanese consumers, they represented part of the stylistic persona

[27] John L. McCreery, *Japanese Consumer Behavior: From Worker Bees to Wary Shoppers* (Richmond, Surrey: Curzon, 2000).

[28] Ivy, "Formations of Mass Culture."

[29] See Tsutsumi Seiji, *Shōhi shakai hihan* [Critique of consumer society] (Tokyo: Iwanami shoten, 1996).

[30] *Akurosu*, no. 136 (July 1985): 2; no. 154 (January 1987): 2; no. 163 (October 1987): 2.

of the Seibu group, which was the most powerful force in the Tokyo consumer market of the time.

Seibu and Parco advertisements gained renown for breaking with traditional marketing. They promoted nonconformism in the 1970s with the slogan "Myself—A New Discovery" and posters showing a photograph of a naked two-year-old child swimming on the surface of a pool, shot from below. Several advertisements in the 1980s featured striking photographs of people from the third world wearing their native dress and standing in stark and mysterious landscapes. "Ah the Origin," read the slogan on a poster showing two Indian girls radiating a magical glow. Parco ads on television featured Faye Dunaway silently eating a boiled egg. No merchandise was mentioned or displayed. Tsutsumi Seiji himself played a direct role in creating these ad campaigns, which purveyed only images, thus seeking to deny that they were advertising while at the same time spreading the image of Seibu as a patron of the avant garde.[31]

Just as the rhetoric of social and cultural critique was echoed in Seibu-Parco publications, the anti-modern position of Edo nostalgia and preservationism could also be absorbed within the cultural repertoire of postmodern marketing. The trade journal of advertising giant Dentsū featured special issues on Tokyo with articles by the leading figures of Edo-Tokyo studies.[32] *Across* ran features on *shitamachi,* on the *Yanesen* neighborhood—which it called "a living urban museum"—and on forgotten examples of postwar architecture under the title "A Study of Remains of the High Growth Era: A Contemporary Archeology [*kōgengaku*] of Mid-Shōwa Era Tokyo in Sepia."[33]

Parco director Masuda Tsūji himself waxed fantastically nostalgic in a dialogue with cartoonist Sugiura Hinako, whose *manga* depictions of life in Edo had contributed significantly to the popularization of Edo studies. The text of their conversation, published in *Across,* began with a sympathetic discussion of historian Haga Tōru's metaphoric pronouncement that "the Edo period was a Sunday," while every day since the establishment of the modern regime had been a Monday. "It could have stayed Sunday a little longer," Sugiura remarked wistfully. She went on to suggest that Japanese had been pushing themselves for a hundred years, but would one day have to return to the Edo way of life. Masuda connected the romantic depictions of Edo in Sugiura's cartoons to life in the tenement row houses

[31] Ueno Chizuko, "Seibu Department Store and Image Marketing: Japanese Consumerism in the Postwar Period," in *Asian Department Stores,* ed. Kerrie L. MacPherson (Honolulu: University of Hawaii Press, 1998), 177–205. See also Thomas R. H. Havens, *Architects of Affluence: The Tsutsumi Family and the Seibu-Saison Enterprises in Twentieth-Century Japan* (Cambridge: Harvard University Press, 1994).

[32] Kitada Akihiro, *Kōkoku toshi Tōkyō: sono tanjō to shi* [Birth and death of advertisement city Tokyo] (Tokyo: Kōsaidō, 2002), 54.

[33] *Akurosu,* no. 146 (May 1986): 39; no. 152 (November 1986): 24–36.

of present-day *shitamachi,* where people remained open and unaffected. "This thing, it's a kind of thoroughgoing everydayness. Recently, I've been feeling this is something really good. . . . If in the end things settle down this way again as you are saying, of course I'm out of business, but . . ." he remarked, laughing. There was nowhere further for this self-contradictory line of thought to go, although obviously a fantasy world in which every day is Sunday would not have been entirely unappealing to a retailer who did his best business on Sundays.[34]

Once marketing strategists recognized widespread interest in forms of public expression that ran counter to the forward movement of capitalism, those expressions themselves could be exploited to generate new market value. *Across* reported a sell-out crowd at an event held in Seibu's Printemps store featuring critical social theorist Asada Akira. Asada, another intellectual of the New Breed generation, wrote abstruse philosophical essays in which he described contemporary society as a "Klein bottle"—an enveloping and cyclical space with neither inside nor outside. He advocated escape as the only means of establishing one's humanity, since human beings were innately distinguished from other creatures by their tendency toward "deviance" (*zure*). These ideas, abstract as they were, had enough appeal to sell over one hundred thousand copies of Asada's opus *Kōzō to chikara* (Structure and Power), prompting the popular press to speak of the "Asada phenomenon."[35]

When critics who challenged the "managed society" enjoyed large audiences, any accidental oddity in the material or social world inevitably became valuable as a sign of what was not "managed." Media coverage of Street Observation Studies brought instant celebrity to an avant-garde artist and an architecture historian. The trend-watchers at *Across* were among the first to pick up on "Street Observation Studies," identifying it as part of a vogue for "fieldwork" and trivia-collecting that characterized the darker, more serious side of the "new era" (in 1985 Japan had entered a new decade of the Shōwa era according to the commonly used calendar based on imperial reigns). Despite the Observationists' quest for the completely uncommodifiable, their own activities quickly gained commercial imitators, and the idea was repackaged in a series of books published by the youth-oriented magazine *Takarajima.*[36]

[34] *Akurosu,* no. 150 (September 1986): 72–79.

[35] Asada Akira, *Kōzō to chikara: kigōron o koete* [Structure and power: Beyond semiotics] (Tokyo: Keisō shobō, 1983); Takeda Seiji, "Asada Akira: chikara, tōsō" [Asada Akira: Power, escape], in *Bessatsu Takarajima 52: Gendai shisō nyūmon II: Nihon hen* [Takarajima supplement 52: Introduction to contemporary thought II: Japan] (Tokyo: JICC shuppankyoku, 1986), 189–91.

[36] The series, originally a column in the back of *Takarajima* magazine, is called *VOW: Machi no henna mono dai katarogu* [Voice of wonderland: Great catalogue of strange things in town] (Tokyo: Takarajimasha, 1987–).

Summing up the growing taste for what *Across* editors called "anachro-modern" goods, the magazine claimed that consumers were buying reproductions of 1930s or 1950s products to "enjoy the gap" (*zure o tanoshimu*) between the sensibilities of the present day and those of the past.[37] This was another sort of "gap," distinct but closely related to the physical gaps in the planned capitalist city that interested practitioners of Street Observation Studies. Anachro-modern consumers had no direct knowledge of the historical eras that attracted them, but they were drawn to them as sources of a modern Japan different from the one they inhabited. Rejecting serious antiquarianism, they took pleasure in the mere juxtaposition of present and past.

Elsewhere, the magazine extended this idea of "enjoying the gap" to various other signs of consumer desire for a place or time outside of prosperous contemporary Japan. Neo-Japanesque, an exoticist taste for traditional Japan as non-Japanese perceived it, was covered in the February 1984 issue, then again at greater length in June, as one of the tastes of the "prodigal generation." *Across* grouped the trend with demand for "No-brand goods," which had gained enormous popularity because, according to the magazine's analysis, this generation found any kind of effort at stylistic coordination uncool.[38] May 1985 saw a special feature on the "Asia Syndrome," in which the writer claimed that young Japanese felt both a "complex" toward Asia (meaning unease about other Asian countries), a result of the negative impression Japan had created among Asians, and a fascination with Asian popular culture as kitsch.[39] In October 1986, the magazine reported on the "ethnic boom" in film, music, and art, as well as in food and fashion, describing it as part anti-modern, part European-inflected colonial fantasy, and part reaction against American-style consumerism. At the outer extreme, staff writer Sakuma Rika reported, were signs of an emerging fascination with communist countries, whose lack of consumer choice offered an antithesis to the consumer-driven Japanese market and suggested a model in accord with the recent buzz in Japan over "moving from material to non-material things [*mono kara koto e*]."[40]

Slumming at home was bound up with these new tastes for the exotic, the antique, and the uncommodified. "B-grade" (*B-kyū*) ("B" as in B-movies)

[37] "Anakuro modan jidai: Shōwa 30 nendai to Taishō jidai o tsunagu kindaishugi no anakuroteki okashisa" [Anachro-modern era: Anachronistic absurdity that links the Shōwa 30s and Taishō era], *Akurosu*, no. 125 (August 1984): 98–99.

[38] "Hōtō eiji no sukizo pawaa" [Schizo power of the prodigal age], *Akurosu*, no. 123 (June 1984): 46–50.

[39] "Ajia shindorōmu" [Asia syndrome], *Akurosu*, no. 134 (May 1985): 26–39.

[40] "Yōropian vs Amerikan ga jidai o yomitoku kagi to naru" ["European vs. American" is the key to reading the era], *Akurosu*, no. 151 (October 1986): 22–29. The "America" being invoked here is an abstraction, a style that by this time had been completely absorbed within Japanese media and everyday life. As Shunya Yoshimi observes in chapter 3 of this volume, this aspect of Americanism had been present in Japan since at least the late 1950s.

Figure 4.2. Cartoonist Kubo Kiriko's *Cynical Hysterie Hour* depicted children of the prosperous 1980s. In an ironic gesture, this scene is set anachronistically in an empty lot—an icon of the "originary landscape" Tokyo had lost. "So how do you play this 'poor folk' game?" "Well, if you come over to our house now we'll show you." Copyright Kiriko Kubo/Hakusensha, Inc. The original cartoon appeared in 1985 in the magazine *LaLa;* it can also be found in *Shinikaru hisuterii awaa* (*Cynical Hysterie Hour*) vol. 2 (Tokyo: Hakusensha, 1998), 98.

was the popular term. The taste of today's prodigal youth, *Across* reported, was consciously "B-grade." Around this same time, the food and lifestyle magazine *Hanako* began publishing *B-Grade Gourmet* (*B-kyū gurume*), a series of pocket guides to cheap restaurants in Tokyo. The series was enough of a hit to have print and television imitators and to establish the phrase in common parlance. The books introduced restaurants of a kind that ordinarily went unreviewed: lunch counters serving distinctly *déclassé* nativized foreign dishes such as ramen, "curry rice," and the unique *omuraisu* (an omelet filled with rice and topped with a dollop of ketchup). In January 1988, *Across* charted the reemergence of taste for Japanese foodstuffs, liquor, and domestic interiors, noting the "limitless desire for 'B-grade' Japanese food" and explaining it in part as playing at being poor (see figure 4.2).[41]

As a generalized search for the unhip, enjoying the gap expanded beyond the choice of discrete commodities to embrace slumming in parts of town that were known to young people only for their lack of appeal. The comedy variety program "Genius Takeshi's TV to Perk You Up!!" (*Tensai Takeshi no genki ga deru terebi*) aired a segment that ridiculed the working-class Tokyo district of Arakawa as the nadir of unfashionability, then turned the joke around in a follow-up program called "Arakawa Ward Kumanomae Shopping District Revitalization Promotion Campaign." This feature, with its tongue-in-cheek bureaucratic title, became a hit, bringing actual

[41] "Wa wa fukkatsu suru ka" [Will Japanese style come back?], *Akurosu,* no. 166 (January 1988): 61–62.

revitalization (presumably only temporary) to the benighted shopping district through fan tourism, and led to subsequent follow-ups in other neighborhoods. The magazine described the vogue as deriving from a fascination with "deviant spaces" (*zure kūkan*), part of what they called the "post-Tokio phenomenon" (using the antiquated romanization "Tokio" to signify the now-passé image of the capital as an icon of westernization). The keywords of the new trend, they reported, were "earthiness, kitsch, and ethnic-ness."[42]

While the proliferation of this kind of hip appropriation of the unhip undoubtedly reveals the canny marketing sense of television studios and magazine publishers, it cannot be written off as their manipulations alone, since the space of cultural production in which it occurred was open and constantly ramifying. Ways of enjoying the gap could extend in time from the imagined premodern Edo to yesterday's lunch counter, in space from working-class Arakawa Ward to the Soviet Union, and in intellectual register from highbrow philosophy to television comedy.

Wanderings of the New Breed

Despite the claims of the Disneyfication thesis, Tokyo itself was not a physically uniform and managed urban environment from which escape was difficult. Japanese writing on postmodernism in architecture reveled in the city's chaotic appearance, pointing to the outlandish juxtapositions of recent high-tech buildings and the stubborn low-tech survivors from the past. The classic instance—and particularly photogenic—was the tiny Shinto shrine tucked into a niche or riding atop a glass-clad office or commercial building. Even Shibuya, ground zero of the new consumer culture, was largely unplanned and shot through with vernacular accidents. A tiny, irregularly shaped bar serving whale meat near Shibuya station became a landmark within a landmark, at least for architectural postmodernists. The establishment had managed to survive on a lot nestled into one flank of the Tōkyū department store's 109 building, one of the district's most conspicuous commercial buildings. For many writers, vernacular architecture and the absence of comprehensive planning became the very definition of Tokyo postmodernism, and this view was reiterated in the pages of *Across*.[43]

According to Parco's trend-watchers, New Breed youth actively sought out these vernacular places. Young people, reported *Across* in 1988, were attracted to unmanaged, unselfconscious places, causing them to move beyond Shibuya to the less developed Ebisu district, where dilapidated old houses stood just behind the main street, and to Shimokitazawa, where

[42] "Datsu TOKIO gensho" [Post-Tokio phenomenon], *Akurosu*, no. 136 (July 1985): 22–23.
[43] See Edward Suzuki interview, *Akurosu*, no. 145 (April 1986): 48–55.

shops displayed a miscellany of unfashionable junk.[44] "Retro" was clearly "in"—and the term "retro feel" (*retoro kankaku*) had become common parlance. Yet the fact that this taste turned toward vestiges of the old city rather than merely thrift-shop clothing and accessories suggests something more deep-rooted than mere retro-kitsch taste. The New Breed was determined to wander into the vernacular interstices in the modern city, perhaps even to walk in the antinomian manner proposed by Michel de Certeau, appropriating and reinventing the forms imposed by capitalist city planning.[45] Their determination bears at least a kinship relation to the preservationist impulse, because it presupposes something authentic outside the bounds of programmed urban space. At some point on the spectrum from thrift-shop chic to open-air museums, playful consumption of the flotsam of earlier waves of urbanization bleeds into an earnest desire for another place and time, not just unfashionable but ineffable, immune to fashion. Indirectly, a taste for the vernacular articulates a sense of unease with the capitalist present. *Across* writers conveyed this sentiment too. A special "white paper" report in the magazine on what they called "Tokyo, City of Overconcentrated Unease" (October 1987) carried the subheadline "The Present Era, Where Even Unease Is Something Consumed" (*fuan mo mata shōhi sareru gendai*). Sensibly heading their list of sources of unease was "land prices/housing."

Other media beside intellectual and trade journals echoed the voices of anti-modern and anti-consumerist critique. Some of the most sophisticated treatments of consumer society appeared in comics (*manga*), which were widely read among youth. Okazaki Kyōko's called her *manga* novel *Pink* a story of "love and capitalism . . . in the boring city of Tokyo." The protagonist, a young woman who is *echt* New Breed, works in a corporate office by day and prostitutes herself by night in order to feed her insatiable pet alligator—a pithy, if outlandish, symbol of consumerism. Midway through the story, she loses her pet and, with it, her sense of meaning in life. As she searches Tokyo, we see her in one brilliantly rendered scene overcome by agoraphobia outside Shibuya Station's north exit. In three frames, the cheerful crowd of shoppers and strolling couples turns sinister, and a familiar landscape gives way to a void evoking utter alienation. Just before she collapses in panic, her face is shown in a close-up profile, framed under the landmark tower of the 109 Building.[46]

Pink is not the tragic story of a young girl forced into prostitution, and it makes no moral pronouncement on the subject. Okazaki's protagonist remains the heroine to the end, without any cathartic break in her selling

44 "B-kyū kankaku afureru machi ga ima, omoshiroi" [Towns overflowing with B-grade feel are in], *Akurosu,* no. 169 (April 1988): 78–85.

45 Michel de Certeau, "Walking in the City," in *The Practice of Everyday Life,* trans. Steven Randall (Berkeley: University of California Press, 1984), 91–114.

46 Okazaki Kyōko, *Pink* (Tokyo: Magajin hausu, 1989). *Pink* originally appeared in serial form in the comic magazine *New Punch Zaurus.*

of herself. The villain is her stepmother, who is buying her boyfriend, but all are equally tainted by commodified sex. Their bodies are simply another form of commodity, whose exchange is both as casual and as fraught with meaning as any other transactions in consumer society. Nor is the heroine portrayed as lost and helpless in the big city. Instead, she appears naturally rootless. Returning to her apartment to feed her alligator provides her temporary respite from the totally commodified environment of the city—until the all-consuming alligator turns out to be commodifiable too. The unrealized happy ending involves an escape to an island in the south Pacific, depicted as a vague dream of jungles and blue skies, the only place that Okazaki's characters can imagine outside consumer society.

Vagueness of the object of longing, or its seeming impossibility, in no way vitiated the language of desire for something beyond the alienation of the affluent crowd. For the New Breed, who lacked a canonized site of loss, the "originary landscape" could be imagined anywhere. Popular singer Yuming (Matsutōya Yumi), whose plaintive voice filled the FM airwaves and was used in many television commercials in the late 1980s, accounted for the success of her music by referring to a "certain sadness" she shared with other middle-class girls who had grown up in Tokyo's new western suburbs and gone to private schools.[47] Cosmopolitanism and privilege permitted Yuming to juxtapose native and non-native landscapes as if both were equally originary for her: "Say I'm writing some lyrics about watching the rain outside the window of a tea shop [*anmitsuya*] in some back street around Shibuya. If someone else wrote it, the loneliness of a 4½ mat Japanese room would probably come out, but with me, the place might be London."[48] Despite her mannered melancholy, Yuming at the same time wholeheartedly embraced her identity as a consumer, in the same breath relating the feeling she shared with other middle-class young women that she would "die" without the money to do what she wanted.

Other instances of this kind of free-floating nostalgia are readily found throughout the cultural products of the era. Yoshimoto Banana, perhaps the most talked-about young novelist to emerge in the 1980s, certainly among the most popular, imbued her teenage fantasy tales with similar melancholy. She too depicted characters who lacked roots in the traditional sense yet formed complex emotional worlds in temporary places and around unconventional relationships.[49] Images of lost utopian pasts and idyllic childhoods pervade the work of animated filmmaker Miyazaki

[47] Ōtsuki Ryūkan, "Ichioku sōchūryū no tōsaku: minna ga 'Yūmin' ni natte shimatta" [Aberration of the total middle-class society: Everyone has ended up being Yuming], *Bessatsu Takarajima 110: 80 nendai no shōtai* [Takarajima supplement 110: True identity of the 1980s] (Tokyo: JICC shuppankyoku, 1990), 34.

[48] Quoted in Ōtsuki, "Ichioku sōchūryū no tōsaku," 47.

[49] John Treat describes Yoshimoto Banana's fiction as "nostalgic for nostalgia." John Treat, "Yoshimoto Banana Writes Home: Shōjo Culture and the Nostalgic Subject," *Journal of Japanese Studies* 19, no. 2 (Summer 1993): 379.

Hayao, whose originary landscapes embraced elements of Mayan civilization, ancient Japan, and early twentieth-century northern Europe, as well as the contemporary Japanese countryside.[50] Among academics, the work of medieval scholar Amino Yoshihiko, who revolutionized Japanese social history in the 1980s by overturning the traditional class analysis of Japanese "feudalism" and became one of Japan's bestselling historians, articulated strong nostalgia for an age before the Japanese archipelago came under unitary political control—implicitly signifying an irreversible step toward the contemporary "managed society." Artists like Miyazaki were influenced by Amino, and in their disparate yet intersecting fields both conjured utopian imagery of landscapes outside the state-controlled, globalized, and commercialized present.

While some popular media projected fantasies of faraway sites of longing, symbolically evoking the lost home of childhood, others idealized sites of private retreat within the city.[51] Peering into the lives and living spaces of young people who occupied tiny private quarters, two projects at the end of the 1980s championed their poverty-amid-plenty as a Japanese aesthetic of hermitage updated for bubble-era urban youth. *Tokyo Living at the Bottom,* a collection of articles originally published in the real estate advertising magazine *From-A,* introduced twenty-two people living in Tokyo and paying less than the low sum of twenty thousand yen (roughly two hundred dollars) monthly in rent. All of the subjects were living alone, and most were in their early twenties.[52] Interviews with these "bottom dwellers" focused on the personal freedom afforded by their inexpensive and minimal abodes. Sketches of the complete contents of their apartments revealed the accumulation of clothing, books, cassettes, videotapes, stuffed animals, electric guitars, and other trappings of youth one might have found in apartments and dormitories in any affluent country in the 1980s. Here these things were transformed from generic ensembles of commodities into expressions of their young owners' personalities and evidence of their mastery of the art of living cheap in the city (see figure 4.3). Tsuzuki Kyôichi's photo essay *Tokyo Style,* published in Japanese and English in 1992, exposed the cluttered tiny interiors of dozens of Tokyo apartments

[50] On Miyazaki and nostalgia, see Yasui Manami, "Shōhi sareru 'furusato'" [Consuming the 'native place'], in *Kokyō no sōshitsu to saisei* [Production and reproduction of native place], ed. Narita Ryūichi et al. (Tokyo: Seikyūsha, 2000), 121–27. On imagery in Miyazaki, see Susan J. Napier, "Confronting Master Narratives: History As Vision in Miyazaki Hayao's Cinema of De-assurance," *Positions: East Asia Cultures Critique* 9, no. 2 (July 2001): 467–93 and Tom Looser, "From Edogawa to Miyazaki: Cinematic and *Anime*-ic Architectures of Early and Late Twentieth-Century Japan," *Japan Forum* 14, no. 2 (2002): 297–327.

[51] See Uchida Ryūzō, "'Kokyō' to iu riariti" [Reality called 'native place'], in *Kokyō no sōshitsu to saisei,* ed. Narita et al., 136–37.

[52] Ōizumi Mitsunari, *Tōkyō saitee seikatsu: yachin niman en ika no hitobito* [Tokyo living at the bottom: People paying rents below 20,000 yen] (Tokyo: Ōta shuppan, 1992).

Figure 4.3. Living at the Bottom: The Minimal Apartment of New Breed Youth Komatsu Chie. Ōizumi Mitsunari, *Tōkyō saitee seikatsu: yachin niman en ika no hitobito* [Tokyo living at the bottom: People with rents below 20,000 yen] (Tokyo: Ōta shuppan, 1992).

absent their occupants. In image after image of rooms overflowing with things, Tsuzuki celebrated the "comfort of that cockpit feeling" afforded by living in tight quarters with all of one's belongings immediately at hand.[53] Tsuzuki's afterword set these scruffy Tokyo interiors in an ascetic native tradition encapsulated in the phrase "a half-mat for sitting, one mat for sleeping."[54] Like *Living at the Bottom,* Tsuzuki's essay proclaimed that true satisfaction lay not in the acquisition of new possessions or better housing but in the security of a small place.

[53] Kyoichi Tsuzuki, *Tokyo Style* (1992; repr. Kyoto: Kyōto shoin, 1997), 19.
[54] Tsuzuki, *Tokyo Style,* 431.

Manufacturing the Gaps

With almost poetic calendrical precision, the Tokyo stock market reached its peak on December 31, 1989, and began its spiral downward in January 1990. Real estate values entered a decline that would continue throughout the decade. Japan remained a rich country, and the shops in Shibuya continued to be busy with young people on the weekends. But national anxiety about the hedonistic "new species" was supplanted in the 1990s by fears of the social consequences of unemployment.

After the economic bubble burst, the tragic confrontation between fragile native tradition and global capitalist modernity took an ironic turn. With the pressure on urban real estate gone, the struggle for the city's soul now appeared less Manichean. But the market value of Tokyo nostalgia had been established. Aided by marketers, crusaders for the vernacular had succeeded in winning the affections of a large enough public that the vernacular city itself was now worth commodifying in Disney fashion as leisure space (with the large investments that this entailed). The search for accidental vestiges in the city was thus domesticated.

This came, however, not in the form of commercially based preservation in the city (what is known as "adaptive reuse" in the United States), but in packaged nostalgic environments, exteriors within interiors, which visitors enjoyed with a sense of irony, either as out-and-out camp or as poignantly tinged humor.[55] These new commercial spaces were called in the trade "staged environment entertainment facilities" (*kankyō enshutsu gata shūkyaku shisetsu*) or, perhaps more mellifluously, "performancescapes" (*pafōmansusukeepu*).[56] Life-sized walk-through recreations of ordinary buildings and streetscapes had already been deployed in un-ironic form at the Edo-Tokyo Museum and other history museums of the late 1980s and early 1990s. The technique was refined and overlaid with a sophisticated self-referentiality in the Shin-Yokohama Ramen Museum, which opened in 1994, presenting a new formula that was soon imitated elsewhere.

By carefully simulating patinae, the Ramen Museum's designers found they could deliver a more potent dose of anti-modern experience than could be achieved in any actual vernacular space. Drawing on Disney techniques, they created an imaginary *shitamachi,* set in circa 1958 (the year instant ramen was invented), and installed eight functioning ramen shops. Visitors to the Ramen Museum pay an admission fee, walk through ground-floor exhibits about the history of ramen noodles, then descend a staircase into this artificial town to wander, look inside houses and shops, and sit

[55] Kitada, *Kōkoku toshi Tōkyō,* 111–16.

[56] Yokohama karee myūjiamu meekingu seisaku iinkai [Yokohama curry museum design planning committee], *Karei naru kūkan dezain: meekingu obu Yokohama karee myūjiamu* [Gorgeous spatial design: Making of Yokohama curry museum] (Tokyo: Sōgō yunikomu, 2001), 54–55.

down to eat. The odd-sounding choice of ramen noodles as a museum theme was not fortuitous: traditionally a street food beloved by young Japanese and bearing lingering traces of "ethnic-ness" from its Chinese origins, ramen was a fitting "B-grade gourmet" item for slumming middle-class consumers.

As the museum's publications explain, the designers did not attempt to reconstruct the past just as it was but as (they believed) people would have it be. They were seeking "an image of authenticity surpassing the real thing."[57] Concretely, this meant that the whole streetscape was stained, streaked, and made to look mildly dilapidated, so that it is more like an old corner of a neighborhood that has happened to survive into the present than a neighborhood as it in fact would have appeared in 1958, when presumably some of the buildings were new. The minutest details of this one-street working-class town were reproduced on the basis of studies in existing *shitamachi* neighborhoods and made to look old through rusticating techniques used on film sets.

The same formula was subsequently repeated by others in several variations. The Namuko entertainment firm was particularly active, producing a series of overtly Disneyfied indoor theme parks with retro or exotic Asian themes, all using low lighting and faux finishes to suggest age and a measure of disrepair. A chain of restaurants called Yataimura replicated a nighttime streetscape lined with traditional food-vendors' carts. Like Parco, Yataimura were actually buildings housing multiple independent outlets coordinated in style and motif. Visitors were invited to imagine that they were in a bustling old downtown district at festival time. Several municipalities created similar museum environments, albeit more didactic in intent, focusing on an urban past recent enough to balance cozy familiarity with exoticism, particularly for young people.

Much of the new nostalgic consumption in the 1990s turned explicitly toward the period between 1955 and 1965, known more widely in Japan as the Shōwa 30s (Shōwa, the name given to the era of emperor Hirohito's reign, began in 1926). This decade is a convenient historical destination for the purpose of marketing. It precedes the trade wars, the oil shocks, and the full emergence into national consciousness of the environmental crisis that marked the end of Japan's postwar rush toward prosperity and, for many, the end of innocence. The Shōwa 30s closed with the Tokyo Olympics in 1964, which were both a national triumph and an urban cataclysm that destroyed countless old neighborhoods. The decade before the Olympics has come to be remembered—or historically reinscribed—as a time of optimism uncomplicated by any questioning of national pur-

[57] Gurafikku ando dezainingu [Graphic and Design Co.], *Meekingu obu Shin Yokohama raamen hakubutsukan* [Making of the Shin Yokohama ramen museum] (Tokyo: Mikuni shuppan, 1995), 32.

pose or personal meaning in life. As Laura Neitzel notes, "Looking back from the 1990s, people felt nostalgia for the feeling of 'looking forward.'"[58] Already in 1992, Kawamoto Saburō, one of the most prolific of Edo-Tokyoologists, had dubbed the era the "Tokyo Belle Epoque."[59] This postwar past incorporated a parade of American products and images, but it was still significantly called "Shōwa" and not "the fifties"; it was a native past, that is, whose symbols of "internationalization" (to use a troubled keyword in 1980s politics) were as benign as hula hoops and women's volleyball teams.

Why this antiquarian desire for patina, then, particularly if the era being recalled represented one of hope, of "looking forward"? Patina is perhaps an inapt word for the simple poverty and decrepitude some of these places conjure. The darkness and grime of the streetscapes at the Ramen Museum and its followers are unpretty evocations of age, reminders of decay and death. Nostalgia, even playful, camp nostalgia, derives its emotional effect from a sense of irretrievable loss. Starting in the mid-1990s, leisure entrepreneurs recognized that the nostalgic investments of critics, artists, historians, celebrities, and consumers during the previous decade of giddy economic speculation had been intensely intimate ones, focused on the small and the fragile and entangled with dreams of childhood. Thus, when the unending cycle of retro fashion came around to the recent past of the late 1950s and early 1960s, the points of reference were not the national icons of achievement in that era (the Olympics themselves, for example) but the fading relics of the era's relative poverty. The "brightness" associated with Japan's postwar economic boom helped revive the era as an antithesis to the deepening economic gloom of the 1990s present, yet popular memory groped instead to recover the sights, sounds, and smells of the back alley and the penny-candy store. Leisure entrepreneurs simply took the ineffable objects of this Proustian reflection and folded them back into commodity forms, making them camp. And visitors to the new performancescapes understood the game, because the exteriors within interiors allowed one easy access behind the façade: the shop fronts in the Ramen Museum, for example, belong to a stationer or a hairdresser, but ramen is served behind all of them, by chefs who make no effort to look or act "in period" (see figure 4.4). Even actors employed to play period figures step readily outside their roles to chat about the good old days of the Shōwa 30s (while acknowledging that they themselves were not yet born at the time). The new nostalgic theme park was thus like an enveloping gestalt of madeleines for a nation of Prousts—but plastic-

[58] Laura Neitzel, "Living Modern: *Danchi* Housing and Postwar Japan," Ph.D. dissertation, Columbia University, 2003, 174.

[59] Kawamura Saburō, *Shōwa 30 nen Tōkyō beru epokku* [Showa 30 Tokyo belle epoque] (Tokyo: Iwanami shoten, 1992).

Figure 4.4. Shop facade in the Ramen Museum with counter, stools, and ramen cook inside. Photo by the author.

wrapped madeleines, showing their artificiality. Since these leisure sites are only the most recent vessels for a fluid nostalgic impulse, and participants' perceptions are shaped by their own actual pasts, we should perhaps view the meticulously reconstructed and rusticated Shōwa 30s streetscapes as a mere moment in the modulation of icons of the city's humbler past across a spectrum running from commodity and camp to noncommodity and critique. The one certainty demonstrated by their success is that their designers knew the iconography, knew which nostalgic buttons to push.

The very consistency of this iconography of the low-tech city of the past should encourage us to take seriously the nostalgic consumerism since the 1980s (even with its overlay of camp) as an expression of desire to retrieve something from beyond the brightly lit confines of overprescribed urban modernity. Without studying the age composition and background of indoor theme park visitors, it is impossible to know precisely how much the 1990s phase of this nostalgia can be explained by the aging of the New Breed. Yet it is clear that the new leisure facilities crystallized a welter of imagery that appeared in the popular media consumed by New Breeders in the 1980s. Efforts in the 1980s to memorialize the vernacular city as the antithesis of the Shibuya of Seibu-Parco set the stage for these post-bubble theme parks. In many ways, the Edo-Tokyo Museum, planned throughout the 1980s and opened in 1993, was the first of the type.

I do not want to derive from this complete commodification of nostalgia only the conclusion that "capitalism swallows all." It may be true, but that doesn't mean it tells us much. On the other hand, I find the portrayal of New Breed consumerism as a form of liberation equally valueless. But these stark antitheses should not be our only choices. In reconstructing the complexly configured relationship among Tokyo's social critics, Seibu's sophisticated marketers, and mass consumers, the attitudes of New Breed youth are the easiest to stereotype, yet the most difficult to fix or know directly. Ambivalence does not mean resistance. We have no reason to believe that attachment to the traces of the past caused either the New Breed of the 1980s or the Proustian noodle-eaters of the 1990s to restrain their consumption of the latest commodities as well. Participation in advanced consumer society is rarely an either-or proposition; the question is rather how individuals or groups negotiate it. In this sense, intimations of ambivalence among the youth consumers who were the targets of both marketing and critical discourse bear significance as a form of contemporary critical commentary as much as any theoretical pronouncement from the intelligentsia. It is evidence that young people too were uneasy about the social and cultural changes of which they were the purported vanguard. If we follow them together with the market researchers, we espy them repeatedly sneaking behind the façades of modernity. In this sense, the cat-and-mouse game between capitalists and critics was actually more complex, as it revolved around a third player who, though lacking the sophisticated tricks of the other two, destabilized the game by constantly shifting its boundaries.

At its most general level, nostalgia is a universal psychological product of the uncertainty of modern life. Japanese critics at both ends of the political spectrum projected onto the new youth illusions of a rootless consumer without personal history or attachments. Yet they mistook the lack of actual experience of an "originary landscape" for the lack of desire for origins and authenticity. The New Breed's ambivalence emerged from the same paradoxical combination of sensibilities that made the critics critical: young Japanese of the 1980s longed for something outside Japan's managed consumer society, yet they were captive to its fashions.

PART II

CONSUMERISM, DEBT, SAVING, AND NATION

In part II, we investigate some of the more concrete manifestations of ambivalence toward consumption. How do households and states balance consumption against other imperatives such as saving, capital formation, and national unity? How do they deal with the phenomenon of consumer credit, which some societies severely regulate yet others embrace as the key to increasing consumption? Furthermore, can we speak of a distinctive Japanese or East Asian approach to consumption and saving? And if so, does it derive from a unique "culture" or a combination of political factors and the transnational emulation of other countries' practices?

These four chapters examine the interconnectedness of consumption, saving, and consumer credit—Andrew Gordon for Japan, Charles Yuji Horioka for Japan and western nations, Laura C. Nelson for South Korea, and Sheldon Garon for Japan, South Korea, Singapore, and Malaysia. Their efforts are particularly important for the study of the Japanese economy. From the heyday of the "Japanese miracle" to the last fifteen years of stagnation, American policymakers and economists have struggled to make sense of the world's second-largest economy. Widely divergent portraits emerge, depending on which element of the household economy is being measured and how. If, for example, we compare long-term Japanese and U.S. personal saving rates, the Japanese appear to be extraordinarily thrifty. On the other hand, if, like Horioka, we focus on the government's recently recalibrated statistics, we see instead a sharp decline in Japanese saving rates since 1991. For additional evidence that the Japanese have abandoned their culture of thrift, many still observe Japanese tourists shopping their way through the boutiques of Europe. Moreover, the Japanese do not look particularly frugal when we examine levels of consumer debt. Since the late 1980s, writes Gordon, Japanese have borrowed to finance their consumption at levels on a par with Americans and far above those of most European consumers. The Japanese, moreover, have a long history of buying consumer durables on the installment plan.

Lest we conclude that the Japanese are fast converging with the free-spending, low-saving American way of life, however, the chapters highlight a complex mix of consumer behaviors that distinguish Japan from the United States. For much of the postwar era, observes Garon, Japanese households steadily expanded consumption while also maintaining high saving rates. Gordon elaborates on the intimate relationship between the seemingly antithetical acts of installment buying and saving in twentieth-century Japan. The installment plan relied upon disciplined households that could make regular payments while rationally budgeting and saving. This enduring discipline helps explain why most Japanese, unlike Americans, remain reluctant to draw upon their credit cards for revolving credit, instead paying their monthly bills in full. Likewise, in Horioka's statistical analysis, Japanese saving rates may have declined over the last decade, but this is not to say that people went on a spending spree; Japanese consumption levels continue to lag behind those of the major western countries.

Indeed, the chapters do much to decenter American consumer culture as the primary reference for studying other countries. By comparing Japanese consumption and saving behavior with that of several western economies, Horioka reveals the United States—not Japan—to be the exception. Like Japan, the major continental European countries save at high rates and consume at levels well below those of the United States. This may not be so surprising, argues Garon in his chapter on the transnational diffusion of ideas and institutions. Historically, the Japanese state emulated Europe's savings institutions and vigorous savings-promotion programs. Nor should we assume that the American model of consumer-driven growth constituted the leading model for developing economies. Leaders of Asia's rapidly growing economies, notes Garon, were more drawn to the "Japanese model" of promoting saving and restraining domestic consumption.

Finally, the chapters explore crucial relations between politics and culture in shaping consumer behavior. They resist the common temptation to ascribe what cannot readily be explained to a timeless "culture"—be it the Japanese character, Confucianism, or "Asian values." With respect to South Korea, Japan, and other Asian nations, Nelson and Garon demonstrate that states and civic groups have played an active role in molding these cultures of thrift. They mounted recurrent campaigns to persuade their peoples to save, avoid "excessive consumption," and buy "national products." Gordon similarly illuminates the interdependence of politics and culture in explaining why Japanese consumers do not commonly borrow against their credit cards: interest-group politics resulted in policies that restricted the practice of revolving credit, which in turn reinforced the "naturalness" of using credit cards only for convenience, not credit. The three chapters further link the formation of these cultures of restraint to Korean and Japanese discourses that constructed women as "housewives" responsible for economizing and managing family finances. Their appreciation of the dynamic nature of "culture" offers insights into the future of Japan and South Korea, as globalization exposes these societies to consumer-centered economics, affluent lifestyles, and greater consumer credit. While Nelson, Garon, and Gordon detect significant changes in these cultures, they are equally impressed by the enduring power of discourses on thrift and "appropriate" consumption.

5

ARE THE JAPANESE UNIQUE?

An Analysis of Consumption and Saving Behavior in Japan

CHARLES YUJI HORIOKA

Japanese people often trumpet their putatively "unique" characteristics vis-à-vis other nations. This is particularly evident with respect to their saving and consumption behavior. According to various public opinion surveys, Japanese respondents overwhelmingly describe themselves as a people who love to save while exercising uncommon frugality in their consumption.[1] By contrast, western observers have generally *criticized* the Japanese for extolling such thriftiness and for saving too much and consuming too little. For example, during the 1980s, when Japan was running record trade and current account surpluses, the United States and Japan's other trading partners urged the Japanese government to promote consumption rather than saving as a way of reducing those surpluses. The conventional wisdom, whether Japanese or foreign, regards the Japanese as big savers who shun borrowing and hold unusually conservative portfolios. The only difference lies in whether they regard such behavior as good or bad.

This chapter marshals comparative data to examine whether Japanese saving and consumption behavior is truly so distinctive. Although we com-

I am grateful to Takatsugu Akaishi, Sheldon Garon, Patricia L. Maclachlan, Sven Steinmo, and the other participants of the two conferences on "Consumer Culture and Its Discontents"; to Shizuka Sekita, Midori Wakabayashi, and the other participants of my graduate seminar for their invaluable comments and insights; and to the Ministry of Education, Culture, Sports, Science, and Technology of the Japanese Government for Grant-in-Aid for Scientific Research number 12124207.

[1] In one government survey, 61.4 percent of the respondents agreed with the statement: "The Japanese are said to be frugal and saving-lovers, and I think this is a good thing." See Tominaga Kenichi and Mamada Takao, *Nihonjin no chochiku: Kōdō to ishiki* [Saving by the Japanese: Behavior and attitudes] (Tokyo: Nihon Hyōronsha, 1995), 25.

monly compare Japan to "the West," the western countries themselves demonstrate considerable variation in their saving and consumption patterns. How then does the saving and consumption behavior of the Japanese compare to that of other industrialized countries, notably the other Group of Seven (G7) countries? If Japan does resemble certain western countries, is it more similar to the English-speaking countries or to continental Europe? By exploring changes in saving and consumption behavior over time, this chapter also challenges the conventional view of Japanese thrift and frugality as static traits.

The Saving Behavior of the Japanese

Are the Japanese Big Savers?

Do the Japanese save more than consumers in other countries? To answer this question, I examine trends over time within Japan, followed by an international comparison. I then seek to explain Japanese saving behavior in the past, present, and future.

Trends over Time. As I have shown elsewhere, Japan's household saving rate was volatile during the prewar, wartime, and early postwar periods.[2] Saving rates were low, sometimes even negative, during about half of the years in this period (1907–15, 1921–30, and 1946–49), but they were high—generally in the double digits—during the other years (1906, 1916–20, 1931–44, and 1950–54). Indeed, household saving rates exceeded 30 or even 40 percent at the height of World War II (1941–44), when goods were scarce or rationed and when the state encouraged and often forced people to save. Thus, there is no simple answer to the question of whether Japan's household saving rates were high or low from 1906 to 1954. Saving rates ranged from negative to astonishingly high.

Before we can assess saving rates in more recent decades, a methodological note is in order. Scholars disagree in their interpretations of recent Japanese saving behavior, in part because in 2002 the Japanese government switched from the United Nations' System of National Accounts 1968 (SNA68) to the U.N.'s System of National Accounts 1993 (SNA93). As a result, a continuous time series for the entire postwar period is unavailable. Figure 5.1 and table 5.A1 show National Accounts data on Japan's household saving rate based on both SNAs for the 1955–2003 period. Data based on both SNAs are available for the 1980–98 period, and, as can be seen in figure 5.1 and table 5.A1, the two series were relatively close from 1980 to 1994 (within 2.6 percentage points of each other), but the gap between the two series widened to as much as 4.9 percentage

[2] Charles Yuji Horioka, "Consuming and Saving," in *Postwar Japan as History,* ed. Andrew Gordon (Berkeley: University of California Press, 1993), 259–92.

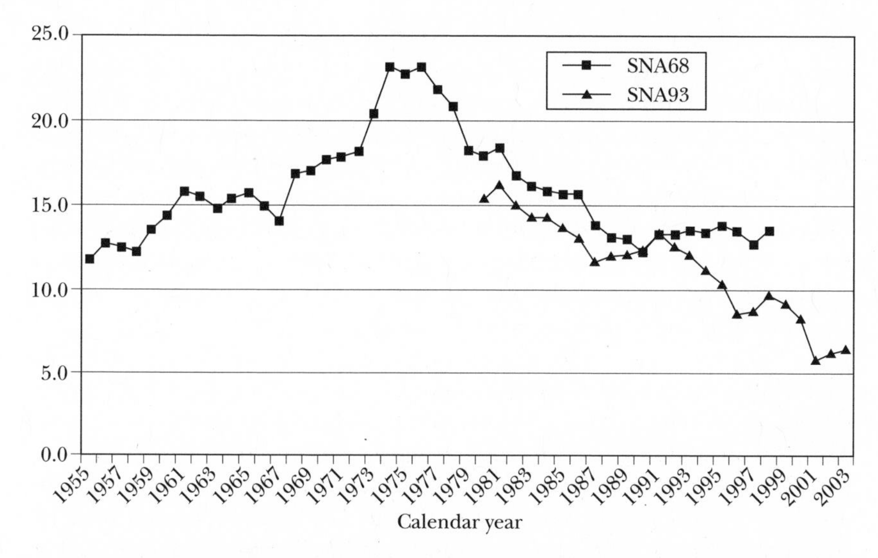

Note: The line marked "SNA68" shows data based on the United Nations' System of National Accounts 1968, whereas the line marked "SNA93" shows data based on the United Nations' System of National Accounts 1993. Payments in kind for medical and other services from social insurance have been added to the denominator of the SNA93 figures to make them comparable to the SNA68 figures.

Source: Department of National Accounts, Economic and Social Research Institute, Cabinet Office, Government of Japan, ed., *Annual Report on National Accounts,* 2005 edition (Tokyo: National Printing Bureau, 2005), and earlier editions of the same.

Figure 5.1. Trends in Japan's household saving rate, 1955–2003

points in the 1995–98 period (with the SNA93 series falling below the SNA68 series except in 1990–91). Moreover, trends over time in the household saving rate after 1991 differ greatly depending on which SNA we use. The SNA68 series leveled off in the 12.6 to 13.7 percent range during the 1991–98 period, whereas the SNA93 series showed a sharp *decline* from 13.3 percent in 1991 to 5.7 percent in 2001 before recovering slightly. Which series are we to believe?

The biggest difference between the two series lies in their treatment of bad loans. The older SNA68 exaggerates the household saving rate for the following reason: under SNA68, write-offs of bad loans to households and unincorporated businesses are treated as a current transfer from financial institutions to households. Thus, bad loan write-offs increase the incomes of households, and because their consumption does not change, their saving appears to increase. By contrast, SNA93 treats write-offs of bad loans to households and unincorporated businesses as a decline in the asset holdings of financial institutions, and thus they do not affect the saving rates of households.

The leveling off of the SNA68 saving rate after 1991 primarily reflects the write-offs of bad loans to households and unincorporated businesses following the collapse of the bubble and thus is a temporary phenomenon. If no write-offs of bad loans had been taken during this period, the SNA68 series would no doubt have exhibited the same sharp decline as the SNA93 series. Thus, it appears that Japan's household saving rate (correctly measured) has continued to decline even after 1991 and that it is no longer high by either absolute or relative standards.[3]

As figure 5.1 and table 5.A1 show, Japan's household saving rate was high (in the double digits) until the mid-1990s, peaking at 23.2 percent in 1974 and 1976 before declining sharply. It exceeded 20 percent during the 1973–78 period, 15 percent during most of the 1961–86 period (only through 1981 in the case of the SNA93 series), and 10 percent during the 1955–98 period (according to SNA68) and the 1955–95 period (according to SNA93). However, the more accurate SNA93 series has been in the single digits since 1996, falling to a paltry 5.7 percent in 2001.

To sum up, Japan's household saving rates *were* high during most of the postwar period (1955–95) but have been low since 1996.

International Comparison. Cross-national comparisons of saving rates present even greater methodological challenges. Data on household saving rates are available for twenty-three of the Organization for Economic Cooperation and Development (OECD) member countries. However, for seventeen of these countries (including Japan), the data measure the net household saving rate, whereas for the other six countries, they measure the gross household saving rate. The difference is significant. In the case of the net household saving rate, the numerator (household saving) and denominator (household disposable income) both exclude the depreciation (consumption of fixed capital) of households and unincorporated businesses, whereas both the numerator and denominator of the gross household saving rate include depreciation. Thus, the two are not comparable, and the gross household saving rate will invariably be much higher than the net household saving rate. Because I wanted to compare the household saving rates of all OECD member countries for which data

[3] The second major difference between the two series is that the series based on SNA68 includes social transfers in kind received, which includes such things as the portion of the cost of medical and nursing care services covered by social insurance and the portion of the cost of day care, textbooks, etc., borne by the government when calculating household disposable income and consumption whereas the series based on SNA93 does not. Since I wanted to make the two series as comparable as possible and since it is conceptually preferable to include social transfers in kind received in household disposable income and consumption, I have added social transfers in kind received to household disposable income when computing the household saving rate from the data based on SNA93.

TABLE 5.1.
Net household saving rates of selected OECD countries, 1985–2003

	1985	1990	1995	2000	2003
Australia	10.8 (7)	9.3 (9)	4.9 (18)	2.9 (18)	−2.2 (22)
Austria	10.5 (8)	14.0 (4)	11.7 (8)	8.4 (10)	8.5 (9)
*Belgium	11.1 (6)	12.1 (8)	13.0 (6)	9.2 (8T)	9.9 (7)
Canada	15.8 (3)	13.0 (7)	9.2 (14)	4.7 (16)	1.4 (18T)
Czech Rep.	N/A	N/A	20.6 (1)	13.0 (2)	11.3 (2)
Denmark	N/A	3.2 (16)	−0.1 (22)	−5.7 (23)	0.3 (21)
Finland	3.4 (14)	1.8 (18)	4.8 (19)	−1.4 (21)	0.4 (20)
France	8.9 (10)	7.8 (12)	11.2 (11T)	10.9 (3)	11.1 (3)
Germany	12.5 (5)	13.9 (5T)	11.2 (11T)	9.7 (6)	10.7 (4)
Hungary	N/A	N/A	15.6 (4)	16.0 (1)	17.3 (1)
Ireland	N/A	7.9 (11)	11.3 (9T)	9.9 (5)	8.3 (10)
Italy	21.5 (1)	24.0 (1)	17.9 (3)	9.2 (8T)	10.5 (5)
Japan	16.5 (2)	13.9 (5T)	11.9 (7)	9.5 (7)	6.3 (13)
South Korea	14.8 (4)	22.0 (2)	18.0 (2)	10.5 (4)	2.5 (17)
Netherlands	5.6 (13)	17.5 (3)	14.4 (5)	6.8 (14)	10.1 (6)
New Zealand	1.3 (16)	0.7 (20)	−3.8 (23)	−4.1 (22)	−6.5 (23)
Norway	−3.3 (17	2.2 (17)	4.6 (20T)	5.2 (15)	7.6 (11)
*Portugal	N/A	N/A	9.5 (13)	7.6 (12)	9.1 (8)
*Spain	7.8 (11)	8.6 (10)	11.3 (9T)	7.5 (13)	7.4 (12)
*Sweden	2.2 (15)	1.1 (19)	6.3 (17)	2.0 (20)	6.0 (14)
Switzerland	N/A	6.7 (14)	8.1 (15_	8.3 (11)	5.7 (15)
*United Kingdom	6.9 (12)	5.6 (15)	7.0 (16)	3.5 (17)	3.9 (16)
United States	9.2 (9)	7.0 (13)	4.6 (20T)	2.3 (19)	1.4 (18T)
OECD mean	9.1	9.6	9.7	6.3	6.1

Notes: The left-hand figures denote the household saving rate, refined as household saving as a ratio of disposable household income, while the figures in parentheses denote the rank of each country. The first figure for New Zealand is the figure for 1986. The last figure for the Czech Republic is the figure for 2002 because the figure for 2003 was not available. The figures include the saving of households as well as that of nonprofit institutions except for the Czech Republic, Finland, France, Japan, and New Zealand. For countries marked by an asterisk, only figures on gross household saving rates were available; the gross figures were converted to a net basis by using a conversion factor of 0.7 (which is the approximate ratio of the average net household saving rate to the average gross household saving rate for the countries and years used in this analysis). In the case of Denmark and Italy, the figures for 1985 were computed from the gross household saving rate.

Source: For 1985 data, *OECD Economic Outlook*, vol. 2003/1, no. 73 (June 2003), Annex Table 24; for 1990, 1995, 2000, and 2003 data, vol. 2004/2, no. 76 (December 2004), Annex Table 23.

are available, I converted the gross household saving rate figures to a net basis using a conversion factor of 0.7 (which is the approximate ratio of the average net household saving rate to the average gross household saving rate for the countries and years used in the present analysis).

My comparative data challenge the conventional view that the Japanese are uniquely thrifty and that they have always been high savers. Table 5.1 presents actual or estimated data on net household saving rates for the 1985–2003 period for the twenty-three OECD member countries for which data are available. The Japanese entered this period as notably high savers, but not uniquely so. As table 5.1 shows, in 1985 Japan's household saving rate (16.5 percent) was second only to Italy (21.5 percent) among the

OECD member countries for which data are available, followed closely by Canada (15.8 percent) and South Korea (14.8 percent). Thereafter, however, Japan's household saving rate fell sharply both in level and rank, from 16.5 percent in 1985 to 6.3 percent in 2003,[4] and from second in 1985 to fifth in 1990 to seventh in 1995 to thirteenth in 2003 among the OECD countries for which data are available. Japan's household saving rate was nearly twice as high as the OECD rate in 1985, but the two were virtually identical in 2003.

Moreover, Japan has shared the distinction of being a big saver with a variety of nations in Asia and the West. Among the OECD member countries for which data are available, the top saver in 1985 and 1990 was Italy, in 1995 the Czech Republic, and in 2000 and 2003 Hungary. Other OECD members that have attained double-digit household saving rates at least once since 1985 include Australia, Austria, Belgium, Canada, France, Germany, Ireland, South Korea, the Netherlands, and Spain. If we confine our comparison to the G7 countries (Canada, France, Germany, Italy, Japan, the United Kingdom, and the United States), Japan ranked second only to Italy during the 1985–95 period (tied with Germany in 1990) but fell to third behind France and Germany in 2000 and to fourth behind France, Germany, and Italy in 2003. Moreover, there are many non-OECD economies in Asia (such as China, Hong Kong, Singapore, and Taiwan) that appear to have higher household saving rates than Japan at present, notwithstanding the absence of comparable data.

In addition, the Japanese government appears to have overestimated Japan's household saving rate vis-à-vis other countries. As Fumio Hayashi and I have demonstrated, there are several conceptual differences and deficiencies in Japan's official data that impart an upward bias in the level of Japan's household saving rate.[5]

Although it is beyond the scope of this chapter, we observe substantial variations in household saving rates among the OECD nations. Ranged against high-saving countries like the Czech Republic, Hungary, Italy, Japan, and South Korea are several OECD members whose household saving rates never exceeded 10 percent during the 1985–2003 period. These low-savers include Denmark, Finland, New Zealand, Norway, Portugal, Sweden, Switzerland, the United Kingdom, and, most notably, the United States.

To sum up, the cross-national data challenge us to reevaluate our un-

[4] The discrepancy between the National Accounts data based on SNA93 and OECD data on Japan's household saving rate is due primarily to the treatment of social transfers in kind received (see note 3).

[5] See, for example, Fumio Hayashi, "Why Is Japan's Saving Rate So Apparently High?" in *NBER Macroeconomics Annual 1986*, ed. Stanley Fischer, vol. 1 (Cambridge: MIT Press, 1986), 147–210; and Charles Yuji Horioka, "Is Japan's Household Saving Rate Really High?" *Review of Income and Wealth* 41, no. 4 (December 1995): 373–97.

derstanding of saving behavior in Japan and elsewhere. First, the Japanese were unquestionably big savers until about 2000, but they were hardly unique and showed household saving rates that were roughly comparable to several major continental European nations as well as South Korea, a country that has long emulated Japan's developmental policies (see Garon, chap. 7, and Nelson, chap. 8). These data present a challenge to those who insist that the Japanese are uniquely thrifty or that East Asians are systematically more inclined to save than westerners.

Second, the data reveal that it is not Japan but the United States and the other English-speaking countries (in particular, New Zealand and the United Kingdom) that stand out as more exceptional, exhibiting the lowest household saving rates among the major industrialized countries. Third, the data demonstrate that, in recent years, Japan's household saving rate has fallen far below those of Europe's leading savers, converging toward the levels in the English-speaking countries, and I argue below that it will decline even more in the future.

Why Were the Japanese Big Savers? Elsewhere, I list more than thirty factors that have been invoked to explain Japan's high household saving rate during much of the postwar period.[6] Here, let's examine what are, in my view, the nine most salient factors.

First, the high rate of income growth during the high-growth era from the 1950s to the early 1970s undoubtedly helped raise Japan's household saving rate. When income grows rapidly or unexpectedly, households often cannot adjust their living standards and consumption patterns at the same pace, and, as a result, saving (the difference between income and consumption) tends to increase, at least temporarily.

Second, household asset holdings were very low in Japan just after World War II because the war destroyed much of Japan's housing stock and the postwar hyperinflation reduced the real value of financial assets to almost nothing. Japanese households presumably saved as much as they did in part to restore their asset holdings to desired levels.

Third, although the Japanese have long made some purchases on the installment plan (see Gordon, chap. 6), consumer credit was not readily available until recently, as I will discuss later. Accordingly, Japanese households often found it necessary to save in advance of purchases of such big-ticket items as houses, automobiles, furniture, and electrical appliances. Moreover, the paucity of credit also increased the need for precautionary saving because Japanese households knew that they would not be able to borrow in times of emergency.

Fourth, Japan's bonus system of compensation, whereby a large chunk

[6] Charles Yuji Horioka, "Why Is Japan's Household Saving Rate So High? A Literature Survey," *Journal of the Japanese and International Economies* 4, no. 1 (March 1990): 49–92. See also Hayashi, "Why Is Japan's Saving Rate So Apparently High?" 147–210.

TABLE 5.2.
Percentage of elderly population in selected OECD countries, 1975–2025

Country	1975	2000	2025
Australia	8.7 (19T)	12.3 (19T)	18.6 (19)
Austria	14.9 (2)	15.6 (10T)	24.3 (7)
Belgium	13.9 (5)	17.0 (4T)	23.7 (8)
Canada	8.5 (21)	12.6 (18)	20.7 (17T)
Czech Rep.	12.9 (9)	13.8 (16)	23.1 (10)
Denmark	13.4 ((8)	15.0 (13)	22.5 (11)
Finland	10.6 (15)	14.9 (14)	25.2 (5)
France	13.5 (7)	16.0 (7T)	22.2 (12)
Germany	14.8 (3)	16.4 (6)	24.6 (6)
Hungary	12.6 (10T)	14.6 (15)	21.2 (16)
Ireland	11.0 (13)	11.3 (22)	16.3 (23)
Italy	12.0 (12)	18.1 (1)	25.7 (3)
Japan	7.9 (22)	17.2 (3)	28.9 (1)
South Korea	3.6 (23)	7.1 (23)	16.9 (22)
Netherlands	10.8 (14)	13.6 (17)	21.9 (13T)
New Zealand	8.7 (19T)	11.7 (21)	18.5 (20T)
Norway	13.7 (6)	15.4 (12)	21.8 (15)
Portugal	9.9 (18)	15.6 (10T)	20.7 (17T)
Spain	10.0 (17)	17.0 (4T)	23.6 (9)
Sweden	15.1 (1)	17.4 (2)	25.4 (4)
Switzerland	12.6 (10T)	16.0 (7T)	27.1 (2)
United Kingdom	14.0 (4.0)	15.8 (9)	21.9 (13T)
United States	10.5 (16)	12.3 (19T)	18.5 (20T)
OECD mean	12.6	16.0	24.4

Notes: The left-hand figures denote the percentage of the population aged 65 or older while the figures in parentheses denote the rank of each country.
Source: United Nations, *World Population Ageing, 1950– 2050* (New York: United Nations, 2002).

of employee compensation is paid in the form of semiannual lump-sum bonuses, is often said to have encouraged saving—or at the very least facilitated it.

Fifth, the age structure of Japan's population was among the youngest among the industrialized countries until recently. As table 5.2 shows, in 1975 the share of the elderly (those aged 65 or older) in Japan's total population was only 7.9 percent. Among the OECD member countries, Japan ranked second to last behind South Korea at 3.6 percent. According to the life cycle hypothesis, the aggregate household saving rate will be higher in a country with a young population because the young typically work and save, whereas the elderly typically retire from work and draw down their existing savings.[7]

[7] On the life cycle hypothesis, see Franco Modigliani and Richard Brumberg, "Utility Analysis and the Consumption Function: An Interpretation of Cross-Section Data," in *Post-Keynesian Economics,* ed. Kenneth K. Kurihara (New Brunswick, NJ: Rutgers University Press), 388–436.

Sixth, the Japanese government introduced many tax breaks for saving such as the *maruyū* system, whereby a portion of interest income on bank and postal deposits and on government bonds was tax-exempt. These tax breaks may have induced Japanese households to save more than they would have otherwise.

Seventh, public old-age pension benefits were relatively low in Japan until 1973. This made it necessary for Japanese households to save on their own to prepare for life after retirement.

Eighth, the Japanese government and the quasi-governmental Central Council for Savings Promotion engaged in a variety of savings promotion activities. In this volume and elsewhere, Sheldon Garon has argued that official savings promotion campaigns helped to raise the household saving rate in Japan.[8]

Ninth, many attribute Japan's high household saving rate to cultural factors. They argue that frugality, considered a virtue in Confucian teachings, is part of the national character of the Japanese people.

However, all of these factors are becoming less applicable over time. Let's run through the list: (1) Double-digit rates of economic growth ended in the early 1970s, and income growth rates have been in the single digits since then, (2) Japanese households have accumulated high levels of assets (see below); (3) consumer credit has become widely available (see below); (4) most companies have scaled back bonuses as a result of the prolonged recession; (5) Japan's population is aging at an unprecedented rate, with the share of the population aged 65 or older rising from 7.9 percent in 1975 to 17.2 percent (third place among the OECD countries) in 2000 (see table 5.2); (6) most tax breaks for saving were abolished in 1988; (7) public old-age pension benefits were dramatically improved in 1973; (8) government savings promotion activities have been scaled back, and the Central Council for Savings Promotion was renamed the Central Council for Savings Information in 1988 and the Central Council for Financial Services Information in 2001, gradually shifting from the active encouragement of saving to providing consumers with information on the array of financial services available; (9) the longstanding culture of thrift may decline over time as foreign lifestyles become more attractive. The weakening of these factors explains why Japan's household saving rate has declined so sharply since the mid-1970s.

Will the Japanese once again Become Big Savers? In my opinion, the most important factor determining future trends in Japan's household saving rate will be the rapid aging of its population. Japan's population is aging rapidly and will soon become the most aged in the world. As table 5.2 shows, the share of the population aged 65 or older in Japan is projected

[8] Sheldon Garon, *Molding Japanese Minds: The State in Everyday Life* (Princeton, NJ: Princeton University Press, 1997), ch. 5.

to increase from 17.2 percent in 2000 to 28.9 percent in 2025, which would make it the highest among the OECD countries. According to the life cycle hypothesis, when individuals are young, they generally work and save a portion of their incomes, while after retirement, they draw down their previously accumulated savings. Thus, the higher the share of the elderly in the total population, the lower the aggregate household savings rate will be, and presumably the rapid aging of Japan's population has contributed to the sustained decline in its household saving rate in recent years. With the aging of Japan's population projected to continue at a rapid rate, its household saving rate can also be expected to continue to decline rapidly. Indeed, a number of authors, myself included, have projected that the rapid aging of Japan's population will cause Japan's household saving rate to decline to zero or even negative levels by around 2010.[9]

I should note, however, that the discussion thus far has focused exclusively on the impact of the aging of the population on the household saving rate. There are, of course, other factors that will influence the household saving rate, so let us turn to four short-term factors that may have been important during the current recession that began in 1991.[10]

First, sharp declines in land and equity prices have led to sharp declines in the value of household holdings of land and equities, and this in turn should have encouraged households to save more in order to make up for the capital losses on their land and equity holdings.

Second, the current recession has undoubtedly increased anxieties about future income and employment prospects, and these increased anxieties should also have encouraged Japanese households to save more.

Third, the profits of individual proprietors have been stagnant during the current recession, and this has lessened their ability to save, thereby lowering the saving rate of the household sector as a whole.

Fourth, consumer price deflation has continued for a number of years, and this, too, should have encouraged households to save more because, in a situation in which consumer prices are declining over time, households can save money by postponing their purchases of consumer goods and services. However, consumer price deflation will also increase the real value of household holdings of financial assets, which in turn will induce

[9] See Charles Yuji Horioka, "Future Trends in Japan's Saving Rate and the Implications Thereof for Japan's External Imbalance," *Japan and the World Economy* 3, no. 4 (April 1992): 307–30. On the question of whether the life cycle hypothesis applies to the Japanese case, see Charles Yuji Horioka, "Saving in Japan," in *World Savings: An International Survey,* ed. Arnold Heertje (Oxford, UK: Blackwell Publishers, 1993), 238–78; and Charles Yuji Horioka, "Are the Japanese Selfish, Altruistic, or Dynastic?" *Japanese Economic Review* 53, no. 1 (March 2002): 26–54.

[10] Charles Yuji Horioka, "The Stagnation of Household Consumption in Japan," Discussion Paper no. 599, Institute of Social and Economic Research, Osaka University, June 2004, downloadable from http://www.iser.osaka-u.ac.jp.

people to consume more and save less. Thus, the net impact of consumer price deflation on the household saving rate is theoretically ambiguous.

In sum, the first and second of these short-term factors should have bolstered Japan's household saving rate during the past decade, the third should have had a downward effect, and the fourth appears to be ambiguous in its impact. Thus, the net impact of these short-term factors on Japan's household saving rate is ambiguous, and I predict that Japan's household saving rate will continue its rapid decline even if the Japanese economy recovers from the current recession and these short-term factors cease to apply.

Are the Japanese Asset-Rich?

High saving rates usually lead to high asset or wealth holdings because wealth is simply the accumulation of past saving. Accordingly, I now turn my attention from saving to wealth and consider whether the asset or wealth holdings of the Japanese are high in absolute terms as well as relative to the other industrialized countries.

Table 5.3 shows data on household wealth and indebtedness for the G7 countries covering the 1990–2002 period. Let us first examine the data on net wealth or net worth (the broadest concept of wealth, defined as financial assets plus nonfinancial or real assets minus liabilities). The net wealth or net worth of Japanese households was the highest among the G7 countries (a whopping 9.5 times household disposable income) in 1990, but it declined sharply thereafter due to the collapse of the bubble (the collapse of land and equity prices), falling to 7.5 to 7.6 times household disposable income in 1995–2002 and, in rank, to second place by 2000, behind Italy. Still, excepting Italy's high ratios during the 1990–2002 period (6.4 to 8.2 times), Japan's ratio of household net wealth or net worth to household disposable income remained significantly higher than those in other G7 countries (5.6 to 7.3 times in the United Kingdom, 5.1 to 6.3 times in France, 5.0 to 5.4 times in Germany, 4.7 to 5.8 times in the United States, and 4.2 to 5.1 times in Canada) throughout this period.

Moreover, Japan has generally ranked much higher in terms of the individual components of household wealth as well. For example, Japan placed first among the G7 countries with respect to financial assets in three out of the four years for which data are shown (1990, 1995, and 2002) and second behind the United Kingdom in the remaining year (2000), with financial asset holdings ranging from 4.0 to 5.0 times household disposable income. Similarly, Japan ranked between first and third among the G7 countries (behind Italy in 1995 and 2000 and behind Italy and the United Kingdom in 2002) with respect to nonfinancial or real assets (land, housing, and consumer durables), with holdings of such assets ranging from 3.9 to 6.8 times household disposable income. Finally, Japan ranked first

TABLE 5.3.
Household wealth and indebtedness in the G7 countries, 1990–2002

Country	1990	1995	2000	2002
Canada				
Net wealth	416.5 (7)	483.7 (7)	505.2 (7)	514.0 (5)
Net financial wealth	177.5 (5)	225.7 (5)	243.4 (6)	233.8 (5)
Nonfinancial assets	239.0 (6)	258.0 (6)	261.8 (6)	280.1 (6)
Financial assets	270.4 (4)	329.1 (4)	356.1 (5)	350.1 (4)
of which: Equities	49.6 (5)	66.3 (4)	94.1 (5)	95.4 (2)
Total assets	509.4 (7)	587.1 (6)	617.9 (7)	630.2 (5)
Liabilities	92.9 (3)	103.4 (3)	112.7 (4)	116.2 (3)
of which: Mortgages	59.2 (3)	68.8 (2)	69.6 (3)	70.9 (4)
France				
Net wealth	541.8 (4)	507.7 (5)	630.2 (4)	606.6 (4)
Net financial wealth	169.6 (6)	195.0 (6)	282.6 (5)	226.5 (6)
Nonfinancial assets	372.2 (5)	312.7 (4)	347.6 (5)	380.1 (4)
Financial assets	248.3 (5)	262.9 (5)	359.2 (4)	302.5 (5)
of which: Equities	114.1 (1)	89.6 (2)	155.7 (2)	100.7 (1)
Total assets	620.5 (4)	575.6 (7)	706.8 (4)	682.6 (4)
Liabilities	78.7 (5)	67.9 (6)	76.6 (6)	76.0 (6)
of which: Long-term loans	53.4 (5)	51.6 (6)	55.2 (6)	56.9 (6)
Germany				
Net wealth	535.6 (5)	496.0 (6)	511.8 (6)	499.5 (7)
Net financial wealth	130.8 (7)	135.4 (7)	162.2 (7)	160.0 (7)
Nonfinancial assets	404.8 (3)	360.6 (3)	349.6 (4)	339.5 (5)
Financial assets	200.7 (7)	236.0 (7)	276.2 (7)	271.8 (7)
of which: Equities	11.6 (7)	43.4 (7)	74.5 (6)	57.1 (5)
Total assets	605.5 (5)	596.6 (5)	625.8 (6)	611.3 (7)
Liabilities	70.0 (6)	100.6 (4)	114.0 (2)	111.8 (4)
of which: Mortgages	53.6 (4)	61.0 (4)	72.2 (2)	73.5 (3)
Italy				
Net wealth	636.9 (2)	739.4 (2)	819.3 (1)	810.9 (1)
Net financial wealth	196.3 (4)	228.3 (4)	314.7 (4)	251.9 (3)
Nonfinancial assets	440.5 (2)	511.1 (1)	504.6 (1)	559.0 (1)
Financial assets	225.4 (6)	254.6 (6)	350.2 (6)	295.5 (6)
of which: Equities	46.0 (6)	46.5 (5)	156.5 (1)	87.9 (4)
Total assets	665.9 (3)	765.7 (2)	854.8 (2)	854.5 (2)
Liabilities	29.1 (7)	30.6 (7)	37.5 (7)	39.3 (7)
of which: Medium and long-term loans	13.7 (7)	18.6 (7)	27.3 (7)	29.7 (7)
Japan				
Net wealth	947.6 (1)	757.0 (1)	764.2 (2)	753.1 (2)
Net financial wealth	268.0 (1)	288.9 (2)	343.0 (3)	361.4 (1)
Nonfinancial assets	679.6 (1)	468.1 (2)	421.2 (2)	391.7 (3)
Financial assets	398.8 (1)	426.1 (1)	478.5 (2)	497.2 (1)
of which: Equities	57.3 (3)	44.7 (6)	41.4 (7)	41.7 (7)
Total assets	1078.4 (1)	894.2 (1)	899.7 (1)	888.9 (1)
Liabilities	130.8 (1)	137.2 (1)	135.5 (1)	135.8 (1)
of which: Mortgages	50.6 (6)	58.6 (5)	59.5 (5)	61.7 (5)
United Kingdom				
Net wealth	611.0 (3)	555.8 (3)	733.4 (3)	674.9 (3)
Net financial wealth	214.1 (3)	285.6 (3)	370.2 (1)	249.9 (4)
Nonfinancial assets	396.9 (4)	270.2 (5)	363.2 (3)	425.1 (2)
Financial assets	329.9 (3)	392.2 (3)	483.5 (1)	378.7 (3)
of which: Equities	61.2 (2)	76.2 (3)	108.7 (4)	56.5 (6)
Total assets	726.8 (2)	662.4 (3)	846.7 (3)	803.8 (3)
Liabilities	115.8 (2)	106.6 (2)	113.3 (3)	128.7 (2)
of which: Mortgages	81.3 (1)	78.1 (1)	81.8 (1)	92.7 (1)

TABLE 5.3—cont.

Country	1990	1995	2000	2002
United States				
Net wealth	474.5 (6)	509.3 (4)	584.7 (5)	506.4 (6)
Net financial wealth	259.0 (2)	305.6 (1)	368.8 (2)	274.3 (2)
Nonfinancial assets	215.5 (7)	203.8 (7)	215.9 (7)	232.1 (7)
Financial assets	345.6 (2)	399.3 (2)	471.7 (3)	385.4 (2)
of which: Equities	52.1 (4)	97.9 (1)	146.7 (3)	91.5 (3)
Total assets	561.1 (6)	603.1 (4)	687.6 (5)	617.5 (6)
Liabilities	86.6 (4)	93.8 (5)	102.9 (5)	111.2 (5)
of which: Mortgages	60.3 (2)	63.5 (3)	68.9 (4)	78.0 (2)

Notes: The left-hand figures denote assets and liabilities outstanding at the end of the year as a percent of nominal disposable income, while the figures in parentheses denote the rank of each country. Most figures are based on the UN System of National Accounts 1993 (SNA93) and, more specifically, for European Union countries, on corresponding European System of Accounts 1995 (ESA95).

Households include nonprofit institutions serving households. Net wealth is defined as nonfinancial and financial assets minus liabilities; net financial wealth is financial assets minus liabilities. Nonfinancial assets include stock of durable goods and dwellings, at replacement cost and at market value, respectively. Financial assets comprise currency and deposits; securities other than shares; loans, shares, and other equity; insurance technical reserves; and other accounts receivable/payable. Not included are assets with regard to social security pension insurance schemes. Equities comprise shares and other equity, including quoted, unquoted, and mutual fund shares. See also *OECD Economic Outlook Sources and Methods* (*http://www.oecd.org/eco/sources-and-methods*).

Primary sources: Banque de France *Flow of Funds Accounts.* Germany: Deutsche Bundesbank, *Monthly Report* and *Financial Accounts for Germany 1991 to 1999,* Special Statistcal Publication, 2000. Italy: Banca d'Italia, *Supplements to the Statistical Bulletin,* Albert Ando, Luigi Guiso, and Ignazio Visco, eds., *Saving and the Accumulation of Wealth* (Cambridge: Cambridge University Press, 1994); OECD, *Financial Accounts of OECD Countries* Japan: Economic Planning Agency, Government of Japan, *Annual Report on National Accounts.* United Kingdom: Office for National Statistics, *United Kingdom National Accounts,* and *Financial Statistics.* United States: Federal Reserve Statistical Release, *Flow of Funds Accounts.*

Source: For 1990 data, *OECD Economic Outlook,* vol. 2003/1, no. 73 (June 2003), Annex Table 56; for 1995, 2000, and 2002 data, vol. 2004/2, no. 76 (December 2004), Annex Table 58.

among the G7 countries with respect to total assets (the sum of financial assets and nonfinancial assets) in all four years, with holdings of such assets ranging from 8.9 to 10.8 times household disposable income.

In terms of trends over time, nonfinancial or real assets declined sharply throughout the 1990–2002 period (from 6.8 to 3.9 times household disposable income) due to the precipitous decline in land prices, yet financial assets continued to increase throughout this period (from 4.0 to 5.0 times household disposable income) despite the sharp decline in equity prices. As a result of these conflicting trends, both total assets and net wealth or net worth declined sharply between 1990 and 1995 but stabilized thereafter.

Indeed, the Japanese are asset-rich in absolute terms as well as relative to the other G7 countries. This enormous wealth of the Japanese presumably resulted in part from high saving rates and in part from rapid increases in land and equity prices during much of the postwar period. However, because Japanese household saving rates are no longer unusually high and because land and equity prices have been plummeting for more than a decade, the level of household wealth in Japan is much lower than it was a decade ago, and the gap in household wealth between Japan and the other G7 countries has narrowed considerably. Moreover, Japan's household wealth can be expected to decline even further in the future.

Do the Japanese Shun Borrowing?

Typically, high saving and low borrowing go hand in hand because both are manifestations of frugality and both are ways of holding down consumption. In this section, I turn my attention to the borrowing side of the ledger. Surprisingly, as table 5.3 shows, Japan ranked first among the G7 countries with respect to outstanding liabilities in all four of the years for which data are shown: outstanding liabilities range from 1.3 to 1.4 times household disposable income in Japan, as compared to 1.1 to 1.3 times in the United Kingdom, 0.9 to 1.2 times in Canada, 0.9 to 1.1 times in the United States, 0.7 to 1.1 times in Germany, 0.7 to 0.8 times in France, and 0.3 to 0.4 times in Italy. Moreover, although conventional wisdom dictates that household liabilities in Japan consist mostly of mortgages (housing loans), the share of mortgages in household liabilities is much *lower* in Japan than it is in all of the other G7 countries in all four years, ranging from 39 to 45 percent in Japan, as compared to 70 to 73 percent in the United Kingdom, 68 to 76 percent in France, 67 to 70 percent in the United States, 61 to 77 percent in Germany, 61 to 67 percent in Canada, and 47 to 76 percent in Italy (see table 5.4). In short, household debt is used to finance consumption to a greater extent in Japan than it is in the other G7 countries.

Data for the more distant past show that outstanding liabilities were a mere 60 and 77 percent of household disposable income in Japan in 1970 and 1980, respectively, indicating that the Japanese, in fact, borrowed relatively little in the past. Moreover, Andrew Gordon's data in this volume corroborate my finding that consumer credit did not "take off" in Japan until the late 1980s. However, Japanese households now borrow more than consumers in the other industrialized countries and have more household debt than in these countries. This dramatic change presumably results from changes in consumer attitudes as well as from the rapid development of credit markets in recent years.

Are Japanese Household Portfolios Unusually Conservative?

As table 5.4 indicates, Japan ranks lowest among the G7 countries with respect to the share of equities in financial assets in three of the four years for which data are shown (1995, 2000, and 2002). In 1990, it ranked second from the bottom (ahead of Germany), but this was during the bubble period when equity prices were temporarily inflated. The share of equities

TABLE 5.4.
Share of equities in financial assets and share of mortgages in liabilities in the G7 countries, 1990–2002

Country	1990	1995	2000	2002
Canada				
Share of equities in financial assets	18.3 (4)	20.1 (3)	26.4 (5)	27.2 (3)
Share of mortgages in liabilities	63.7 (5)	66.5 (4)	61.8 (6)	61.0 (6)
France				
Share of equities in financial assets	46.0 (1)	34.1 (1)	43.3 (2)	33.3 (1)
Share of mortgages in liabilities	67.9 (4)	76.0 (1)	72.1 (3)	74.9 (2)
Germany				
Share of equities in financial assets	5.8 (7)	18.4 (5)	27.0 (4)	21.0 (5)
Share of long-term loans in liabilities	76.6 (1)	60.6 (6)	63.3 (5)	65.7 (5)
Italy				
Share of equities in financial assets	20.4 (2)	18.3 (6)	44.7 (1)	29.7 (2)
Share of medium- and long-term loans in liabilities	47.1 (6)	60.8 (5)	72.8 (1)	75.6 (1)
Japan				
Share of equities in financial assets	14.4 (6)	10.5 (7)	8.7 (7)	8.4 (7)
Share of mortgages in liabilities	38.7 (7)	42.7 (7)	43.9 (7)	45.4 (7)
United Kingdom				
Share of equities in financial assets	18.6 (3)	19.4 (4)	22.5 (6)	14.9 (6)
Share of mortgages in liabilities	70.2 (2)	73.3 (2)	72.2 (2)	72.0 (3)
United States				
Share of equities in financial assets	15.1 (5)	24.5 (2)	31.1 (3)	23.7 (4)
Share of mortgages in liabilities	69.6 (3)	67.7 (3)	67.0 (4)	70.1 (4)

Notes: The figures in parentheses indicate the rank of each country.
Source: See Table 5.3.

in financial assets has ranged from 8 to 14 percent in Japan, as compared to 33 to 46 percent in France, 18 to 45 percent in Italy, 15 to 31 percent in the United States, 18 to 27 percent in Canada, 15 to 23 percent in the United Kingdom, and 6 to 27 percent in Germany.

These data confirm that Japanese households are the most conservative in the G7, investing only a small share of their assets in equities and a correspondingly large share in bank and postal deposits. This conservative portfolio can be explained in large part by such factors as: (1) the high brokerage fees charged by securities companies, (2) the large minimum lot sizes when buying and selling equities, (3) consumer mistrust of securities companies arising from widely publicized scandals involving securities companies, (4) tax breaks for saving, which applied mostly to bank and postal deposits, (5) the lack of consumer financial education, and (6) a higher degree of risk aversion in Japan. The collapse of equity prices in the early 1990s and their continued stagnation since then also partially explain the low share of equities in Japan. Indeed, the decline in the share of equities in financial assets from 14.4 percent in 1990 to 8.4 percent in 2002 is largely attributable to the collapse and continued stagnation of equity prices. However, the collapse of the Tokyo stock market cannot be the only explanation of the low share of equities because Japan had the second-lowest share among the G7 countries in 1990 even before the collapse of equity prices.

To summarize, the Japanese used to be big savers, but they no longer are. They used to rely relatively little on borrowing, but they now borrow at high levels. The Japanese do, however, continue to possess a high level of assets and to hold conservative portfolios.

The Consumption Behavior of the Japanese

To what extent has consumption behavior in Japan changed over time, and how does it compare to that in the other industrialized countries? Let us now examine data on both consumption levels and the composition of consumption.[11]

Are the Japanese Big Spenders?

How do Japanese consumption levels compare to those in the other G7 countries? Since the figures for each country are expressed in the currency of that country, it is necessary to convert the figures for each country into a common currency (say, U.S. dollars) when making inter-country comparisons. If this is done using market exchange rates, the figures will be biased to the extent that price levels vary from country to country. Indeed, because of Japan's high price levels, market exchange rates would lead us to the erroneous conclusion that the Japanese consume at levels far above the average of both the G7 and OECD countries.[12] It is therefore prefer-

[11] For data over a longer time period and on more countries, see Horioka, "Consuming and Saving," and Charles Yuji Horioka, "Japan's Consumption and Saving in International Perspective," *Economic Development and Cultural Change* 42, no. 2 (January 1994): 293–316.

[12] If market exchange rates are used to convert the figures for each country to U.S. dollars, consumption levels in Japan in 2003 were 77.3 percent of U.S. levels (as opposed to 63.5 percent when purchasing power parities are used to make the conversion), 103.2 percent of

able to convert the figures for each country to a common currency using purchasing power parities, which take account of differences in price levels among countries.

Table 5.5 presents data on per capita household final consumption expenditure in Japan and the other G7 countries during the 1970–2003 period in U.S. dollars, with the conversion to U.S. dollars being done using purchasing power parities. Japanese consumption levels showed considerable improvement during much of this period but continued to lag far behind the free-spending Americans and also behind the other G7 and OECD member countries. Consumption levels in Japan improved sharply from 54.0 percent of U.S. levels in 1970 to 60.8 percent in 1985, from 73.8 percent of the G7 average in 1970 to 80.8 percent in 1985, and from 78.7 percent of the OECD average in 1970 to 89.0 percent in 1985. However, it is noteworthy that Japanese consumption levels have not improved relatively since then, remaining at 61 to 63 percent of U.S. levels, 81 to 84 percent of the G7 average, and 89 to 92 percent of the OECD average. With respect to Japan's rank among the G7 countries, Japan ranked last in all years and has not improved its relative position at all.

By contrast, the United States stands out as a colossus of consumption throughout this period (see Cohen, chap. 2). Although the G7 countries all expanded their consumption, no other G7 country managed to consume at more than 86 percent of U.S levels during the 1970–2003 period. To be sure, Japanese consumption levels have remained at the bottom of the G7 countries, but notwithstanding Japan's reputation for uniqueness, it is the United States that jumps off the charts when it comes to consumption.

Are Japanese Consumption Patterns Unique?

Having established that Japan, like the other G7 countries, consumes at levels far below that of the United States, let us compare the composition of consumption in Japan to the other G7 countries. The most important indicator of consumption patterns is the so-called Engel coefficient (defined as the budget share of food and non-alcoholic beverages). Needless to say, a lower Engel coefficient indicates a higher standard of living. As the (current-price) data I analyze elsewhere show,[13] Japan's Engel coefficient was very high (70.2 percent) just after World War II, but it has shown a phenomenal decline (improvement) during the postwar period, falling to 50.1 percent in 1955, 35.2 percent in 1965, 28.4 percent in 1975, and 22.5 percent in 1985.

---

the G7 average (as opposed to 83.4 percent), and 115.9 percent of the OECD average (as opposed to 92.0 percent).

[13] Horioka, "Consuming and Saving," Tables 10–2 and 10–4.

TABLE 5.5
Consumption levels in the G7 countries, 1970–2003

Country	1970		1985		2000		2003	
Canada	2,895	83.55 (2)	10,342	82.82 (2)	18,882	72.77 (3)	21,186	72.77 (3)
France	2,542	73.36 (3)	9,193	73.62 (3)	18,218	70.22 (5)	21,175	72.73 (4)
Germany	2,293	66.18 (5)	8,834	70.75 (5)	18,628	71.80 (4)	20,170	69.28 (5)
Italy	2,216	63.95 (6)	8,752	70.09 (4)	18,182	70.08 (6)	19,830	68.11 (6)
Japan	1,870	53.97 (7)	7,596	60.83 (7)	16,371	63.10 (7)	18,473	63.45 (7)
United Kingdom	2,461	71.02 (4)	8,626	69.08 (6)	20,606	79.42 (2)	25,029	85.97 (2)
United States	3,465	100.00 (1)	12,487	100.00 (1)	25,946	100.00 (1)	29,115	100.00 (1)
G7	2,535		9,404		19,548		22,140	
OECD mean	2,376		8,536		17,781		20,087	

Notes: The left-hand figures show per capita household final consumption expenditure at current prices and current purchasing power parities (U.S. dollars), the right-hand figures show the ratio of the left-hand figure to the figure for the United States, and the figures in parentheses show the rank of each country. The OECD means exclude the Czech Republic, Hungary, Poland, and the Slovak Republic.

Source: Organization for Economic Cooperation and Development, *National Accounts of OECD Countries,* vol., 1 1990–2003; *Main Aggregates* (Paris: OECD, 2005), 346–47.

Table 5.6 shows a twelve-way breakdown of the final consumption expenditure of households by purpose for the G7 countries for 1990 and 2002. As this table indicates, Japan's Engel coefficient declined further to 16.8 percent in 1990 and to 14.5 percent in 2002. Thus, Japan's Engel coefficient is now only about a quarter of what it was a half century ago.

Despite this marked improvement, Japan's Engel coefficient was still the second highest among the G7 countries in both 1990 and 2002. In 1990, it was 16.8 percent, behind first-place Italy (19.4 percent) but well above the G7 average of 14.2 percent and the last-place United States (8.9 percent). In 2002, Japan's Engel coefficient was 14.5 percent, behind first-place Italy (14.7 percent) but well above the G7 average of 11.7 percent and the last-place United States (7.0 percent). Moreover, although Japan's Engel coefficient improved (declined) somewhat between 1990 and 2002 in absolute terms, it deteriorated in relative terms during this time period: the ratio of Japan's Engel coefficient to the G7 average increased slightly from 1.18 to 1.24, and its ratio to the U.S. figure increased slightly from 1.88 to 2.08 and is now more than twice the U.S. figure.

In terms of other categories of consumption, the most unusual features of consumption patterns in Japan are the relatively low shares of "transport" and "furnishings, household equipment and routine maintenance of the house" in both 1990 and 2002, the relatively high share of "recreation and culture" in 1990, and the relatively high share of "housing, water, electricity, gas and other fuels" in 2002 (see table 5.6).

At first glance, Japan's consumption patterns look more "backward" than those of most other G7 countries inasmuch as the budget shares of necessities such as food and housing are relatively high and the budget shares of luxuries such as transport and furnishings/household equipment/etc. are relatively low (although the share of recreation/culture, a luxury, is relatively high). However, Japan's consumption patterns are heavily influenced by factors other than income levels. For example, Japan's high Engel coefficient is due in large part to the much higher food prices in Japan, which in turn may be explained by the scarcity of arable land, government regulation of food prices, and restrictions on food imports. Similarly, the high budget share of housing in Japan results in large part from high rents, which in turn are due in large part to the scarcity of land. The low budget share of transport is due in large part to the low automobile ownership rate, which in turn is related to high gasoline prices, high expressway tolls, high parking fees, and the widespread availability of public transportation.

As in the case of consumption levels, it is the United States that stands out with respect to consumption patterns, with the share of "food and nonalcoholic beverages" being by far the lowest of any G7 country and the share of "health" and "miscellaneous goods and services" being by far the highest of any G7 country. The high share of spending on "health" is re-

TABLE 5.6.
Household final consumption expenditure by purpose for the G7 countries, 1990 and 2002

Purpose of consumption	Canada	France	Germany	Italy	Japan	UK	US	G7
1990								
Food and nonalcoholic beverages	11.53	16.14	13.98	19.39	16.77	12.54	8.92	14.18
Alcoholic beverages, tobacco, and narcotics	4.82	3.01	4.27	2.66	3.36	4.37	2.34	3.55
Clothing and footwear	6.50	6.59	7.87	10.33	7.68	6.30	5.92	7.31
Housing, water, electricity, gas, and other fuels	24.23	21.43	20.08	16.60	20.60	16.38	18.44	19.68
Furnishings, household equipment, and routine maintenance of the house	7.34	6.93	8.08	10.08	5.36	5.91	5.40	7.02
Health	3.58	3.33	3.13	2.21	3.19	1.31	15.16	4.56
Transport	14.78	15.48	15.51	12.21	11.24	15.38	11.51	13.73
Communications	1.78	1.78	1.78	1.76	1.26	1.93	1.75	1.72
Recreation and culture	9.56	8.64	9.93	7.70	11.75	10.92	8.02	9.50
Education	0.48	0.62	0.61	1.02	2.26	0.96	2.18	1.16
Restaurants and hotels	7.75	7.41	5.76	8.37	6.21	12.04	6.66	7.74
Miscellaneous goods and services	7.65	8.63	8.99	7.65	10.31	11.95	13.68	9.84

2002								
Food and nonalcoholic beverages	9.91	14.53	12.14	14.67	14.54	9.30	6.99	11.73
Alcoholic beverages, tobacco, and narcotics	3.97	3.40	4.01	2.41	3.19	4.02	2.23	3.32
Clothing and footwear	5.24	4.64	6.11	9.23	4.97	5.76	4.72	5.81
Housing, water, electricity, gas, and other fuels	23.40	23.51	24.87	19.86	26.42	18.05	17.81	21.99
Furnishings, household equipment, and routine maintenance of the house	6.67	6.07	6.76	8.96	4.18	6.60	4.87	6.30
Health	4.55	3.62	4.16	2.97	3.71	1.59	18.15	5.54
Transport	15.01	15.02	14.39	11.95	10.66	14.96	11.40	13.34
Communications	2.28	2.35	2.85	3.05	2.53	2.27	1.91	2.46
Recreation and culture	10.87	9.05	9.34	7.48	9.65	12.12	9.09	9.66
Education	1.26	0.62	0.71	0.93	2.27	1.29	2.54	1.37
Restaurants and hotels	7.55	7.67	4.69	9.78	7.49	11.68	5.99	7.84
Miscellaneous goods and services	9.28	9.54	9.97	8.70	10.38	12.36	14.30	10.65

Notes: The figures show consumption for each purpose as a share of the final consumption expenditure of households in the economic territory, both at current prices. The figures for Germany are for 1991.

Source: For 1990 data, Organization for Economic Cooperation and Development, *National Accounts of OECD Countries,* vol. 2, 1990–2002; *Detailed Tables* (Paris: OECD, 2003); for 2002 data, vol. 2, 1991–2003: *Detailed Tables* (Paris: OECD, 2004).

lated to high medical costs and the lack of universal health insurance coverage in the United States, but U.S. consumption patterns primarily reflect the much greater affluence of American consumers.

To summarize, Japan showed phenomenal improvement in consumption levels and consumption patterns during the postwar period. As a result, its consumption levels and consumption patterns are now roughly comparable to those of the other G7 countries but are still well behind those of the United States.

Conclusions

This chapter has analyzed the saving and consumption behavior of the Japanese, examining trends over time as well as comparisons with the other industrialized countries (mostly the G7 countries). Is the conventional wisdom about Japanese saving and consumption behavior correct? Yes and no, depending on which behavior and which period one is discussing. The Japanese *were* big savers during parts of the prewar, wartime, and early postwar periods and throughout the 1955–95 period, yet at other times they were not and they no longer save at high levels, and household saving rates can be expected to decline even further in the future. The Japanese *did* borrow relatively little at one time, but not any longer. The Japanese *are* still wealthy despite the decline in equity and land prices, and the Japanese *do* continue to hold conservative portfolios. Finally, although the Japanese steadily increased their consumption levels during the postwar period, they still do *not* consume quite as much as most other G7 countries and far less than Americans, and their consumption patterns lag behind those of most other G7 countries and far behind those in the United States. However, many of the differences in saving and consumption behavior that persist between Japan and the other industrialized countries can be largely explained by economic, institutional, and demographic factors.

Are the Japanese unique? No. Japanese saving and consumption behavior is admittedly quite different from that of the English-speaking countries (Canada, the United Kingdom, and the United States), which have low household saving rates, high financial assets, low real assets, high consumption levels, and low Engel coefficients. However, Japanese saving and consumption behavior is surprisingly similar to that of the continental European countries—France, Germany, and especially Italy, all of which exhibit high household saving rates, high real assets, low consumption levels, and high Engel coefficients. At the same time, Japan generally differs from the continental European countries in its greater financial assets and liabilities.

An analysis of the striking differences in saving and consumption behavior between continental Europe and Japan on the one hand and the

English-speaking countries on the other awaits another paper. However, one explanation may be that high land/housing prices—combined with capital market imperfections and a strong desire for homeownership—in both continental Europe and Japan led to the high household saving rates and high real assets. If this explanation is correct, it suggests that cross-national differences in saving and consumption behavior can be explained by economic factors without resorting to sweeping cultural explanations. In any event, all too often, scholars compare Japan only to the United States, but such narrow comparisons create the false impression that Japan is unique. We should bear in mind that Japan and continental Europe are quite similar in many ways, and we would do well to avoid exaggerating the distinctiveness of Japan. When it comes to saving and consumption, it is *American* exceptionalism (together with that of Canada and the United Kingdom) that demands further study.

Appendix

TABLE 5.A1.
Trends in Japan's household saving rate, 1955–2003

Calendar Year	SNA68	SNA93
1955	11.9	
1956	12.9	
1957	12.6	
1958	12.3	
1959	13.7	
1960	14.5	
1961	15.9	
1962	15.6	
1963	14.9	
1964	15.4	
1965	15.8	
1966	15.0	
1967	14.1	
1968	16.9	
1969	17.1	
1970	17.7	
1971	17.8	
1972	18.2	
1973	20.4	
1974	23.2	
1975	22.8	
1976	23.2	
1977	21.8	
1978	20.8	
1979	18.2	
1980	17.9	15.4
1981	18.4	16.2
1982	16.7	14.9

TABLE 5.A1—cont.

Calendar Year	SNA68	SNA93
1983	16.1	14.3
1984	15.8	14.3
1985	15.6	13.7
1986	15.6	13.0
1987	13.8	11.5
1988	13.0	11.9
1989	12.9	12.0
1990	12.1	12.3
1991	13.2	13.3
1992	13.1	12.5
1993	13.4	12.0
1994	13.3	11.1
1995	13.7	10.4
1996	13.4	8.5
1997	12.6	8.6
1998	13.4	9.6
1999		9.2
2000		8.2
2001		5.7
2002		6.1
2003		6.3

Note: See Figure 5.1 for notes and data sources.

6

FROM SINGER TO SHINPAN

Consumer Credit in Modern Japan

ANDREW GORDON

Japan has been famous as a nation of savers since the 1950s. But with much less fanfare, Japan has also become a nation of borrowers and spenders. Since the late 1980s, Japanese consumers have been no less in debt than their American counterparts. In 1989, outstanding per capita consumer debt in Japan surpassed American totals when measured as a percentage of net disposable income. It remained greater for most of the 1990s (see figure 6.1). The statistics underestimate debt in both societies, but the evidence is suggestive and surprising. In this chapter, I seek to make sense of it by tracing the rise of consumer credit across the twentieth century, with emphasis on the installment plans used to finance the purchase of so many household consumer durables.

The *economic practice* of consumer credit in Japan from roughly 1900 through the 1950s primarily followed the catch-up trajectory of the late developer. It began to spread widely a few decades after comparable practices took root in the United States and has only in recent years come to rival the American practice quantitatively. By contrast, the *cultural construction* of consumer credit must be understood as a story of virtually simultaneous development in dialogue with American culture.[1] From the earliest days of widespread installment selling and buying, the discourse of consumer credit in Japan exemplifies this volume's theme of the ambivalent stance toward consumerism found in modern culture and politics around the world. It has been sophisticated in its appreciation of the com-

[1] See H. D. Harootunian, *Overcome By Modernity* (Princeton: Princeton University Press, 2000), xvi.

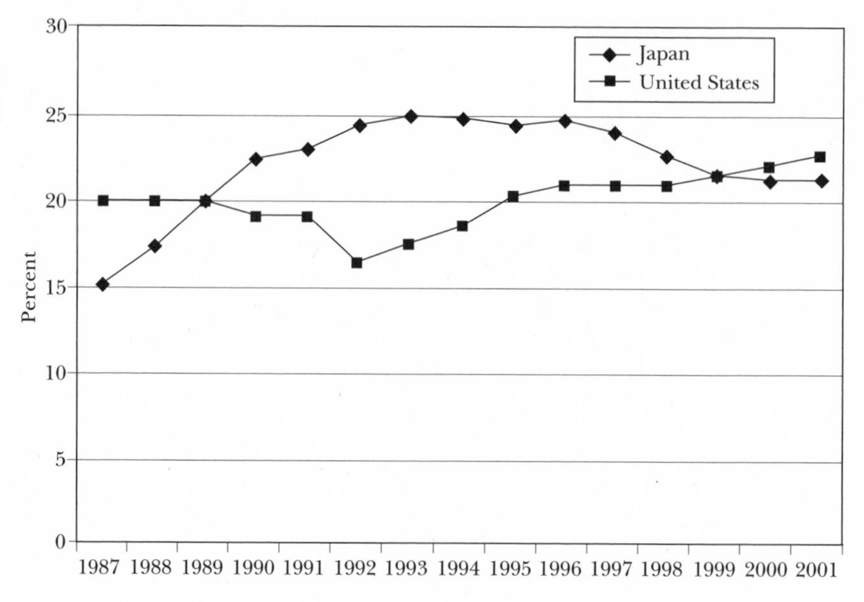

Source: Annual volumes of Nihon kurejitto sangyō kyōkai, Nihon no shōhisha shinyō tōkei, 1988–2002.

Figure 6.1. Consumer credit balance as a proportion of disposable income, Japan and United States, 1987–2001

plex balance of risk and gain, of excess and discipline, that has marked consumer borrowing worldwide in the past century.

The Early Days of Consumer Credit: 1890s–1920s

Modern consumer credit is a practice based on the assumption that the borrower is a wage earner, required and able to make regular installment payments. Such credit emerged in Japan in the late nineteenth century. During the 1880s and 1890s in the lacquer industry, indigenous sellers, who for decades had peddled their ware on credit to rural households, shifted from seasonal or open-book credit to regular installment plans.[2] These businesses evolved into "installment department stores" selling additional household goods such as furniture, bedding, *tatami,* and clothing.[3] Like the "borax stores" that spread in the United States starting in the

[2] See *Geppu kinkyū* [Installment studies] 1, no. 1 (April 15, 1957): 3; 1, no. 3 (June 15, 1957): 3.

[3] Tōkyō shōkōkaigishō, *Geppu hanbai seido* [Installment selling system] (Tokyo: Tōkyō shōkōkaigishō, 1929), 212–13.

1880s, these sellers sold shoddy products to a relatively impoverished customer base.[4]

Around 1900, foreign corporations, including National Cash Register and the Encyclopedia Britannica, provided a second source of modern installment credit. Of these, the Singer Sewing Machine Company was most important. It took the lead in spreading the practice of installment buying to a new clientele: middle- to upper-class urban families, in particular women. Unlike the native installment sellers, Singer used detailed written contracts; the period for repayment was longer, the cost of goods was high, and the credit premium was modest. In 1924, a Singer machine selling for 112 yen in cash cost a total of 140 yen on a two-year installment plan, at roughly a 12 percent annual interest rate. Buying "on time" was essential for most Singer customers because such a machine represented about two months' wages for an ordinary "salaryman" (this ratio held roughly constant from 1900 through the 1950s). The company first offered machines on an installment plan in Japan in 1907. By 1918 Singer was importing 50,000 machines per year, a level it maintained with some fluctuation throughout the 1920s. About 80 percent of its machines were sold on the installment plan.[5]

As it was around the world, installment selling was central to Singer's drive to create a new household market in Japan. In its advertising, the ease of the "modern" practice of installment purchase was a major selling point, but the company also framed its appeal in terms of progress for the individual and the nation. An early Singer leaflet from 1908 proclaimed, "Japan is the country of progress."[6] A leaflet from about 1912 echoed the theme of installment credit as progressive and modern:

> The past quarter century has seen all sorts of impressive progress in Japan. . . . [In every country] the sewing machine has completely revolutionized the household economy. . . . Singer Sewing Machine Company's monthly installment method makes it possible for any sort of family to purchase this great economic good. The Singer Model 28 Hand Turned Machine can be purchased for the incredibly cheap price of 3 yen per month, for 16 months, in other words 10 sen a day. In this way you can make a useful lifelong investment.[7]

[4] Lendol Calder, *Financing the American Dream* (Princeton: Princeton University Press: 1999), 56–57.

[5] Janome mishin shashi hensan iinkai, *Janome mishin sōgyō 50 nen shi* [Fifty-year history of Janome Mishin] (Tokyo: Janome kabushiki kaisha, 1971) and Kuwahara Tetsuya, "Shoki takokuseki kigyō no tainichi toshi to minzoku kigyō" [Early multinational corporations' investment in Japan and domestic corporations], *Kokumin keizai zasshi* 185, no. 5 (February 2002): 50.

[6] Singer sales leaflet, Autumn 1908, Edo-Tokyo Museum.

[7] Singer sales leaflet, ca. 1912, Edo-Tokyo Museum.

It is no surprise that Singer advertising presented installment buying in unambiguously positive terms, linked to the virtues of national pride and progress, as well as individual economy and investment. Of greater interest is that women's magazines, which often framed articles in didactic and moralistic terms, generally echoed this positive view. In January 1920, one female columnist proclaimed that "All Daily Clothes for Children Should be Western": "First, one must increase the efficiency of the housewife or servant by boldly switching over to Western clothes for children. To this end, one must furnish the home with a sewing machine. As this is in recent years possible for a small monthly installment payment, it is not that difficult for an ordinary family."[8]

Articles such as this were typical. They framed buying on time in positive terms as an element in a modern life of discipline, economy, and investment. To such themes of economy and investment, Singer advertising brochures of the 1920s added an appeal to liberation and pleasure: a sewing machine bought on time offered access to a new world of convenience and the freedom enabled by western dress.[9]

At the same time, from the early days of installment selling, one finds concern or anxiety about the practice, linked in some cases to a scornful middle-class appraisal of the unreliable lower classes. The Tokyo Chamber of Commerce conducted the first systematic survey of installment selling in 1929. It lamented abuses such as poor quality goods sold "on time" at high prices. Combined with a World War I scandal over the fraudulent sale of securities by monthly payments, such practices gave installment selling a bad name. Buyers, the report noted, came to see purchasing on time as shameful. Major department stores concluded that installment sales were beneath their dignity.[10]

Fragments from the history of slang reveal a negative, class-based view of the practice. A pun in the early 1900s dubbed the high-interest loans of the installment department stores "crushed ice," a plebian refreshment that was also a homonym for "usury" (both were pronounced *kōri gashi*). By the 1920s a cleverer play on words labeled installment selling as "*ramune.*" *Ramune* (the word derived from "lemonade") was a popular carbonated soft drink, first introduced in the 1870s, which naturally caused those who imbibed it to *geppu* (burp), a homonym for the most common term for "installment sales" (Takao Nishimura also mentions this in chap. 11). The derisive pun suggests that installment credit by the mid-1920s was viewed as a low-class practice, even as sewing machine sales soared among the middle class. In such slang one detects anxiety that practices

[8] Imura Nobuko, "Kodomo no nichijō fuku wo zenbu yōfuku ni" [Make all children's daily dress Western dress], *Fujokai* 21, no. 1 (January 1920): 213–15.

[9] Singer sales leaflet, ca. 1922, Edo-Tokyo Museum.

[10] Tōkyō shōkōkaigishō, *Geppu hanbai seido,* 227.

of lower-class society were infecting the world of respectable ladies and gentlemen.[11]

The Rise of the Installment Plan Nation: 1920s–1950s

The world of consumer credit changed in two related ways in the 1920s. The volume and range of goods sold on time began to increase sharply, a trend that continued well into the 1930s. And in the late 1920s the first systematic analyses of the phenomenon appeared, conducted by public and private organizations and made available to a broader public as well as to policymakers and the business community. After a wartime interruption, the practice resumed its vigorous spread in the late 1940s even before economic recovery gained momentum, and to some extent it fueled the upswing.

The pioneering survey of consumer credit in the nation's capital undertaken by the Tokyo Chamber of Commerce in 1929 was based on a substantial sample of retailers; it is noteworthy as well for its even longer discussions of consumer credit in the United States and Britain. It drew on state-of-the-art analyses, such as E. R. A. Seligman's important opus, *The Economics of Installment Selling* (1927), for the account of the American scene.[12]

The report notes that installment selling had been limited to a small number of products until the mid-1920s, when it expanded dramatically.[13] The "relatively organized present day practice which can be called installment sales" started with Singer. At about the same time, improvised practices of traditional credit emerged for household goods such as furniture, ceramic or lacquer products, and clothing (especially men's western suits). Another new entrant was Nihon Gakki (Yamaha), selling pianos and organs starting in 1924. In addition to a scattering of other household appliances, suburban homes were sold, with mortgages lasting several years, along the newly opened commuter railway lines as harbingers of the "modern, cultural" life. Automobile sales in moderate numbers began in the early 1920s; by the end of the decade the annual market stood at about 30,000 car sales. By the mid-1930s, a third of all cars were bought on installment plans, and autos constituted the largest installment market in total sales value. But most were purchased by taxi drivers, not ordinary consumers.[14] Overall, retailers noted two motives for the expansion of the

[11] Fukushima Hachirō, "Geppu, wappu, kurejitto" [Installment credit], *Gekkan kurejitto*, no. 200 (1973): 20.

[12] On Seligman, see Calder, *Financing the American Dream*, 237–48.

[13] Tōkyō shōkōkaigishō, *Geppu hanbai seido*, 227.

[14] Tōkyō shōkōkaigishō, *Geppu hanbai seido*, 211–18; Tōkyō shiyakusho, kōgyōkyoku, shōgyōka, *Wappu hanbai ni kansuru chōsa* [Survey on installment selling] (Tokyo: Tōkyō shiyakusho, 1935), 63–64.

installment plan: to break out of the prolonged recession and to compete with the established department stores, which were reluctant to offer installment credit.[15]

The Chamber of Commerce thus explicitly divided consumer credit into two streams from about 1900 through the 1920s: the imported American practice, starting with Singer, and a modernized form of traditional credit practices centered on clothing, furniture, and dining ware. Of the two, the "imported" practice drew more attention. Based on a survey of 254 installment sellers in Osaka and Tokyo, an academic article in 1933 claimed that the salaried urban life "was perfected" in the mid-1920s, a "cultured life" centered on "so-called 'American goods'" such as sewing machines and pianos. The author presented a supply-driven rationale for the sudden spread of payment plans: installment sellers needed to find new customers because their output had increased due to greater manufacturing efficiency.[16]

The next major survey, conducted by the city of Tokyo in 1934, quantified the relative proportion of retail installment and cash sales for the first time, estimating that 10,000 of 130,000 retailers in greater Tokyo offered their goods on time. Overall, the survey estimated that 8 percent of all Tokyo retail sales were made on installment. Both municipal authorities and the press considered this to be a remarkably high number for a relatively new practice.[17]

Consumer credit took on a new class and nationalistic dimension in the 1930s with the advent of what was called a "Japanese-style" and "populist" practice in installment sales, especially for sewing machines. By the late 1920s a number of entrepreneurs, machinists, and disgruntled Singer salesmen had founded several domestic sewing machine makers. The most successful was the Pines Company. Like the patriotic leaders of other new sewing machine makers, the first president of Pines, Ose Yosaku, believed Singer had alienated potential buyers and developed a reputation as arrogant because of stringent credit requirements and a tendency to avoid lower-income buyers. Ose set his sights on what he called the "plebian [*shomin*] class" with a modified installment plan that fit "the Japanese situation."

As Ose told the tale, he had been inspired by the "smiling savings plan" offered by the Japan Real Estate Savings Bank, a popular loan plan for small businesses since 1916; a saver made installment deposits to his savings account up to an agreed target. At this point he qualified for a loan, to be repaid in monthly installments. This was a successful way to offer par-

[15] Tōkyō shōkōkaigishō, *Geppu hanbai seido,* 221–22.

[16] Hirai Yasutaro, "Honpō ni okeru bunkatsu barai seido no genjō ni oite" [Installment sales system in Japan today], *Kokumin keizai zasshi* 43, no 2 (1933): 69–73, 81.

[17] Tōkyō shiyakusho, *Wappu hanbai ni kansuru chōsa,* 62.

tially secured loans to small borrowers, as the borrower had already demonstrated the discipline to save on a regular basis.[18] In similar fashion, Ose offered customers who could not afford a down payment the chance to "reserve" their machines by contributing 5 yen a month for six months *before* taking possession. By that time, Pines had its down payment in hand, and the customer had the choice of paying cash in full, converting the remaining obligation to a series of ordinary installment payments (including interest) or continuing the layaway without taking the machine home until it was fully paid off. In the latter case, the customer would be offered a discount against the cash price, in effect earning "interest" on the money deposited with Pines over the course of two years. Pines (later renamed Janome) touted the plan as especially suited to a family with young daughters. The parents could start paying at birth. When the youngster was ready to learn to sew, she would own her own machine.

Pines first offered this layaway-installment scheme, which it called "monthly reservation payments," in December 1930. The Ministry of Finance objected that Pines was violating banking laws by acting as a savings bank. But Ose reportedly overcame these objections with an appeal to national interest. He argued that it was more important to nurture a domestic sewing machine industry than to worry about such legal niceties. In the words of Shimada Taku, a key Janome salesman and later its president, the company was cultivating "the bottom of the social pyramid," the "ordinary masses" such as "the wife in a back-alley tenement who carries her baby half-asleep on her back to go shopping." This strategy slowly bore fruit. Janome, renamed Teikoku (Imperial) Mishin in 1935, began to compete with Singer with only modest success for several years. With a network of stores offering the layaway and installment plans, it sold 6,000 machines in 1937 and about 9,000 in 1938 (versus 40,000 and 13,000 respectively, for Singer). Only after Singer was shut out of the Japanese market by wartime currency controls did sales by Imperial Mishin and other domestic makers begin to rise significantly.[19]

This creative financing strategy offered the maker a cash-flow advantage; the prepayments essentially financed the subsequent installment credit. Prepaid orders allowed the company to calibrate production schedules to future demand. And a customer sufficiently disciplined to make regular prepayments—in essence a saver and not a spender—was likely to be able to continue to meet the installment obligations. Marketing rhetoric notwithstanding, this was not a unique Japanese practice. The Ford Motor Company in 1923 had offered a poorly received layaway program called the "Weekly Purchase Plan," which required customers to pre-

[18] *Janome mishin sōgyō 50 nen shi,* 194–200.

[19] *Janome mishin sōgyō 50 nen shi,* 277. For the Singer numbers, see Kuwahara, "Shoki takokuseki kigyō," 50.

pay the entire cost of the car. Chevrolet responded with a "6 percent purchase plan" that anticipated Janome's effort precisely. Purchasers prepaid installments into a trustee bank account. When the down payment was completed, the customer took the car and continued paying normal installments.[20] It is unclear whether Pines executives were aware of this precedent.

In the late 1930s, the Japanese economy shifted to a war footing. Under such propaganda slogans as "luxury is the enemy," the state mounted vigorous savings campaigns, even prohibited women's permanents, and forced textile manufacturers to produce airplane parts. In the face of these stringent policies, the consumer economy—credit included—contracted and then virtually vanished. Imperial Mishin was forced by state order to stop layaway sales in late 1940. The company discontinued installment sales in 1942.[21]

After the war, however, sewing machine producers quickly revived, promoting themselves as a quintessential peacetime industry. Output soared from 45,000 machines in 1946 to just under one million by 1950 (about half exported), making sewing machine production one of the most successful industries in the devastated postwar economy. Installment sales of these machines revived quickly as well, leading the way to the recovery and then the dramatic expansion of consumer credit in the overall economy. Industry publications mention installments prominently for the first time in late 1948; such credit was in great demand by individuals, schools, and home economics teachers on behalf of schools. Even a group of policemen reportedly purchased machines on time (presumably for their wives), pledging mutual responsibility for each other's installment contracts. In other cases as well, groups of buyers collectively guaranteed each other's purchases in a creative strategy to establish credit with reluctant sellers or lenders.[22] Offering the potential for women, war widows especially, to earn money as dressmakers, the sewing machine was both productive investment and a consumer good.

Scarcely able to believe how good business had become, sewing machine makers initially appeared uneasy over aggressive credit offers. Competitors criticized Riccar Corporation when it first offered what it touted as "easy, American style" terms—installment sales with no money down and no prepayments. Riccar developed a reputation as a lone wolf and refused to join the industrial association.[23] Yet by 1950, sewing machine producers, together with makers of autos, bicycles, motorbikes, refrigerators, washing machines, and farm machines, were speaking of installment sales

[20] Calder, *Financing the American Dream,* 195–99.

[21] *Janome mishin sōgyō 50 nen shi,* 286–302.

[22] *Nihon mishin taimusu* (*NMT*) [Japan sewing machine times], no. 48 (November 11, 1948): 2.

[23] *NMT,* no. 87 (December 11, 1949): 2

as the key to "healthy" and "rational" growth; they called on the Ministry of International Trade and Industry (MITI), without success, for preferential tax treatment and a state-funded line of credit for sellers of approved installment goods.[24]

Janome resumed layaway and installment selling in 1953 to good effect: sales overshot projections by 10 percent.[25] Juki entered into a partnership in 1953 with Tokyo Mutual Bank as its finance company. To protect itself against default, the bank kept the customer's down payment in escrow until one-fourth of the installment payments were made, at which point it turned the down payment over to Juki.

Although sewing machines led the way in the revival of installment sales to ordinary consumers, by the end of the 1950s purchasing "on time" had become the method of choice for consumers seeking a wide range of "cultural" goods that defined the bright new consumer life of postwar and peacetime.[26] Their collective shopping binge transformed sewing machines and radios—then washing machines, televisions, refrigerators, vacuum cleaners, cameras, motorbikes, and (later) automobiles—from luxuries to the necessities of the burgeoning middle-class masses. One 1959 survey enumerated the proportion of goods bought on monthly payments: bicycles, 80 percent; televisions, 75 percent; automobiles, 70 percent; motorbikes, 68 percent; refrigerators, 66 percent; sewing machines, 60 percent; washing machines, 59 percent. According to a 1960–61 MITI survey of 6,200 retail sellers offering credit for a broad spectrum of goods including clothing, from half to two-thirds of all sales at these stores were made on installment.[27]

In these same years, an important new form of consumer credit, and a harbinger of the credit card, emerged as well: "ticket" sales. The ticket industry offered a form of credit halfway between a small loan to be used at the consumer's discretion and an installment loan tied to the purchase of a particular good. As with a credit card company, the ticket company contracted on one hand with its member retail stores and on the other hand with consumers. The latter were given books of yen-denominated tickets to be used in lieu of cash to purchase goods at member stores. Tickets denominated at 500 and 1,000 yen were typically sold in books of 10,000 or 20,000 yen. The repayment obligation, divided into installments ranging from three to twelve months, commenced the moment a ticket was used to make a purchase. Ticket companies charged interest as part of the monthly installments at annualized rates of 1 to 9 percent depending on

[24] *NMT,* no. 112 (August 21, 1950): 1.

[25] *Janome mishin sōgyō 50 nen shi,* 392.

[26] *NMT,* no. 249 (August 21, 1953): 7.

[27] Nihon mishin sangyō kyōkai, *Nihon mishin sangyō shi* [History of Japanese sewing machine industry] (1961), 9; Tsūshō sangyōshō, *Wappu hanbai jittai chōsa [Survey on the state of installment sales]* (Tokyo: Tsūshō sangyōshō, 1962), 9.

the number of payments. They charged member stores from 5 to 10 percent of the value of purchased goods.[28]

Retailers were divided into two competing sectors. Clustered in numerous shopping districts in all major cities, the small neighborhood stores constituted one sector. Most ticket companies were likewise small-scale, serving a limited number of local retail centers. Opposed to these small retailers were their archrivals, the department stores. The willingness of the latter to join hands with a handful of the largest ticket companies was a new postwar departure. With the exception of the slightly déclassé "installment department stores," the mainline emporiums such as Mitsukoshi had made cash-only selling a point of pride since the turn of the century.

These two segments of the retail industry jumped on the credit bandwagon in 1949 and 1950. Each presented its tactic as a defensive response to the other.[29] But the company that sparked the full-scale takeoff and the political contention in this industry was Nihon Shinpan (Japan Credit Sales), to this day the largest such firm. It was founded in July 1951 in partnership with the Tokyo outlets of four venerable department stores: Takashimaya, Matsuya, Shirokiya, and Keihin. The great majority of ticket associations linked to small retailers were founded in the following two years.

The practice spread at a terrific pace. Three months after Nihon Shinpan began operations, the *Nihon mishin taimusu* (Japan Sewing Machine Times) reported that local merchants had started offering ticket sales in reaction to department stores doing likewise. The paper added a cautionary note that customers might avail themselves of such credit to buy useless goods (rather than sewing machines, presumably).[30] The *Asahi shinbun* in 1952 headlined the contest of "Department Stores and Retailers Competing over Installments." It noted a surge of ticket groups serving small retailers and reported as well Nihon Shinpan's record monthly sales volume of 37 million yen, with 26,000 customer-members.[31]

The most creative aspect of the ticket industry was the practice of contracting *collectively* with credit customers. Not until the late 1950s did any ticket company offer its product directly to individuals. Instead, a ticket company would reach an agreement with a government office or a private firm to offer tickets to its employees, or it would arrange with a neighborhood association to offer tickets to its members. A work group agent, usually a manager in a company's welfare or general affairs section, would issue the ticket books to employees and handle the subsequent payment collections via payroll deduction. Nihon Shinpan, for example, collected

[28] Takagi Kunio, "Chiketto hanbai no keitai" [Forms of ticket selling], *Jurisuto,* no. 382 (October 15, 1967): 68–69.

[29] See *Asahi shinbun,* April 10, 1950, p. 2.

[30] *NMT,* no. 54 (October 21, 1951), part 2 of series on installment selling.

[31] *Asahi shinbun,* March 18, 1952, p. 2.

the used tickets from the department stores on the fifteenth of each month. Shinpan staff stayed up all night to sort the tickets, write up invoices for each individual buyer, and deliver tickets and invoices to the workplace or neighborhood agents the next day. At the company, tickets and invoices were stuffed into pay envelopes, deductions were taken on payday, and the proceeds were remitted to Nihon Shinpan. In most cases in the 1950s, the workplace agents did not charge the ticket company for this considerable effort, although Nihon Shinpan would express appreciation in the form of theater tickets or other gifts.[32]

This was a win-win situation for both the credit companies and the customers. At a time when a rigorous credit-check industry scarcely existed, major *shinpan* companies were able to use employers to guarantee their loans and handle their paperwork. In the 1960s, Nihon Shinpan reported a loss ratio of just 0.1 percent of total credit volume.[33] Customers received relatively low-cost credit, usually less than a 10 percent annual rate, for use in purchasing a wide range of goods in local retail shops or department stores. This form of credit grew steadily through the 1950s, reaching a total of 6.6 billion yen ($18 million) in Tokyo in 1959. The six major finance companies, which dealt mainly with department stores, grew at a particularly dramatic rate, up 93 percent in sales volume over the previous year.[34] As the 1960s began, well over half the consumer durables transforming daily life and driving economic growth were bought "on time." The "ticket" companies offered a portion of this credit, and they appeared to be evolving toward the credit card industry as we know it today. The Japanese people in the early years of the high-growth era had become an "installment plan nation."[35]

The Cultural Construction of Consumer Credit

Consumer credit, like the consumer economy as a whole, took off in Japan as part of a catch-up project of economic development. Observers commonly noted that the new "cultural life" of the 1920s was a limited phenomenon in comparison to the United States or Western Europe. But even in these early days, and certainly in the postwar era, observers in Japan were not playing "catch-up" in their cultural framing of modern consumer

[32] Nihon shinpan, *Za bunka: Nihon shinpan no hanseiki* [Culture: Fifty-year history of Nihon Shinpan] (Tokyo: Nihon shinpan kabushiki gaisha, 2001), 1; Takagi, "Chiketto hanbai no keitai," 68–69.

[33] Takagi, "Chiketto hanbai no keitai," 69.

[34] Tōkyō shōkōkaigishō, *Tōkyō ni okeru wappu hanbai no genjō to mondai* [Situation and issues of installment selling in Tokyo] (Tokyo: Tōkyō shōkōkaigishō, 1960), 37.

[35] Compare to the recent American variant, described in Robert D. Manning, *Credit Card Nation* (New York: Basic Books, 2000).

life; they were participating in a contemporaneous global dialogue. As with the discourse of consumer credit in the United States, anxieties about hedonistic excess or loss of discipline and moral fiber coexisted with the celebration of credit for enabling the nation to enjoy a new life of abundance.[36] If anything, one finds in Japan a relatively precocious presentation of an affirmative case for installment buying as a practice that promotes sober discipline and modern rationality.

Certainly, the commentary was often negative. Having surveyed 55 articles in the *Asahi shinbun* indexed under the keyword *geppu* from 1926 to 1941, I found a strong minority of articles that present credit purchases as either a promising or a neutral practice (19 stories), countered by many articles that depict installment selling as corrupt or problematic (23 stories).[37] In one 1930 story typical of the latter, the headline announces "Outlook Poor for Development of Installment. Too Expensive and Risky." The writer claims the practice is poorly developed compared to the United States. Costs run 30 to 50 percent above cash prices due to poor credit checks and high collection costs. Consumers are portrayed as notorious for late payments and poor discipline. A 1933 story similarly cautions: "No room for carelessness. Ads for home purchase on installment. What method to choose?" It explains that everything these days is bought on installment, from clothes and furniture to homes, in particular among the "salary-man installment class." Later that year, readers were told to "be prepared when buying on installment." Although fraud is less common than before and sellers are making efforts to reform their image as "overpriced and shoddy," the article warns, the buyer still must beware.[38]

Even a booster like Matsunami Tadayuki, author of a bestselling "how-to" guide to installment selling, warns that such credit can make buying too easy, extending a consumer beyond the ability to pay and leading producers to flood the market to their detriment. His example is the "one-yen book"—the collected works by noted writers that poured into the market on installment plans at such low prices that publishers could not make a profit.[39]

Overall, these and other popular prewar assessments offer some contrast to the picture one takes away from Lendol Calder's account of the American scene. The Japanese critics dwelled less on the problem of the moral hazard to buyers, who might fall into hopeless debt or hedonistic abandon, while directing their scorn at the shadiness and shoddiness of sellers who were cutting their own throats by excessive competition. Of course, the two perspectives cannot be neatly separated; a corrupt seller

[36] Calder, *Financing the American Dream.*

[37] *Asahi shinbun senzen Shōwa deeta beesu* [Asahi newspaper prewar Shōwa data base].

[38] *Asahi shinbun,* February 11, 1930, p. 4; March 4, 1933, p. 5; September 18, 1933, p. 5.

[39] Matsunami Tadayuki, *Sugu yaku ni tatsu geppu hanbai hō* [Immediately useful installment selling methods] (Tokyo: Banrikaku shōbo, 1930), 149–50.

could ensnare an unsuspecting buyer in dangerous debt. Nonetheless, the weight of criticism seems to differ.

In postwar as well as prewar Japan, undertones of ambivalence can be heard even in basically positive assessments of the new world of mass consumption. An editorial column in *Japan Sewing Machine Times* from 1951 described installment purchasing as benefiting the "national economy" while nonetheless posing dangers in its excess: "When [this method] is made too convenient, the installment buyer tends to wastefully purchase items of little necessity, but if one sets a credit limit and has the employer stand as guarantor, one can solve this problem."[40] Among Japanese critics of credit, the predicted damage fell primarily into one of several categories of "excess": excessive pressure on consumers by unscrupulous sellers, excessive purchases plunging consumers into deep debt, excessive consumption sparking runaway inflation, and excessive competition ruining the credit providers or retail sellers. Some of these accounts were decidedly fearful, echoing the sorts of criticism found in Europe or America.[41] Yet one sees two differences. One is a matter of tone. Japanese consumer critics were usually less hysterical in their denunciation than the anxious American commentators presented by Calder. Neither does the Japanese discourse present the same degree of anxiety that lay at the core of European critiques of consumer credit. One also discerns a difference in substance. When observers in Japan stressed the benefits of credit, they pointed mainly to gains to the national economy and only secondarily to easier lives for individual consumers.

The year 1957 saw a significant escalation of credit talk, pro and con, sparked by new surveys, intensified political struggle between small retailers and department stores, and more fundamentally the continued expansion of installment credit. In March the Credit Industry Association founded its own monthly journal (*Installment Studies*). That September, Satō Sadakatsu, a counselor in the government's Small and Medium Enterprise Agency, offered a typically ambivalent analysis of the dangers and benefits of installment selling in a lecture for corporate financial officers, later published in *Installment Studies*.

Although the editors noted great interest in the potential of installment selling to "raise the cultural standard of living of ordinary people, a truly revolutionary technique for the world of commerce," Satō himself began cautiously. Taking a dim view of indiscriminate consumer credit offered via tickets for the cheap necessities of daily life like food and drink, Satō judged that only relatively expensive products should be sold on install-

[40] "*Geppu hanbai, eejii peemento*" [Installment selling, easy payments], *NMT*, no. 154 (October 21, 1951): 2.

[41] See, for example, Calder, *Financing the American Dream*, 166–83, 212–30; and Rosa-Maria Gelpi and François Julien-Labruyère, *The History of Consumer Credit* (New York: St. Martins Press, 2000), 99–101.

ment. He recalled that in the early days of ticket sales, around 1952–53, consumers saw these tickets as a marvelous convenience, especially the payroll deduction feature. But "this [purchase of perishables] is a form of credit that obviously cannot work well." Many went overboard and ended up bringing home thin paychecks.[42] He reminded his audience that if terms were too easy, credit would be inflationary. In this sober bureaucrat's telling, "it is not acceptable for retailers to place their own profits first at the expense of the nation's interest."[43] Satō also lamented excessive "useless competition," a situation he found endemic in this industry. His office aimed to consolidate local installment sellers into single city-wide organizations so that consumers were not overwhelmed with four or five different ticket books and company personnel offices were not overwhelmed with paperwork. He reported having made the rounds of Kobe, Niigata, Kanazawa, Omuta, and Yotsukaichi to urge ticket organizations to join forces and offer common tickets. All parties, he claims, were delighted.[44]

The mainstream press joined the debate with similarly divided views. In a feature titled "Advent of the Installment Age?" in 1957, an *Asahi* reporter fretted that "one hears installment is more expensive [than buying with cash], and people overspend, but still all sorts of goods are selling this way: TVs, sewing machines, refrigerators, washing machines. . . ." Though convenient for salaried workers, installment purchases not only risk ruining the household's finances if overdone, they could harm the "national kitchen," meaning the economy. The writer lamented that some credit tickets could even be used in movie theaters and coffee shops. Although banks and the Finance Ministry could easily regulate the flow of capital to industry when authorities saw need to slow down the expansion, they could not so easily regulate the decentralized providers of consumer credit to head off inflation, he worried.[45] A 1959 *Asahi* opinion column on "expanding installment sales" recognized that installment sales, for good or ill, were here to stay, having "eaten deeply into the salary class." The column concluded pessimistically that such credit led the salaryman to spend income before having it in hand: if he went overboard just a little, he would fall hopelessly into debt.[46]

Similar fears were expressed in the media and by key figures in the business and bureaucratic elite. A vice president of the Japan Productivity Center writing in 1958 recognized that consumer credit helped industry by generating mass demand, lowering unit costs, and raising productivity.

[42] Satō Sadakatsu, "Wappu hanbai no shidō ni tsuite" [Guidance for installment selling], *Geppu kenkyū* 1, no. 6 (September 15, 1957): 3.

[43] Satō, "Wappu hanbai no shidō ni tsuite," *Geppu kenkyū* 1, no. 8 (November 15, 1957): 5.

[44] Satō, "Wappu hanbai no shidō ni tsuite," *Geppu kenkyū* 2, no. 2 (February 15, 1958): 4.

[45] "Kuru ka? geppu jidai" [The age of installments: Has it arrived?], *Asahi shinbun,* November 21, 1957, p. 5.

[46] *Asahi shinbun,* July 27, 1959, evening, p. 1.

But, he warned, increased consumption must be kept in line with increased exports and accumulated savings, or else trade imbalances will plague the resource-poor nation. As a cautionary tale, he cited press reports of a schoolteacher overcome by excessive installment debt. His solution was to distinguish good from bad installment buying. Expensive durable goods properly required credit; food and drink would not. This distinction between the productive use of credit and its economically and morally suspect "consumptive" use had long been typical in the United States and would significantly inform Japanese policymaking in the 1950s and 1960s.[47]

For all their worries, journalists and officials from the 1920s through the 1950s appeared more cautionary than condemnatory. Their rhetoric promoted what they defined as good or responsible consumer borrowing, rather than rejecting or dramatically restricting the practice. Remarkably, none of the first generation of credit surveys made any effort to measure delinquency, default, or repossession or even discuss such problems in any detail.[48] And, balancing the concerned voices above, one finds a forceful positive case from the earliest days of the discourse on credit. Matsunami's "how-to" book of 1930 grandly proclaimed that credit selling would "democratize mass access to commodities, spread human happiness more equally, and relieve troubling class struggles." The "property-less intellectual class" would be able to afford a 100-yen phonograph only on installment, and the practice thus "elevates the level of daily life." Also, installment purchase would bring economic security to households by encouraging families to budget their expenses.[49]

On this last point, Matsunami took his cue from the most noteworthy prewar case for consumer credit, made by the Tokyo Chamber of Commerce in 1929. Affirming the importance of "rationalizing" industrial management, the business association then offered a parallel case for the "household consumer." Its precocious appreciation of the benefits of installment selling merits quotation:

> In order to support the development of our national people's economy, it is necessary to reform the consumer economy, increase the efficiency of consumption, eliminate waste, lower the expense of daily life, and thus rationalize daily life. . . . [To this end, installment buying] is not only extremely useful in order to lead a disciplined life, planning a monthly budget of expenses; it also raises standards of living by allowing purchase of goods otherwise too expensive. . . . For that class of people who have regular monthly

[47] Kagawa Sanroku, "Antei shita keizai kakudai no tassei" [Achieving stable economic growth], *Geppu kenkyū* 2, no. 1 (January 15, 1958): 2.

[48] Matsunami, *Sugu yaku ni tatsu geppu hanbai hō,* 193–200 is a rare prewar exception.

[49] Matsunami, *Sugu yaki ni tatsu geppu hanbai hō,* 148, 160.

> incomes, installment purchase is far more rational than either cash or [open book, seasonal, or other less formal] credit purchases, and it also is beneficial to expand sales. . . . In sum, skillful operation of installment selling will contribute in no small measure to rationalization of both daily life and [business] management, and is most appropriate for those who are selling to the working salaried classes.[50]

The most striking aspect of this passage is the view of installment credit as a form of social discipline. Lendol Calder's study of the United States, published seventy years later, centers its revisionism on the argument that credit reinforced social discipline rather than promoted hedonism. He asserted that both prewar and recent analysts in the United States had failed to appreciate this critical point.[51] This claim is not quite fair. No less a figure than E. R. A. Seligman, in his classic 1927 treatise on consumer credit, stated quite clearly that "the installment plan induces the consumer to look ahead with greater care and to plan his economic program with a higher degree of intelligence. Many persons who would otherwise give little or no thought to the planning of future receipts and expenditures are virtually compelled by installment buying to construct what is in effect a personal budget."[52] What is striking is that these Tokyo authors—who read Seligman carefully and probably took a cue from this passage—were even more forthright than he was in stressing the rationalizing, disciplining function of installment credit. Seligman had buried this insight in the middle of a chapter toward the back of the book; they placed it front and center in the preface.

As postwar installment credit took off, a second generation of surveys of consumer installment credit, conducted between 1957 and 1961, echoed prewar installment studies in stating that the practice would promote economic growth and affluence on the one hand, and social discipline on the other. As early as 1952 an economist contributing to a sewing machine industry newspaper called installment selling "a great weapon for increasing demand and blazing the trail to new markets" that "clearly brings planning into daily life and regulates consumption."[53] Culture, spending, and savings were part of a connected bundle of virtuous concepts and behaviors; one sewing machine company called its layaway-installment plan "cultural savings."[54]

[50] Tōkyō shōkōkaigishō, *Geppu hanbai seido,* 1–2.

[51] Calder, *Financing the American Dream,* 29–33.

[52] E. R. A. Seligman, *The Economics of Installment Selling* (New York: Harper and Brothers, 1927), 1:267.

[53] Kawauchi Mamoru, "Geppu hanbai no keizaigaku" [Economics of installment selling], *NMT,* no. 172 (March 21, 1952): 9.

[54] "Wappu hanbai hō" [Installment selling methods], *Janome shanaihō* 7, no. 37 (March 1962): 9.

The Tokyo Chamber of Commerce likewise prefaced its survey of 1957 by describing the congruent interests of manufacturers, sellers, and consumers. Installment selling helped all of them by expanding commodity markets, stabilizing sales volumes, and "bringing the benefit of raising the standard of living to consumers and rationalizing consumer outlays." It is not only the installment purchaser who enjoyed the benefit of the practice; even the cash purchaser benefited from the cost savings enabled by mass production.[55]

Such upbeat accounts of the economic stimulation and disciplinary effects of consumer demand appeared in the media and academic analysis as well. The leading authority of consumer credit from the 1950s through the 1980s was Waseda University's Yajima Yasuo, who argued in a prolific body of work that installment selling was the key to expanding mass production. He described a positive ethos of consumerism as well as positive feedback among demand for these goods, installment sales, and more demand via a demonstration effect.[56]

The history of consumer credit illuminates the relationship between "catch-up" and simultaneity in Japan's modern history. On the one hand, American-style installment selling was exported to late-developing Japan several decades after it took off in the United States. Yet, by the late 1920s, Japanese observers were fully abreast of global trends, and indeed precocious in their insight into the significance of the expanding practice at home and abroad.

All these voices in institutional and academic reporting and in mainstream journalism were male. However, the overwhelming majority of users of some of the most popular modern credit goods, especially the sewing machine, jewelry, and pianos, were female.[57] Is there a gendered history of installment buying in Japan? Scattered evidence suggests that the answer is yes. At the same time, the cultural construction of the female shopper remained different from that found in the American discourse, even as it changed over time.

The balance of household power is contentious among historians and contemporary analysts in Japan. The prewar evidence for decisions about installment purchases does not support the common view that women have always been household financial managers enjoying significant au-

[55] Tōkyō shōkōkaigishō, *Wappu hanbai ni kansuru jittai chōsa* [Survey on the state of installment sales] (Tokyo: Tōkyō shōkōkaigishō, 1957), 1.

[56] Mishima Akira, "Kokumin keizai ni okeru geppu no igi" [Significance of installment selling in national economy], *Geppu kinkyū* 2, no. 6 (June 15, 1958): 2; Yajima Yasuo, "Wappu hanbai no keizaiteki igi" [Economic significance of installment selling], *Jurisuto*, no. 382 (October 15, 1967): 76–78.

[57] Tōkyō shiyakusho, *Wappu hanbai ni kansuru chōsa,* 63.

tonomy and power.[58] A 1929 testimonial ad in a women's magazine, for example, prominently offers a collection of books on western dress and sewing for sale on the installment plan. It tells a fictional story of a woman distraught over her poor physique, ill-suited to western clothes. Scorned by a clothing salesperson, she resolves to learn to sew her own clothes. Only with considerable importuning is she able to convince her husband to open his wallet and buy both a sewing machine (probably on time) and the set of books (definitely on the installment plan). This is a tale of gendered household governance in which the man makes the spending decisions, even for goods that benefit the wife and daughters. It is also a tale in which easy payments and hard work are the twin keys to a fashionable life, pride, and domestic bliss: the wife's new look even leads her husband to propose they go for walks together.[59] A 1937 training manual for Janome salesmen with the (English) title "Our Salesmanship" offers additional evidence of male decision-making. The manual admits it is hard to sell a sewing machine, which costs more than 100 yen, even if it is a household necessity: "In a family, typically the first things bought are for the children, then men's necessities for the husband, and finally goods for the wife." Salesmen are advised to stress that though it is a "woman's good," the sewing machine is the only production machine in the home providing goods for the whole family.[60]

As consumer credit in the United States reached giddying heights in the 1920s, anxious critics depicted women as the source of the credit problem, vulnerable by nature to credit addiction and abuse.[61] In contrast, the scornful view of women as self-indulgent, undisciplined shoppers is not a major theme in prewar and early postwar Japan. Rather, the marketing of the sewing machines "on time" connected women with two sets of eminently modern behaviors: (1) sober rationality, prudence, and investment and (2) pursuit of a new life of abundance and pleasure. In one striking ad in 1936, Janome buyers were told "Just 10 sen a day [on the layaway plan], convenient and beneficial. . . . And [one can support oneself] just in case." The text evoked themes of desire and pleasure, together with science and prudent rationality, in a single grand sweep:

[58] See Haruko Wakita, "The Medieval Household," in *Women and Class in Japanese History,* ed. Hitomi Tonomura, Anne Walthall, and Haruko Wakita (Ann Arbor: Center for Japanese Studies, University of Michigan, 1999), 81–98; and Sumiko Iwao, *The Japanese Woman* (New York: Free Press, 1993), 80–88.

[59] "Taikaku ga hinjaku na watakushi ga yōsō suru made wa" [Until I dressed my poor physique in Western clothes], *Fujokai* 39, no. 1 (January 1929): 293.

[60] Cited in *Janome mishin sōgyō 50 nen shi,* 246–47.

[61] Calder, *Financing the American Dream,* 181–83, 217–20. On the postwar United States, see Lizabeth Cohen, *A Consumers' Republic: The Politics of Mass Consumption in Postwar America* (New York: Knopf, 2003), 278–86.

> The women who play more, socialize more, and earn more than any in the world are Americans. In our country, in 1936, the new trend for women is to earn a ton of money, and buy whatever they like without hesitation. But, you say, how can I earn money? I need to take care of washing and sewing and cooking. There is only one way to solve this problem, brilliantly, by putting a little bit of science into daily life . . . buy a sewing machine.[62]

The layaway and installment plans of Janome and its competitors on the eve of war thus nurtured disciplined female *saver-consumers* who might pursue pleasure, but whose impulse to shop was balanced by the obligation to pay and whose purchases were likewise valued for building the national economy.[63]

In the early postwar discourse of consumer credit, women were framed differently, as household managers who make major decisions. A 1963 panel of Janome salesmen turned on its head the company's sales advice of 1937. The salesmen emphasized that the key to selling is to cultivate the women who, after all, hold the power of the household purse.[64] But if women had gained power, they were not presented as abusing it. Independent as well as industry sources echoed the prewar view that women are far from excessive spenders ignorant of the cost of compound interest or decadent hedonists entranced by useless baubles. They were portrayed as prudent consumers often victimized by irresponsible men. Counselor Satō from the Small and Medium Enterprise Agency saw unmarried young *men* as a particularly irresponsible lot prone to binging on credit.[65] Ticket companies usually sold their products through companies to male employees, and married men could use ticket credit unbeknownst to their wives. The latter would then only find out when a pay envelope came home filled with cancelled tickets and no money, leading to many a "domestic struggle," in Satō's telling.[66]

Because housewives were the most active members, Satō found neighborhood associations quite reliable as the intermediary between *shinpan* and ticket customers. Rather than fall behind—and, one assumes, suffer the scorn of their peers—these women would "go pawn something the night before, to be able to make the payment that day."[67] The daily press made the same points with the same images, dressed in the cultural clichés

[62] *Tōkyō asahi shinbun,* February 26, 1934, p. 5; January 19, 1935, p. 7; January 9, 1936, p. 5.

[63] See also Kawamoto Teruo, "Mishin no maebarai shiki wappu hanbai keitai" [Prepaid credit sales for sewing machines], *Jurisuto,* no. 382 (October 15, 1967): 57–59.

[64] *Janome shanaihō* 8, no. 51 (June 1963): 10–11.

[65] Satō, "Wappu hanbai no shidō ni tsuite," February 15, 1958, p. 4.

[66] Satō, "Wappu hanbai no shidō ni tsuite," September 15, 1957, p. 3. For an identical point in the press about housewives left with nothing but tickets in a husband's pay envelope, see "Kuru ka? geppu jidai."

[67] Satō, "Wappu hanbai no shidō ni tsuite," *Geppu kinkyū* 1, no. 7 (October 15, 1957): 2.

of the 1950s. The *Asahi* noted that ticket companies could rely on female customers in "neighborhood" groups enrolling five or six housewives: "After all, from the standpoint of collective responsibility, these women are really fierce gossips. If you fell behind, the neighbor group was unrelenting; one makes the payment on time, whatever it might take."[68]

The Political Regulation of Consumer Credit

In the late 1950s, consumer credit stood on the brink of taking off to a new level. Installment sales were booming with the overall domestic and export economy. And roughly fifteen years before the rise of bank cards in the United States (the parents of today's MasterCard and Visa), a creative system of credit tickets usable at thousands of member stores was surging in popularity. Observers, including state officials, recognized the benefits for industry of extending credit to masses of customers, and some understood the monthly payment as a form of social discipline rather than an invitation to excess and unsustainable debt. But they simultaneously worried about inflation, default, and the socially erosive impact of "consumptive credit."

Against this complex backdrop of support and ambivalence, MITI in 1959 issued an administrative order to restrict the ability of the major "ticket" finance companies and department stores to offer consumer credit. This obscure order was arguably the most consequential decision in the history of postwar consumer credit. The years around 1960 are a bit like the far more famous era of abortive European revolutions of 1848—a moment of transformation that failed to happen.

This episode also illustrates nicely the contingencies of turning points in history, since the direct impetus for the order was a political struggle between large and small retailers, which intersected only tangentially with the worries of MITI mandarins about excess credit. The contest pitted local and national federations of small retailers and their allied ticket sellers against department stores and a handful of major ticket companies, the *shinpan.* The aggressive growth of the largest finance company, Nihon Shinpan, was the proximate cause of the struggle. In 1956 the company expanded beyond its Tokyo-Yokohama base by opening branches in Nagoya and Osaka. Federations of small-scale retailers and 200 ticket companies with 10,000 member stores launched a fierce lobbying campaign against this move. They heckled the Nihon Shinpan president as "Godzilla" when he visited Osaka. They complained that many members were on the verge of collapse. They wanted the government to limit the type and value of

[68] "Chiketto hanbai ni shin te: Okusan no mie wo riyō" [New tactic for ticket selling: Using the wife's vanity], *Asahi shinbun,* June 28, 1954, p. 8.

goods that department stores could offer on credit. They wanted to restrict the *shinpan* from issuing tickets that were valid nationwide. Nihon Shinpan and the department stores countered that the minimum purchase of 2,000 yen per item proposed in 1959 was too high: only 40 percent of their ticket sales exceeded that. The large department stores also argued that the problem was exaggerated since only 3 percent of their sales were through tickets. The struggle ultimately came down to what sort of regulation would be acceptable, and to whom. Nihon Shinpan warned it would go bankrupt if tickets purchased were limited to 1,000 yen and up, and the National Federation of Consumer Groups supported this position, claiming that tickets were important in enabling ordinary consumers to shop at department stores. But the consumer group did not oppose credit limits in principle. It could live with prohibition of ticket purchases at the 100- to 200-yen level. And it opposed ticket credit for the purchase of perishables, fearing reckless spending.[69]

After a year of intensive lobbying, the small stores won the battle. In October 1959 MITI sent 106 department stores and 19 *shinpan* companies its "Order Concerning Self-Restraint by Department Stores." The ruling prohibited stores from selling, and credit companies from financing, installment goods priced below 500 yen, with a stricter floor of 1,000 yen in six major cities. It banned department store installment sales of services, food, drink, plants, and pets. And it outlawed the use of tickets outside the prefecture of issue.[70] The small retailers had won a monopoly on installment credit for low-priced goods, and nationally or regionally portable consumer credit had been ruled illegal. The intense battle between large department stores and small retailers had been raging in Japan since the 1920s in other arenas as well.[71] It had now spilled over to restrain the spread of consumer credit.

Three years later, the Installment Sales Law—also drafted by MITI—took effect. It reinforced the administrative constraints.[72] The law stipulated that "if it is judged that a department store or manufacturer will cause great harm to the business of small scale installment sellers, the relevant ministry can refuse to allow the former [to sell on installment]." And to prevent irresponsible use of credit, the law mandated that the government, by administrative order, would designate a list of the "specified goods" that could legally be sold on installment credit. The initial list of approved goods, issued in 1961, was quite extensive. It allowed credit purchase of

[69] Nihon shinpan, *Za bunka,* 3; and "Momeru hyakkaten no geppu uri" [Argument over department store installment selling], *Asahi shinbun,* November 4, 1958, p. 4.

[70] *Asahi shinbun,* October 31, 1959, p. 1; October 24, 1959, p. 4.

[71] Sheldon Garon and Mike Mochizuki, "Negotiating Social Contracts," in *Postwar Japan as History,* ed. Andrew Gordon (Berkeley: University of California Press, 1993), 148–55.

[72] For text of the law and Diet deliberations, see http://kokkai.ndl.go.jp/cgi-bin/KOKUMIN/www_login.

items such as toys and cosmetics—hardly "consumer durables." But it prohibited "consumptive" credit—food, drink, and tobacco—and credit for services.[73]

Over the following four decades, this set of regulatory restraints reinforced customary practice and ideology to institute an enduring system of consumer credit. Incredibly, the 1959 order remained in force until 1992. This combination of regulation and habit accounts for key features of Japanese consumer credit as it expanded in volume from the 1960s. First, single-purchase transactions remained the dominant focus of consumer credit into the 1980s. Most were "installment" contracts, and some (purchases made with just one or two credit payments) were defined as "non-installment" credit (see figure 6.2). Even through the mid-1990s the combined total of these two categories was roughly comparable to total credit card volume. To this day these two categories together exceed the volume of credit card purchases paid in installments or in revolving fashion. Second, and related to the previous point, the proportion of consumer credit provided through cards remained relatively low. Only the *shinpan* were allowed to offer what came to be called revolving credit. They replaced credit ticket books with credit cards in the mid-1960s, subject to the same regulations. For several decades, banks were allowed to enter the consumer credit market only in limited ways, with convenience "credit cards" that had to be cleared monthly by automatic deduction from a linked savings account. These features of the regulatory past have proved resilient to the present day.

In broad outlines the story unfolded as follows. In the wake of the MITI order of 1959, Nihon Shinpan closed its Osaka and Nagoya offices, set up a separate corporation to develop its business in Kansai, and saw total credit volume in 1960 fall to 1957–58 levels.[74] When one considers how quickly the economy as a whole was growing, this was indeed a dramatic setback. But in 1963, Nihon Shinpan and other finance companies devised a clever new tool to circumvent the 1959 order: "shopping credit." On a purchase-by-purchase basis, any customer (not necessarily a pre-enrolled *shinpan* customer) who entered a member store anywhere in Japan could apply for credit from Nihon Shinpan and pay for that good on installments. Since there were no tickets or cards involved, MITI's 1959 order was not applicable; neither the regional restriction nor the price floor applied, and the ministry did not move to halt or regulate the practice. Although not as convenient as pre-approved tickets or credit cards, this innovation sufficed to spark a second wave of growth for the company and its com-

[73] See Shinada Seihei, *Wappu hanbai no hōritsu, kaikei, zeimu* [Installment sales: Law, accounting, and financing] (Tokyo: Dayamondosha, 1961), 63–218.

[74] Nihon shinpan kabushiki gaisha, *Nihon shinpan 35 nen no ayumi* [Thirty-five-year history of Nihon Shinpan] (Tokyo: Nihon shinpan, 1961), 135–36.

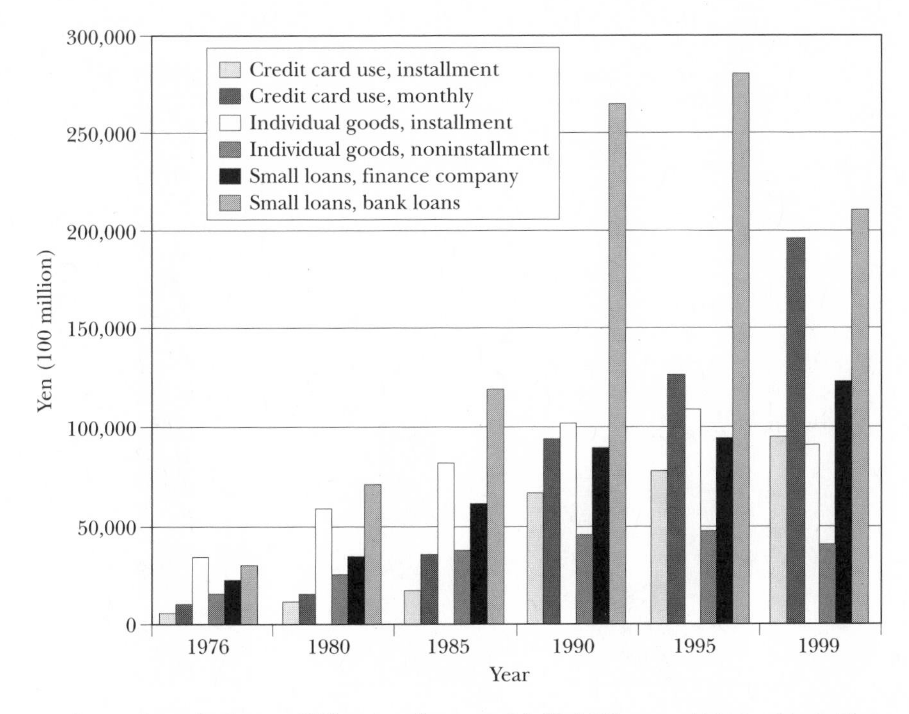

Source: Annual volumes of Nihon kurejitto sangyō kyōkai, Nihon no shōhisha shinyō tōkei, 1988–2002.

Figure 6.2. Consumer credit use by type of credit

petitors. In sum, the regulatory context of the 1959 order and the installment credit law channeled the expansion of consumer credit toward two practices: limited short-term (one- or two-payment) credit, often linked to salary bonuses, and single-good installment purchases.

At the same time, regulation guided the newly emerging bank cards away from revolving credit and down the path of least resistance, to the "convenience" type of credit cleared on a monthly basis. Every bank card had to be linked to a savings account from which payments were deducted in full each month. Although MITI had no legal basis for its action—the Finance Ministry regulated banks—MITI refused to allow banks to offer coupon, ticket, or shopping credit and enter the long-term installment business dominated by the *shinpan*. Short-term credit cleared monthly, on the other hand, fell outside the scope of the 1959 order and 1962 law, and MITI made no claim against banks that offered it. For its part, the Ministry

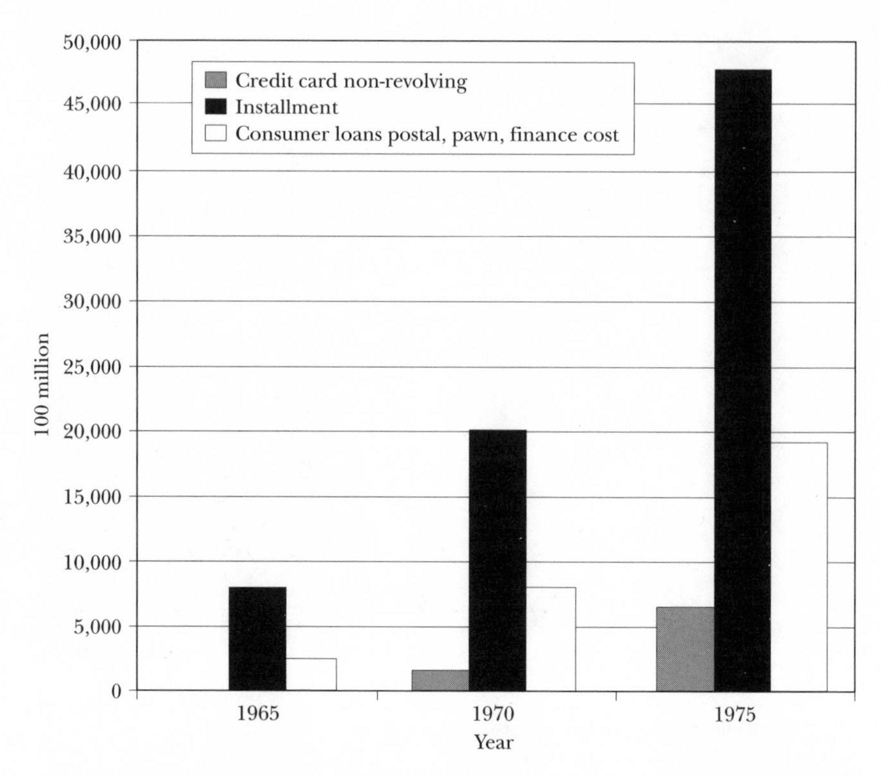

Source: Annual volumes of Nihon kurejitto sangyō kyōkai, Nihon no shōhisha shinyō tōkei, 1988–2002.

Figure 6.3. Breakdown of credit by type

of Finance maintained that longer-term, card-based consumer credit—whether revolving or installment—amounted to unacceptable unsecured loans. As a result, from around 1970, bank credit cards cleared monthly began to spread widely (see figure 6.3). Regulators and credit providers institutionalized this practice. Card users came to see it as so "natural" that most continue to use cards for convenience, not credit, even though the requirement to do so has vanished.

The 1959 ordinance was finally revoked in 1992 as part of a compromise form of deregulation involving MITI, the Ministry of Finance, the *shinpan,* and the major banks. The banks were allowed to issue revolving or installment credit via cards. In exchange for surrendering their monopoly on this instrument, the *shinpan* won access to the bank ATM network. Since 1992, both banks and *shinpan* have been free to issue consumer credit via

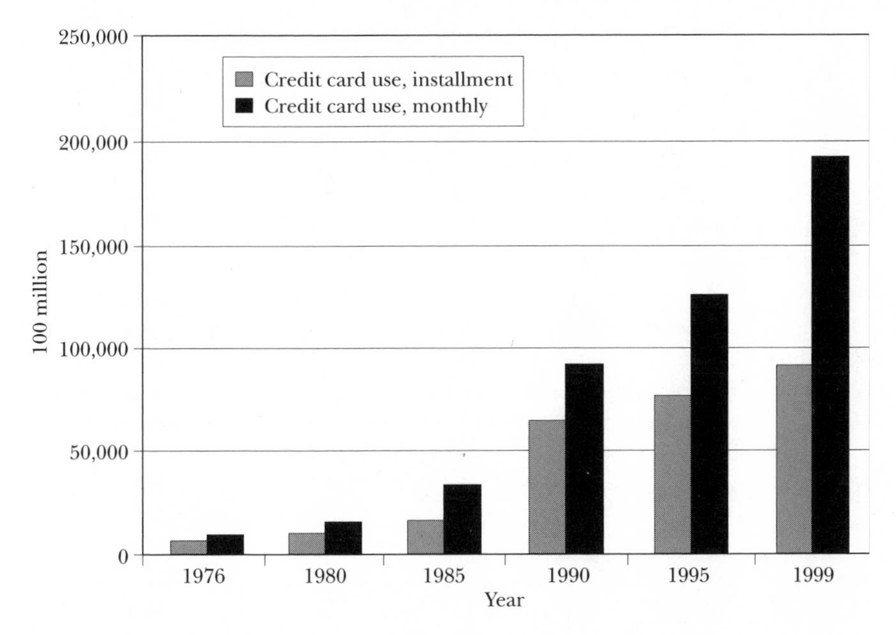

Source: Annual volumes of Nihon kurejitto sangyō kyōkai, Nihon no shōhisha shinyō tōkei, 1988–2002.

Figure 6.4. Breakdown of credit card debt, 1976–2000

cards in three forms: credit cleared on a monthly basis, installment credit (typically ten payments), or revolving credit, where the consumer can decide the amount of the monthly repayment of an outstanding balance. The customer specifies which type of credit she or he wants at the point of purchase (rather than the moment of payment, as in the United States). What is intriguing is that even after twelve years of this deregulated practice, the vast majority of consumers choose—or simply accept as the "natural" default practice—the monthly clearing of outstanding balances. In 1999, roughly two-thirds of total credit card charges were cleared monthly; only one-third was paid on installment (see figure 6.4). According to a 2001 survey of 1,455 credit card users, 71 percent reported making full payments monthly; 12 percent chose to make installment payments; 4 percent made payments linked to semi-annual bonuses; and just 4 percent opted for payment on a revolving basis.[75] Compared to this preponderance of "conve-

[75] Nihon kurejitto sangyō kyōkai, *Kurejitto ni kansuru shōhisha chōsa* [Survey of consumers on credit] (Tokyo: Nihon kurejitto sangyō kyōkai, 2001), 245.

nience" over "loan" users, the American case is very different; less than 40 percent of consumers clear their balances monthly at present.[76] And figure 6.4 makes clear that much of the increase that has taken place in installment-type card credit in Japan (this graph includes credit offered through *shinpan* or bank cards) actually predates the 1992 deregulation.[77]

Returning, then, to the initial surprise that Japanese consumers use credit at American levels relative to income, two points should be clear. A large, though decreasing, proportion of this credit has long taken the form of installment purchases of durable consumer goods. And, to this day, a very small proportion has taken the form of card-based revolving credit. Neither of these trends can be explained solely with reference to culture and custom, on the one hand, or politics and regulation, on the other. Clearly one cannot explain a practice such as consumer credit in a zero-sum fashion, where either culture or regulation is designated the independent causal factor. Culture and politics are interdependent. The regulations of the 1950s were shaped by anxieties and expectations concerning healthy and risky consumer behavior and economic development, themselves already articulated in dynamic fashion for several decades. These regulations in turn shaped or reinforced subsequent consumer attitudes about what constitutes obvious or natural choices. Consumer behavior was changing even in advance of deregulation, as installment use of credit cards spiked up from the late 1980s (figure 6.4). And even as regulations change, certain basic patterns—such as the default use of monthly credit—remain "natural" choices for many Japanese. Habit emerges as the hybrid product of these crosscutting pressures.

[76] Manning presents industry estimates that between 1990 and 2001, roughly 30 to 40 percent of American credit card users cleared their balances monthly. *Credit Card Nation,* 102.

[77] Unexamined here is the huge spike in small loans to consumers from banks and finance companies in the 1990s (figure 6.3). On the supply side, the bubble and aftermath surely led banks to focus on individual consumers as well as (or rather than) corporate borrowers.

7

THE TRANSNATIONAL PROMOTION OF SAVING IN ASIA

"Asian Values" or the "Japanese Model"?

SHELDON GARON

Viewed from abroad, the United States appears a nation obsessed with the expansion of consumer spending. Since the late 1940s, Americans have embraced mass consumption as an economic and political panacea (see Cohen, chap. 2). It has become axiomatic that personal consumption drives the U.S. economy and that government policy should stimulate spending not only in bad times, as Keynes recommended, but in boom times as well. So intoxicating has this vision been that few Americans expect other nations to approach consumption differently. As Walter Russell Mead of the Council on Foreign Relations put it in 1998, "To keep their economies growing, Asian societies must develop the consumer mentality of the West. If history is any guide, Asian governments will encourage the mass retreat from thrift, just as Washington did. . . . There's no getting around it; Asia's little emperors [the young] are going to have to get charge cards, just like their decadent, spendthrift, individualistic counterparts in the West."[1]

Perhaps Mead is right, and consumer culture will inevitably triumph in Asia as it has in the United States. But to do so, the history that is his guide must overpower alternative histories in those East and Southeast Asian economies that have grown so rapidly in recent decades. As in much of the rest of the world, Asian governments and publics have understood consumption in complex ways that go far beyond the simple act of spending money. On one hand, these governments have encouraged greater consumption both to improve living standards and to bolster their legitimacy.

[1] Walter Russell Mead, "The Real Asian Miracle; Asia Devalued," *New York Times Magazine,* May 31, 1998, p. 38.

At the same time, most Asian states and their peoples remain openly ambivalent about unfettered consumption for a variety of economic, social, political, and moral reasons.[2] In Japan, postwar officials and women's publications have urged the nation to strike a balance between consumption and saving. There and elsewhere in Asia, consumption is often regarded as a behavior that must be "rationalized." One should engage in "rational" spending, refrain from wasting money on luxuries, and not indulge in excessive consumption. Moreover, Asians have frequently understood consumption to be a test of one's patriotism, measured by whether one buys "national products" or imported goods (on consumer nationalism, see Nelson, chap. 8).[3] Conspicuous consumption is also widely represented as a threat to social stability. In Malaysia, where officials strive to maintain a delicate balance among ethnic groups, the state today has worked to inculcate thrift and "positive spending habits" in the majority Malays to raise their living standards to those of the Chinese minority.[4]

I have chosen to illuminate Asian attitudes toward consumption by focusing on its inverse—the pervasive efforts to restrain spending and encourage saving. Under conditions of modern economic growth in East and Southeast Asia, discourses on consumption have been bound up not so much with messages of frugality but more positively, with the imperative to manage personal spending so as to augment household and national savings. As an influential World Bank study noted in 1993, every successful economy in the region boasts high household saving rates. The massive pool of savings has in turn provided ready sources of low-cost capital for industrial investment.[5]

Yet few have rigorously examined why many Asian nations are so thrifty in their consumer and savings behavior. This important topic has largely been left to popular and official interpretations. Asian leaders and people alike have come to see thrift as deeply embedded in their cultural traditions. Although the Japanese have long judged "diligence and thrift" to be a uniquely Japanese trait, other Asians are more inclined to present a high saving rate as the product of a common regional heritage. By the early 1980s, "Confucianism" emerged as the supposed magic bullet that would explain why South Korea, Taiwan, Singapore, Hong Kong, and later China had followed in Japan's footsteps of rapid economic development. Together with overseas Chinese scholars, western observers highlighted the

[2] See Beng-Huat Chua, ed., *Consumption in Asia: Lifestyles and Identities* (London: Routledge, 2000), 9–10.

[3] See also Laura C. Nelson, *Measured Excess: Status, Gender, and Consumer Nationalism in South Korea* (New York: Columbia University Press, 2000).

[4] "Savings Promotion Campaign," PowerPoint presentation, Financial Management and Savings Secretariat, Bank Negara Malaysia, June 25, 2001.

[5] The World Bank, *The East Asian Miracle: Economic Growth and Public Policy* (London: Oxford University Press, 1993), 16.

role of Confucianism in what two American political scientists termed "the Eastasian urge to save." One account is typical in summing up the tradition as follows: "Confucian philosophy . . . hailed prudence and frugality, demanded sacrifice for future employment, and condemned parents who failed to provide for their offspring."[6] The putative link between Confucianism and the East Asian variant of capitalism soon strongly influenced South Koreans and ethnic Chinese. Notably in Singapore, the government promoted "Confucian Ethics" in schools and society. Subsequent economic growth in the predominantly non-Chinese nations of Malaysia, Indonesia, and Thailand gave rise in the early 1990s to the new discourse of "Asian values." As formulated by Singapore's former prime minister Lee Kuan Yew and Malaysia's then prime minister Mahathir bin Mohamad, "thrift" figures prominently among the cardinal Asian virtues—along with "hard work," the "deferment of present enjoyment for future gain," and the subordination of the individual to the family.[7]

To be sure, many East and Southeast Asian societies appear culturally disposed toward thrift, but I question the timelessness and uniqueness of these so-called Asian values regarding saving and consumption. Accordingly, this chapter historicizes the self-conscious *formation* of these cultures. First, I look at how Asian states and various groups have actively worked to stimulate saving and inculcate thrift among their respective peoples. In recent decades, they have expanded government-run savings institutions, mounted recurrent savings campaigns, organized grass-roots savings associations, and mobilized the schools and media to encourage thrift. Second, I highlight the transnational diffusion of knowledge regarding savings promotion in Asian developmental strategies. That is, the widespread urge to save in Asian economies probably has less to do with their shared "Asian-ness" and may be more related to their common adoption of savings-promotion models and practices from other countries. Although the European colonial powers implanted some of the methods and thinking behind thrift promotion in Asia, the seldom-recognized catalyst has been Japan and its historic efforts to increase national saving. Before 1945, Japanese imposed the "Japanese model" on their colonies and occupied territories. More recently, Asian nations have consciously emulated the policies underlying postwar Japan's "economic miracle."

This chapter focuses on savings-promotion programs in three leading Asian economies—South Korea, Singapore, and Malaysia—because these cases best exhibit (1) the concerted use of state power to encourage thrift

[6] Roy Hofheinz Jr. and Kent E. Calder, *The Eastasia Edge* (New York: Basic Books, 1982), 120–22.

[7] Fareed Zakaria, "Culture is Destiny: A Conversation with Lee Kuan Yew," *Foreign Affairs* 73, no. 2 (March/April 1994): 113–14, 116; Mahathir, in *Straits Times* (Singapore), October 4, 1997, p. 62.

and (2) the indispensable role of Japanese knowledge in their developmental strategies.

A Short History of the "Japanese Model"

The Japanese state's efforts to mold a culture of thrift may be traced as far back as the Tokugawa era (1603–1868), when the authorities and reformers exhorted the people to practice "diligence and thrift." Nonetheless, the savings institutions and programs that would later influence the rest of Asia were in large part modeled after several European innovations. Following the Meiji Restoration (1868), Japanese officials became fascinated by the efforts of contemporary European nations to create thrifty, hardworking, and patriotic citizens. Seeking to establish Japan as a great power, they assiduously emulated such statist European policies as postal savings banks, school savings programs, and war savings campaigns.[8]

In 1875, Japan became only the third nation in the world to institute a system of postal savings in emulation of Britain's Post Office Savings Bank (established 1861). Designed to attract the small savings of the populace, postal savings emerged as a major source of finance for the Japanese state's military, colonial, and developmental projects. The Ministry of Finance assumed total control over investing the growing pool of postal savings deposits in 1884. To this day, finance bureaucrats manage the vast funds of the postal savings system, which make it the largest bank in the world.

The postal savings system provided Japanese bureaucrats with powerful incentives to persuade households to restrain their consumption and deposit their savings in the state-controlled postal savings bank. The authorities encouraged thrift not simply as a moral virtue but as a means to national power. Poor access to foreign capital at favorable rates plagued Japan after 1868, during World War II, and again in the immediate postwar era. The state's mobilization of popular savings often substituted for foreign investment in financing the nation's ambitious military and industrial projects.

Having instituted accessible savings institutions, the Japanese state and various societal groups cooperated to encourage saving along two distinct fronts. The earliest programs aimed at organizing communities into "savings associations." Typically a savings association required members to tender small, but regular, deposits to the association representative, who would deposit the monies in the member's name in a savings institution. Employing group pressure and offering convenience, the savings associa-

[8] See Sheldon Garon, "Saving for 'My Own Good and the Good of the Nation': Economic Nationalism in Modern Japan," in *Nation and Nationalism in Japan*, ed. Sandra Wilson (London: RoutlegeCurzon, 2002), 97–114.

tion proved an effective mode of boosting saving. At the height of World War II, new legislation enabled the authorities to organize the entire populace into national savings associations, which played a central role in compelling Japanese to save at punishing rates (estimated at 40 percent of disposal income in 1944). Following the Japanese defeat in 1945, the national savings associations remained an important vehicle for mobilizing small savings until the 1960s.

During the 1920s, the savings campaign surfaced as another potent means of persuading Japanese to save. Officials modeled the campaigns after World War I savings drives in the western nations—particularly Britain's centrally organized National Savings Movement. Like their western counterparts, the Japanese campaigns employed the mass media—including radio, posters, and advertisements—and they worked closely with women's groups, housewives' magazines, religious organizations, teachers, local civic groups, and the savings associations. The savings drives became most intrusive during Japan's wars with China and the Allied powers between 1937 and 1945. Wartime campaigns were administered by the Ministry of Finance's National Savings Promotion Bureau and the advisory National Savings Promotion Council.[9]

In the wake of World War II, Japanese governments mounted a new series of savings campaigns to finance recovery and economic growth. In 1952, the Bank of Japan and the Ministry of Finance founded the Central Council for Savings Promotion, which encouraged thrift in cooperation with local committees, schools, women's groups, the media, and local governments. The Central Council still functions, though it changed its name to the Central Council for Savings *Information* in 1987. Renamed again in 2001, the present Central Council for Financial Services Information no longer aims to increase savings. Rather, in this era of financial liberalization, it seeks to provide the public with the knowledge necessary to make informed financial decisions. Nonetheless, one could argue that the Central Council for Financial Services Information continues to reinforce a culture of thrift in Japan. The organization still provides households with "advice on life planning," and in schools it sponsors financial education programs designed to teach children how to spend and save wisely (see Nishimura, chap. 11).[10]

While the state encouraged saving, postwar officials by no means discouraged the general expansion of consumption. As Japanese incomes grew, households became capable of significantly increasing *both* saving and spending (see Horioka, chap. 5). By the end of the 1950s, notes Simon

[9] Sheldon Garon, "Luxury is the Enemy: Mobilizing Savings and Popularizing Thrift in Wartime Japan," *Journal of Japanese Studies* 26, no. 1 (Winter 2000): 41–78.

[10] Central Council for Financial Services Information, August 2005, http://www.saveinfo.or.jp.

Partner, economic planners and industrialists regarded consumption as a "key ingredient in the political economy of high growth." Exports alone would not sustain rapid growth, they recognized; Japanese industry also required a vibrant home market. Japanese consumers rapidly acquired television sets, refrigerators, and washing machines—many of them purchased on the installment plan (see Gordon, chap. 6). In 1959, the Economic Planning Agency officially acknowledged the existence of a "consumer revolution," and the government-sponsored Japan Productivity Center promoted consumer demand for Japanese products.[11]

We must not, however, conflate the growth of consumption in Japan with the rise of an American-style consumer culture privileging consumption over thrift. Japanese consumers often afforded costly durables only by severely cutting back on other expenditures, including housing.[12] Savings-promotion efforts further discouraged certain types of consumption by instructing households to distinguish "sound" or "rational" spending from "wasteful" consumption (see figure 7.1). This discourse had first surfaced in the 1920s among officials, progressive thinkers, home economists, and editors of housewives' magazines. These figures instructed the masses to "improve daily life" by "rationalizing" consumption and keeping detailed household account books. They advised households that it was good to spend money on nutritious foods and modern, efficient kitchens but irrational to buy luxuries. Because modern Japan confronted endemic trade *deficits* until the 1960s, the savings campaigns often coded "luxuries" as imports. The populace was repeatedly exhorted to avoid purchasing fancy imported goods and instead augment their savings, which would then be invested in Japanese industry. The 1920s and early 1930s also witnessed the beginnings of the "buy national products" campaigns (*kokusan aiyō undō*). Government-related groups revived these campaigns during the 1950s, and savings campaigns urged Japanese to eschew foreign goods under the slogan "Promote Exports and Conserve Foreign Exchange." In the early 1960s, even after proclaiming the "consumer revolution," the government exhorted households to economize because excessive consumption had worsened Japan's trade deficit.[13] As late as 1997, the Central Council for Savings Promotion still advised households to live a "life that strikes a balance between saving and consumption."[14] Mired in a protracted economic

[11] Simon Partner, *Assembled in Japan: Electrical Goods and the Making of the Japanese Consumer* (Berkeley: University of California Press, 1999), 3, 168–70; and Patricia L. Maclachlan, *Consumer Politics in Postwar Japan: The Institutional Boundaries of Citizen Activism* (New York: Columbia University Press, 2002), 86, 94.

[12] Partner, *Assembled in Japan,* 163–65.

[13] Sheldon Garon, "Japan's Post-war 'Consumer Revolution,' or Striking a 'Balance' between Consumption and Saving," in *Consuming Cultures, Global Perspectives: Historical Trajectories, Transnational Exchanges,* ed. John Brewer and Frank Trentmann (Oxford: Berg, 2006); and Garon, "Saving for 'My Own Good,'" 106–7, 113.

[14] Chochiku kōhō chūō iinkai, "Chochiku kōhō chūō iinkai undō hōshin" [Program of Central Council for Savings Information], 1997 (mimeo), 1.

これからも
家計のプランに
創業八十周年
郵便貯金

Figure 7.1. "I'll Keep Planning Our Household Finances." The housewife as saver and rational consumer (Postal savings poster, Japan, 1955). Poster XD-C 50, Communications Museum, Tokyo.

slump since 1991, Japan's ubiquitous housewives magazines have reinforced official messages by routinely instructing housewives in techniques of saving and economizing.[15]

A final element in this story has been the recent effort to export the Japanese model of savings promotion to the rest of Asia. Following World War II, international organizations and economists advised developing nations to "mobilize domestic savings" to finance growth.[16] By the 1960s, Japan had become the poster child in this international campaign. Led by the influential planner Ōkita Saburō and his Japan Economic Research Center, Japanese economists touted high saving rates and "low consumption" in explaining their nation's rapid economic growth—and "its implications for developing countries."[17] Although at the time the Japanese govern-

15 E.g., "Watashitachi no tame-teku & setsuyaku waza" [Our techniques for saving and economizing], *Shufu no tomo* [Housewife's companion] 86, no. 10 (July 2002): 68–85.

16 "Measures for Mobilising Domestic Saving for Productive Investment," *Economic Bulletin for Asia and the Far East* (United Nations) 13, no. 3 (December 1962): 1.

17 Saburo Okita, *Causes and Problems of Rapid Growth in Postwar Japan and Their Implications for Newly Developing Economies* (Tokyo: Japan Economic Research Center, 1967), 2, 12–14, 20–29.

ment did not systematically seek to shape Asian developmental strategies, it embarked on a more missionary course after the yen sharply appreciated against the U.S. dollar from 1985 to 1987. As Japanese businesses heavily invested in Southeast Asian production and the government rapidly increased aid to the region, Japanese officials confidently counseled Southeast Asian states to mobilize household savings. Japan's Postal Savings Bureau played a leading role, funding yearly meetings of Asia's government savings bank officials (primarily from Southeast Asia). In such forums, Japanese bureaucrats trumpeted the applicability of postal savings to other nations, citing its historical successes in establishing the "idea of saving in the minds of the people," curbing inflation, accumulating capital, stabilizing the "livelihood of the depositor," and bringing about the "stabilisation of society at large."[18] Similarly, the Bank of Japan sponsored working seminars on "Savings Promotion" that brought together central bank officials from Asia and the Pacific.[19]

We next turn to the impact of Japan's decades-long promotion of saving and economizing on its Asian neighbors.

South Korea

South Korea most faithfully emulated Japanese programs for encouraging saving. This is hardly surprising. Under Japan's colonial rule (1910–45), the Japanese trained most of those who would later staff the Republic of Korea's bureaucracy, schools, businesses, and military. Indeed, Japanese-trained officers dominated the South Korean military as late as 1980. Even after independence, despite official anti-Japanism, Korean elites continued to study Japanese policies. They read and spoke Japanese better than any other foreign language, and many admired postwar Japan's rapid economic growth.[20]

Moreover, the South Korea regime inherited the infrastructure of savings promotion from Japanese colonial rule. Japan's postal savings system more deeply influenced colonial Korea than any of Japan's other overseas territories. By the end of 1944, Korea boasted more than 13 million postal

[18] "Fourth Meeting of the Advisory Committee and Meeting of ISBI Members in the Asia-Pacific Region, Tokyo, Japan, 25–27 May 1989: Minutes," doc. 371, pp. 47, 50, Archives of International Savings Banks Institute, Brussels.

[19] E.g., the 3rd Bank of Japan/World Bank Joint Seminar for Central Bankers from Asian Countries in Transition: Savings Promotion, February 25–March 3, 1998, Tokyo; also, 19th Bank of Japan Seminar for SEANZA Central Banks: Savings Promotion, September 16–23, 1997, Tokyo. See papers held by Savings Information Division, Bank of Japan.

[20] Bruce Cumings, "The Legacy of Japanese Colonialism in Korea," in *The Japanese Colonial Empire, 1895–1945,* ed. Ramon H. Myers and Mark R. Peattie (Princeton: Princeton University Press, 1984), 479, 495; and John Lie, *Han Unbound: The Political Economy of South Korea* (Stanford: Stanford University Press, 1998), 59–61.

savings accounts—five times the number in Taiwan.[21] Even if each depositor held two or three accounts, some 5 or 6 million Koreans had become accustomed to saving at the post office. After 1945, the new South Korean regime quickly moved to make postal savings a Korean institution. In addition, Korean officials continued the colonial state's practice of organizing the people into national savings associations and other semiofficial associations. Many of these associations dated back to the 1930s, when under the Rural Revitalization Campaign the colonial authorities and local elites formed village-level bodies to encourage Koreans to plan their finances, reduce debts, and increase saving.[22]

In the course of the Korean War, the Republic of Korea also reinstated the type of war savings campaign experienced under Japanese rule. Faced with the urgent need to finance rebuilding after the massive destruction of the war's first months, the government in 1951 mounted the "Campaign to Save for Certain Victory." Organizers adopted the old Japanese slogans nearly verbatim, and they set a national savings target, as had their former colonial masters.[23] And just as Japan's wartime regime had established the National Savings Promotion Council, the South Korean state instituted its own National Savings Promotion Council in 1952. The council worked closely with the Bank of Korea's new Savings Section, sitting atop a hierarchy of organizations reaching down to village and town savings-promotion committees. True to the wartime Japanese model, Korean officials concentrated on increasing the number of national savings associations in neighborhoods and workplaces.[24] In one government-issued handbill, "How to Develop the National Savings Campaign" (1955), campaign organizers unwittingly revealed the profound legacies of Japanese practices (see figure 7.2). The illustration depicted various methods of propagating thrift: lectures and discussions with residents, touring squads to enlighten the villages, blaring sound trucks, oratorical contests, children's banks, stronger savings associations, and badges of honor and commendations for good savers.

Although the campaigns of the 1950s expanded the grass-roots organization of savings promotion, they did little to increase household savings.

[21] Postal Division, "Survey of the Postal Savings Bank System," May 3, 1947, Civil Communications Section, Box 3181, Supreme Commander of the Allied Powers, RG 331, National Archives and Records Administration, College Park, Maryland.

[22] Gi-Wook Shin and Do-Hyun Han, "Colonial Corporatism: The Rural Revitalization Campaign, 1932–1940," in *Colonial Modernity in Korea,* ed. Gi-Wook Shin and Michael Robinson (Cambridge: Harvard University Asia Center, 1999), 70, 83, 87–88.

[23] Hanguk ŭnhaeng [Bank of Korea], *Chigŭm ŭn jŏchuk I jolsil I pilyohan tae imnida* [Now is the time to save] (Seoul: Bank of Korea, 1997), 5, translated for the author by Soyoung Lee.

[24] Korea taehakkyo kyŭngjae yonguso [Korea University, Economics Institute] *Kukmin jŏchuk undong banghyang gwa chujin jogik ui palchŏn bangan* [Proposal for development of promotional organizations of national savings campaigns] (Seoul: Korea taehakkyo kyŭngjae yonguso, 1996), 21, 24–26, translated for the author by Sangho Ro.

Figure 7.2. "How to Develop the National Savings Campaign," by Kim Yong-hwan (Korea, 1955). Hanguk ŭnhaeng, *Chigŭm ŭn jŏchuk I jolsil I pilyohan tae imnida* (Seoul: Bank of Korea, 1977), 8.

Most Koreans were too poor to put aside much, and high levels of inflation further discouraged saving. Moreover, unlike early postwar Japan, where low-cost foreign capital was scarce, the South Korean government and economy relied on massive U.S. aid and loans.[25]

The cause of savings promotion took on new vigor under the authoritarian rule of President Park Chung-hee. Park came to power in a military coup in 1961 and governed until his assassination in 1979. Like many South Korean officers, the president had earned his spurs in the Japanese-led Manchurian Army in World War II. During the 1960s, Park became enamored of not only Japan's postwar model of economic development but also the prewar Japanese regime's revolutionary success in molding a people willing to sacrifice for the nation-state. He promptly established a Japanese-style National Reconstruction Movement to mobilize youth groups, women's associations, and other semiofficial organizations. The movement's nationwide network promoted a "self-help spirit," the "elimination of empty courtesies and rituals," "rice saving," and the "rationalization of living." Park described these activities as part of a "New Life system." This was a clear reference to postwar Japan's "New Life movement," which similarly aimed at persuading people to improve their daily lives by "rationalizing consumption" and saving money.[26]

Soon after taking power, President Park declared his leading models to be Japan's "Meiji Reform" and West Germany's "Miracle on the Rhine." To

[25] Korea taehakkyo, *Kukmin jŏchuk,* 21; and Alice H. Amsden, *Asia's Next Giant: South Korea and Late Industrialization* (New York: Oxford University Press, 1989), 39.

[26] Chung Hee Park, *The Country, the Revolution and I,* 2d ed. (Seoul: Hollym Corp., 1970), 93, also 111, 120. For the New Life campaigns in Japan, see Sheldon Garon, *Molding Japanese Minds: The State in Everyday Life* (Princeton: Princeton University Press, 1997), ch. 5.

achieve a comparable "'miracle' on the Han River," Koreans would need to adopt "an austere living atmosphere" in which "spending should be checked in favor of savings." In his first Five-Year Plan for Economic Development, Park pledged to boost domestic savings—"the most promising of domestic resources"—in order to finance high growth, export-led development, and an "independent economy" that would be less reliant on foreign capital. For his role model of frugality Park initially chose the West Germans, who might have seemed more appealing than the less popular Japanese. These Germans were "sparing in eating, clothing and spending. Austerity and savings were ruthlessly practiced by every individual." Park particularly praised German financiers for their patriotic patterns of consumption: "They rode in German cars while traveling, ate German bread, used German film and German waste paper." Traveling to Italy and Switzerland, they "left nothing but waste paper and excrements."[27]

By the late 1960s, Japan had replaced West Germany as Park's working model. Within the South Korean bureaucracy, emulation of Japanese economic policies became standard operating procedure following the normalization of Japanese-Korean relations in 1965. If there were any doubts that the Republic of Korea had adopted the Japanese approach to encouraging saving, the president would dispel them in 1969, when he created the Central Council of Savings Promotion within the Bank of Korea. The similarity in name with the Bank of Japan's own Central Council for Savings Promotion was more than a coincidence. Savings-promotion officials in the two central banks actively shared information in the inauguration and subsequent operation of Korea's Central Council.[28] Like its Japanese namesake, the Central Council of Savings Promotion sought to promote a "voluntary savings movement" and the people's "enlightenment in the spirit of thrift."[29] The Korean council also sponsored nationwide activities to encourage saving in the schools, model savings districts, companies, and the *Saemaŭl* (New Community) organizations. Personal saving rates steadily rose in the 1970s and 1980s during the heyday of the Central Council's campaigns (from 9 percent in 1975 to 17.6 percent in 1989). These increases in part reflected rising real incomes, but Korean economists and officials also cite the contributions of the government's moral suasion drives and the introduction of attractive savings instruments.[30]

Women's groups provided most of the foot soldiers in the savings cam-

[27] Park, *The Country, the Revolution,* 176–77, also 66–67, 111, 147.

[28] Chochiku zōkyō chūō iinkai, *Chochiku undōshi: Chozōi 30 nen no ayumi* [History of savings campaigns: 30 years of Central Council for Savings Promotion] (Tokyo: Chochiku zōkyō chūō iinkai, 1983), 84.

[29] Korea taehakkyo, *Kukmin jŏchuk,* 22–23.

[30] Interview with Park Jongkyu, June 4, 2001; Jongkyu Park and Jin-Yeong Kim, *Declining Saving Rate: Macroeconomic and Microeconomic Evidences* [in Korean] (Seoul: Korea Institute of Public Finance, 2000), 11; Bank of Korea, *Annual Report, 1979* (Seoul: Bank of Korea, 1980), 8.

paigns, much as they did in Japan. In 1967, officials formed the Women's Central Council for Savings Life, incorporating some twenty women's associations. This women's council became an integral part of the Central Council of Savings Promotion. The convergence between Korean and Japanese practice extended to everyday gender relations and norms. Korean officials and women's organizations alike trumpeted the housewife as the household's primary saver and financial manager, just as Japanese had done a generation or two before. Likewise, the Korean savings campaigns achieved considerable success in normalizing the practice in which housewives keep highly detailed household account books.[31] Called *kakeibo* in Japanese and *kagaebu* in Korean, the government-issued account books were nearly identical, revealing the large degree of Korean emulation. In both nations, the household account book has served as a crucial tool in motivating households to contain consumption and increase savings.

While encouraging saving, Korea's Central Council of Savings Promotion and allied groups went further than their Japanese counterparts in inculcating critiques of consumption itself. Korea's most visible campaigns from the 1970s to the mid-1990s went by the name of "frugality campaigns," with the emphasis placed on the restraint of consumption. The frugality campaigns communicated several imperatives: (1) eliminate "excessive consumption" and wasteful ceremonial expenses, (2) improve the nation's trade balance by buying Korean products and eschewing foreign "luxuries," and (3) augment national savings and investment in national production by curbing unnecessary purchases. In a typical poster in 1988, the Central Council of Savings Promotion warned shoppers to "Give End-of-the-Year and New Year's Presents Only According to Your Standing" (basically, "Don't Try to Keep up with the Joneses"). As recently as 1996, another Central Council poster cast "consumption" as impeding national progress:

> We are right now at the crossroads. At the threshold of the advanced countries.
> Are you turning away from saving, thinking of consumption as a virtue?
> Now is the time to wise up to thrift.
> Save!
> This is our bright future.[32]

The frugality campaigns did not curb the growing consumer appetites of Koreans. Yet as levels of consumption rapidly rose in the 1980s, these drives did reinforce popular anxieties that the burgeoning consumer culture was widening the gap between the nouveaux riches and the poor while eroding Korean's national identity. The recurrent frugality campaigns

[31] Korea taehakkyo, *Kukmin jŏchuk,* 21–22.

[32] The two posters appear in Hanguk ŭnhaeng, *Chigŭm ŭn jŏchuk I jolsil I pilyohan tae imnida,* 19, 21.

played an important role in persuading South Koreans to work long hours and make consumer choices based on a calculus of what would be good for the nation (see Nelson, chap. 8).[33]

It is worth exploring the origins of South Korea's aggressive measures toward shaping popular consumption. The Japanese imprint is unmistakable. The anti-import messages were surely influenced by Japan's "buy national products" campaigns of the interwar era and 1950s. Likewise, imperatives to "rationalize" consumption and reduce the costs of weddings and funerals owed much to the prewar Japanese "daily life improvement" campaigns and the postwar New Life movement. Even the term for "frugality" used in the Korean campaigns derives from the twentieth-century Japanese word for "economizing" (*setsuyaku*) rather than older East Asian terms for "frugality."

In addition, indigenous and western thought interacted with Japanese influences to produce Korea's "consumer nationalism." The frugality campaigns accentuated their Koreanness by building on neo-Confucian ideals from the Yi Dynasty (1392–1910). The era's *yangban* elite (scholar-officials) extolled the virtues of simplicity, frugality, and austerity. And in their resistance to imported goods, the recent campaigns modeled themselves not only on Japan's "buy national products" drives but also, ironically, on colonial-era Korean movements that had urged the Korean people to boycott *Japanese* goods and buy Korean manufactures. Notable were the activities of the Korean Products Promotion Society, founded in 1922 by Cho Mansik, the Presbyterian secretary-general of the Pyongyang YMCA. Indeed, Korean Protestants played a prominent role in the historical development of the frugality campaigns. As in prewar Japan, Christians melded Confucian and Protestant ideals of austerity and thrift, often serving as leading spokesmen in the regime's savings campaigns. Yet whereas Japanese Christians never accounted for more than 1 percent of the population, Christianity in Korea has grown steadily to embrace roughly one-fourth of the South Korean population today. The Seoul YMCA worked closely with the government in the frugality campaigns of the last two decades. In 1986, the Seoul YMCA sponsored the "Social Forum for the Cultivation of the Consciousness of a Wholesome Consumer Lifestyle." Bemoaning Korean society's "extravagance [*sach'i*] and an all-out dedication to pleasure," speakers advocated "ascetism" and saving to solve the nation's problems.[34] When the U.S. special trade representative in 1990 attacked one frugality campaign for obstructing American imports, it was a Korean Presbyterian minister who rebuked her for maligning Koreans' dedication to hard work, providence, and frugality.[35]

[33] See also Nelson, *Measured Excess,* 2, 18–19, 23–25, 114.

[34] Nelson, *Measured Excess,* 115–16, also 107–11.

[35] *Los Angeles Times,* November 25, 1991, sec. D, p. 3.

The South Korean state was actively promoting saving and discouraging "excessive consumption" as late as 1996 and 1997, at the time of the most recent frugality campaign. Western manufacturers and governments vociferously complained that this frugality drive amounted to an official anti-import campaign. The Korean government denied any involvement by the Bank of Korea, insisting disingenuously that the "frugality campaign is a voluntary movement by civic groups with a view to encouraging rational and reasonable consumption. It was not intended to discriminate [against] imports."[36] Yet beyond the western gaze, Korean officials were not only encouraging saving but also lauding the Japanese model. In its savings-promotion measures, commented one government-sponsored study in 1996, contemporary Korea "resembles Japan of the old days." Korea had "followed" the Japanese model in many respects, and it would likely do so in the future. Even as foreigners in the 1980s complained about Japan's growing balance of payments surpluses, noted the researchers, the Japanese campaigns continued to urge people to save—no longer to accumulate capital, but for the needs of a rapidly aging society. "There is much for us to study here," the report concluded.[37]

The vision of South Korea's Japanese trajectory soon proved to be wildly off the mark. The financial crisis of late 1997 opened up South Korea's economic governance to unprecedented outside scrutiny once the nation accepted a massive emergency loan from the IMF. Fearing western protests, the Bank of Korea quietly disbanded the thirty-eight-year-old Central Council of Savings Promotion at the end of 1997. American-trained officials and economists began to advocate a more consumption-driven economy, and the government and banks did an about-face by providing large amounts of consumer credit to the public (see Nelson, chap. 8). While the Japanese economy of thrifty consumers remained mired in stagnation, the South Korean economy reignited, in part because of expanding consumer credit and spending in 2001–02. Reflecting a common American view, the IMF's resident representative confidently predicted, "With its increased efficiency, restructured banking sector, and blooming consumer culture, Korea is emerging as the new model for Asian economies."[38] Yet as credit card and other household debt rose to American levels in 2003, Korean growth ground to a near-halt.[39] Whether the South Koreans will fully embrace the American model of high-level consumption remains to be seen. But its remarkable emulation of Japanese savings-promotion practices is likely a thing of the past.

[36] Ministry of Finance and Economy, "Korean Government Statement on Frugality Campaign on May 9, 1997," http://www.mofe.go.kr/P_R/ep051301.html.

[37] Korea taehakkyo, *Kukmin jŏchuk,* 48.

[38] Paul F. Gruenwald, "Korea and the IMF," in *Korea's Economy 2003* (Washington, D.C.: Korean Economic Institute, 2003), 11.

[39] Thomas Byrne, "The Korean Banking System Six Years after the Crisis," *Korea's Economy 2004* (Washington, D.C.: Korean Economic Institute, 2004), 17.

Singapore

Like the South Korean state before 1997, the government of Singapore has been no less impassioned about promoting saving over the past four decades. Nonetheless, Singapore has developed a unique approach that combines Japanese-style state encouragement of voluntary saving with an elaborate system of *compulsory* saving. The linchpin in the regime's promotion of savings is the Central Provident Fund. The CPF dates back to 1955 when Singapore was still under British colonial rule. It began life as an old-age pension fund into which employees and employers were each obligated to deposit a small fixed proportion of wages or salary. Beginning in 1968, members received permission to withdraw funds from their individual CPF accounts for the purposes of purchasing public-housing apartments and paying monthly mortgage installments. Thereafter contribution rates rose dramatically, peaking in the mid-1980s at 25 percent each from employee and employer (in 2005, the contribution rates are 20 percent from employee and 13 percent from employer). Besides financing housing and retirement, CPF funds may be withdrawn—with restrictions—to pay for medical and educational expenses.[40]

As the state expanded this compulsory savings program during the 1970s and 1980s, it also actively encouraged voluntary saving in banks and particularly the Post Office Savings Bank (POSB; later the POSBank). Singaporean households have managed to save relatively high percentages of their income even after making hefty contributions to their CPF accounts. By 1988, voluntary saving had reached 11 percent of gross income. The postal savings system lured savings by means of school savings programs, attractive "POSBank Girl" tellers, and other types of marketing schemes seen in Japan and elsewhere.[41]

Nowhere else in the world has the mobilization of savings been at the center of governance as much as in Singapore. The CPF and voluntary savings accounts first and foremost function as self-financed systems of social security in the absence of generous state-funded programs. Ideologically, the leadership of the ruling People's Action Party (PAP) has long touted these institutions as Singapore's self-help alternative to degenerate western welfare states. Politically, leaders envisioned the CPF and its encouragement of home ownership as giving the people "a deep and abiding stake in the country."[42] Economically, the Singaporean state has exercised complete control over the massive funds of both the CPF and POSB. The success of Singapore's industrial and social development policies owes much to the government's investment of these funds. For the purpose of

[40] Linda Low and T. C. Aw, *Housing a Healthy, Educated and Wealthy Nation through the CPF* (Singapore: Times Academic Press, 1997).

[41] Richard Lim, *Banking on a Virtue: POSBank, 1972–1997* (Singapore: POSBank, 1997), 21–22, 59, 75; and Low and Aw, *Housing a Healthy, Educated and Wealthy Nation,* 95, 99, 119.

[42] Labor Minister S. Rajaratnam, in *Straits Times,* June 2, 1973.

macroeconomic stabilization, the regime has often manipulated CPF contribution rates to improve Singapore's competitive position in world markets. Confronted by recession in 1986, the government sharply reduced labor costs by cutting only the *employer's* contribution rate from 25 to 10 percent.[43] Similarly, the authorities halved the employer's rate in the wake of the 1997 financial crisis.

The origins of Singapore's passion and institutions for promoting saving are by no means obvious. Were one to ask former prime minister Lee Kuan Yew (now the retired "Senior Minister"), he would invariably speak of the "Confucian values" of thrift that prevail among Singapore's Chinese majority. Beginning in the 1990s, the government shifted to promoting "Shared Values" in an effort to appeal to all of Singapore's three major ethnicities—the Chinese, the Malays, and the Indians. The Ministry of Education's current civics and moral education curriculum teaches the value of thrift by highlighting traditional sayings and folktales from each of the three cultures.[44]

Many western observers are skeptical of explanations based on Confucian or Asian values. A historical examination of Singaporean savings promotion lends credence to their suspicions. As in most countries, the modern encouragement of thrift in Singapore developed from the interplay of external and indigenous influences. We begin with the British legacy. It was, after all, the British who introduced the Post Office Savings Bank to colonial Singapore in 1877, just two years after the advent of Japan's own system.[45] The British also founded the Central Provident Fund in 1955 at a time when the government-run National Savings Movement back home was encouraging schoolchildren and adults to save. British attitudes profoundly shaped Lee Kuan Yew and several other English-educated leaders of the postcolonial People's Action Party. Called "Harry" until his thirties, Lee imbibed the paternalism of the former colonial masters in seeking to civilize the tropical inhabitants of his city-state. He disdained the Chinese business community as venal and backward during the 1960s. Not until the late 1970s would he discover the virtues of Confucianism.[46] As for Chinese culture's putative thriftiness, in the early 1970s Lee still had little faith in Singaporean workers, who "spend freely and save less." "So it is necessary," he concluded, that "we should *enforce* savings through CPF contributions."[47]

[43] Low and Aw, *Housing a Healthy, Educated and Wealthy Nation,* 86; and "Speech by Dr. Richard Hu, Minister of Finance, at the World Economic Forum Meeting in Geneva," September 8, 1987, Singapore Government Press Releases, National Archives of Singapore.

[44] "'Thrift' in Our Idioms, Sayings and Folktales" (typescript), Civic and Moral Education curriculum, Singapore, Ministry of Education, ca. June 2001.

[45] The Post Office Savings Bank, *The First Hundred Years of the Post Office Savings Bank of Singapore* (Singapore: Post Office Savings Bank, 1977), 10–11.

[46] Kian Woon Kwok, "How to be Singaporean, Chinese and Modern All at Once," *Straits Times,* October 25, 1998, p. 37; Zakaria, "Culture is Destiny," 125.

[47] Emphasis mine. *Straits Times,* April 28, 1974.

In addition, the Japanese model of savings-promotion significantly shaped Singapore's programs at several historical junctures. During World War II, Japan occupied Singapore for three and a half years. The Japanese, of course, mounted savings campaigns, and they expanded the colonial postal savings system throughout Malaya. Despite its harshness, the Japanese occupation's reliance on popular mobilization impressed those who would later lead independent Singapore. In the late 1950s and 1960s, Japanese direct investment in Singapore significantly increased, and Lee Kuan Yew and the new leadership eagerly sought the assistance of the Japanese government in industrializing the country. Singaporean planners studied the lessons of the Japanese developmental state, which had overcome resource limitations and lack of capital by mobilizing the savings of its people.[48]

Institutionally, the Japanese model of a mammoth postal savings system undoubtedly inspired the Singaporean officials who devised the mechanisms that similarly channeled popular savings to developmental projects. Although the CPF differs from Japanese postal savings, its role in financing Singapore's industrial policy closely followed Japan's successful example of the 1950s and 1960s. The influential finance minister Goh Keng Swee frequently cited postwar Japan's investment of a substantial part of its income in industrial expansion. In 1967, Goh set about to transform the moribund Post Office Savings Bank into an effective instrument for mobilizing national savings. As he envisioned it, the POSB—together with the compulsory CPF—would soak up the people's purchasing power and "provide the Government with a non-inflationary source of funds for the development of the infrastructure." Between 1972 and 1974, the government went beyond Japanese precedents to make the Ministry of Finance responsible not only for the investment of POSB funds, but for the bank itself.[49]

Goh opted for a path of development that nicely combined Japanese experience and Victorian virtues: "If I may be so presumptuous as to give advice to others [developing countries] . . . , I would ask them to throw away all the books published on economic growth since World War II. I would advise them instead to read the essays of Samuel Smiles—his exhortations to thrift, industry, ambition, honesty, perseverance, etc."[50] When later recalling how his "small island nation with no natural resources" achieved annual growth rates comparable only to contemporary Japan and South Korea, Goh singled out "one crucial element . . . to which inadequate attention was paid in the past. This is the role of domestic savings."[51] In the

[48] Hiroshi Shimizu and Hitoshi Hirakawa, *Japan and Singapore in the World Economy: Japan's Economic Advance into Singapore, 1870–1965* (London: Routledge, 1999), 4, 113, 161, 183–84.

[49] Lim, *Banking on a Virtue,* 20–21, 29–30, 34.

[50] Keng Swee Goh, *The Economics of Modernization* (1972; repr. Singapore: Federal Publications, 1995), 35, also 220.

[51] Keng Swee Goh, *Wealth of East Asian Nations* (Singapore: Federal Publications, 1995), 78.

realm of education as well, elementary schoolchildren recently studied "The Story of Japan's Industrial Development," from which they were expected to learn "about the qualities of the Japanese such as a thrifty people and positive work attitude."[52]

Lastly, Singapore's ambitious promotion of saving has had much to do with the dynamic, self-confident leadership of the People's Action Party. The PAP's founding fathers not only mediated transnational influences from Britain, Japan, and other nations but repeatedly innovated as they expanded the CPF. The leadership deftly drew on a string of successes to cultivate among the public a myth of themselves as infallible visionaries.[53] Goh Keng Swee in 1972 likened PAP leaders to Moses leading the Israelites to the Promised Land, having "to exhort the faithful, encourage the fainthearted and censure the ungodly." Lee Kuan Yew was blunter still in 1986: "I am often accused of interfering in the private lives of citizens. Yet, if I did not, had I not done that, we wouldn't be here today. . . . We decide what is right. Never mind what the people think."[54]

Like Japanese and South Korean officials, Singaporean leaders have been wary of too much consumption. In 1974, Lee warned that the nation was "caught in the meshes of consumer society"; ads urged people to "buy what they do not really need, as finance companies and other mechanisms encourage people to buy now and pay later."[55] Concerned about rising consumer credit, especially among the young, the government today strictly controls the issuance of personal loans and credit cards, requiring substantial income to qualify. The Ministry of Education recently redoubled its efforts at thrift education in the conviction, as one official explained, that "now, more than ever, we must arrest consumerism."[56] Nonetheless, to restrain consumption, the Singaporean state has relied less on moral suasion than in South Korea and Japan. With a population of less than five million, the city-state thrives on free trade, depending on both exports and entrepôt trade. Mounting a series of "buy national products" drives would have been economic suicide. Moreover, the one-party regime recognized early on that sustained improvements in consumption could buy popular support in lieu of permitting genuine democratic participation. In this "air-conditioned nation," comments Cherian George, the government at first provided basic public housing but was then compelled to cater to the

[52] "'Thrift' in Our Syllabuses" (typescript), Singapore, Ministry of Education, ca. June 2001.

[53] Low and Aw, *Housing a Healthy, Educated and Wealthy Nation*, 86.

[54] Goh and Lee, quoted in Low and Aw, *Housing a Healthy, Educated and Wealthy Nation*, 86, 11–12.

[55] *Straits Times*, 28 April 1974.

[56] Interview with Lee Kah Chuen (deputy director, Humanities and Aesthetics Branch, Curriculum Planning and Development Division), Ministry of Education, Singapore, June 21, 2001.

growing consumer appetite for, among other items, air conditioning.[57] Not that the leadership has encouraged unrestrained consumption. Singapore's government simply has less need to dissuade the people from extravagance because—through the CPF—it retains the capacity to drain purchasing power (by raising contribution rates) while directing much of a family's consumption toward housing.

Malaysia

Of the cases presented, Malaysia's emulation of Japanese-style campaigns is the most recent. At the beginning of the twenty-first century, this Southeast Asian nation was Japan's most enthusiastic student. Like Singapore, the former British colony inherited a compulsory savings program, the Employees Provident Fund (EPF). However, unlike Singapore, the EPF permits only limited withdrawals to finance home buying. Its rates of contribution have, moreover, been below those of the CPF (in 2005, 11 percent from employees and 12 percent from employers). Nonetheless, the EPF's accumulations are quite large, functioning as "the major source of non-inflationary funding for the government's development expenditure needs."[58]

Similarly, the Malaysian state has devoted substantial resources to stimulating voluntary savings. In 1974, the government transformed the sleepy colonial-era Post Office Savings Bank into the National Savings Bank (Bank Simpanan Nasional), which became the leading force in mobilizing small savings and encouraging school savings. As in Japan and Singapore, National Savings Bank funds have directly financed national economic development.[59] Indeed, the National Savings Bank expanded during the late 1980s in conscious emulation of the postal savings institutions of the successful Asian developmental states. Information-sharing among the region's economic bureaucracies occurred in a number of forums, including ASEAN (Association of Southeast Asian Nations). Malaysia's National Savings Bank derived the most useful knowledge from the little-known but influential Regional Office for Asia and the Pacific, part of the International Savings Banks Institute (ISBI). The ISBI's leading members represented European postal savings systems and associations of local savings banks as well as Japan's gargantuan postal savings bank. As new theories of eco-

[57] Cherian George, *Singapore: The Air-Conditioned Nation: Essays on the Politics of Comfort and Control* (Singapore: Landmark Books, 2000), 15–17.

[58] Al' Alim Ibrahim, ed., *Generating a National Savings Movement: Proceedings of the First Malaysian National Savings Conference, Kuala Lumpur, July 8–10, 1993* (Kuala Lumpur: ISIS Malaysia, 1994), iii.

[59] Bank Negara Malaysia, *The Central Bank and the Financial System in Malaysia: A Decade of Change* (Kuala Lumpur: Bank Negara Malaysia, 1999), 513.

nomic development emphasized the mobilization of domestic savings, the ISBI supported the expansion of savings promotion in Southeast Asia, founding its regional office in Bangkok, Thailand, in 1973. Beginning in the mid-1980s, representatives of Asia's government savings institutions (primarily postal savings banks) met annually and routinely exchanged information and personnel in ISBI-sponsored forums. The Southeast Asian nations of Malaysia, Singapore, Thailand, and Indonesia assumed leadership in the transnational organization—financially assisted, as we have seen, by Japan's Postal Savings Bureau.[60]

Not until the 1990s, however, did the Malaysian state develop significant interest in the Japanese model of savings promotion. Malaysia had not been one of the "Four Dragons" (South Korea, Taiwan, Hong Kong, and Singapore) that exhibited dramatic economic growth in the 1970s. The Malaysian economy's high growth became apparent only in the late 1980s. By the early 1990s, officials worried that savings were insufficient to sustain investment in the surging economy. Stepping up its commitment to the "promotion of savings and the savings habit," the central bank exhorted consumers to fight inflationary pressures: "Spending on luxuries and unnecessaries should be discouraged and prudence in spending would be necessary."[61] At the government-sponsored First Malaysian National Savings Conference in 1993, organizers observed that the newly industrialized East Asian economies illustrated "a direct and casual correlation between high national savings and high economic performance." Finance Minster Anwar Ibrahim voiced additional concerns about declining saving rates as Malaysians spent more on "luxury goods" and engaged in "conspicuous consumption": "It is important that our society becomes more disciplined."[62]

Ideology has been central to Malaysia's mobilization of domestic savings. Mahathir bin Mohamad, the charismatic prime minister who ruled from 1981 to 2003, championed pan-Asian unity as a counterweight to western hegemony. Throughout the 1990s, he warned of the political dangers of relying on foreign capital:

> Countries that are too dependent on their foreign capital for their investment activities will be vulnerable to the interests of foreign countries, their

[60] "International Savings Banks Institute ISBI Regional Office in Southeast Asia," *Savings Banks International* (International Savings Banks Institute, Geneva), no. 3 (Autumn 1980), 46; and "Meeting of the Advisory Committee and Meeting of ISBI Members in the Asia-Pacific Region, Kuala Lumpur, Malaysia, 15–18 January 1991: Minutes," doc. 373, Archives of International Savings Banks Institute, Brussels.

[61] Bank Negara Malaysia, *Annual Report, 1990* (Kuala Lumpur: Bank Negara Malaysia, 1991), 125, 127.

[62] Anwar Ibrahim, "Keynote Address," in *Generating a National Savings Movement,* ed. Al' Alim Ibrahim, xi–xii, translated for the author by Janine Yoong. See also "Introduction," i–ii.

> economic movements, and global finance. As can be seen from the world economy recently, the sentiments of foreign investors can change according to developments that have nothing to do with domestic economic developments. Although we will continue to welcome foreign investments into Malaysia, we need to be prepared to have our own capabilities that we determine ourselves.[63]

In 1996, the government established the Cabinet Committee on the Promotion of Savings, and proceeded to launch a national savings campaign. In the face of the next year's Asian financial crisis, Malaysia alone eschewed IMF assistance, and Mahathir imposed currency controls to shield Malaysia's economy from the vicissitudes of international finance. The new national savings campaign became all the more important in advancing his goal of a more self-sufficient Malaysian economy. Besides promoting thrift, the campaign instructed the nation to avoid imported goods and "buy locally made products" in order to advance economic recovery.[64]

Moreover, the savings campaigns formed part of Mahathir's efforts to assist ethnic Malays (the Bumiputra) in catching up to the wealthier Chinese and Indian minorities. In the year 2000, some 58 percent of the population was ethnically Malay, 24 percent Chinese, and 8 percent Indian. This program was as much social policy as political patronage. In the wake of murderous communal violence in 1968, leaders of all ethnic groups embraced the goal of closing the economic gap between Malays and Chinese. Since the late 1970s, the government has attempted to build up the assets of Malays through special banks and unit trusts that provide highly attractive, above-market rates of returns. The state also manages "Islamic banking," which encourages thrift within Islamic strictures. Among other things, Islamic banking promotes saving to enable Malays to make the pilgrimage (*Hajj*) to Mecca. Officials have made it one of their key missions to persuade the Bumiputra to abandon their traditional spendthrift ways.[65]

In devising the savings campaigns, Malaysian leaders freely acknowledged the importance of the Japanese model. Mahathir was Asia's most outspoken admirer of Japan. In 1981, he announced Malaysia's "Look East" policy, aimed at introducing a Japanese work ethic and managerial attitudes. Economically, Mahathir employed this policy to lure considerable Japanese foreign direct investment to Malaysia.[66] Culturally, he envi-

[63] "Speech of the Prime Minister Y. A. B. Dato Seri Mahathir Bin Mohamad at the Launching Ceremony of the National Savings Campaign," December 16, 1996, trans. Janine Yoong, http://www.bnm.gov.my/feature/sav/spch_PM.htm.

[64] "People Helping in Economic Recovery: Dr. Mahathir," *Bernama* (Malaysian National News Agency), August 29, 1998; and Bank Negara Malaysia, *Annual Report, 1996,* p. 71.

[65] Bank Negara Malaysia, *Central Bank and the Financial System,* 243–53, 530–31; and interview with Hasbullah bin Abdullah (Manager, Financial Planning and Savings Secretariat), Bank Negara Malaysia, Kuala Lumpur, June 25, 2001.

[66] Hua Sing Lim, *Japan's Role in Asia,* 3d ed. (Singapore: Times Academic Press, 2001), 1.

sioned Japan as the leader and teacher of Asia, standing up to a degenerate West plagued by family breakdown and "hedonistic values."[67]

At the policy level, Malaysian bureaucrats in the central bank—the Bank Negara Malaysia—gravitated toward the Japanese model of savings promotion for a number of reasons. Japan, they noted, had achieved a high saving rate despite the lack of resources. It offered the example of a central agency dedicated to promoting saving by means of an extensive grassroots network. Also, as a substantial investor in Southeast Asia, Japan enjoyed significant influence in the region.[68] Following the establishment of the Cabinet Committee on the Promotion of Savings, Bank Negara officials visited the Bank of Japan's Central Council for Savings Information in 1997, returning with a trove of savings campaign materials. In 1998, the Bank Negara set up a Japanese-style Savings Promotion Secretariat to coordinate the campaigns. It was during those years that Japan's Central Council for Savings Information sponsored major conferences on savings promotion for Asian central bank officials, of whom the Malaysians were the most enthusiastic.

Having chosen the Japanese model, the Bank Negara's staff set about translating the core documents and objectives of Japanese savings campaigns. Like their Japanese counterparts, the Malaysian campaigns targeted women, students, and workers. In 1998, the Savings Promotion Secretariat began distributing translated household account books to women and "pocket money books" to schoolchildren—aiming in the latter case at "inculcating the savings habit" and assisting students in "monitoring their spending habits." Nor did the translations stop there. As in Japan, officials sponsored national training programs in "household financial management" for leaders of women's organizations. There, the women were taught the importance of budgeting, "life planning," and "economizing and conserving resources." Benefiting from the long experience of Japanese campaign organizers, Malaysian bureaucrats sought to assure households that it was possible both to save and to spend, as long as one consumed "efficiently." The key, as it had been in Japan, was to recognize "the importance of the need to balance consumption and savings."[69]

Malaysian savings-promotion officials face the challenge, as one put it, of "tropicalizing" Japanese campaign techniques.[70] Many of the problems of adapting the Japanese model to Malaysia lie in differences in social

[67] Mahathir Mohamad and Shintaro Ishihara, *The Voice of Asia: Two Leaders Discuss the Coming Century* (Tokyo: Kodansha International, 1995), 46–47, 80–81, 130–32.

[68] Interview with Vijayaledchumy Veluppillai (director, Economics Department), Bank Negara Malaysia, Kuala Lumpur, June 25, 2001.

[69] "Savings Promotion Campaign," PowerPoint Presentation, Financial Management and Savings Secretariat, June 25, 2001.

[70] Interview with Hasbullah bin Abdullah, June 25, 2001.

structures, notably in gender relations. Malaysian society generally lacks the Japanese or South Korean norm of the full-time housewife who takes control of her husband's salary and manages household finances. In the absence of such Malaysian housewives, the Bank Negara–issued household account books have often failed to stimulate saving. In an effort to persuade Malaysian women to keep regular accounts, the Bank Negara simplified its household account book from the original Japanese version. Even then, Malaysian women and their organizations have not been as enthusiastic about the savings campaigns as the organizers would have liked. In 2001, I visited two high-ranking officials of the Ministry of Women and Family Development tasked with mobilizing the nation's women's organizations behind the Bank Negara's savings campaign. When the conversation turned to the distribution of household account books, one of the officials—a woman—shrugged and replied: "Oh, I tried keeping one of those account books myself, but it's so much work. I gave up after three months."[71]

Whither the "Japanese Model"?

Finally, we must consider the current predicament of the Japanese developmental model in Asia after a decade of Japanese economic stagnation punctuated by the Asian financial crisis of 1997. One would have expected the universal repudiation of Japanese-style savings promotion in the capitals of Asia. Yet the story is not so straightforward. To be sure, the last few years have witnessed many Asian economists questioning the utility of aggressively promoting saving. Within the Malaysian government itself, while some officials work hard to inculcate habits of thrift, there are as many or more who argue for stimulating domestic *consumption* in view of the slackening demand for Malaysian products in the United States and Japan.[72] In South Korea, rising consumer credit, ample foreign capital, and the end of statist savings promotion may portend an American-style political economy.

Nonetheless, years of concerted savings promotion in these Asian nations have left most leaders and ordinary people with a suspicion of the American economic norms that appear to privilege "excessive consumption." Widespread ambivalence toward consumption remains, even in South Korea. In the year 2000, President Kim Dae-jung himself exhorted the public to engage in "voluntary frugality." A "forcible anti-import drive" would be impossible due to foreign pressure, the president grudged, yet

[71] Interview with Amon Azla, Ministry of Women and Family Development, Kuala Lumpur, June 26, 2001.

[72] Interview with Vijayaledchumy Veluppillai, June 25, 2001.

the people needed to be warned that imports were growing "too fast."[73] Four years later, the Korean media was abuzz with stories of the "credit card problem," reporting on the sharp rise in indebtedness among millions of consumers. Although the government itself had actively encouraged credit card usage in 2002 by easing regulations, Bank of Korea Governor Park Seung recently blamed the ensuing slump on "inappropriate consumption" by individuals: "During the 2001–2002 period, people increased their spending excessively with credit cards and borrowing from financial services companies, neglecting savings (for a rainy day)." More saving, he concluded, would be needed to "fuel the nation's main growth engine of research and development investment."[74]

The Japanese, too, remain ambivalent about consumption. Most economic bureaucrats appreciate the need for expanded consumption if Japan again is to achieve significant growth. Yet among economists, bureaucrats, and politicians, one does not detect a new consensus on behalf of more robust American-style consumption, especially if it means a sharp decline in saving. On the contrary, the logic of saving remains remarkably strong in Japan, as elites and ordinary people worry that too little saving will impair Japanese households' ability to respond to economic downturns and the rapid aging of society. Witness the media response to the recent news that Japan's household saving rate plummeted from 9.8 percent in 2000 to a reported 6.9 percent in 2001. Rather than applaud the growth of consumption, the liberal *Asahi shinbun* warned of dire consequences: lower saving would result in less capital for Japanese industry and export production, and it would vastly increase the costs of government borrowing. Furthermore, declared the daily in not so neutral terms, a declining saving rate meant that Japan was becoming like America.[75] Japan may someday become a consumption-driven society like the United States, but it is also possible that Japanese anxieties about such a future could be mobilized to reinforce propensities to save.

Thrift is not a timeless Asian value, nor is it unique to Asians. But influenced by the pervasive moral suasion efforts of governments and allied groups, many Asian peoples have come to embrace thrift as what they perceive to be an enduring Asian value and a key marker of their national identities. As the head of Singapore's POSBank remarked in 1997, "promoting thrift" forms part of his "country's core values" and the national educational system's program to "nurture the Good Singaporean."[76] Moreover, for all the problems in the Japanese economy today, the Japa-

[73] "EU, U.S. Automakers Condemn S. Korean 'Frugality' Campaign," Kyodo News Service, Japan Economic Newswire, February 29, 2000.

[74] *Korea Times,* October 27, 2004.

[75] "Chochikuritsu kyūraku, Bei ni sekkin" [Savings rate plummets, approaches U.S.], *Asahi shinbun,* May 19, 2003, p. 5.

[76] Dileep Nair, in Lim, *Banking on a Virtue,* 86.

nese state's historical management of economy and society may still seem a better fit to many Asians than the American free market model. Leading Asian economies retain the institutional and ideological foundations upon which governments could revive the managed consumption and savings promotion of the recent past. And should the U.S. economy appear to stagnate or decline, they may do just that.

8

SOUTH KOREAN CONSUMER NATIONALISM

Women, Children, Credit, and Other Perils

LAURA C. NELSON

What people buy—as individuals and in the aggregate—and how they feel about buying things and spending money speaks volumes about cultural beliefs, history, social coherence, and personal values.[1] Moreover, changes in consumer culture both reflect and influence broader social phenomena. In times of rapid cultural change, an examination of consumer discourse and practices offers a grounded methodology for understanding the implications of diffuse cultural transformation. In the context of industrial development, changes in consumption (both as practice and as a domain of discourse) illuminate the struggles among state, business, and personal domains and forms of power. As this volume demonstrates, while these struggles may appear similar in various national and historical circumstances, the similarities may simultaneously reflect the transmission of ideas and practices among nations (see Garon, chap. 7) and mask distinct, local contests. In each case, the shifting domain of consumption calls up new images of appropriate citizenship, incorporating idealized traditions as well as novelty and cosmopolitanism, remaking cultural diversity in the context of globalization.

[1] This approach to studying consumption has a rich history including, perhaps foundationally, Thorstein Veblen's *The Theory of the Leisure Class* (1899; repr. Mineola, NY: Dover Publications, 1994). In the past two decades, the topic of consumption has attracted a number of scholars and generated some important work, including Pierre Bourdieu, *Distinction: A Social Critique of the Judgment of Taste* (London: Routledge and Kegan Paul, 1984); Arjun Appadurai, ed., *The Social Life of Things: Commodities in Cultural Perspective* (Cambridge: Cambridge University Press, 1986); Daniel Miller, *Material Culture and Mass Consumption* (Oxford: Basil Blackwell, 1987); and Victoria de Grazia, ed., *The Sex of Things: Gender and Consumption in Historical Perspective* (Berkeley: University of California Press, 1996).

The domain of consumption in South Korea has been politically charged since the first years of the nation's push to industrialize in the 1960s. At that time the Republic of Korea (South Korea) was one of the world's poorest countries, grouped (according to the United Nations) with Burma, the Congo, and India; average per capita annual income was less than $125.[2] The "economic miracle" that brought South Korea to its present level of affluence was achieved through capitalizing on certain geopolitical advantages, catching some lucky breaks in the rhythms of global commerce, and carefully orchestrating the activities of South Korean corporations and citizens in support of a particular kind of economic development. This last factor was of critical importance to South Korea's development strategy, and one of the principal tools for engaging citizen support was an appeal to patriotism through "appropriate" consumer behavior. This appeal, backed up with economic policies that restricted wages and stifled the consumer market, helped to keep labor costs low and saving rates high and muted the appearance of class differences through the early 1980s. In the process, the modest social role of "the consumer" (*sobija*) and a category of social behavior defined as the "consumer lifestyle" (*sobi saenghwal*) came to be central symbols in public discussions of mutual responsibility and the importance of preserving the (South) Korean character.

In this chapter I outline the development of a specific discourse of *responsible* consumer behavior in South Korea, examining the ways in which the terms of this discourse shifted with changing local circumstances. This discourse—a campaign against "excessive consumption" (*kwasobi*) and an attempt to define "appropriate consumption" (*ol parŭn sobi saenghwal*)—has had remarkable longevity in the face of enormous changes in South Korean cultural, political, and economic circumstances. Even as South Koreans pursue economic recovery and growth in the aftermath of the 1997 Asian financial crisis, old discursive themes reappear. Despite improvements in income distribution, anxiety about class divisions and a perceived growing gulf between rich and poor persist. Criticism of women consumers, prevalent in the 1980s and 1990s, is recapitulated in the current focus on the consumer practices of children and youth. And the recent proliferation of consumer credit cards—and a looming social and financial debacle around credit card defaults—has revived criticism from consumers who lack the idealized Korean consumer qualities of humility, patience, and frugality. The current discourse also reveals important changes in the ways South Korean consumers now weigh the present against the future—their own, and their nation's. These are all examples of the various qualities of the "discontent" produced by the achieve-

[2] United Nations, Department of Economic and Social Affairs, "Industrialization for Economic Development in the Under-Developed Countries," *World Economic Survey 1961* (New York: United Nations, 1962).

ment of prosperity and the attendant ability to engage in discretionary consumption.

South Korean Economic Development Strategies and Responsible Consumption: 1960–1980

It is impossible to understand the attitudes and behaviors of contemporary South Korean consumers without a brief background in Korean history. When Japan took control and then formally colonized Korea between 1905 and 1910, it seized a country that had been wrenched from a feudal system just thirty years earlier. Nineteenth-century Korea was largely a country of peasants and a limited group of *yangban* (persons of hereditary nobility). There were few cities worthy of the term, and there was little in the way of a professional, commercial, or urban artisanal class. The last decades of the nineteenth century and the first decades of the twentieth altered Korea dramatically. Even before the colonial period, foreign interests established rail lines, built up the cities, and founded banks. Continuing this process, the Japanese colonial authorities shaped the Korean economy to the needs of the Japanese state, mining coal and other minerals in the northern mountains, extracting rice from the fertile paddies of the south, and turning Seoul, Pyongyang, and a few other towns into industrial centers. While a few Koreans profited and some of the changes benefited the general populace, many suffered either in the stressed countryside or in the urban slums. Although a primitive consumer infrastructure developed, Koreans remained largely impoverished, owning few possessions and living nearly self-sufficient lives. At the same time, the colonial period served as an important learning phase for Korean consumers, as urban Koreans became exposed to Japanese-style goods and services.[3] They were also introduced to Japanese savings programs (see Garon). Within colonial Korean society, many affluent Koreans developed a taste for modern consumption, while some dissenters discouraged patriots from adopting Japanese ways and, at the very least, encouraged Koreans to live and consume with a consciousness of preserving Korean culture and society.[4]

The partition of Korea in 1945, the establishment of two separate Korean nations in 1948, and the war between the two nations (1950–53) left

[3] See, for example, Michael Robinson, "Broadcasting, Cultural Hegemony, and Colonial Modernity in Korea, 1924–1945," in *Colonial Modernity in Korea,* ed. Michael Robinson and Gi-Wook Shin (Cambridge: Harvard University Asia Center, 1999), 52–69; and Kenneth M. Wells, "The Rationale of Korean Economic Nationalism Under Japanese Colonial Rule, 1922–1932: The Case of Cho Man-sik's Products Promotion Society," *Modern Asian Studies* 19, no. 4 (1985): 823–59.

[4] Carter Eckert, *Offspring of Empire: The Koch'ang Kims and the Colonial Origins of Korean Capitalism, 1876–1945* (Seattle: Washington University Press, 1991).

South Korea in economic ruins. The war itself destroyed more than 40 percent of the housing and over one thousand factories in Seoul alone. The remaining years of the 1950s (under the administration of Syngman Rhee) were characterized by political corruption and economic stagnation. During this period, the United States and the United Nations propped up the South Korean economy with large aid grants and shipments of food. In 1961, General Park Chung-hee led a coup that overturned a short-lived democratic regime. He established a military dictatorship and a pattern of rule by generals that lasted until 1993, fourteen years after his assassination and eight years after the establishment of democracy in South Korea. One of his regime's central goals was economic development. Park recognized that a strengthened economy was critical not only to the stability of his own control of power but also to the security of the nation: the Democratic People's Republic of North Korea stood ready to capitalize on any weakness in its conjoined twin. Economic competition between South Korea and North Korea was more than symbolic. Park believed that South Korea needed a strong industrial base and a healthy citizenry to discourage North Korean aggression. Park established weekly and monthly meetings with the heads of major South Korean corporations (the *chaebŏl*) in which he set priorities for both national- and corporate-level production and sales. During the eighteen years of his presidency, the central government took a leading role in setting a national economic development agenda and in allocating industrial and trade opportunities to specific corporations.

Park's interest in economic development was not limited to issues of production and trade. The president took a personal role in establishing a discourse of responsible consumption. After assuming power, Park moved quickly to arrest and publicly humiliate the businessmen who had profited during the 1950s, primarily through their possession of precious import licenses. Establishing a public preference for frugal modesty, he accused these men of "illicit profiteering" and lambasted their luxurious lifestyles.[5] Park viewed consumption as a key element of the economy, but not necessarily a positive one. Rather than encourage household spending, he promoted the *restraint* of consumption as vital to national economic growth. He abhorred waste and encouraged thrift and saving on both moral and practical grounds. His Council of National Reconstruction imposed rationing of rice to restaurants, and it outlawed the sale of goods on the black market.[6] Throughout his rule, Park often spoke of the virtues of frugality, as in his 1968 New Year's message:

[5] Jung-en Woo, *The Race to the Swift: State and Finance in Korean Industrialization* (New York: Columbia University Press, 1991), 83.

[6] John Lie, *Han Unbound: The Political Economy of South Korea* (Stanford: Stanford University Press, 1998), 12.

> When a frugal spirit permeates homes, schools and offices, making all citizens watchful against waste and loss, no matter how trivial it will be, this will display formidable power in economic construction: as the proverb says, "Little and often make a heap in time." It should be recognized deeply that a frugal life, doing away with waste and practicing economy, will act as a "hidden force," benefiting not only housekeeping in individual homes but the whole national economy.[7]

In the same message, he calculated the danger of even a small degree of carelessness: "If each of our 30 million people wastes 10 wŏn a day, the daily loss will amount to 300 million wŏn, and if the daily waste continues year round, a huge sum of 100 billion wŏn will be lost. The latter figure corresponds to half the national budget."[8] Park envisioned a nation in which the minute acts of citizens improved the country's economic outlook by facilitating the efficient use of scarce resources. During the Park years, the regime involved South Koreans in ongoing campaigns to collect scraps of metal and paper and to save electricity, all for the national economy. Children, in particular, were recruited to participate in these activities at school. Many of those children, now adults, recall the sense of communal mission inspired by the practice of socially focused frugality.

Park's embrace of frugality echoed similar discourses in Japan, and many of the policies and programs around frugality were inspired by Japanese efforts (see Garon). Park had volunteered for service in the Japanese Imperial Army and had trained in Japan during the colonial period. His program for South Korean development was influenced by his admiration for Japan as well as by his brief membership in a communist cell.[9] President Park's strategic economic goals depended not on increased domestic consumption but rather on exports to bring in foreign currency with which to buy essential inputs, such as technology, know-how, and minerals and metals for industrial development. Given the poor quality of South Korean products and the low prices they could command in foreign markets, the profitability of South Korean exports depended heavily on low labor costs. Accordingly, the Park administration participated actively in holding down urban wages. During the 1960s and 1970s, South Korean

[7] Chung Hee Park, *The Major Speeches by Korea's Park Chung Hee,* compiled by Shin Bum Shik (Seoul: Hollym Publishers, 1970), 135.

[8] Park, *Major Speeches,* 134.

[9] For Japanese policies toward consumers during the imperial period and in the immediate postwar period, see Gordon, chap. 6, and Garon, chap. 7; Sheldon Garon, "Luxury is the Enemy: Mobilizing Savings and Popularizing Thrift in Wartime Japan," *Journal of Japanese Studies* 26, no. 1 (Winter 2000): 41–78; and Sheldon Garon, *Molding Japanese Minds: The State in Everyday Life* (Princeton: Princeton University Press, 1997). The ideal of frugality was also shaped from the late nineteenth century on by Protestant Christian ideologies; see Wells, "Rationale of Korean Economic Nationalism."

police often backed up private strikebreakers and management thugs in battles between factory workers and employers.[10]

Even so, profit margins on South Korean exports remained low, leading Park to compensate the *chaebŏl* by facilitating the overpricing of domestic consumer goods. Among other strategies, the government limited foreign competition in the domestic market. This suppressed the consumer market enough so that middle-income South Koreans and the poor generally *felt* as though they were in the same boat during the Park years—notwithstanding actual income differences in the population. Even members of the middle class have childhood memories of cold winters without sufficient heat and days without enough to eat. The suppression of the consumer market shielded feelings of shared deprivation from potentially disturbing displays of income difference. There were few goods to be had; most people made do with similar items. South Korean sociologist Baek Uk-in recalls that in the 1960s and 1970s, "for ramen, toothpaste, clothes and such things, names and brand labels had not yet become a problem. If it was ramen, it was ramen; if it was toothpaste, you understood it was toothpaste. Even though we were at the center of mass-production/mass-consumption, because of chronic low wages and the shortages of goods, the brand names of things could not play such an important role."[11]

Sacrificing for the National Future, Achieving Prosperity, and the Perils of Consumption: 1980–1997

The Park years were not free from protest and social unrest.[12] Nevertheless, most South Koreans quietly worked hard and sacrificed their own happiness not only out of necessity but also for the good of the nation's future—a future they believed their children would inherit. Park's propaganda spoke explicitly about a prosperous future South Korea: "The economic, social and political goals . . . are: promotion of the public welfare, freedom from exploitation, and the fair distribution of income amongst the people. It is obvious that these goals cannot be reached overnight; they are, nonetheless, the fundamental aims of the economic order toward which we must move."[13] Often, the image of the Korean future was of a

[10] George Ogle, *South Korea: Dissent within the Economic Miracle* (London: Zed Books, 1990).

[11] Baek Uk-in, "Taejung'ŭi samgwa han'guk sahoe pyŏnŭi yoch'e" [The secret of mass culture and Korean society], in *Han'guk sahoe undongŭi hyŏksinŭl wihayŏ* [On the reform of Korean social movements], ed. Kim Chŏl-mi (Seoul: Paeksan Sŏdang, 1993), 35.

[12] See, for example, Ogle, *South Korea;* Lie, *Han Unbound,* 120 ff.; and Donald N. Clark, ed., *The Kwangju Uprising: Shadows over the Regime in South Korea* (Boulder: Westview Press, 1988).

[13] Alice H. Amsden, *Asia's Next Giant: South Korea and Late Industrialization* (New York: Oxford University Press, 1989), 49.

unified Korean peninsula.[14] These two ideals—a prosperous, egalitarian society and a unified nation—were powerful motivational icons for South Koreans during the first two decades of industrial development. They were, in fact, key foundations of the particular contours of nationalism in South Korea.

A great deal has been written in the last twenty years about the forms and processes of nationalism and national identity.[15] Several scholars have examined the ways that nationalism is often built upon a created history—a past that combines fiction and interpretation with bits of facts to spin a compelling tale of essentialism. "The cultural shreds and patches used by nationalism," wrote Ernest Gellner, "are often arbitrary historical inventions. Any old shred and patch would have served as well."[16] South Korean nationalism shares many of the themes of nationalism found elsewhere: a focus on language, history, tradition, culture, and ethnic homogeneity. South Koreans certainly draw upon their history to foster a sense of shared identity. Nationalistic stories span very recent history (the Kwangju uprising, the Seoul Olympics), history now remembered only by older South Koreans (the division of the peninsula, the Korean War, shared privation), dim contemporary history (the colonial period, the March 1st rebellion of 1919), and distant history (the Hideyoshi invasion of 1598 and the victory of the Turtle ships, the glory of the Shilla dynasty, and Tangun's founding of Korea some 5,000 years ago). These stories invoke shared anger, sorrow, or satisfaction. But the past is imperfect material for national pride in South Korea. The recurrent themes of foreign invasion, ambivalence about the legacy of the long Chosŏn period, shame in the face of Japanese colonial domination, anger over the division of the peninsula and the occupation by the United States, sadness in the wake of the war and its devastations, and discomfort with the decades of authoritarian rule—all tarnish the material of history. Moreover, the very memory of "Korea" calls up the pain of division—any historical stories predating 1945 refer to a unified Korea, and stories after division simply remind South Koreans of the amputation of their northern territory. In contrast to the functional "narration" of a unified history (which, as Homi Bhabha wrote, "'singularizes'

[14] Roy Richard Grinker, *Korea and Its Futures: Unification and the Unfinished War* (New York: St. Martin's Press, 1998).

[15] Eric Hobsbawm and Terence Ranger, eds., *The Invention of Tradition* (Cambridge: Cambridge University Press, 1983); Brackette Williams, "A Class Act: Anthropology and the Race to Nation Across Ethnic Terrain," *Annual Review of Anthropology* 18 (1985): 401–44; Ernest Gellner, "Nations and Nationalism," in *Nationalism*, ed. John Hutchinson and Anthony Smith (Oxford: Oxford University Press, 1994); Partha Chatterjee, *The Nation and its Fragments: Colonial and Postcolonial Histories* (Princeton: Princeton University Press, 1993); and Benedict Anderson, *Imagined Communities: Reflections on the Origins and Spread of Nationalism* (London: Verso, 1983).

[16] Gellner, "Nations and Nationalism," 64.

the nation's cultural totality"), South Koreans cannot narrate their history without spotlighting the current distress of division.[17]

Perhaps for these reasons, South Korean nationalism appears to have been constructed as firmly on images of the future as it is on ideas of the past. There has been little written about how the future can be mobilized as the basic material for national identity formation. Yet the future can be a superior substance for generating a feeling of national community. Like the past, the future distracts from the present—a convenient feint when current political or economic conditions are somehow unsatisfactory. In Park's South Korea, when the majority of South Koreans were working long hours and living in various states of hardship, the carrot of a more equitable, wealthier, democratic, and unified Korea was dangled before the population by the government and its media and institutions. Unlike the past, the future is itself intrinsically motivating. A compelling picture of an attractive future can inspire action at various social levels. From a political perspective, the future is a stabilizing discourse compared to the past, for the future must be achieved through leadership of the government in partnership with the public. Government plans are appeals for faith, patience, and cooperation; they stake out a role for the government, implicitly demanding a deferral of judgment and engaging the citizenry in the project of accomplishing the envisioned nation.

This future-oriented nationalism has one weakness, however, compared to a nationalism built on the "shreds and patches" of the past: if the future is judged to have "arrived" without the promised results, the spirit of national unity diminishes. For example, in South Korea, a national orientation toward the future fit neatly into a preexisting pattern of intergenerational sacrifice. Korean anthropologist Cho Hae-jŏang has written about how Korean mothers, often deprived of domains of personal agency, tended to invest themselves in their children's future and to develop prodigious patience.[18] During the period of rapid industrialization, mothers—as well as fathers—demonstrated tremendous powers of endurance in the hope of a better future for their children. Yet by the middle of the 1980s, the generation that had been young in the early years of the Park administration was beginning to measure the returns on their own personal sacrifices as their children reached adulthood.

This moment of intergenerational assessment coincided with the blossoming of the South Korean consumer market. Beginning in the 1980s, South Korean *chaebŏl* began to produce large quantities of consumer electronics, appliances, and automobiles. Although the ultimate goal was to

[17] Homi K. Bhabha, "DissemiNation: Time, Narrative, and the Margins of the Modern Nation," in *Nation and Narration,* ed. Homi K. Bhabha (London: Routledge, 1990), 317.

[18] Haejoang Cho, "Male Dominance and Mother Power: Two Sides of Confucian Patriarchy in Korea," in *The Psycho-Cultural Dynamics of the Confucian Family: Past and Present,* ed. Walter H. Slote (Seoul: International Cultural Society, 1986).

reach lucrative export markets, many of these manufactures found their way into the South Korean marketplace.[19] This increase in consumer options, combined with a runaway real estate market that made some families rich while consigning others to squatter housing or substandard apartments, cracked the veneer of egalitarian suffering. Gazing upon luxurious new high-rise apartments, increasing numbers of cars on the road, and fancy restaurants, many South Koreans became aware that the era of shared poverty was behind them.

For a government that had depended on a sense of national unity, the shattering of the illusion of common destitution left it vulnerable to accusations of false promises of shared prosperity. Dissatisfaction and dissent reached an apogee in the mid-1980s, when popular uprisings pushed the dictator Chun Doo-hwan from office. But government economic planners still believed in the keen need to keep personal saving rates high and to limit expenses on imported consumer goods to support continued economic growth. In this context, a renewed *ol parŭn* (appropriate) consumption campaign arose. Surprisingly, despite widespread disillusion with both government and the *chaebŏl,* this campaign involved both government agencies and private civic organizations, reflecting a consensus on the importance of consumer restraint. The key themes in this campaign were: eschew imports, cultivate a frugal character because it is a *Korean* character, and defend against the erosion of South Korean moral unity through appropriate consumer decisions that would hide differences in affluence.

Elsewhere I have described in depth the ways that women were targeted by the *kwasobi ch'ubang* (eliminate excessive consumption) campaigns.[20] In the late 1980s and early 1990s in particular, anti-consumption discourse focused heavily on women as both the principal agents of consumption (South Korean women were overwhelmingly responsible for all household purchasing decisions) and as a weak link in the moral fabric of South Korean society. Women were viewed (and depicted) as vulnerable to the temptations of personal indulgence. A deluge of newspaper, magazine, and television pieces focused on the debauched lifestyles of rich housewives. One shocking article was published by the generally left-leaning journal *Mal* (word). In it, a philosophy professor discussed the growing problem of income disparity in South Korea, and he criticized the anti-*kwasobi* movement as distracting the public from the more fundamental structural causes of inequality. Nevertheless, the author passed along his own commentary on a then widely circulated story about a sexual assault on the wealthy wife of an unnamed company president. The author was

[19] Laura C. Nelson, *Measured Excess: Status, Gender, and Consumer Nationalism in South Korea* (New York: Columbia University Press, 2000), see esp. 186–89.

[20] Nelson, *Measured Excess.*

less outraged by the crime than he was by the value of the jewelry the woman reported stolen at the time: "A 40,000,000 wŏn [approximately $50,000] three-karat diamond ring; a gold Rolex watch (18,000,000 wŏn [$22,500]); a diamond and gold bracelet, and about five pearl items, all worth about 70,000,000 wŏn [$90,000]. . . . It seems absolutely impossible to imagine the ultraluxurious lifestyle of such a woman."[21] He observed bitterly that the jewelry amounted to twice the value of the security deposit he put down on his apartment.

Similar stories were common in the media in the late 1980s and early 1990s, and they frequently fused criticism of women's wealth with indictments of their moral and sexual character. There was often a salacious edge to stories criticizing wealthy women. Expensive health clubs were seen as a kind of rich women's sexual spa, where clients could swim, work out, relax in a sauna—and make assignations with the male employees. A famous article carried in *Newsweek* in 1991 touched off an obsessive public debate about college women who spent hundreds of dollars on lingerie.[22] Rich women were lightning rods for resentment over increasingly visible disparity in wealth. Women often managed the household's financial investments (including buying and selling stocks and real estate) and were therefore particularly visible agents in these extremely sensitive economic domains. Affluent South Korean women faced conflicting expectations. Their families' wealth depended upon their aggressive management of household finances, while (in contrast to the upright image of the salaried jobs of their "productive" husbands) the realm of investment was associated with scandal, greed, and wealth gained at the expense of others (particularly in the real estate arena). The common term for investment income is *bullosodŭk,* or "unearned income," implying that such income is undeserved. Stories such as the one in *Mal* were as much expressions of popular disillusionment with the fantasy of a future of shared prosperity as they were misogynistic barbs at women who had attained a level of independence afforded by affluence.[23]

It is instructive to note that *men's* spending habits attracted relatively little criticism during this period. Occasional campaigns against political corruption would focus on the huge bribes some men paid to politicians, yet rarely did the money men spent on sexual services incur censure. Overall,

[21] Ch'oi Chong-uk, "Kwasobiwa 90 nyŏndaep'an ojŏk" [Excessive consumption and the five thieves of the 90s], *Mal* (November 1991): 151.

[22] Tony Emerson with Bradley Martin, "Too Rich, Too Soon," *Newsweek* (Pacific International Edition), November 11, 1991, pp. 12–16.

[23] A similar gendering of consumption, and in particular of consumer *responsibilities,* occurred in Europe. See Leora Auslander, "The Gendering of Consumer Practices in Nineteenth-Century France," and Victoria de Grazia, "Nationalizing Women: The Competition between Fascist and Commercial Models in Mussolini's Italy," in *The Sex of Things,* ed. De Grazia, 79–112, 337–58.

men as a category escaped the anti-consumption diatribes, perhaps both because they left to their wives the responsibility for household management (including most of the spending decisions), and because men's *kwasobi*—in particular money spent on politics, drinking, and sex—was an almost sacred aspect of South Korean male homosocial activity.

A complex coalition of actors formulated the anti-*kwasobi* discourse. The state engaged in public education campaigns, producing posters, pamphlets, and a variety of materials distributed through schools and residential committees or displayed in public spaces. Civic organizations, including consumer protection organizations, some of which had close links to the South Korean government, as well as civil justice groups, published consumer magazines and pamphlets. They also mounted exhibits of appropriate and excessive consumption. Christian organizations preached about the virtues of frugality and the sins of indulgence, also drawing connections between the comfortable lifestyles of the well-to-do and the misery of South Korea's poor. The YMCA was a particularly strong voice in the *kwasobi ch'ubang* movement in the 1980s and 1990s. The media, including women's magazines, television and radio programs, and newspapers, offered a constant stream of both exposés of unimaginable luxury and homey suggestions about how to save more and spend less. The ideal of frugality was embraced by political conservatives and progressives alike. The gendered slant of anti-*kwasobi* messages appears not to have been produced exclusively by male agents, and certainly the pointed criticism of consumer practices of women and mothers was *re*produced by both women and men in their own discussions of contemporary social ills.

Although women were the primary targets of *kwasobi* criticism, they were not the only consumers who attracted disapproving attention. The campaigns also occasionally singled out *children's* consumer practices. Children and youth endangered national unity in a variety of ways. First, to the extent that well-off children were indulged by their parents, their possession of fancy electronics, stationery items, and designer clothing created visible distinctions between wealthier and less wealthy children. In the discourse of appropriate consumption, the *appearance* of income differences is generally seen as socially damaging. It gives the lie to the promises of an equitable future. The affluent are discouraged from flaunting their wealth in order to avoid sparking class envy. A more concrete threat here was the potential to create a system of class reproduction through the access of wealthier youths to superior extracurricular (private) educational programs; many media stories focused on extracurricular education as a problem of *kwasobi*. The Korean Educational Development Institute estimated that by 1990, 9.4 trillion wŏn (U.S. $13.4 billion) were being spent annually on extracurricular lessons, compared to a total of 8.7 trillion wŏn ($12.4 billion) spent on public education.[24] These extracurricular classes

[24] *Korea Herald*, June 23, 1992.

gave students an advantage in public school examinations; in my own fieldwork, children told me that some public school teachers assumed that some of their students had already learned the basics of a lesson in their private, extracurricular classes and so went directly to questions and testing. The media also criticized the anti-progressive practice of affluent parents offering teachers "white envelopes" (gifts of money) to secure for their children extra attention or a seat closer to the front of the classroom.

As with the women-focused *kwasobi* discourse, while wealthy youth were of particular concern, it was not only *affluent* youth who endangered the nation through their consumer practices—*all* children posed a threat to national cultural integrity because they were seen as poorly rooted in a Korean tradition of appropriate consumer behavior. Children were considered to be particularly vulnerable to the seductions of Japanese cultural imports. Although it was illegal until the mid-1990s to import Japanese games and comics, smuggled goods were not hard to find, and many households installed illegal satellite dishes precisely so that they could pick up Japanese TV broadcasts. To allay concerns about the cultural pollution of South Korean youth, in the early 1990s the government cracked down on the sale of foreign magazines near schoolyards. Children were also seen as susceptible to American cultural influences; newspaper editorials bemoaned children's preferences for pizza or hamburgers over Korean food. At a higher level of cultural abstraction, children were thought to be developing new and unwelcome (that is, un-Korean) consumer habits. One journalist commented, "Nowadays the new generation doesn't know how to use things sparingly, and they lack a frugal character."[25]

Like women, children were portrayed as less firmly rooted than men in the national ethos and as more vulnerable to an animal-like tendency to indulge one's whims and desires. A pamphlet published by the Seoul YMCA, a leading institution in the civic *ol parŭn sobi saenghwal* (appropriate consumption) campaign, warned that it was no longer only men who indulged their carnal desires: "This same tide has also infiltrated family, sex, and every generation to reach even women and youth. It is reported that housewives and middle school students are drug addicts, and women of all ages sell their bodies; it can be said that this is concrete proof of the atmosphere of indulgence that promotes exactly this depraved pleasure."[26] Moreover, women's and children's consumption practices were often linked. Women weighed the good of the nation against their children's best interests when making household consumer decisions; women's self-indulgence was portrayed as coming at the expense of the well-being of their children; women had the primary responsibility for teaching their

[25] Chŏng Chae-ryŏng, ed., *Sinsaedae: Kŭdŭrŭn nuguinga?* [The new generation: Who are they?] (Seoul: Hanguk Ilbo, 1990), 35.

[26] Seoul YMCA, "Hyangnak sanŏpgwa kwasobi" [Pleasure industry and excessive consumption], photocopied manuscript report, July 1989, p. 19.

children appropriate consumption behaviors. In a sense, criticism of the inappropriate consumer inclinations of the young was yet another way to criticize women, this time in their role as mothers, because they had not taught their children how to live frugally in the Korean manner.

The anti-*kwasobi* campaigns of the late 1980s and early 1990s expressed a widespread unease about several aspects of South Korean society. The sense of camaraderie built around a shared history of poverty and a shared future of prosperity—albeit never wholly convincing—dissipated as a new generation came of age. This new generation not only had *not* shared the same level of deprivation, it did not share the expectation that the entire nation should sacrifice for a *future* goal. While older parents whose children had not achieved affluence were disillusioned, their children—now young adults—were inclined to value family over nation, and they identified less with the future than with the present. The uneasiness is not surprising: many South Koreans felt they were losing not only the feeling of national unity but also an identifiably "Korean" way of life. (In this sense, prosperity generated a perplexing longing for an idealized and impoverished past, similar to the commodified nostalgia described by Jordan Sand in chap. 4) The affluence for which the nation had struggled had arrived, but for many South Koreans it brought with it a sense of anomie and uncertainty.

Consumer Nationalism in the Post-1997 Period: Buy Now, Pay Later

The 1997 Asian financial crisis hit the South Korean economy hard. Faced with foreign exchange–denominated debt and insufficient reserves, the South Korean government agreed to an IMF restructuring program and narrowly avoided complete economic collapse. Nevertheless, South Koreans saw the value of their assets drop by as much as half; corporations and the government laid off hundreds of thousands of employees; many small and medium-sized businesses went bankrupt. Domestic consumption shriveled, undermining the profitability of the businesses that remained. This downward spiral of shrinking demand, reduced profitability, more layoffs, and lower wages threatened to deal long-term damage to the nation's industrial base.

The crisis prompted the government to rethink the national economic strategy. Initially, the IMF encouraged a tightening of the money supply (in large part in reaction to the extreme levels of indebtedness of the major corporations), but the sharp contraction of the South Korean economy led the government to decide, by the end of 1998, to pursue a different course of action. In an unpromising global market for South Korean exports, it expressed the hope that domestic consumers would help breathe life back into the economy. This was a subtle, but important, departure from the expectations placed on consumers in the past. Despite the critique of "excessive" consumption, *appropriate* consumption had come to be seen as an increasingly important element in the economy through the 1980s and early 1990s, but it remained widely understood that the vitality of the national economy depended upon export success. In the post-1997 period, by contrast, consumers themselves were recruited to the economic frontlines to take up the slack of global demand. Domestic consumption would be the vanguard for economic revitalization.

Yet at a time when citizens felt uneasy about the economy, consumers needed encouragement and a hand up. Unemployment reached over seven and a half percent in 1998, and even many of the lucky ones who had held onto their jobs experienced salary cuts, while households experienced steep losses in the value of their assets. Because potential consumers were deficient in their ability to pay and their will to spend, the government rapidly liberalized the consumer credit sector.

Before the Asian financial crisis, almost all private transactions in South Korea were conducted using cash (or cashier's checks, essentially a cash medium). As in Japan, consumer credit had most commonly taken the form of purchasing on installment (see Gordon, chap. 6). Credit cards were not entirely unknown. The first credit card in South Korea was a Shinsaegye department store card, issued in 1967. The Korea Exchange Bank began issuing Visa International charge cards in 1978, and in 1982 several banks joined together to create a domestically owned charge card, the BC card. Nevertheless, credit cards were not a large part of the South Korean economy and were not widely accepted before the late 1990s. While stores, restaurants, and hotels catering to foreign visitors or to the South Korean elite had generally accepted credit cards, elsewhere cash was essential. With limited forms of legitimate consumer credit, curb-market moneylenders would conspicuously count bundles of cash as they waited for customers in the alleys of Seoul's outdoor markets. Many tenants even paid their annual rent deposit—sums equivalent to tens or hundreds of thousands of dollars—in cash. Before 1997, the cash economy went hand in hand with a tendency to save for large expenditures, and this was reinforced by South Korean banks' emphasis on corporate loans over retail lending and consumer credit—pushed by government directives to the banks to channel money to the *chaebŏl*.

However, in a landmark policy reversal following the 1997 crisis, the South Korean government lowered interest rates (which had climbed to over fifteen percent by 1998) and unveiled policies to encourage private consumption, particularly by promoting the use of consumer credit. These policies relaxed oversight and restrictions on credit card issuance and utilization: banks and other financial institutions were not required to check the creditworthiness of card applicants; delinquencies were uncapped;

merchants were required to install card readers; cash advances were unlimited; and cardholders who spent 10 percent or more of their income using credit cards were eligible for a 20 percent deduction on their income taxes. (The South Korean government also viewed credit card transactions as a way to gather better information on income, which they would then use to improve tax collection.) These policies instantly transformed the patterns of credit card use in South Korea: agents on commission recruited customers on street corners, offering toys and kitchenware as well as discounts on purchases as incentives to sign up for a credit card. Applicants needed to provide little more than a name and address to qualify. The number of credit cards skyrocketed. In 1996, before the Asian financial crisis, there were 40.25 million credit cards in use in South Korea; by 2002, there were more than 100 million credit cards in circulation, a number more than twice the population of the nation, or approximately four cards per working person.[27] The value of credit charges jumped from 90 trillion wŏn in 1999 (the year credit policies were changed), to 443 trillion wŏn in 2001 and 622 trillion wŏn in 2002.

At first, South Korean consumers seemed to have succeeded in resuscitating the economy. Domestic and international observers lauded South Korean economic growth, noting that "pocketbook power" had helped the country achieve the highest growth rates in Asia (except for China) in a remarkably short span of time.[28] Consumer spending in the last quarter of 2001 was more than 9 percent higher than in the previous year, fueled in large part by the easily available credit. Economic growth tracked consumer spending: in 1999, GDP rose 10.9 percent, and the next year it continued expanding at 9.3 percent. Booming sales of big-ticket items like refrigerators, cars, and computers buoyed consumer confidence and bolstered the profitability of South Korean corporations. After the doldrums of 1997 and 1998, this spending spree was widely welcomed. Only a few murmured criticisms of *kwasobi* appeared in the media.

This credit-driven boom, however, had built-in weaknesses. The recklessness with which credit card companies issued cards to all applicants meant that many cards were issued to people without the means to pay the bills, and the charge ceiling on most cards was shockingly high—often higher than the average annual per capita GDP. Moreover, most credit cards in South Korea require full payment of all charges each month rather

[27] Yong-yil Kim, "Adjusting Consumption to Diminished GNP," *Korea Focus* (May-June 1998): 54; David Scofield, "South Korea Loses its Nerve on Credit," *Online Asia Times*, October 9, 2003, http://www.atimes.com/atimes/Korea/EJ09Dg01.html; and Yoolim Lee, "Consumer Debt Weighing on South Korean Economy," *International Herald Tribune*, September 23, 2003.

[28] *Time Magazine*, "Veni, Vidi, Gucci," March 18, 2002; and Andy Xie, "South Korea: Party On?" *Global Economic Forum*, November 21, 2001, http://www.morganstanley.com/GEFdata/digests/20011123–fri.html.

than allowing customers to accumulate balances and make low minimum monthly payments.[29] Given the easy access to cards, however, many cardholders found that they could emulate a "revolving" card by using one card to pay off another card's bill. This practice came to be known as "bicycling," and it goes a long way in explaining why South Koreans have acquired so many cards in such a short time. It also partially explains the high utilization of the cash advance service.

The enthusiasm that greeted the consumption-driven economic expansion quickly faded. Already by 2001, more and more anxious essays concerned with credit card–related overconsumption appeared in popular magazines. One law professor criticized the false promise that credit cards are an "Aladdin's Lamp."[30] Reports of increasing rates of delinquency worried economic researchers.[31] By 2002, the tide had turned: many more articles discussed the problems caused by credit card access than trumpeted the importance of consumer spending in the South Korean economy. Credit card debt was threatening the economic security of individuals, families, and the South Korean financial system as a whole.[32]

Some of this will sound familiar to North American readers. In the United States, credit card–related personal bankruptcies, particularly among low-income cardholders, is a well-known problem. The circumstances in South Korea are similar, but with certain key distinctions. The expansion of consumer credit occurred in a highly compressed timeframe and swept up a large fraction of the population. This amounted to a real transformation of an essential element of consumption: the mode of payment. In 1998, 12.9 percent of consumer purchases were made with credit cards; that percentage grew to 16 percent in 1999, 26 percent in 2000.[33] One researcher wrote, "Nowadays it is difficult to imagine consuming without the use of credit cards."[34] The transition from a norm of making immediate cash payments to one where consumers postponed payments is a profound one, enabling higher levels of spending and altering the temporal psychology of consumption. As many South Korean consumers dis-

[29] This system is not unique to South Korea; it is also common in Japan, and a similar system is the norm in the (as yet) miniscule charge card market in China.

[30] Kim Sŏng-ch'ŏn, "Singyongbulryangjaŭi palsaengwŏningwa daech'aek" [Origins of and countermeasures toward credit delinquency], *Sobija Sidae* (April 2001): 24.

[31] Kim Dae-ik, "Kagyedaech'ul Jŭlga'e Ddarŭn Yŏnghyang'gwa Daeŏng," [Regarding influences and confrontations on market lending], *Sinyong Kadŭ* (December 2002).

[32] The South Korean government did not take action to restrain the expansion of the credit card market until one of the largest credit card issuers, LG Card, lurched to the brink of default in a liquidity crunch resulting from too many overdue accounts. Even the LG Card crisis resulted only in a government-brokered deal in which the card company's major creditors lent LG Card additional money to avert bankruptcy.

[33] Kim Kyŏng-ja, "Sinyong sahwoeran muŏsin'ga?" [What is credit society?], *Sobija Sidae* (April 2001): 22.

[34] Kang Chang-hwa, "Sinyongk'adŏwa Sobijamunje" [Credit cards and consumer problems], *Sobija* (October 2002).

covered, although their first purchases were soberly made (just as if they were paying in cash), as they grew more accustomed to charging, they became more likely to spend money on unaffordable luxuries.[35] Between 2002 and 2003, household debt in South Korea grew by 30 percent as consumers experienced the pleasure of enjoying today and paying later.

Many of the articles that condemn reckless credit card utilization follow the familiar pattern of blaming housewives and youth for a significant portion of the delinquencies; the two groups had long been the targets of *kwasobi* criticism. Now, sensational stories of heavily indebted consumers feature students and women who hold seven, eight, even ten cards and, tragically, consumers who commit suicide over their inability to pay their debts. When analysts criticize the card companies for issuing cards without assessing risk, they often point to the ease with which students and housewives—people who do not earn their own income—can secure credit cards. Yet clearly the problem of overextension is widespread among South Korean cardholders, not only students and women.

Ideas of *kwasobi* and appropriate consumption have also evolved since the pre-1997 era. *Kwasobi* criticism, quieted for a few years as consumers played the role of national heroes, has returned to public discourse. One shift is that women are no longer the principal target of anti-consumption campaigns. The discussion of excessive consumption tends to be framed in general terms, with less emphasis placed on the woman as household manager. But at the same time, the focus on the consumer habits of children and youth has become even more intense, with entire issues of consumer magazines dedicated to this topic. For example, the leading consumer journal, *Sobija Sidae* (consumer era) ran a special issue on children's consumption in May 2002. The principal message of the issue was that "in order to achieve an appropriate consumer lifestyle when one is mature, it is important to cultivate [good] consumer habits."[36] The magazine voiced concern about the reasons young people gave for purchasing things with their pocket money: "When children purchased things, rather than buying something out of necessity, the survey shows that children purchased things to keep up with their friends in a form of interdependent consumption."[37] Unwholesome patterns of consumption on the part of young South Koreans were seen as demanding urgent attention as children and youth make up an increasingly large proportion of South Korean consumers. One of the articles in the issue argued for the importance of structured lessons in "appropriate" (*ol parŭn*) consumption for students at all levels of school. The article outlined a proposed "consumer education"

[35] "Veni, Vidi, Gucci."

[36] Kim In-suk, "Wangdda p'iharyŏgo ch'inguga gatgo nonŭn mulgŏn guip" [Upon comparing, children purchase the same things their friends have], *Sobija Sidae* (May 2002): 4.

[37] Kim In-suk, "Wangdda p'iharyŏgo ch'inguga gatgo nonŭn mulgŏn guip," 5.

curriculum, with lessons in "the value and behavior of consumers," "consumers in the marketplace," and "consumer rights and responsibilities." While at elementary school, lessons in the last category focus on consumer rights, but high school students study how to understand their responsibilities as consumers to their families and to the wider public.

A typical newspaper article in 2001 opens with an anecdote about an absurdly expensive dress for a child. The shopper is told that the dress is a popular item, and only one is left in that particular size. Kim Hye-kyong of the Korea Youth Counseling Institute comments, "The so-called X-generation parents are spending way too much money raising their children. This type of extravagance is hurting our economy, particularly since many of the preferred products are imported. But it's also dangerous in that the kids will probably grow up to be very materialistic and socially irresponsible."[38] The article notes that the falling birth rate—in 1999, birth rates were below the replacement rate—allows parents to spend more money on each child and that the current generation of parents has a tendency to teach their children the materialistic habits that they themselves acquired while growing up. As in earlier *kwasobi* criticism, the list of examples of immoderate consumerism includes such extraordinary items as golf wear and equipment for toddlers, and party dresses priced at more than 500,000 wŏn ($395). This post-1997 article also targets more reasonable things, like private babysitters and parents' decisions to preserve newborn babies' umbilical cord blood for future medical use.

These post-1997 critiques differ significantly from the earlier era of appropriate consumption campaigns in two ways. First, domestic consumption is no longer simply one pillar of the economy; it is now the motor of the economy. This is true as long as conditions remain unfavorable for South Korean exports: for example, if the global market is suppressed, the wŏn appreciates relative to the dollar, or the Japanese *yen* falls. This places consumers in a new position. No longer is consumer patriotism primarily defined as frugality; in this new era, consuming itself can be a nation-saving act. This makes criticism of *kwasobi* much less persuasive, as the line between enthusiastic patriotism and dangerous or unpleasant self-indulgence blurs. It remains to be seen whether this is a fundamental, permanent shift in the position of consumption in the South Korean economy or a temporary response to the extreme circumstances following the 1997 crisis. In addition, while it seems likely that the credit card industry will undergo some reforms, consumer credit is now rooted in South Korean consumer practice. The old days of saving in order to make a purchase are past; now consumers have a taste of what it is like to consume in the present what they can only afford in the future.

Moreover, the credit card industry is less amenable to South Korean

[38] Kim Mi-hui, "X-gen Parents Raising Kids Like Royalty," *Korea Herald,* May 15, 2001.

state control—or persuasion—than corporate entities generally had been in the past. While the *chaebŏl* did not always meekly obey state commands, in general the relationship between South Korean corporations and the South Korean government has been mutually supportive.[39] In the context of the globalized financial market and the growing dominance of U.S. financial institutions, however, even South Korean credit card companies are subject to foreign interests. When, in late 2003, LG Card, the largest of the South Korean card issuers, came close to defaulting, the South Korean government stepped in to broker a deal among LG Card's sixteen largest creditors, securing loans to rescue the company from its liquidity crisis. A few months later, two of LG Card's creditors, Korea Exchange Bank and Koram Bank—both formerly Korean banks but now U.S.-owned—pulled out of the deal, placing a greater burden for the rescue on domestic banks.[40] The expansion of consumer credit in the late 1990s has added a new, powerful element to the dynamism of the South Korean economy—an element that continues to loosen the potential for direct state control.

Conclusion

Most analyses of South Korean economic development highlight the intersection of government policies, *chaebŏl* productivity, and export success. South Koreans' own perceptions of their economy's growth focus on the major corporations. Yet the success of South Korean business would have been impossible without the orchestrated cooperation of South Korean citizen-consumers. From the early decades of frugality to the recruitment of consumers to rescue the near-bankrupt nation, consumers have played an increasingly visible and active role, becoming more self-conscious as "consumers" over time. Consumers have also gained significant freedoms. Consumers now have access to credit and a more open market. A whole generation has come of age having experienced comfort and pleasure without tremendous sacrifice or guilt. And yet, despite South Korea's growing political sophistication and economic complexity, the appeals to consumer patriotism endure. Remarkably, pundits, scholars, and ordinary people continue to discuss what kinds of consumption are appropriate—in terms of individual morality, national character, and mutual (that is, patriotic) responsibility. In South Korea, consumers now are synonymous with "citizens," much as they are in the United States (see Cohen, chap. 2), but they are burdened with responsibilities defined not by belief in the magic of the marketplace but by explicit instructions in appropriate practice.

[39] Jung-en Woo, *Race to the Swift,* see esp. 148–75.

[40] Ji-hun Lee, "U.S.-owned KEB says no to LG Card," *Digital Chosun,* February 4, 2004, http://english.chosun.com/w21data/html/news/200402/200402050032.html.

No act of consumption is innocent in South Korea. The society is permeated with debates and anxieties about appropriate consumption, excessive consumption, "Korean" consumption, and patriotic consumption. Each decision about a brand of rice or a type of automobile may be fraught with meaning, burdening the simple pleasures of shopping and ownership with a sense of responsibility. While many people resist this framework, it appears again and again in newspaper and magazine articles, television programs, government propaganda campaigns, and everyday conversations. South Korea's economic miracle, so often seen as a miracle of industrial development and export success, is founded upon a nation of self-conscious consumers.

PART III

THE POLITICS OF CONSUMPTION

If politics is understood as the competitive allocation of resources, then consumption is by definition a political act. Ideally, what we consume in a free-market economy should determine what is produced; this in turn should place consumers in a powerful position within the broader political economy. In practice, consumers are often marginalized by producers and retailers, who control the flow of information in the marketplace and narrow the parameters of consumer choice. This distortion of consumer expectations is a significant wellspring of ambivalence in the modern world.

While political themes permeate much of this volume, they take center stage in the chapters in part III. One such theme concerns the responsibilities of states for the well-being of consumers and the tradeoffs that often result. Takatsugu Akaishi and Sven Steinmo examine how the Swedish and Japanese states have linked consumption taxes to the expansion of the welfare state. Institutional incentives inherent in the corporatist political system enabled the Swedish state to strike a bargain among various actors in the political economy: consumers pay high consumption taxes in return for comprehensive social welfare benefits. Because Japan's particularistic political system precluded such a bargain, consumers there receive fewer social welfare benefits from the state. Patricia L. Maclachlan analyzes state responses to consumer demands in her study of consumer attitudes toward genetically modified foods in the United States, Japan, and Britain. For cultural, historical, and political reasons, she explains, Japan's pro-biotech government has been unexpectedly proactive in regulating the flow of transgenic foods in the marketplace, whereas the United States has done relatively little. The British government, meanwhile, struggles to find a workable balance between angry consumers and a biotechnology industry determined to expand.

Several of the chapters explore the political contests surrounding consumer rights. Deborah S. Davis's study of Chinese homeowners underscores a deep-seated tension between two state-initiated visions of what it means to be a consumer in contemporary China. When it first embarked on economic liberalization more than two decades ago, the Communist state viewed consumers as passive, apolitical beings who contributed to economic growth simply by striving for greater material satisfaction. More recently, by contrast, the party-state has endowed consumers with a surprising number of rights and privileges that may enable them to achieve higher degrees of power and autonomy in the marketplace. The regime's reluctance to allow Chinese homeowners to implement these rights fully, however, suggests that it is not yet ready to cede power to ordinary consumers. In Japan, notes Takao Nishimura in his analysis of consumer education, the conflicts often revolve around whether the consumer possesses a right to know. As education programs empower consumers and enhance their self-sufficiency in the marketplace, he observes, consumer education threatens the supremacy of business interests that has long been a hallmark of the postwar political economy. The dissemination of information likewise figures prominently in the story of the consumer's right to safe food. As Maclachlan notes with reference to the Japanese and British cases, the more that consumers learn about genetically modified foods, the more they tend to clash with biotech firms and their state sponsors, even though the evidence suggests that these foods are reasonably safe. The specter of political conflict may be one of the reasons why the American government refuses to inform consumers of the presence of genetically modified organisms in their food supply.

The chapters have important implications for the ongoing debate about globalization and the future of the nation-state. Free trade advocates are quick to predict that economic deregulation and the elimination of national trade restrictions will erode state powers over the economy. The findings here suggest that this need not be the case. As national economies become increasingly interdependent, consumers have made new demands for protection on their nation-states. In so doing, consumers strive to protect their national political, economic, and cultural traditions from the leveling effects of globalizing trends, which many equate with American economic hegemony.

Finally, these chapters underscore the broader intellectual utility of studying consumer politics. The case studies here offer new insights into the shifting relations between states and their societies in response to new economic and political challenges. Nishimura, Davis, and Maclachlan further highlight some of the processes and consequences of economic deregulation. The chapters also have implications for the study of citizenship, in democratic and nondemocratic systems alike. In sum, and as other chapters in this volume attest, consumption is far more than an isolated act performed at the tail end of the production cycle; it is deeply embedded in the broader cultural, social, and political values of a given society. The politicization of consumption, then, can be viewed as an illuminating metaphor for how those values are implemented, contested, and, in some instances, transformed.

9

CONSUMPTION TAXES AND THE WELFARE STATE IN SWEDEN AND JAPAN

TAKATSUGU AKAISHI AND SVEN STEINMO

"The art of taxation is one of plucking the goose so as
to get the greatest amount of feathers with the least amount of hissing."
JEAN MICHAEL COLBERT

As the modern state has grown, so has its need to raise revenue. In all democratic countries this means that governments must find ways to generate revenue without alienating voters. This is no easy task. Citizens like government spending but are deeply suspicious of government's attempts to raise the taxes needed to pay for it. There are, in short, no popular taxes.

The political challenges of taxation have been nowhere more apparent than in the recent attempts of many democracies to introduce or raise consumption taxes. Consumers tend to dislike consumption taxes because they raise the prices of what they want to buy; governments tend to like them because they are highly efficient sources of revenue which are often less visible than direct income and capital taxes. In this chapter, we examine two advanced industrialized democracies that have met the challenges of consumption taxation in dramatically different ways: Sweden and Japan. In so doing, we highlight the significance of consumption tax politics for the political economy more generally. By emphasizing the particular political compromises that have encouraged or hindered consumption taxation in Sweden and Japan, moreover, we hope to explain the relationship among consumption, taxation, and the size and effectiveness of the welfare state.

Takatsugu Akaishi gratefully acknowledges the financial support of the Japan Society for the Promotion of Science (Grants-in-Aide for Scientific Research (C) 15530220).

Consumption Taxes and Consumption

What are consumption taxes? This is not as simple a question as one might think. The Organization for Economic Cooperation and Development (OECD) has difficulty categorizing consumption taxes, because while many taxes directly affect consumption, only some of them are paid directly by the consumer.[1] It is easy to understand that a classical sales tax is a consumption tax. Other consumption taxes such as tariffs, however, are more difficult to place, even though they are ultimately shouldered by consumers. The OECD lists over forty-two different categories of consumption tax in its inventory of taxes. These range from the general Value Added Tax (VAT), which can apply to all goods sold in a country, to specific taxes on things like salt, wigs, videocassettes, gasoline, advertising, gambling, fur coats, and *sake*. Most countries have literally hundreds of different consumption taxes on specific goods and services. In fact, they are among the oldest and most widely used taxes in history for the obvious reasons that they are relatively easy to collect and can generate enormous revenues. But consumption taxes have also been the source of intense political controversy. In the North America and India, to cite two extreme examples, opposition to consumption taxes on tea and salt, respectively, triggered major revolutions.

In recent years, taxes on general consumption have grown enormously while taxes on specific goods and services have declined across the advanced capitalist world. There appears to be a growing consensus among tax policy elites that the revenues generated by specific taxes do not justify their high administrative costs. Moreover, the liberal consensus that swept the world in recent decades posits that governments should not be in the business of shaping individuals' consumption choices.[2] General consumption taxes, by contrast, are now the single most important source of revenue in the OECD, accounting for 29.9 percent of total government tax revenues in member nations on average.[3] Given the increasing difficulty of taxing income and profits in a globalizing world economy, most analysts agree that broad-based consumption taxes are likely to grow in importance as a major source of state financing.

As table 9.1 illustrates, some countries tax their societies much more than other countries. Sweden takes in 54.2 percent of GDP and has the world's heaviest tax burden, while the Japanese tax burden of 27.1 percent

[1] OECD, *Taxing Consumption* (Paris: OECD, 1988), 22–25.

[2] Vito Tanzi, *Globalization and the Future of Social Protection* (Washington, D.C.: International Monetary Fund, January 2000), 1–22.

[3] Personal income tax accounted for an average of 26.5 percent of total tax revenue in 2001. Corporate profits taxes accounted for 9.4 percent and social security charges an average of 25.1 percent. OECD, *Revenue Statistics, 1965–2002* (Paris: OECD, 2003), tables 11, 13 and 15.

TABLE 9.1.
Sources of tax revenue, as a percentage of GDP, 2001

	Consumption	Income and profits	Social security	Total taxes
OECD avg.	11.1	13.4	9.2	37.4
Sweden	12.6	19.3	14.5	54.2
Japan	4.6	8.9	9.9	27.1

Source: OECD Revenue Statistics 1965–2002 (2003), table 3.

of GDP is the lowest of any democracy in the world (as of 2001). But the single biggest difference between the tax structures of these countries is the amount of revenue each collects in consumption taxes. Japan is at the bottom of the OECD, collecting only 2.4 percent of GDP in general consumption taxes (VAT), while Sweden is near the top, collecting 9.1 percent of GDP with its VAT (see table 9.2).

These data reveal only the most general differences in the ways countries have raised, lowered, and used consumption taxes. In the following pages we explore the politics of consumption taxes in Sweden and Japan, the world's most dissimilar democratic welfare states. Despite their obvious differences, we believe that comparing these two countries makes a lot of sense. First, each has achieved admirable levels of economic prosperity and wealth. Counted among the poorer countries of the world only a century ago, they are now two of the richest and most technically advanced countries. Second, both countries achieved this economic growth and prosperity while reducing economic inequality. Third, both countries are noted for having strong states—governments that have actively directed their economies toward widely accepted social and economic goals. That said, the ways in which Sweden and Japan have developed their politico-economic systems have been remarkably different.

While Sweden has built the world's most generous (and expensive) welfare state, Japan's welfare state is one of the least developed in the industrialized world. Sweden established a universal social insurance system that offers "cradle to grave" social insurance coverage to all citizens. Conversely,

TABLE 9.2.
Consumption taxes as a percentage of GDP, 1965 and 2001

	Tax on general consumption		Tax on particular goods and services	
	1965	2001	1965	2001
Sweden	3.6	9.1	6.7	3.5
Japan	0	2.4	4.6	2.1
OECD avg.	3.3	6.9	5.8	4.0

Source: OECD Revenue Statistics 1965–2002 (2003), tables 28, 30.

Japan has constructed a minimalist welfare state that relies heavily on the private sector (either family or company networks) to provide most social services. Sweden has financed its generous welfare state in large part by heavily taxing workers and consumers, while Japan has taxed its workers and consumers at very low rates by international standards. We find this interesting—and worth explaining—because the Swedish government has been dominated for roughly six decades by a self-defined socialist party whose rhetoric is generally pro-worker, pro-consumer, and anti-capitalist. The Japanese government, by contrast, has been controlled for most of the past half-century by the conservative Liberal Democratic Party (LDP), which has long emphasized economic growth objectives over the rights or interests of consumers and workers. We would expect, in other words, the Japanese government to tax consumers and workers at much higher rates than its Swedish counterpart. By exploring the politics of consumption taxes in these two countries, we hope to better understand these puzzling outcomes. As Sheldon Garon and Patricia L. Maclachlan observe in the introduction, our story highlights the fact that while rising consumption is considered an important objective in most countries, it may often play second fiddle to other social, political, and economic issues that are important in specific national contexts.

We argue that these different tax systems are best understood through an institutionalist lens. Specifically, we show how political institutional structures contributed to fundamentally different consumption tax policy choices in these two countries. Briefly stated, the structure of Swedish corporatist decision-making institutions (themselves the products of both the electoral system and the existence of powerful producer groups) encouraged political and economic elites to strike a distinctive political bargain. In this bargain, labor and consumers were required to shoulder tax increases that would in turn allow the construction of a generous welfare state. This welfare state would support higher and more equitable standards of living—and thus higher levels of consumption for society's poorest individuals. In Japan, by contrast, the multi-member electoral system (in existence from 1948 to 1994) has prevented elites from imposing short-term costs (taxes) on citizens, thereby hindering the expansion of social programs that would benefit these same citizens. Although there have been many attempts over the years to increase consumption taxes for social welfare purposes, most have been undermined by politicians who face short-term electoral incentives. In short, what Sheldon Garon and Mike Mochizuki call the "social contract" is quite different in Japan and Sweden.[4] Our study hopes to explore why this is so and what the consequences are in terms of funding these two social welfare states.

[4] Sheldon Garon and Mike Mochizuki, "Negotiating Social Contracts," in *Postwar Japan as History,* ed. Andrew Gordon (Berkeley: University of California Press, 1993), 145–66.

Taxing Consumption in Sweden

We begin this section with the curious fact that Sweden, which has been dominated by a (self-proclaimed) socialist party for most of the past six decades, imposes some of the heaviest and most regressive consumption taxes of any country in the world. Leftist parties typically oppose regressive taxes because they place a heavier burden on the poor than progressive taxes. There is a simple explanation for the Swedish anomaly: the Social Democrats believe that taxing general consumption is necessary to finance the expansionist welfare state. We have found no evidence to suggest that the Swedish government uses general consumption taxes to reduce consumption levels and promote savings; instead, the Social Democrats use these taxes, along with other forms of taxation, to *redistribute* consumption. By taxing all citizens heavily and then redistributing that income, the government is effectively "churning" income within society. The result is that even the poorest have relatively high levels of real and disposable income, good housing, and the ability to take periodic vacations. At the same time, however, the Swedes have taxed "sins" very heavily in the hopes of reducing certain kinds of consumer behavior. But this type of tax appears to be an exception to the general tax rule in this country.

Despite the nominally socialist label held by the Swedish Social Democrats, tax policy in Sweden is about generating revenues to build a redistributive and just social welfare state *without interfering in the capitalist economy any more than necessary.*[5] To be sure, taxes on income and profits are used to encourage general investment in Sweden, but tax policy is not manipulated to encourage or discourage particular patterns of consumption in favor of Swedish manufacturers or industries.

The key to understanding these curious policies lies in the particular character of Swedish corporatist decision-making institutions. In this highly centralized system, business, labor and political elites meet in (literally) closed-door sessions to coordinate annual wage demands, tax policy, and social welfare spending policy. Like politicians everywhere, Social Democratic elites are continually faced with pressures to increase public spending. In Swedish corporatism, the government is able to go to the very agents of these demands (the unions) and offer them a deal: increased spending on health care or public housing in return for increased taxes. The employers' federation (SAF), which is also sitting at the table, will oppose increases in corporate profits taxes because they reduce investment levels and thereby jobs. Another option is to increase income taxes on workers by lowering tax thresholds and increasing rates at lower income levels. But since labor union officials do not want to be held responsible

[5] Ernst Wigforss, *Skrifter und urval, vol. III: financeministern* [Writings and selections, vol. III: The Finance Ministry] (Stockholm: Tiden, 1980).

for the direct taxation of their own workers, the government generally finds it preferable and less politically painful to increase general consumption taxes.

Electoral Rules, Corporatism, and Tax Policy

When the Social Democratic Party (SAP) attained power in 1932, it promised its supporters (particularly labor unions) that it would create a more equitable tax system. But the mid-1930s were difficult economic times, of course, so tax increases had to wait until circumstances would allow them. Time, it so happened, was what the Social Democrats had plenty of. They would remain in office from 1932 to 1976.

What accounts for the enormous stability of the Swedish government? Up until 1974 Sweden had a bicameral legislature in which lower house seats were filled every three years in a proportional representation (PR) electoral system, while representatives in the upper house were selected on a regional basis (also a PR system), but with only an eighth of the members up for election in any given term. Thus, once a party controlled both houses of parliament, as the Social Democrats did by the 1940s, it could be quite confident that it would *continue* to dominate the government—*even if it lost seats in the next election.* This institutional fact is the cornerstone for understanding the development of tax policy in twentieth-century Sweden.

Precisely because of its enormous electoral stability, the Social Democrats were able to engage in long-term tax planning. Equally important, stability allowed them to make deals with interest groups and other political parties in ways quite unimaginable in countries with more fluid or uncertain electoral outcomes. Put bluntly, the minister of finance could (and did) force both labor unions and companies to the negotiating table and promise them that deals struck in this corporatist setting would be enforced for many years to come. At the same time, however, Sweden's PR system made it unlikely that the Social Democrats would control the parliament as an absolute majority.[6] This effectively constrained the SAP. Even if the Social Democrats wished to impose radical redistributive policies, they would probably not be able to push those policies through parliament unless they happened to be in alliance with another smaller party. In short, Sweden's particular electoral institutions had a profoundly stabilizing and regularizing effect on the government's political choices because they dramatically shaped the strategic context of all the major political actors involved.

One should note that in 1974, under significant pressure to "democra-

[6] Olof Ruin, "Patterns of Government Composition in Multi-Party Systems: The Case of Sweden," *Scandinavian Political Studies* 4 (1969): 71–87.

tize" the political system, the Social Democrats agreed to a major constitutional revision. The key feature of this revision was elimination of the upper chamber. Significantly, in the next election (1976) the Social Democrats were removed from government for the first time in forty-four years. Though most of the basic systems and structures underlying the Swedish tax and social welfare system were well in place by then, there can be no doubt that politics became more "politicized" over the next several years. But one should not overemphasize the effects of this change. Sweden's system of proportional representation continues to this day and still provides enormous political stability—especially when compared to single-member district systems like those found in the United States and Britain.[7]

The most dramatic and obvious consequence of these institutional incentives on Swedish tax policy was apparent by the late 1930s. In 1938–39 the SAP decided to bring the unions and employers to the negotiating table. Up to that point, Sweden had the highest strike rate of any country in Europe; strikes and lock-outs were severely damaging the country's economic performance. The SAP offered both the unions and employers incentives to bargain together more peacefully. After a series of negotiations that were far too complex to reiterate here, the unions received a set of recruiting tools, including the power to distribute unemployment insurance. Large corporations, meanwhile, obtained generous tax breaks that virtually eliminated their tax burdens as long as they reinvested their profits in Sweden. This was the beginning of Sweden's famous "historic compromise" or "corporatist" system—a system in which tax policy always played an important part.

In Sweden, as in most countries, World War II resulted in large tax increases and an expanding public debt. A temporary sales tax was introduced at this time, as were increases in a variety of excise taxes (taxes on particular items). Probably the most important innovation was the introduction of the mass-based income tax. Income taxes had been a fixture in Sweden since early in the century but had been levied mostly on the wealthy. During the war, finance officials realized that as average wages increased, they could tax these incomes and generate huge revenues. And these taxes could be collected very conveniently through the "Pay As You Go" (PAYG) system in which employers deducted taxes from their employees' paychecks. This system proved to be an enormously efficient and effective means for raising revenue. To balance the new working-class taxes, the government also increased inheritance taxes, wealth taxes, special wartime "excess profits" taxes, and income tax rates on high-income earners. The rates and levels of each of these taxes were negotiated annually in the corporatist setting discussed above. And since it was wartime, the

[7] Sven Steinmo, *Taxation and Democracy* (New Haven: Yale University Press, 1993), 179–84.

government had few problems convincing the participants that everyone had to sacrifice to keep Sweden strong and neutral.[8]

To the surprise and disappointment of many, taxes were not dramatically scaled back at the end of World War II. Although the temporary sales tax was abolished, there was a widespread understanding that as long as the government shouldered its enormous war debts, taxes must remain high. The Swedish economy was also rapidly modernizing, which meant that the need for government spending would grow. At the same time, Swedish workers had begun to demand benefits like higher pensions and public health care. Against this backdrop, cutting back taxes was simply not an option. But the Social Democrats also understood that taxing Swedish firms too heavily would kill the goose that laid the national income egg.[9] Fortunately, the new mass-based income tax generated enormous revenue growth. Effectively, then, the politics of taxation in Sweden (as elsewhere in the 1950s) became the politics of tax cuts. And as annual negotiations among labor, business, and the state were institutionalized, potentially explosive tax, wage, and public spending policies grew remarkably depoliticized.[10]

Consumption Taxes and the Welfare State

The major exception to the depoliticization of fiscal policy occurred vis-à-vis consumption taxes. As the Swedish economy developed, the Social Democratic elite reasoned that they would not be able to depend forever on the "automatic" revenue growth generated by bracket creep and inflation because of the political backlash that would inevitably arise. At the same time, they fully believed that social justice required the construction of more comprehensive and better-financed social welfare policies.

By the late 1950s, Finance Minister Gunnar Sträng had concluded that if Swedish workers were going to have the social programs they wanted, they would have to pay for them through increased taxes. By this point, Ministry of Finance officials were committed to promoting Swedish capital in the international marketplace and saw no alternative but to revive the consumption taxes that they had earlier repealed. These elites understood that if the Swedish welfare state were to grow, Sweden would need to shift its tax burden toward consumption taxes and social insurance charges. The fundamental economic problem with direct income taxation was the same problem that had confronted consumption taxes several decades before, namely, that after a certain level you cannot increase rates

[8] Enrique Rodriguez, *Offentlig inkomstexpansion* [Expansion of state revenues] (Uppsala: Gleerup, 1980).

[9] Sven Steinmo, "So What's Wrong with Tax Expenditures: A Re-evaluation Based on Swedish Experience," *Journal of Public Budgeting and Finance* 6, no. 2 (1986): 27–44.

[10] Lars Magnusson, *Sveriges ekonomiska historia* [Swedish economic history] (Stockholm: Tiden/Athena, 1997).

and generate more revenues. If marginal tax rates on income were to exceed 80 percent, for example, either people would stop working (and investing) or they would leave the country. Neither scenario would be good for the economy, jobs, or the working class. In response to these fiscal realities, the Ministry of Finance concluded that they would have to reintroduce a consumption tax.[11] In this instance, the consumption tax was seen as a way to raise revenue, which was deemed more important to the government than the short-term dampening effects that the tax would have on consumption.[12] Because the Social Democrats were philosophically committed to redistributive policies and because he had specifically argued that the SAP should *lower* taxes paid by the working classes, Sträng had to clear several hurdles before introducing a general consumption tax. Consumption or sales taxes are clearly regressive. Sträng had to convince his working-class base that *they* needed to pay higher taxes if they wanted to receive more social welfare programs in the future. Swedes, like citizens everywhere, believe that they pay too much in taxes and that the rich do not pay enough; if the government needs more money for social programs, why not tax the rich more? In public opinion polls taken at the time, it was clear that the majority of voters—and even stronger majorities of Social Democratic voters—opposed the sales tax.[13]

Sträng was undeterred by these political problems. He strongly believed that a large welfare state was in the interests of the working class and that the working class would have to pay for it if the capitalist economy were to remain internationally competitive. He launched a vigorous "education" campaign and personally attended local party and labor union meetings around the country in order to convince the Social Democratic base of the need for a new sales tax. In 1959, when he felt that he had generated sufficient support, he moved to introduce the new tax in parliament.

Once introduced, the government increased the 4.2 percent sales tax almost immediately. From the start, nearly all parties understood that the sales tax would become a major revenue source in the long run. Why? Because it is a "hidden tax" that is much easier to increase than income or profits taxes.

In 1970 the sales tax was converted to the Value Added Tax (VAT) for reasons of administrative efficiency. Whereas a sales tax is added at the point of retail sale, the VAT is integrated into the price of goods. Those involved understood that the move would make it even easier to increase this

[11] Enrique Rodriguez, *Den svenska skattehistorien* [Swedish tax history] (Lund: Liber laromedel, 1981).

[12] Donald Hancock, *Sweden: The Politics of Post-Industrial Change* (Hindsdale, IL: Dryden Press, 1972).

[13] Bo Särlvik, "Party Politics and Electoral Opinion Formation," *Scandinavian Political Studies* 2 (1967): 171.

revenue source in the future. Consequently, the VAT has grown from 10.3 percent of total tax revenue in 1970 to 17.7 percent in 2001.[14] As in other European countries, it is a major source of income.

One should not assume that these tax increases have always been uncontroversial. In fact, each major attempt to increase the general consumption tax has met with considerable opposition from both the left and the right. The left (especially the unions) has opposed increases on the grounds that the tax is regressive and places an uneven burden on those least able to pay. The right has consistently opposed consumption tax increases not because of their effects on consumption but because these taxes generate revenue too easily. The right (even in Sweden) is philosophically opposed to growing the welfare state: "hidden" taxes enable this growth. At each of these junctures, various Social Democratic governments have met the objections of the left by balancing tax increases with increases in specific programs meant to offset the burden shouldered by the poor in society. To address the concerns of the right, governments have simply argued that it is better for Swedish industry to increase taxes on consumption than to increase income and profits taxes and that increasing the public debt is not an option.[15]

Of course, consumption taxes have been only one revenue instrument in the Swedish government's arsenal. We have emphasized the consumption tax here, but many of the dynamics discussed above can be applied to income and social security taxes as well. Again, with the exception of profits taxes, most taxes in Sweden are high compared to those of other OECD nations. The bottom line is that Swedes believe that taxes should be used not as instruments of *direct* redistributive policy but rather as a means to generate revenues for social programs. Thus, all taxes should be levied in ways that generate the most revenue with the least amount of social and economic disruption. The Swedish elite have concluded that to the extent the government wishes to intervene in society and the economy, it should do so through direct public spending. In short, it is more economically efficient and socially just to directly subsidize individuals' incomes than to create a distortional tax system.

Sin Taxes

This is not the whole story. Even though the general trend has been toward a decline in taxes on specific goods and services, there has also been strong and consistent pressure to increase taxes on certain items—not so much

14 OECD, *Revenue Statistics, 1965–2002,* table 29.

15 Thomas Frazen, "Skatternas effect pa arbetsviljan" [Taxation's effect on the willingness to work], *Oversyn av skate systemet* [Overview of the tax system] 91 (1977): 357–96.

for their revenues as for their regulatory effects on consumption. One of the curious effects of Sweden's system of proportional representation has been that the relatively smaller parties will sometimes have more political influence than one might expect given their size. This is because their votes in parliament can be crucial to holding a coalition together. This has been particularly true for the traditional Farmer's Party (now Center Party), which has occasionally supported the Social Democrats in exchange for support from farmers and other groups that espouse traditional values. Many of the "traditionalists" in Scandinavia have been strongly anti-alcohol, and the government has accommodated their preferences by increasing taxes on alcohol. Clearly, these groups wanted to increase taxes on alcohol (and tobacco) as a way to discourage consumption. The Social Democrats, however, were less concerned with the moral function of these taxes but clearly enjoyed the revenues that they would bring in.[16] Consequently, Sweden (along with its neighbor Norway) has long had the distinction of having the heaviest liquor taxes in the world. As anyone who has spent time in these countries knows, a bottle of vodka costing eight dollars in the United States costs over forty dollars in Sweden. Over time, these taxes (and the state liquor stores that have a monopoly on liquor sales) have become an important source of revenue in their own right. In recent years, the Social Democrats have also accommodated the demands of younger "green" interests in society by introducing "green" carbon taxes. In 2001, excise taxes made up 3.5 percent of GDP, down from 6.7 percent of GDP in 1965 (see table 9.2).

Summing Up

With the exception of taxes on "sinful products," the politics of consumption taxes has not really been about consumption in Sweden—at least not directly. Instead, as we have tried to show, policymakers have thought of consumption taxes as a means to generate revenues which could then be redistributed back to taxpayers in the form of either direct or indirect subsidies. Although we have not seen specific discussions of these policies in such terms, the Swedish welfare state has effectively redistributed consumption. The system takes more from the rich than from the poor, since the rich consume more. Public spending, meanwhile, favors those at the lower end of the income scale in that the poor are provided with health care, public education, and other "goods" that they cannot afford to "buy" themselves. There is, in short, a close and dynamic interrelationship among consumption, consumption taxes, and social welfare benefits in Sweden that will no doubt persist in the future.

[16] Rodriguez, *Offentlig inkomstexpansion.*

Taxing Consumption in Japan

Japan offers an interesting comparison to Sweden for a variety of reasons. Japan, like Sweden, has had a strong commitment to economic equality since World War II. With the exception of a very brief period during the 1990s, moreover, its political system has been dominated by a single party for the past five decades. In terms of tax policy outcomes, however, Japan is the virtual opposite of Sweden. Japan has the lowest overall tax burden in the OECD today. It also has very low (regressive) consumption taxes and very high (progressive) corporate profits taxes compared to other advanced nations. This is surprising when we consider that Japan has pursued a policy that discouraged consumption in favor of stimulating household savings for most of the postwar period (see Garon, chap. 7). In the pages that follow we attempt to make sense of these curious facts.

As in Sweden, the key to understanding Japanese policy outcomes lies in the particular structure of the country's political institutions. First, under the old multi-member district system, the political balance of power in the national legislature, the Diet, strongly favored the countryside in that rural electoral districts were given three to five seats without much correlation to population size. Rural areas tend to have far fewer citizens per district than urban centers. They also tend to have populations that are considerably older and poorer than those of cities and tend to be dominated by small and/or traditional producers.[17] Although the electoral reforms of 1994 redressed some of the worst of these inequities, the fundamental problem of urban underrepresentation persists today. This has contributed to a tax system that excessively favors rural citizens and small businesses.

Second, pre-1994 electoral rules encouraged politicians to run for office as semi-independent political entrepreneurs. In this system, politicians were primarily responsible to their home electoral districts rather than to the parties to which they nominally belonged. In many ways the electoral incentives facing Japanese politicians are quite similar to those facing American political elites. Consequently, the parties (and the LDP in particular) were little more than groups of politicians who were committed more to the needs of their constituents than to specific ideologies or political agendas. In this ideological vacuum, national bureaucrats tended to assume ultimate responsibility for the details of policymaking.

Japan's political institutions have had enormous consequences for consumption tax policy and for the structure of the Japanese welfare state. Faced with these electoral realities and a broad national consensus in support of strong, successful industries, bureaucrats established a system that

[17] Andrew DeWit and Sven Steinmo, "Policy Vs. Rhetoric: The Political Economy of Taxation and Redistribution in Japan," *Social Science Japan Journal* 5, no. 2 (2002): 159–62.

uses the economic wealth generated by Japan's successful international firms to subsidize the interests of the rural voters and small businessmen who make up the electoral core of the LDP.

Whereas the dominant political party in Sweden has been ideologically committed to promoting long-term social and economic equity, the LDP has been driven almost entirely by short-term electoral incentives. In both cases, bureaucrats (especially in the ministries of finance) have had to balance the demands of different interest groups as represented by elected politicians. In Sweden, bureaucrats have convinced politicians of the need to sacrifice short-term benefits in favor of longer-term structural change. Japanese officials, however, have been far less successful in this regard.

Japan's Postwar Tax Policy

At the end of World War II, American reformers set out to "modernize" Japan's tax system. The Shoup Commission, led by U.S. fiscal policy expert Carl Shoup, believed that social equity was necessary for the development of a successful democracy in Japan. The commission therefore pressed for the adoption of the "ability to pay" principle, in which those with higher incomes would pay higher rates of tax. The commission also believed that consumption taxes were inefficient and unfair and that they should be avoided in almost all circumstances.

The Japanese Ministry of Finance (MOF), which was searching for ways to fuel economic reconstruction, had other ideas. The MOF could not depend on income tax revenues given the poverty-stricken state of ordinary citizens, industrial stagnation, and the burgeoning black market, which made some incomes nearly impossible to pinpoint. Instead, the ministry believed that indirect taxes could provide government with a lucrative and immediate source of revenue.[18] In 1948, the MOF imposed a type of general sales tax called a "transactions tax." But the tax was soon scrapped following protests from small firms fearing increased governmental interference in their affairs and from the Shoup Commission itself, which viewed the tax as a violation of the equity principle.[19] After failing to introduce a broad-based consumption tax, the MOF increased taxes on specific goods—particularly luxury goods. In this way, it hoped to raise revenues while assuaging the Shoup Commission's commitment to pro-

18 Kurt Steiner, *Local Government in Japan* (Stanford: Stanford University Press, 1965), 265; and Hiromitsu Ishi, *The Japanese Tax System*, 3d ed. (Oxford: Clarendon Press, 2001), 264.

19 See General Headquarters, Supreme Commander for the Allied Powers, *Report on Japanese Taxation by Shoup Mission*, vol. 2 (Tokyo: GHQ, SCAP, 1949), 166; and Miyajima Hiroshi, "Kansetsuzei to fukakachizei" [Indirect taxes and value added taxes], in Nihon sozei kenkyū kyōkai, ed., *Shaupu kankoku to wagakuni no zeisei* [Shoup recommendations and the Japanese tax system] (Tokyo: Nihon sozei kenkyū kyōkai 1982), 280–81.

gressive taxation.[20] But in incorporating new items into the tax net or increasing the rates of existing taxes, the MOF faced strong opposition from small business groups that feared an increase in their tax burdens. These groups successfully pressured their Diet representatives not to impose taxes on new items and not to increase tax rates.

The MOF's attempts to raise tax revenues over the next several years were met with stiff opposition from politicians, who offered all manner of tax breaks to their constituents. Politicians also demanded substantial spending increases—particularly for programs that would alleviate the economic and social plight of Japan's rural (and declining) communities. In 1957, finance officials attempted once again to introduce a general sales tax, only to confront insurmountable resistance from small producers, retailers, and rural interests.

A key point to note here is the lack of strong political leadership in Japan. No one has the ultimate political authority to balance costs against benefits for the budget as a whole. Nor does Japan have an equivalent to Sweden's Gunnar Sträng—someone who can bring diverse interests together and convince them of the need to make short-term sacrifices for long-term gains. As we have seen, Japanese politicians are primarily concerned about the immediate interests of their constituents and have almost no incentive to promote the longer-term interests of the nation as a whole. Although the MOF often took on this responsibility, its policy prescriptions were usually rejected by shortsighted elected officials.

The conflict between the MOF and the Diet was further complicated by the growing influence of the Ministry of International Trade and Industry (MITI) during the early postwar period. Not surprisingly, the MITI saw tax policy as a potent instrument for directing the economy. At first, the MITI attempted to manipulate taxes in order to promote targeted industries and firms early in their life cycles, and the MOF tolerated this strategy.[21] By the mid-1950s, however, its tax policies also embraced costly subsidies for ailing industries and regions.[22] Although the MOF had been increasingly dis-

[20] For a discussion of this period in Japanese public finance, see Yoshida Shintarō, "Zeisei kaikaku to kansetsuzei" [Tax reform and indirect taxes], *Keizaigaku ronshū* 19, no. 6–7 (1950): 94–108; Suzuki Takeo, *Gendai nihon zaiseishi* [History of public finance in contemporary Japan] (Tokyo: Tokyo daigaku shuppankai, 1960), 4:372–73; Takagi Katsuichi, "Shaupu kankaku to kansetsuzei" [Shoup recommendations and indirect taxes], in *Zaisei no genri to genjitsu* [Principles and practice of public finance], ed. Ide Fumio, Obuchi Toshio, Ishimura Chōgorō, and Nakamura Kazuo (Tokyo: Chikura shobō, 1986), 182–92.

[21] See Yoshida Shintarō, "Shaupu chihō zeisei no seiritsu to kaitai" [Establishment and dismantlement of the Shoup local tax system], in *Sengo chihō zaisei no tenkai* [Development of postwar local public finance], ed. Fujita Takeo kyōjū kanreki kinen ronshū kankō kai (Tokyo: Nihon hyōronsha, 1968), 116, 123.

[22] See Nobuhiro Hiwatari, *Organized Markets and the Restrained State: Institutions for Industrial Policy, Incomes Coordination, and Political Quiescence in Postwar Japan*, Ph.D. dissertation, University of California, Berkeley, 1989, pp. 67–68; and Noguchi Yukio, *1940 nen taisei: saraba senji keizai* [1940 regime: good-bye wartime economy], 2d ed. (Tokyo: Tōyō keizai shinpōsha, 2002), 117–22.

satisfied with its rival's policies, the newly formed Liberal Democratic Party endorsed the MITI's backward-looking approach to taxation since it reinforced the party's efforts to consolidate its base of support among farmers and the petite bourgeoisie.[23]

Economic Growth as a National Goal

As Japanese administrators obsessed about economic growth during the 1950s and 1960s, ordinary consumers strived to assume American lifestyles. The media bombarded consumers with information about consumer durables such as refrigerators, vacuum cleaners, washing machines, television sets, and cars. Domestic firms advertised these products with catch phrases like "The Three Sacred Treasures," "The First Year of the Electrification Era," and "The First Year of the Motorization Era." Consumers were encouraged through public education and tax incentives to save for major purchases of consumer goods.[24] At the same time, the government facilitated investment in plants and equipment by providing firms with low-interest loans funded by public savings, while mass production and rapid innovation led to economies of scale and large price cuts for durable goods.[25] But as Garon points out in this volume, there is a tradeoff between savings and consumption. In this case, Japanese citizens were essentially told to "save now, buy later."

As incomes rose and living standards improved, social class distinctions dissolved and the populace increasingly thought of itself as middle class. Rural areas suffered, however, as economic rationalization spurred a massive movement of labor away from agriculture and traditional industries toward the large export-oriented manufacturing firms of large cities.[26] In its attempts to redistribute the benefits of increased national growth and shore up its traditional base of political support, the LDP expanded public works projects in rural districts. Travelers from crowded cities like Tokyo or Osaka are often surprised to find large but deserted highways, bridges, and tunnels in Japan's outlying areas. These facilities were built not to alleviate any real traffic burden but to boost employment in Japan's powerful local construction industry; as such, they constitute a major drain on the country's tax revenues. There may be no better example of the inherent producer bias of Japanese public policy.

As the economy evolved and the LDP grappled with declining popular support levels, the party began gradually to incorporate workers into its

[23] Garon and Mochizuki, "Negotiating Social Contracts," 152.

[24] Sheldon Garon, *Molding Japanese Minds: The State in Everyday Life* (Princeton: Princeton University Press, 1997), 154–57.

[25] Maki Atsushi, *Nihonjin no shōhi kōdō* [Japanese consumer behavior] (Tokyo: Chikuma shinsho, 1998), 78–82.

[26] Yoshikawa Hiroshi, *Kōdo seichō: Nihon o kaeta 6,000 nichi* [High economic growth: 6,000 days that changed Japan] (Tokyo: Yomiuri shinbunsha, 1997), 184–85.

base of political support. This pro-labor orientation was consolidated in the LDP's "Labor Charter" (1966), which promoted full employment, better working conditions, and enhanced social welfare.[27] Later, the LDP's "Report on the Circumstances of the LDP" (1969) encouraged the party to engage labor in more dialogue. Accordingly, labor participation in the policymaking process increased during the early 1970s, and the unions grew more demanding of government.[28]

The 1973 oil crisis dramatically altered the focus of Japanese politics. For one thing, it transformed budgetary politics from a positive-sum to a zero-sum game. Consequently, the LDP could no longer rely on automatic revenue growth—generated by bracket creep and economic expansion—to fund public programs. At the same time, unions and big business interests were starting to bristle after years of footing the national bill for social and economic subsidies. It is one thing for firms and urban workers to subsidize the less fortunate in society when they are steadily becoming richer; it is quite another when subsidies force the payee to make significant financial sacrifices.

In response to this new political reality, big business and moderate labor unions joined forces to prevent further expansion of the welfare state.[29] During the early high-growth years, many corporate managers had come to regard corporate taxes not so much as "expenses" as profit allotments earmarked for the advancement of the public good. By the 1970s, however, business interests feared that increased public-sector growth would inevitably mean increased corporate taxes—even as profit margins fell. Thus, big business became deeply skeptical of public-sector growth and demanded administrative reform and fiscal restraint.[30]

We saw in the Swedish case how labor union elites came to accept increases in their own tax burden *in exchange for* social welfare and social safety-net programs. In Japan, in part because private-sector unions were organized inside companies (the "enterprise unions"), workers in large successful firms were able to extract from their employers generous benefits, including lifetime employment, housing subsidies, health care, and bonus and retirement payments. The Japanese firm, in short, became the employee's welfare state. Large Japanese businesses gave their workers added incentives to place their trust in the company by linking salaries to total corporate sales.[31] For as long as big businesses continued to prosper, therefore, these workers neither needed nor wanted an expanded public

[27] Garon and Mochizuki, "Negotiating Social Contracts," 160.

[28] Hiwatari, *Organized Markets and the Restrained State,* 54; Ikuo Kume, *Disparaged Success: Labor Politics in Postwar Japan* (Ithaca: Cornell University Press, 1998), 116; and Yoshikawa, *Kōdo seichō,* 185.

[29] Kume Ikuo, *Nihongata rōshi kankei no seikō* [Success of Japanese-style labor-management relations] (Tokyo: Yūhikaku, 1998), 190–95; and Itō Mitsutoshi, "Daikigyō rōshirengō no keisei" [Formation of the business-labor alliance], *Leviathan* 2 (Spring 1988): 59–66.

[30] Itō, "Daikigyō rōshirengō," 61–62.

[31] Hiwatari, *Organized Markets and the Restrained State,* 40–43.

welfare state. To complicate matters, labor was politically weak. Whereas Swedish unions were organized by craft at the national level and had strong confederal leadership, Japanese worker interests were divided along vertical lines. In Sweden, unions fought for the rights of all workers (and thus consumers) because they represented nearly all workers (and consumers). In Japan, union elites had strong incentives to negotiate for the interests of their workers primarily at the firm level. These structural differences encouraged Japanese labor to see its interests more narrowly than Swedish labor.

But the internationalization of the Japanese economy and the first oil crisis prompted the private-sector union leaders—*Dōmei,* the International Metalworkers' Federation–Japan Council (IMF-JC), and the Council for Policy Promotion Unions (CPPU)—to moderate their demands and to participate in political negotiations with the LDP. Their strategy was to maintain real wage levels through income tax cuts and an anti-inflation policy, and they were willing to restrain their nominal wage increases to ensure employment. Public sector unions (*Sōhyō*) were not so accommodating. Since they did not feel the pressures of international competition, they advocated high wage increases and demanded improvements in welfare policy. Since the mid-1970s, however, moderate, private-sector union leaders eventually supplanted the left-leaning leaders of Japan's union movement as it became increasingly necessary to gain the support of the centrist parties and to negotiate with the LDP over issues that could not be solved at the company level.[32]

Because Japanese workers employed in large, successful firms received higher wages than those outside the economically successful "core," they paid higher taxes. The government then redistributed this income to small business owners, farmers, and rural workers. The inequity of this situation was exacerbated by the open secret that wealthy farmers and small business owners rarely paid taxes. Urban workers soon resented what they perceived to be an unfair tax system. Whereas Swedish unions regarded public spending as a mechanism for increasing the consumption levels of the workers and the poor, Japanese unions saw public spending as subsidies to the unproductive (but politically powerful) rural and small business interests.

At this time, the LDP's traditional supporters were facing international pressures to liberalize the domestic economy, including the agricultural and large retail sectors. The LDP had no choice but to respond to such pressures, and it tried to secure the support of private-sector unions as it did so. This enhanced the labor-management coalition's influence, accelerated the decline of the left within the labor movement, and helped

[32] For more on these trends, see Tsujinaka Yutaka, "Kyūchi ni tatsu rōdō no seisaku kettei" [Policy decisions by labor in crisis], in *Nihongata seisaku kettei no henyō* [Transformation of Japanese policymaking], ed. Nakano Minoru (Tokyo: Tōyō keizai shinpōsha, 1986), 289–90; and Kume, *Disparaged Success,* 141–42.

weaken opposition to administrative reform from both the bureaucracy and *Sōhyō*. It was also at this time that Prime Minister Nakasone Yasuhiro put forth his own proposals for administrative reform, first as the minister of the Administrative Management Agency and then as prime minister (1982–87).[33] Among his objectives was the introduction of a consumption tax. This proved to be an onerous task, however, given the conflicting demands of the LDP's traditional supporters, on the one hand, and the labor-management coalition, on the other.

The Long Road to a Consumption Tax (VAT)

In the context of labor's resistance to higher income taxes, MOF officials increased their efforts during the 1970s to introduce a general consumption tax that would be evenly distributed across society. Like their Swedish counterparts, they recognized that consumption taxes were necessary components of a more stable financing system at a time when demands for government spending were increasing. Unlike the Swedes, however, Japanese officials could not find a strong political ally to help fight for this new tax. Instead, they faced resistance from small businesses, workers, middle-income housewives, and the politicians who represented them.[34] Women's groups were particularly vocal in their opposition to the consumption tax, arguing that it was unfair to tax items that consumers needed and used. It would be far more equitable, they believed, to tax luxuries while leaving the ordinary consumer's hard-earned cash alone.[35]

Despite the public's opposition, MOF officials intensified their pressure on LDP elites to introduce a general consumption tax. They eventually convinced Prime Minister Ohira Masayoshi, himself a former MOF official, to sponsor a general consumption tax proposal in the months leading up to the 1979 general election. From the party's point of view, this was a big mistake. Public opposition to the tax swelled immediately, the LDP did poorly in the election, and the general consumption tax was shelved. The MOF then turned its attention to spending cuts—at least for the time being.

Japan clearly faced a trilemma: the fiscal realities of a maturing welfare state conflicted with the political resistance to increased income and profits taxes, which in turn conflicted with the Diet's proclivity to increase subsidies for Japan's least productive sectors and regions. To cope with this

[33] Kume, *Disparaged Success,* 192–94, 203–4.

[34] For the best discussion of the politics of the VAT in this era, see Junko Kato, *The Problem of Bureaucratic Rationality: Tax Politics in Japan* (Princeton: Princeton University Press, 1994). See also Junko Kato, *Regressive Taxation and the Welfare State* (New York: Cambridge University Press, 2003).

[35] Ozaki Mamoru, *Zaisei seisaku e no shiten* [Viewpoint on fiscal policy] (Tokyo: Ōkura zaimu kyōkai, 2001), 309–11.

trilemma, the MOF tried to change the understanding that commodity taxes are a kind of luxury tax by broadening the list of taxable items to include word processors, fax machines, copy machines, personal computers, and other office equipment. Despite these changes, its attempt to introduce such a tax in 1984 failed on the heels of strong opposition from related industries and their politicians. And so the MOF redoubled its efforts to introduce the broad-based consumption tax, believing that once introduced it could be increased without too much opposition from industry and politicians.[36]

In defiance of his promise during the 1986 election not to introduce a general sales tax, Prime Minister Nakasone succumbed to pressure from the MOF and proposed a major tax reform package that offered income tax cuts in exchange for a general sales tax. Fearing that the MOF would increase the profits tax to finance income tax cuts—as it had done in 1984—big business supported the proposal in the hopes of avoiding possible tax hikes in the future.[37] In the face of strong opposition from the opposition parties and a voter backlash in local elections, however, all seven of Nakasone's bills were defeated.

In the midst of a mushrooming budget deficit, MOF officials grew increasingly frustrated by the Diet's inability to exercise fiscal discipline and continued to press for a broad-based (universal) consumption tax. Eventually, they convinced key LDP members that the current tax system, which relied heavily on income taxes, could not be sustained given Japan's rapidly aging society. Japan, they argued, had to make a very difficult choice: introduce a consumption tax or scale back the social security system—a system that was of particular benefit to the LDP's more traditional constituents.

The MOF's tax crusade touched the population's heartstrings. By this point, most middle-class consumers were feeling anxious about their retirements. A 1988 NHK opinion survey revealed that approximately half the population agreed that a general consumption tax was necessary given Japan's demographic circumstances. Respondents also stated that correcting inequities in the tax system should be settled before a consumption tax was introduced.[38]

Prime Minister Takeshita Noboru, a former LDP tax expert with a history of cooperating with MOF officials, finally agreed in 1988 to introduce

[36] Kishiro Yasuyuki, *Jimintō zeisei chōsakai* [LDP's tax commission] (Tokyo: Tōyō keizai shinpōsha, 1985), 1–9.

[37] Ōtani Hirochika, "Atsuryoku dantai no taiō" [Responses of pressure groups], in *Zeisei kaikaku o meguru seiji rikigaku* [Political dynamics of tax reform], ed. Uchida Kenzō, Kanazashi Masao, and Fukuoka Masayuki (Tokyo: Chūō kōronsha, 1988), 102–3.

[38] Ōkuma Sadao, "Fukōhei zesei/shōhizei ni kibishii hyōka: zeisei kaikaku chōsa kara" [Harsh criticisms of unequal taxes and consumption taxes: From the survey on tax reform], *Hōsō kenkyū to chōsa* 38, no. 9 (September 1988): 9.

a 3 percent consumption tax, effective in April 1989. Unfortunately, the proposed tax package offered income tax cuts that surpassed in value the projected returns from the consumption tax. The package also increased public spending for the poor and the elderly. These two items were designed to alleviate the regressive nature of the consumption tax and to obtain the support of the two centrist parties, the Komeitō and the Democratic Socialist Party.[39] The bill also contained loopholes for small businesses that simply exacerbated the inequity problem. Since small companies would be permitted to pocket taxes collected from consumers, the tax effectively functioned as a direct subsidy of small business by consumers. Not surprisingly, consumers—led by the housewives' associations—vehemently opposed the new tax.[40]

The political struggle surrounding the final stages of the decision-making process intensified as thousands of consumers took to the streets in protest. Despite these developments, the Diet passed the tax package. Takeshita, who was also under siege in the wake of the Recruit stocks-for-favors scandal, was forced to resign in April 1989. While many agreed with the principle of a consumption tax *in order to finance a more secure retirement system in the future,* few voters liked what the Diet had passed. As before, salarymen would be subsidizing small businesses, farmers, and, in this case, the self-employed. They were furious. In July 1989, the LDP was decimated in the upper house election.

By the early 1990s, Japan was in political and economic crisis. The enormous economic bubble of the mid- to late 1980s had finally burst, and the economy desperately needed restructuring. To combat the recession, the government introduced a series of income and corporate tax cuts and increased public works spending. Then, in 1994, Prime Minister Hosokawa Morihiro proposed raising the consumption tax rate to 7 percent and renaming it the "National Welfare Tax." Revealed to the public at a spur-of-the-moment midnight press conference, the proposal accommodated the demands of big business groups, the MOF, and MITI by exchanging income and corporate tax cuts for consumption tax increases. But as a result of vehement opposition from the Social Democratic Party of Japan (SDPJ, formerly the Japan Socialist Party), which threatened to leave the coalition if the increase were introduced, an embarrassed Hosokawa was forced to withdraw the proposal. In keeping with the demands of small business groups, the SDPJ supported income and corporate tax cuts financed by public debt rather than the consumption tax.[41]

[39] Mizuno Masaru, *Shūzei kyokuchō no 1,300 nichi* [1,300 days as chief of the tax bureau] (Tokyo: Ōkura zaimu kyōkai, 1993), 261–67.

[40] Yokoyama Shigeru and Kawano Hiraku, "Jimin antei tasū/shakai yakushin no haikei; dai 39kai shūgiin senkyo" [Background of the LDP's stable majority and the JSP's progress: the 39th lower house election], *Hōsō kenkyū to chōsa* 40, no.5 (May 1990): 9.

[41] Hiwatari Nobuhiro, "Zaisei seisaku" [Fiscal policy], in *Ryūdōki no nihon seiji* [Japanese

But the pressure to restructure the Japanese tax system was still on. In 1995 Hosokawa's successor, Prime Minister Murayama Tomiichi of the SDPJ, introduced income tax cuts and, in a complete reversal of his party's previous stance on the issue, raised the consumption tax from 3 to 5 percent, effective in 1997. The government had originally intended to raise the consumption tax to 7 percent, but this was scaled back in response to intense opposition from consumers and small businesses. One percent of the consumption tax was to be automatically transferred to local government authorities as part of a general devolution of the MOF's power.

When all was said and done, the government increased the general consumption tax not to finance the welfare state but to compensate for income and corporate tax cuts.[42] The government had embraced the neoliberal economic philosophy that tax cuts for business and high-income earners would stimulate the economy. But the strategy backfired. Fearing that the government could not be trusted with their retirement funds, consumers began saving more and spending less. Meanwhile, tax revenues continued to decline, the budget deficit soared, and the economy slipped into recession.[43]

Consumption Taxes and the Future of the Japanese Welfare State

The combined long-term debt of the central and local governments is expected to hit 774 trillion yen by the end of fiscal year 2005. Buoyed by the LDP's landslide victory in the September 2005 general election, Koizumi seems determined to delve deeper into fiscal reform. However, he has not provided a clear vision of how comprehensive tax reform should be carried out.

Japan still lacks the economic and political advantages that enabled Sweden to revamp their tax and social welfare systems four decades ago. Swedish elites operated within a context of high growth, public confidence in government, and an institutional structure that facilitated conciliation and compromise. Conversely, while the Japanese economy appears on the road to recovery, there is no reason to expect that the high growth rates of the 1960s will return. In addition, the government does not yet have enough public support to raise the consumption tax; the public's high regard for Koizumi notwithstanding, they still harbor a deep-seated distrust of political elites and a belief that the political process is rigged in favor of producers.

---

politics in the era of political mobility], Hiwatari Nobuhiro and Miura Mari (Tokyo: Tōkyō daigaku shuppankai, 2002), 208–9.

[42] Unlike their Swedish counterparts, Japanese governments have consistently increased taxes on specific products like *sake* and tobacco not so much for their regulatory effects on consumption as for their revenues.

[43] See Kato, *Regressive Taxation,* 181.

Fortunately for the tax-reform camp, however, their ranks are expanding. Determined to shift the burden of welfare policy from the private sector to the public sector, Keidanren supports consumption tax hikes earmarked for pension benefits. Rengō, Japan's leading labor federation, favors consumption tax—but not social security or income tax—increases because it wants to keep pension benefits at current levels. Finally, a recent poll reveals that the public's understanding of the need for a consumption tax increase has begun to grow since the recent general election; among those surveyed, 48 percent responded that the move was either acceptable or inevitable given current economic conditions.[44]

Meanwhile, there are signs that postwar political dynamics have been changing since Koizumi became prime minister in 2001. The 1994 changes to the electoral system, for instance, have encouraged parties to focus more on policy issues during election campaigns and less on particularistic favors to voters and interest groups. This in turn has legitimized Koizumi's attempts to introduce a top-down leadership system within the government and the LDP. Furthermore, the broad decision-making mandate of the Council on Economic and Fiscal Policy, which was created within the new Cabinet Office during the reorganization of government ministries and agencies in 2001, has made it easier for the cabinet to press forward with politically sensitive policies like tax reform. Finally, Koizumi has taken steps to loosen the influence of special interests over government budgeting as he prepares to cut spending—a move that should also have positive ramifications for future tax reform plans.

Nevertheless, problems remain. For over a decade, Japanese finance officials have pressed for consumption tax increases. But as of early 2006, the LDP remained split over whether or not to support the ministry on this issue. As they prepare for the post-Koizumi era, many LDP lawmakers are understandably worried about the effects of a tax hike on the party's popularity. Despite Koizumi's progress toward building a more effective top-down decision-making system, moreover, the government still lacks the institutional mechanisms for forging agreements across bureaucratic and party lines. As long as these conditions persist, tax reform will remain an uphill battle.

Conclusion

In this chapter, we have demonstrated that consumption tax policies in Sweden and Japan have followed quite different patterns. By the middle of the twentieth century in Sweden, the Social Democratic Party concluded that it should defy the left's historical opposition to regressive tax-

[44] *Nihon keizai shinbun*, November 2, 2005, morning edition, p. 1–2.

ation and raise consumption taxes in order to finance a generous welfare state. An egalitarian society, they believed, could be had through an extensive social welfare system, while the regressive effects of consumption taxes could be overcome by direct public subsidies to those in need. Although Swedes did not speak of it in these terms, the result of this policy was a positive redistribution of consumption. In Japan, by contrast, the conservative government has been unable or unwilling—at least until recently—to increase consumption taxes over the opposition of consumers and small producers. As a result, the government has failed to raise the revenue needed to fund an expanded social welfare state. The weakness of the social welfare state has in turn contributed to consumers' distrust of the government's ability to use their tax money wisely as well as deep suspicion of any tax changes that might increase the burden on lower-income groups.

In contrast to Sweden, Japanese consumption taxes have been used to shape economic outcomes in favor of producer groups rather than to improve the welfare of ordinary consumers. And to the extent that consumption has been redistributed, it has been through a net transfer of income and wealth from the productive sectors of the economy to the less competitive small business and agricultural sectors. The fiscal consequences of these political circumstances are clear. As Japanese society ages, more and more individuals will stop paying income taxes and place increasing demands on the welfare state. Without major new sources of revenue, Japan's fiscal future looks grim indeed.

Our case studies show quite clearly that while consumption taxes have had an impact on consumer behavior, they have rarely been used intentionally—or effectively—in this regard. Instead, these taxes are more accurately seen as the product of a broader set of political and economic agendas.

10

GLOBAL TRENDS VS. LOCAL TRADITIONS

Genetically Modified Foods and Contemporary Consumerism in the United States, Japan, and Britain

PATRICIA L. MACLACHLAN

In recent years, the specter of genetically modified foods has galvanized postwar consumer activism as no other event since Ralph Nader's mid-1960s crusade against General Motors. At first glance, the similarities between the two "anti-GM" campaigns are striking. Both embody the information gap between consumers and manufacturers, the inability (or unwillingness) of governments to respond to the specific demands of consumers, and the consumers' quest for more control over the products they purchase. But while Nader's campaign against General Motors' sale of an unsafe product—the Corvair—was limited to the American market and backed by middle-class consumers, the campaign against agricultural biotechnology crosses national borders to embrace consumers of many nationalities and socioeconomic classes. As such, it may very well be the largest, most global consumer movement in modern history.

The movement against GM foods is intriguing because there is no conclusive evidence that these foods are unsafe for human consumption. So, why the uproar? One reason is that GM foods have become a highly potent symbol of the "consumer condition" in the context of economic globalization. One of my purposes in this chapter is to identify the ethical, economic, and political forces that have shaped consumer discontent vis-à-vis these products at the international level.

Consumer opposition to GM foods has also been shaped by very local concerns. To illustrate this point, I compare and contrast consumer attitudes toward genetically modified organisms (GMOs) in three countries where the biotechnology industry has become an important economic player: the United States, Britain, and Japan. In the United States, a so-called bastion of consumer power, many consumers seem surprisingly complacent about biotechnology and have done comparatively little to stem the flow of GMOs into the marketplace. The Japanese, by contrast, are highly distrustful of the biotech industry and have managed to wrest small but significant concessions from their otherwise pro-business government. British consumers, who enjoy more representation in policymaking institutions than the Japanese, are equally distrustful of biotechnology but are fighting an uphill battle against the biotech industry and its government backers. As the following pages illustrate, these national discrepancies are the product of cultural and historical factors, consumer awareness of agricultural biotechnology, and of the particular institutional contexts of national consumer politics.

The Promises of Agricultural Biotechnology

Since Watson and Crick discovered the double helix structure of DNA a half-century ago, scientists have made remarkable progress in creating more resilient plant strains. By the 1970s, molecular biologists had mastered the now routine procedure of transferring genes among different plant species, making them permanent parts of the host's genome.[1] These developments spawned the meteoric growth of the American agricultural-biotechnology industry, which has invested billions of dollars into the research and development of plant-based genetic modification. By the early to mid-1990s, American regulatory agencies had approved genetically engineered corn, soybeans, rapeseed, cotton, and a number of other crops for cultivation in the United States. Within a few short years, food products with genetically modified components were being distributed to food processors and retail shops around the world.

Two types of GM crops dominate the industry. The first is crops engineered to contain a gene from *Bacillus thuringiensis,* also called *Bt,* a natural, soil-based bacteria that is toxic to moths and other pests but, according to most scientific studies, is safe for human consumption. The other is the so-called Roundup Ready strains of maize, soybeans, and cotton produced by Monsanto, the world's leading biotech corporation. Roundup is the trade name for glyphosate, a chemical herbicide introduced by Monsanto in 1974 that does not pose any known risks to humans.[2] Roundup Ready crops can tolerate having glyphosate sprayed directly on them.

The actual and potential benefits of agricultural biotechnology are at least threefold. First, GM crops allow farmers to cut costs and, in the case

[1] Mark L. Winston, *Travels in the Genetically Modified Zone* (Cambridge: Harvard University Press, 2002), 3.

[2] "Roundup Unready," *New York Times,* February 19, 2003.

of *Bt* crops, reduce the application of chemical substances during the growing process. By contributing to the development of sturdier plant strains and facilitating intensive cultivation, moreover, genetic engineering promises to meet the expanding global demand for food.[3] Third, although GM foods now on the market are nutritionally equivalent to their conventional counterparts, this may soon change. Scientists are developing varieties of crops containing nutrient-producing genes that may help redress vitamin-related malnutrition syndromes, including childhood blindness in developing countries, and even stave off disease.[4]

By all accounts, agricultural biotechnology stands at the forefront of scientific progress. Consumers in many countries praise biotechnology's accomplishments and willingly consume its products. Others, however, fear that in their zeal to promote progress, scientists, industry, and government may be unleashing a Frankenstein into the international food supply.

The Movement against "Frankenfoods": Participants, Tactics, and Common Themes

Genetically modified organisms sparked opposition from a diverse array of citizen groups even before those foods hit the consumer market. Included in the movement are a variety of organizations, including Consumers International (the world's leading consumer umbrella organization), the Sierra Club, Friends of the Earth International, Greenpeace, and a number of other radical and conservative environmental organizations and networks. The movement also encompasses national and international nongovernment organizations (NGOs) covering food-related issues; groups of scientists, including the U.S.-based Council for Responsible Genetics; and church and farmers' organizations.[5]

The range of tactics employed by the movement is as diverse as the people who employ them. At the fringes of the movement are radical groups that trumpet their cause by destroying field trials, demonstrating in the nude, surreptitiously affixing anti-biotechnology messages to GM products in supermarkets, and disrupting official meetings of the World Trade Organization (WTO) and other international organizations. Far more prevalent, however, are groups that apply more mainstream tactics such as

[3] See Jonathan Rauch, "Will Frankenfood Save the Planet?" *Atlantic Monthly* 293, no. 3 (October 2003): 103–8.

[4] See Peter Pringle, *Food, Inc.: Mendel to Monsanto—The Promises and Perils of the Biotech Harvest* (New York: Simon and Schuster, 2003), ch. 2.

[5] Rachel A. Schurman and William A. Monroe, "Making Biotech History: Social Resistance to Agricultural Biotechnology and the Future of the Biotechnology Industry," in *Engineering Trouble: Biotechnology and Its Discontents,* ed. Rachel A. Schurman and Dennis Doyle Takahashi Kelso (Berkeley: University of California Press, 2003), 115–16.

political lobbying and sponsoring peaceful demonstrations, petition drives, public seminars, and scientific studies designed to counter the arguments of the biotech industry.

Safety Issues and the Question of Consumer Risk

The consumer critique of plant-based genetic modification embraces several interrelated issues, the most obvious of which is safety. Two fears drive consumer doubts about GM foods and their impact on human health. One is that GMOs may accelerate the already alarming trend of antibiotic resistance of some bacteria. In many instances, agricultural biotechnologists use antibiotic genes as selection markers to identify the hosts for new genetic material. Some scientists suspect that once ingested, the genes may jump to disease-causing bacteria in the human digestive system and cause these bacteria to develop a resistance to certain kinds of antibiotics.[6] Consumers are troubled by the lack of conclusive evidence to disprove this theory.

Consumers also fear the possibility that GMOs may contain allergens, a concern that recently made newspaper headlines in the United States and Japan. At issue was StarLink corn, a strain containing a novel form of the *Bt* toxin that was produced by Aventis and authorized in the United States for use as animal feed.[7] In the summer of 2000, Friends of the Earth discovered that taco shells produced by Taco Bell contained small amounts of StarLink corn, proof that the substance had gotten mixed up with conventional corn supplies. The discovery led to one of the largest product recalls in American history. A few months later, a Japanese consumer group uncovered trace amounts of StarLink in processed foods that contained corn imported from the United States. The Japanese government subsequently banned imports of *all* American corn. Outraged consumers in both countries were reacting to scientific allegations that the *Bt* gene found in StarLink corn contained an allergenic protein. The U.S. Food and Drug Administration (FDA) responded to these findings in 2001 by banning the distribution and use of StarLink seeds in the United States.[8]

The StarLink scandal underscores important consumer attitudes toward risk. For more than a century, consumers in the advanced industrialized world have been bombarded with food-related scandals and disasters, the most recent of which involved outbreaks of mad cow disease in Britain, Japan, Canada, and the United States. In response to these episodes, more and more consumers have adopted an attitude of low or "zero tolerance"

[6] Marion Nestle, *Safe Food: Bacteria, Biotechnology, and Bioterrorism* (Berkeley: University of California Press, 2003), 176–77.

[7] Nestle, *Safe Food,* 5.

[8] Nestle, *Safe Food,* 10–12.

toward food-related risk. This is not to suggest that consumers are completely risk averse; to the contrary, many will happily eat unpasteurized cheeses or raw fish in the understanding that these foods could contain harmful bacteria. Consumers are more likely to object to artificial substances like synthetic additives or to foods—including genetically modified products—that are produced via scientific processes that are poorly understood. These are, moreover, foods that are not always clearly labeled, may be consumed involuntarily, and, for the time being, lack added nutritional benefits.

Many—if not most—scientists contend that GM foods may carry with them a small degree of risk. But they also argue that risk can be definitively assessed only when the overall impact of new technologies is fully known. Since plant-based genetic engineering is still a relatively new field, they reason, some ambiguity about the long-term impact of GMOs on human health is to be expected.[9] For the time being, scientists and government regulators are content to base their approval of GM foods on the absence of any known dangers. This, as one expert concluded, is about "as certain as food science can get."[10]

Many consumers find this argument unacceptable. Confused by conflicting scientific findings on the safety of genetic engineering and, in some cases, driven by a historically conditioned aversion to food-related risk, they insist that GMOs should be banned until proven absolutely safe. In a remarkable show of distrust of science, some consumers even condemn the application of the "rational scientific method" to the approval processes of GM foods, arguing that the method measures risk almost solely in terms of the costs and benefits borne by producers.[11]

While American scientists and regulators in the biotech sphere continue to adhere to the rational scientific method in their approval processes, the European Union responded to the public's mounting complaints by adopting the "precautionary principle" as the guiding principle for the regulation of potentially hazardous substances.[12] The precautionary principle allows regulators to ban the marketing of a food product on the basis of that product's *potential,* as opposed to its established, risks. It shifts the burden of proof from member governments, which heretofore had to show that GMOs and their production were probably not harmful, to industry, which must now prove that the substances and processes are safe.[13] Much to the dismay of American industry and government regulators, the

[9] *The Politics of GM Food: Risk, Science, and Public Trust* (Sussex: ESRC Global Environmental Change Program, University of Sussex, 1999), 5.

[10] David C. Victor and C. Ford Runge, "Genetically Modified and Healthy," *International Herald Tribune,* February 23, 2003.

[11] Nestle, *Safe Food,* 17.

[12] Frederick H. Buttel, "The Global Politics of GEO's: The Achilles' Heel of the Globalization Regime?" in *Engineering Trouble,* ed. Schurman and Kelso, 163.

[13] Buttel, "The Global Politics of GEO's."

institutionalization of the precautionary principle led to an EU moratorium on imports of GM foods and the adoption of some of the world's strictest labeling standards.

Concerns about the Industry

For many consumers, the mere mention of the term *GM food* conjures up images of Monsanto, the St. Louis–based firm that by the end of the twentieth century controlled over 80 percent of the world's transgenic crops.[14] Monsanto has manufactured several controversial products in the past, including polychlorinated biphenyls (PCBs) and the herbicide Agent Orange, both of which were subsequently linked to certain cancers and other health hazards.[15] Although Monsanto has struggled to improve its tarnished reputation over the years, many consumers continue to view the firm as the embodiment of all that is wrong with the biotech industry.

Critics have been quick to condemn the level of concentration within the industry. Once characterized by a substantial degree of competition, the industry today is governed by only a handful of firms, many of which are based in the United States. Adding insult to injury, industry leaders are extending their control over other actors in the food chain. Monsanto now completely controls its seed distributors and, by extension, much of the growing process itself.[16] These trends, many lament, have alarming implications for the future of independent farmers.

Equally troubling to some consumers is the tendency of governmental regulators—particularly in the United States—to base their decisions about the safety of GM foods on manufacturers' data. Consumers further bemoan the close relationship between industry and government regulators in the United States and elsewhere, a relationship that often excludes the consumer interest.[17] Against this politico-economic backdrop, more radical consumers criticize the increasing commodification of food and predict the advent of a global "biotechnocracy" or "agrotyranny."[18]

Ecological Concerns

Environmental concerns have also galvanized the anti-GM movement. Advocates fear the appearance of "superweeds" that are resistant to herbicides, a phenomenon that has already plagued the effectiveness of some

[14] William Boyd, "Wonderful Potencies? Deep Structure and the Problem of Monopoly in Agricultural Biotechnology," in *Engineering Trouble,* ed. Schurman and Kelso, 28.

[15] Pringle, *Food, Inc.,* 115.

[16] Boyd, "Wonderful Potencies?" 30.

[17] See Marion Nestle, *Food Politics: How the Food Industry Influences Nutrition and Health* (Berkeley: University of California Press, 2002).

[18] Michael W. Fox, *Beyond Evolution* (New York: Lyons Press, 1999), 43; and Winston, *Travels in the Genetically Modified Zone,* 107.

Roundup Ready crops developed by Monsanto.[19] Some also suspect that *Bt* crops will eventually create *Bt*-resistant insect populations.[20] Finally, many worry that wind-blown pollen from GM crops will infect conventional or organic plaint strains, producing new hybrid crops or killing non-target organisms that are beneficial to the growing process. There have already been documented instances of this.[21]

Industry opponents also worry about biotechnology's impact on global biodiversity. Scientists all over the world fear monocultures—vast areas of farmland dominated by a single crop that could, over time, develop vulnerabilities to certain types of disease. With the organizational force of companies like Monsanto behind them, critics complain, farmers in the developing world could find themselves growing the most environmentally hazardous crops of all.

Finally, critics take issue with the industry's assertion that GM foods are the solution to mass starvation caused by global food shortages, arguing that hunger is the result not of inadequate supply but of problems within third world distribution systems. These problems include natural disasters, armed conflict, political corruption, and the absence of effective transportation methods.[22] Consequently, critics see no need to mess with the natural order of things by expanding the acreage of transgenic crops. Instead, they demand the expansion of more efficient international aid programs and incentives for third world leaders to take better care of their citizens.

Ethical and Cultural Issues

Ethical concerns also motivate the anti-GM movement. Some critics of agricultural biotechnology wax nostalgic for a bygone era when agriculture was centered on the autonomous family farm. Vandana Shiva, a prominent spokesperson for traditional agricultural methods, pits the family farm against the farming conglomerate in a veritable battle of good against evil. Small farmers, she argues in a metaphor drawn from her native India, are like "sacred cows" that live in harmony with their environments and bestow benefits on their communities. "Mad cows," by contrast, are products of capitalism run amok, reflecting the commodification of basic resources,

[19] "Roundup Unready."

[20] Alan McHughen, *A Consumers' Guide to GM Food: From Green Genes to Red Herrings* (Oxford: Oxford University Press, 2002), 108.

[21] "Spread of Gene-Altered Pharmaceutical Corn Spurs $3 Million Fine," *New York Times*, December 7, 2002.

[22] Testimony of Jean Halloran, Director, Consumer Policy-Institute/Consumers Union, before the Senate Foreign Relations Committee, European Affairs Subcommittee, on "U.S. Relations with a Changing Europe: Differing Views on Technology Issues." See http://www.consumersunion.org/pub/core_food_safety/.

the construction of mass markets, and the quest for consumer uniformity on a global scale.[23]

Others contend that biotechnology represents the latest phase in the separation of mankind from the natural environment that began with the Enlightenment and accelerated during the Industrial Revolution. In the words of one author, "the integrity and future of creation is threatened more by this new technology than by any other past human invention or activity, including nuclear fission and the development and release of petrochemicals into the environment."[24] Similarly, many, including the late Pope John Paul II, have expressed uneasiness about producing and consuming foods by scientifically manipulating "God's work."[25] Included in this camp is Britain's Prince Charles, who proclaimed that "we should show greater respect for the genius of nature's designs. . . . The idea that the different parts of the natural world are connected through an intricate system of checks and balances which we disturb at our peril is all too easily dismissed as no longer relevant."[26]

The Big Picture: Consumer Democracy in the Era of Globalization

Driving many of the critiques of biotechnology is the widespread fear that local consumers are losing control over the foods they consume as national agricultural markets become increasingly interdependent. Those who espouse such views tend to be highly critical of WTO rules and regulations that enable the unfettered trade in GMOs and render the organization a mere "handmaiden" of American free trade policy. Of particular concern has been the WTO agreement on sanitary and phytosanitary measures. The agreement allows member countries to regulate crops and food products in order to protect human health and the environment, but only on the basis of sound "scientific" evidence.[27] Requirements like these, many argue, constitute a wholesale repudiation of the precautionary principle and pave the way for American domination of local food supplies.

These critiques would seem to suggest that the anti-GM movement is anti-capitalist in orientation. To be sure, many radicals in the movement associate the diffusion of GM foods with the meteoric ascension of the profit motive in human affairs. It appears, however, that most activists are more moderate, calling for the assertion of state power over economies

[23] Vandana Shiva, *Biopiracy: The Plunder of Nature and Knowledge* (Boston: South End Press, 1999).

[24] Fox, *Beyond Evolution*, 17. For a similar argument, see Shiva, *Biopiracy*.

[25] Pope John Paul II, "Jubilee of the Agricultural World," reprinted in *Genetically Modified Foods*, ed. Michael Ruse and Davis Castle (Amherst: Prometheus Books, 2002), 112–13.

[26] Charles, Prince of Wales, "Reith Lecture 2000," reprinted in *Genetically Modified Foods*, ed. Ruse and Castle, 13.

[27] http://www.usda.gov/news/releases/2003/08/ustr03–54.htm.

through stricter regulation of GM products, more democratic control over political and economic institutions governing the food supply, and a check on the influence of multinational corporations over local traditions—culinary or otherwise. As such, the anti-GM forces can be interpreted as a new social movement, one that focuses on quality-of-life issues rather than material concerns and that challenges those in authority to fulfill the fundamental political and economic principles of postindustrial democracies.

This emphasis on democracy and consumer sovereignty at the local level is evident in the agenda of Consumers International. CI champions four basic consumer rights vis-à-vis food (the rights to safety, health, choice, and food security) and actively promotes the establishment and growth of consumer organizations that can represent these rights at the national, regional, and international levels. For several years, biotechnology has been one of CI's top priorities and a recurring theme of its World Consumer Rights Day (March 15). For the March 2003 event, the organization proclaimed that "while key safety and environmental questions remain unanswered, we believe it is also important to look beyond these to the ways that corporations are using GM technology to consolidate their control over global food production."[28] When all is said and done, the primary issue for anti-GM activists is not so much safety as consumer sovereignty over the production and sale of food.

National Trends: The United States, Japan, and Britain

While the consumer campaign against GM foods is remarkable in terms of the many values and objectives shared by consumers in different national contexts, the story would not be complete without a look at the very local dimensions of this otherwise global movement. What follows are brief analyses of consumer activism in the United States, Japan, and Britain. How do consumers in each of these countries view GM foods? And what impact have the opponents of biotechnology had on governmental responses toward the industry?

The United States

Since the mid-1960s, when Ralph Nader's "Raiders" leapt into the American national consciousness, the United States has been widely regarded as the bastion of consumer power. By all accounts, the accomplishments of the American consumer movement have been remarkable. The movement was instrumental in introducing some of the world's strictest product safety legislation, opening American courts to more consumer-initiated lawsuits,

[28] http://www.consumersinternational.org.

and enhancing corporate and governmental accountability to consumers. By the early 1970s, it appeared that the consumer interest—for many a revealing measure of the "public interest"—had come to prevail over producer interests within the American democratic process.

Why, then, have American consumer advocates lagged so far behind their European counterparts in terms of achieving stricter safety criteria and tighter labeling requirements for GM food products?

The answer certainly does not lie in the size and activism of the organized movement. Virtually all the major consumer organizations, including the Consumers Federation of America and Consumers Union, have long upheld food safety as a major priority and have adamantly opposed the development and sale of GM foods. They also participate in a number of networks, including the "Campaign to Label Genetically Engineered Foods," that pressure the government for stricter regulatory rules governing agricultural biotechnology.

A more valid explanation for the relative weaknesses of the American anti-GM movement lies in its relationship to the public at large: American consumers are less inclined to support the movement than their counterparts abroad, or so the argument goes, because of their relatively high tolerance of agricultural biotechnology. There is plenty of circumstantial evidence to support this hypothesis. As Lizabeth Cohen illustrates in her chapter in this volume on the "Consumers' Republic," Americans tend to prioritize product choice and low prices—two values that biotechnology promises to fulfill. Consider, too, that American consumers have experienced fewer tainted-food scandals and are less supportive of the organic food movement than their European or Japanese counterparts. These facts alone suggest that ordinary Americans are less predisposed to question the safety of their food supply and the practices of the food-processing industry. Public tolerance of agricultural biotechnology may also reflect Americans' historically high degree of respect for both science and free enterprise, sentiments that may enhance the willingness of consumers to shoulder more risk for the sake of progress. Finally, recent public opinion polls indicate that Americans are more trusting of their regulatory agencies than consumers in Europe.[29] This suggests that if a food product is approved by the FDA for sale in the United States, consumers will tend *not* to question the safety of that product.[30]

It is tempting to conclude that American consumers are distinctive in terms of their attitudes toward food-related risk. But before we jump to conclusions, we must consider the state of American consumer knowledge about agricultural biotechnology. In a 1999 Angus Reid poll of more than

[29] Andrea Knox and Susan Warner, "Americans, Europeans Divided on Use of Genetically Altered Foods," *Philadelphia Inquirer*, June 27, 1999.

[30] http://pewabgiotech.org/research/2003update.

5,000 consumers in eight countries, 95 percent of German respondents stated that they had heard about GM foods, and 80 percent said they were less likely to buy them than conventional foods. By contrast, only a third of American respondents stated that they were aware of GM foods, and only 57 percent said that they were less likely to buy them.[31] Awareness levels rose after the StarLink scandal of late 2000. One study revealed that American consumers were split on the issue, with 45 percent responding that they were "not too confident" in the safety of these foods.[32] But more recent statistics show that awareness actually *declined* after that. In 2001, 44 percent of respondents had heard some or a great deal of information about GM foods, a level that dropped to only 34 percent in 2003. In addition, only 26 percent of Americans surveyed in a recent poll believed that they had eaten GM foods, even though many informed observers maintain that nearly 80 percent of all processed foods sold in U.S. supermarkets contain some genetically modified components.[33] Americans, in short, know comparatively little about GM foods and the controversies that surround them. This helps explain why more knowledgeable consumer advocates have not attracted the popular followings that have characterized many of the anti-GM campaigns in other parts of the world.

Another reason for the failure of consumer groups to curb the marketing of bioengineered foods in the United States lies in the nature of the country's regulatory regime for such foods and the underlying relationship between government and the biotech industry. Grafted onto an institutional structure that was designed to regulate chemical contaminants and weeds, that regime is controlled by three agencies with overlapping jurisdictions: the FDA, the Environmental Protection Agency (EPA), and the United States Department of Agriculture (USDA), with the FDA taking the lead.[34] Briefly stated, a new plant-derived genetically modified product will be approved as "substantially equivalent" to a corresponding conventional product if it is "generally recognized as safe." If this cannot be established, the FDA is authorized to treat that product like a "food additive" by subjecting it to strict regulation.[35]

Critics contend that this system does little to advance basic consumer rights, including the right to know. For example, the government allows

[31] *Economist*, January 15, 2000.

[32] "Poll: Confidence in Biotech Regulation Mixed," Pew Initiative on Food and Biotechnology, *PR Newswire*, June 27, 2001, re-released by *Consumer Choice* (2001). http://www.biotech-info-net/confidence.html.

[33] Study by the Food Policy Institute at Rutgers University, reported in *The Campaign Reporter* (November 2003).

[34] Thomas O. McGarity and Patricia I. Hansen, "Breeding Distrust: an Assessment and Recommendations for Improving the Regulation of Plant Derived Genetically Modified Foods," a report prepared for the Food Policy Institute of the Consumer Federation of America (January 11, 2001), 8.

[35] McGarity and Hansen, "Breeding Distrust," 9.

industry, rather than independent scientists, to determine whether a particular product is "generally recognized as safe," and the data used to generate these decisions are not readily available to the public. Consumer advocates are also troubled by the fact that the FDA has refused to apply strict regulatory measures to most foods suspected of containing allergens on the grounds that the presence of such allergens has yet to be scientifically established. Consequently, when the FDA and other government officials learned well before the scandal's outbreak that StarLink corn had entered the conventional food supply, they did little to correct the problem.[36] These actions, critics contend, are evidence of a government that has been partially "captured" by the very firms they are supposed to control.

Collusion between national regulatory agencies and the agricultural biotechnology industry is the latest episode in a long history of close relations between the American government and domestic food producers. As Marion Nestle notes, the American food industry is characterized by intense competition resulting from an overly abundant food supply and an affluent consuming public. Determined to recoup their multi-billion investments in R&D and satisfy stockholders, biotech firms have successfully lobbied congressional committees, regulatory agencies, and the White House for subsidies or favorable regulatory rules.[37] Producers made great headway in this regard during the 1980s, when deregulation and the retreat of the public interest movement enabled industry in general to flourish.

The government-business relationship in the biotech sphere helps explain the low levels of awareness of GM products among ordinary American consumers. As others have shown, the media are key to public information flows relating to genetic engineering in that they "alert consumers to formal government policies and draw attention to issues and themes pertaining to genetic engineering emanating from the general public."[38] In the United States, however, the media has done relatively little to disseminate the details not only about government policies pertaining to biotechnology but also about the industry's behind-the-scenes pressure on the policy process. The industry has even taken legal steps to prevent controversial stories from reaching consumers. To cite just one example, lawyers for Monsanto recently prevented Fox Television in Florida from broadcasting a four-part documentary on local dairy farmers' use of the com-

[36] Nestle, *Safe Food,* 12.

[37] Nestle, *Food Politics,* 1.

[38] George Gaskell, Martin W. Bauer, and John Durant, "The Representation of Biotechnology: Policy, Media and Public Perception," in *Biotechnology in the Public Sphere: A European Source Book,* ed. John Durant, Martin W. Bauer, and George Gaskell (London: Science Museum, 1998), 7.

pany's rBGH (reconstituted bovine growth hormone) to boost milk production.[39]

Mindful of the industry's tactics and the revolving door between biotech firms and American regulatory agencies, consumer advocates have insisted on more rigorous testing of GM foods and the introduction of strict labeling standards. The labeling issue in particular has garnered strong support from the attentive public. In 2001, an ABC News telephone poll revealed that 93 percent of 1,024 consumers supported labeling.[40] While American consumers appear almost complacent about bioengineering, they are overwhelmingly in favor of regulations that uphold the consumer's right to know. In a nod to industry, however, the Bush administration refused to introduce tighter regulations on the grounds that labeling products as genetically modified would suggest to consumers that those products were in some way inferior to conventional foods. And this, the government argues, would encourage consumers to base their purchasing decisions on paranoia rather than on rational calculations of risk.

As global opposition to biotechnology mounts, will American consumers remain complacent about GM foods? There is good reason to believe that they will not. The expansion of Christian religious movements and the ethical controversies surrounding stem cell research may eventually prod more consumers to think twice about these products. Indeed, the popularity of novels like Ruth Ozeki's *All Over Creation,* which addresses biotechnology and ecoterrorism, as well as very recent upsurges in the organic food movement, suggest that this is already happening. As the consuming public continues to learn about GM foods, the United States may very well witness the protests that have characterized the politics of biotechnology in Japan and Britain.

Japan

As in the United States, biotechnology enjoys the strong support of both business and government in Japan. For well over a decade, private enterprise and government-sponsored organizations have carried out field trials of a variety of genetically modified crops, including rice, soybeans, corn, potatoes, rapeseed, tomatoes, wheat, tobacco, and certain fruits and flowers.[41] Although Japanese GMOs are not yet distributed commercially, Japanese consumers have been regularly consuming GMOs since 1996, when the government first authorized imports of these substances. Not surprisingly, the vast majority of GMOs are imported from the United States.

Increasing numbers of Japanese consumers have mobilized against GM

[39] Nestle, *Safe Food,* 202.
[40] http://www.thecampaign.org/education.
[41] See http://www.s.affrc.go.jp/docs/sentan/guide/edevelp.htm.

foods in the context of food-related and environmental scandals. Over the past decade alone, the public has grappled with the discovery of dioxins in their urban environments, the mislabeling of beef products, tainted dairy foods, outbreaks of *E. coli,* and the appearance of mad cow disease on domestic farms. These experiences weakened already low levels of consumer trust in the government's ability to guarantee the safety of the public food supply. In a 2003 government survey, 77.7 percent of consumers stated that Japanese civil servants and scientists were insufficiently attentive to consumer wishes regarding food safety.[42] Small wonder, then, that many Japanese view the proliferation of GM foods with suspicion and even fear.[43]

To a greater extent than their American counterparts, Japanese consumers and their representatives in the cooperative movement, the housewives' organizations, and other leading consumer organs have upheld food safety as their top priority. The reasons for this are both cultural and historical. Conditioned by centuries-old Shinto traditions and rituals, the Japanese have developed a strong penchant for cleanliness and purity that is manifest in everything from housekeeping practices to nutritional standards. Traditional beliefs about the origins of disease also come into play. As Emiko Ohnuki-Tierney argues, the Japanese have viewed disease as the product of contaminants emanating from outside controlled environments and have gone to great lengths to eliminate those contaminants through ritualistic cleansing practices.[44] These religious and etiological considerations inform consumers' "zero tolerance" of food-related risks.[45]

Consumer opposition to GM foods also reflects the country's growing dependence on food imports. Today, Japan imports approximately 60 percent of its total food supply; by contrast, the United States and many West European countries are almost completely self-sufficient in food production. It just so happens that import dependence is especially high for soybeans, corn, and other crops that are most likely to be genetically modified. Between 1950 and 1995, soybean imports grew from 50 to 98 percent of total domestic consumption.[46] Japan has also become the world's largest

[42] Government of Japan, *Survey for Safety Monitors: Attitudes toward Food Safety* (Tokyo: Food Safety Commission, September 2003), 15.

[43] In 1998, 96.6 percent of 231 consumer groups surveyed in the Tokyo metropolitan area alone were keenly aware of the potential "problem" of GM foods. Tokyo Shōhisha Dantai Renraku Sentaa, *Idenshikumikae shokubutsu mondai ni taisuru tōnai shōhisha dantai no ishiki chōsa* [Opinion survey of consumer organizations in the metropolitan area toward the issue of genetically modified foods] (Tokyo: Tokyo shōhisha dantai renraku sentaa, 1998), 2.

[44] See Emiko Ohnuki-Tierney, *Illness and Culture in Contemporary Japan: An Anthropological View* (Cambridge: Cambridge University Press, 1984), 21–50.

[45] Patricia L. Maclachlan, *Consumer Politics in Postwar Japan: The Institutional Boundaries of Citizen Activism* (New York: Columbia University Press, 2002), ch. 7. See also David Vogel, "Consumer Protection and Protectionism in Japan," *Journal of Japanese Studies* 18, no. 1 (1992): 119–54.

[46] Shōdanren, *Dai 36 kai zenkoku shōhisha taikai* [36th National Consumer Rally] (Tokyo: Shōdanren, 1997), 10.

importer of corn, most of which is produced in the United States.[47] As dependence on these imported transgenic crops intensifies, so too have consumer doubts about the safety of both GMOs and the overall food supply. According to a public opinion poll conducted by the Tokyo Metropolitan Government in 2000, *96.3 percent* of those surveyed were either very (60.1 percent) or moderately (36.2 percent) worried about GM foods.[48]

These doubts are fanned by media organizations that have been far more attentive to food-related issues than the American media. Food warrants close media attention in Japan for a number of reasons, not least of which are the cultural concerns and recent food-related scandals noted above. Food has also been at the center of intense political conflicts, from the mass demonstrations by starving citizens during the immediate postwar years and the protests against synthetic food additives during the 1980s to the recurrent stand-offs between the Japanese and American governments over Japanese agricultural protectionism. Food, in short, makes for good copy in Japan.

For Takeuchi Naokazu and others, the solution to Japan's food-related problems has been a return to Japanese-style basics. A former official of the Ministry of Agriculture, Forestry and Fisheries (MAFF), Takeuchi founded the Japan Consumers Union (Nihon Shōhisha Renmei), one of the country's most prominent consumer organizations. From the late 1960s, he repeatedly called on consumers to decrease their dependence on potentially unsafe foreign imports by upholding their culinary traditions and eating domestically produced foods, including Japanese rice for breakfast.[49]

The culinary nationalism inherent in Takeuchi's recommendations symbolizes not so much the centrality of indigenous foods in Japanese culture as a marked distrust of free trade principles and economic globalization led by the United States. Takeuchi maintained that in their determination to use food exports as a weapon in their quest for global economic domination, Americans were subjecting food products to the same free trade rules that govern other commodities.[50] This, he complained, was morally wrong; food should be treated not as a commodity to be bought and sold but rather as a "life resource" (*seimeiza*), like water and air, subject to governmental protection.[51] Complying with American pressures, warned Takeuchi, would be tantamount to allowing the United

[47] "StarLink Find Sparks Consumer Fears, Import Chaos," *Japan Times,* November 25, 2000.

[48] Tōkyōto seikatsubunkakyoku, *Tōkyōto shōhiseikatsu monitaa anketto: "idenshikumikae shokuhin"* [Tokyo consumption lifestyle monitor survey: genetically modified foods] (Tokyo: Tōkyōto seikatsubunkakyoku, 2000), 3.

[49] Takeuchi Naokazu, *Tabemono wa shōhin janai* [Food is not a product] (Tokyo: Nantsumori shokan, 2002), 26–27.

[50] Takeuchi, *Tabemono wa shōhin janai,* 16, 17.

[51] Takeuchi, *Tabemono wa shōhin janai,* 3.

States to "occupy the stomachs of the Japanese," a provocative allusion to Japan's political emasculation during the American occupation (1945–52).[52]

The Japanese anti-GMO movement has simply augmented these safety and geopolitical concerns. Activists routinely criticize the United States for imposing genetically modified products on Japan when their safety and environmental impact are still uncertain and, in a show of economic nationalism, for threatening the livelihoods of domestic farmers. Accordingly, activists have pressed for a complete ban on all imports of GM foods. Although the Japanese government has shut out specific GM products like StarLink corn when doubts arise about their safety, it has refused to impose a blanket ban on GM products for fear of sparking a trade dispute with the United States.

Consequently, networks of consumers and environmentalists have resorted to other tactics to reduce Japanese dependence on imported GMOs and to prevent the marketing of homegrown GM foods. They joined forces with local farmers to expand the already vibrant organic food movement, declared certain agricultural areas "GM free zones," and established agricultural trusts in areas targeted for field trials of genetically modified soybean crops. Meanwhile, watchdog groups, including the one that discovered StarLink corn in the Japanese food supply, routinely supervise the importation and distribution of GMOs. One such group recently caused a media stir after discovering genetically modified rapeseed growing wild in areas adjacent to eleven Japanese ports, the evident result of spillage from incoming foreign shipments.[53]

Some citizen groups are also pressuring government to introduce strict regulations governing the growth, importation, and marketing of GMOs.[54] The government first responded in April 2001 by introducing comprehensive labeling standards for GM foods. As critics are quick to point out, however, few companies have complied with these standards, which cover only a small number of GM products.[55] Two years later, the government passed another law to regulate the use of GMOs, this one in conformity with the 2000 Cartagena Protocol on Biodiversity, an international agreement for the regulation of trade in biotech products. Among other things, the law subjects all handlers of GMOs in Japan to governmental approval processes; the penalties for noncompliance are fairly strict.[56] Those who would like to see GMOs banned altogether condemn the law as a gov-

[52] Takeuchi Naokazu, *Nihon no shōhisha wa naze okoranai no ka* [Why don't Japanese consumers get angry?] (Tokyo: San'ichi shobō, 1990), 104.

[53] "Seeds of Dispute: Crop Crusaders," *Asahi Newspaper,* February 25, 2005.

[54] Shōdanren, *Idenshikumikae shokuhin no hyōji to ryūtsū ni kansuru yōseisho* [Requests regarding labeling and circulation of genetically modified foods] (Tokyo: Shōdanren, 1999).

[55] "Shiranu aida ni shōhisha no kuchi ni" [They're in consumers' mouths before they know it], *Tōkyō shinbun,* April 29, 2002; and "Hyōji de wa handan dekinu kōnyū" [Making purchases on the basis of labels that tell us little], *Mainichi shinbun,* June 29, 2002.

[56] "Law to Regulate GMO Usage Passed By Diet," *Japan Times,* June 11, 2003.

ernmental endorsement of both imports of GMOs and domestic biotech firms.

Although these laws are flawed in the eyes of some consumers, it is remarkable that they were enacted at all given the political economy's historical bias toward the interests of producers. As I illustrate elsewhere, the power of producers in the Japanese political economy is entrenched in the institutions of consumer-related policymaking processes, which often exclude consumer participation and pay little more than lip service to consumer interests.[57] How, then, did consumers manage to achieve as much as they did with regard to GM foods?

Part of the answer has to do with changes in the Japanese political climate since the mid-1990s. Since briefly falling from power in 1993, the ruling Liberal Democratic Party (LDP) has grown far more solicitous of consumers and other diffuse societal interests as it struggles to diversify its electoral support base. Accordingly, the past decade has witnessed the enactment or amendment of several laws that address consumer concerns as well as bureaucratic reforms to make government more responsive to consumer demand. For food safety, these developments include the 2003 establishment of the Food Safety Commission within the Cabinet Office to oversee the evaluation of risks pertaining to food products, including GMOs, and the recent enactment of the Basic Law on Food, Agriculture and Rural Areas, which commits the state to "increase domestic agricultural production" as a means to secure a more stable food supply.[58]

Second, consumer advocates faced comparatively little opposition from mainstream food manufacturers and retailers, many of whom embraced pro-consumer regulations in principle (if not in practice). The reason for industry compliance is simple: firms that defy consumer wishes risk losing market share to the vaunted consumer cooperative movement. Over the past six decades, the cooperative movement—one of the largest of its kind in the world—has done far more than its mainstream competitors to manufacture and sell foods that meet the high safety and cleanliness standards of consumers. Since GMOs first entered the domestic market, the coops went to great lengths to eliminate or at least limit GMO use in their food products. They also labeled products containing GMOs well before the government introduced its new labeling standards in 2001. These trends appear to be having a copycat effect on mainstream firms, many of which have been struggling to shore up their reputations among consumers following the recent scandals over tainted food. Put simply, taking a stand on GMOs now makes good business sense.

Meanwhile, the government strives to strike a balance between con-

[57] For more on those processes, see Maclachlan, *Consumer Politics in Postwar Japan,* esp. ch. 5.

[58] "Food Safety Commission Launched," *Journal of Japanese Trade and Industry* 22, no. 5 (September/October 2003): 3. The Basic Law replaces the 1961 Agricultural Basic Law.

sumer and producer interests with regard to GM foods. Its new labeling standards, as we have seen, can be interpreted as a concession to consumers who worry about the safety of these products. The government is also cooperating with other countries under the auspices of the 165-member Codex Alimentarius Commission to hammer out international standards governing the distribution of GM products. At the same time, the government is quietly taking steps to promote domestic agribusiness. Government-supported field trials of GM crops, as we have seen, have been in the works for over a decade. In 2002, the government set up the Biotechnology Strategy Council to deliberate on the future of the industry in Japan at Prime Minister Koizumi Jun'ichirō's initiative. In its report, the council recommended the expansion of research and development in biotechnology, support for the establishment of new biotech firms, and—in marked contrast to American policy—the systematic promotion of consumer awareness of the nature and advantages of this growing industry.[59] Although some advocates view these policies as evidence of an irreconcilable double standard, the government has been relatively successful in finding a middle ground between the interests of consumers and producers in the biotech sphere.

Britain

British responses to GM foods have been far more polarized than those in either the United States or Japan. At one extreme stands a government intent on approving the domestic production of GM crops in order to cultivate the biotech industry—already the largest of its kind in Europe—and boost the economy; at the other is a vast array of consumer, environmental, and farmers' groups, politicians, and concerned scientists that will go to almost any lengths to keep the country free of "Frankenfoods." The high degree of conflict in the British case is surprising. In keeping with the European Union's controls over agricultural biotechnology, Britons consume far fewer GMOs than either the Americans or the Japanese. They also seem to have more opportunities to voice their demands to government than consumers elsewhere.

Historically rooted attitudes toward food help explain the British case. As in Japan, food has been at the center of British consumer politics for generations.[60] In 1875, Britain introduced the world's first food-related law (Sale of Food and Drugs Act) in response to a host of problems resulting from the growth of mass markets and the steady internationaliza-

[59] "A Bridge from Science to Life," *Japan Times*, December 25, 2002.

[60] For an in-depth analysis of British food politics in the late nineteenth and early twentieth centuries, see Frank Trentmann, "Bread, Milk, and Democracy: Consumption and Citizenship in Twentieth-Century Britain," in *The Politics of Consumption*, ed. Martin Daunton and Matthew Hilton (Oxford: Berg, 2001), 129–63.

tion of food production. Over time, however, that law proved incapable of dealing with food-related health hazards. Concerned about nutrition and public health, consumers throughout the twentieth century pressured the government for stricter controls over the food supply with mixed results. Today, Britons are nearly as concerned about food safety as the Japanese, and food safety remains a top priority for British consumer organizations.

The politics of food in British history reflect longstanding debates about food security. Like the Japanese, the British are keenly aware of their geographical status as an island nation and are anxious to secure a stable food supply. Unlike the Japanese, however, Britain was once the world's leading power in the international political economy of food, a position now occupied by the United States. Accordingly, the British state has on many occasions over the past century extolled the virtues of free trade in food products. At the turn of the twentieth century, many consumers embraced free trade as a mechanism for securing cheap food.[61] Today, however, most Britons view free trade with countries outside the European Union as a recipe for declining national control over food and intolerable risks to its safety.

GM foods have been at the center of this latest shift in consumer attitudes toward free trade in food. More and more Britons have come to equate "free trade" in these products with American multinational control over the British food supply—especially after Europe's refusal to import hormone-treated American beef products during the mid-1990s and the Bush administration's May 2003 decision to file suit at the WTO against the EU's moratorium on GMO imports.[62] They also fear that backing their own government in its determination to nurture the domestic biotech industry will increase the country's vulnerability to foreign economic forces, since some of the corporations currently engaged in R&D in plant-based biotechnology in Britain are foreign-owned.

Britons' doubts about GM foods reflect a growing distrust of government and scientific "experts" following a string of food-related scandals, the most notorious of which involved governmental responses to the outbreak of mad cow disease. Despite repeated warnings from the scientific community during the 1980s and early 1990s that bovine spongiform encephalopathy (BSE) posed a significant risk to human health, the government delayed the introduction of safeguard measures while continuing to

[61] Patricia Maclachlan and Frank Trentmann, "Civilising Markets: Traditions of Consumer Politics in Twentieth-Century Britain, Japan, and the United States," in *Markets in Historical Contexts: Ideas and Politics in the Modern World,* ed. Mark Bevir and Frank Trentmann (Cambridge: Cambridge University Press, 2004), 171–77. This point is attributable to Frank Trentmann.

[62] For an analysis of the importation of hormone-treated beef and related issues, see Christina L. Davis, *Food Fights over Free Trade: How International Institutions Promote Agricultural Trade Liberalization* (Princeton: Princeton University Press, 2003), 321–38.

publicly support the domestic beef industry.[63] The incident fueled popular suspicions that the government had become a handmaiden of industry. Consumer trust in the scientific community is also eroding. In 1998, the public was bombarded with stories about Dr. Arpad Pusztai of the Rowett Institute in Aberdeen; his scientific experiments had revealed a potential health hazard in genetically modified potatoes. After his research methods became the focus of controversy within the scientific community, including the esteemed Royal Society of London, Dr. Pusztai was abruptly suspended from his position.[64] Although there was in fact good reason to question Dr. Pusztai's methods, many consumers interpreted the incident as an unwarranted attack on a maverick scientist who had dared to defy the conventional scientific wisdom that GMOs were not unsafe, sentiments that in turn helped deepen consumer misgivings about science itself.[65]

Once it became clear that only a third of consumers trusted their government to make responsible decisions about biotechnology, the government finally took steps to placate the nervous population.[66] In 1999, it placed a minimum three-year moratorium on commercial plantings of GM crops. Then, as its own field trials neared completion in the summer of 2003, the government sponsored a six-week public debate on whether or not GM crops should be grown commercially in Britain. The ensuing discussions included more than 650 meetings around the country and nearly 40,000 comments from concerned consumers. The discussions did not, however, produce the results that the government had hoped for. In *GM Nation?*—the official report on the debates published the following September—the government admitted that only 2 percent of participants were unconditionally willing to consume GM foods.[67] Meanwhile, ordinary consumers demonstrated in the streets in opposition to the biotech industry, towns and villages declared themselves "GM-free" zones, and thousands of citizens—including university professors, clergymen, and politicians—signed a "Green Gloves" pledge to take part in or support efforts to destroy GM crops grown in Britain.[68] As of this writing, the sabotage of commercial field trials has been so effective that many British companies are transferring their trials to Eastern Europe and China.[69]

[63] See Nestle, *Safe Food,* 250–52.

[64] See Alan McHughen, *A Consumer's Guide to GM Food: From Green Genes to Red Herrings* (Oxford: Oxford University Press, 2000), 117–18; and Andrew Rowell, *Don't Worry: It's Safe to Eat* (London and Sterling, VA: Earthspan Publications, 2003), 78–102.

[65] "Believe in Facts Not Fads," *Guardian,* March 12, 2005.

[66] Marie Woolf, "People Distrust Government on GM Foods," *Sunday Independent,* May 23, 1999.

[67] "Most Britons 'Oppose GM Crops,'" *BBC News,* September 24, 2003. http://news.bbc.co.uk/1/hi/sci/tech/3134278.stm

[68] John Vidal, "Pull Together—Protesters Vow to Root out GM Crops," *Guardian,* September 27, 2003.

[69] "Fears of Extremists Kill Off GM Tests," *Guardian,* March 20, 2005.

The steady escalation of consumer opposition suggests that ordinary British consumers are far more aware of the issues surrounding agricultural biotechnology than American consumers. This opposition reflects in part the media's willingness to cover the subject. Between 1973 and 1996, British newspapers published 5,471 articles on biotechnology and genetics—far more than the EU (and, we can safely assume, the American) average.[70] During the summer of 2003, when the public debate about GM foods began to peak, the subject made headline news in nearly all the major newspapers. The more Britons learn about these products, the more anxious they become—a relationship underscored by a government-commissioned focus group intended to gauge the position of the "silent majority" on agricultural biotechnology. Although prepared to acknowledge the benefits of GM foods at the beginning of the proceedings, the members grew increasingly negative as the study unfolded.[71]

Public opposition to GM foods received further validation in October 2003 when the government released a long-awaited report on the results of its field trials. The report found that some GM crops were indeed likely to damage the British countryside by destroying essential weeds and insects.[72] Undeterred, the Blair government announced in March 2004 that it would license Bayer CropScience to produce genetically modified maize in Britain. The move sparked protest from both members of the House of Commons and ordinary consumers. Ironically, Bayer subsequently announced that it would not proceed with the plantings on the grounds that government regulations would render the project economically unviable.[73]

At the center of British opposition to GM foods is the conviction that the democratic system has failed ordinary consumers. As one irate demonstrator commented in October 2003, "This is the freedom movement in our country now. There is no more basic human right of people than to decide what food they are going to eat."[74] Curiously, such criticisms occur amid unprecedented levels of public debate and a decision-making process that is more open to consumer input than either their Japanese or American counterparts. How can we explain this? In addition to the public's growing distrust of government and of the scientific and biotech sectors, we must also take account of the structure of British policymaking.

Unlike the United States, where policymaking tends to open or close to

[70] Martin W. Bauer, Jon Durant, George Gaskell, Miltos Liakopoulous and Eleanor Bridgman, "United Kingdom," in *Biotechnology in the Public Sphere,* ed. Durant et al., 166.

[71] Michael McCarthy, "Britain Delivers Overwhelming Verdict after Unprecedented Public Opinion Exercise,' *Independent,* September 25, 2003.

[72] Victoria Fletcher and Ed Harris, "Report on GM Crops is Damning," *Evening Standard,* October 16, 2003.

[73] "GM Crop Growth Unlikely for 'Foreseeable Future,'" *Guardian,* March 31, 2004.

[74] Threat of Civil Unrest over GM," *Western Morning News,* September 25, 2003.

consumer demands depending on the cohesiveness of business opposition and the general political climate, or Japan, where policymaking historically has been heavily biased toward large manufacturers' interests, British consumer policymaking institutions accommodate a diverse spectrum of consumer and producer interests. In the biotech sphere, this means that significant power is given to retailers, who tend to be more attentive to consumer demand than the large manufacturers who dominate the politics and marketing of GM foods in the United States. And while the consumer interest in Japan or the United States is articulated primarily by private consumer organizations located outside formal policy processes, British consumers also have a prominent advocate *within* the policy process. An independent, nondepartmental body funded by the Department of Trade and Industry, the National Consumer Council (NCC) is mandated to articulate and defend consumer rights within the various branches of government and works closely with private organizations toward that end.

Unfortunately, the formal institutions of British consumer policymaking have raised—but failed to meet—consumer expectations in the biotech sphere. The NCC, for instance, has consistently opposed the commercial production of transgenic maize and other crops in Britain, citing safety and environmental issues and the lack of consumer demand.[75] But as the government's recent approval of commercial plantings of transgenic maize illustrates, council opinion is often overruled by producer interests. Also noteworthy is the Food Standards Agency (FSA), which was established in 1999 in response to consumer demand for greater attention to food security following the mad cow disease scandal. The FSA, which has ultimate authority for deciding the safety of GM foods, openly defied public opinion by siding with the government on the question of commercial plantings.[76] These observations suggest that despite a formal system of "bureaucratic accommodation," the government will not hesitate to bypass majority opinions if they run counter to the interests of producers.[77]

As we noted earlier, British consumers today eat virtually no genetically modified foods. And yet they complain about these foods far more than their counterparts in the United States and perhaps even Japan. Fueling their discontent is a government determined to promote the British biotech industry despite longstanding consumer worries about the safety and integrity of the domestic food supply. Also important is a policymaking system that frustrates the public's expectations about governmental responsiveness to consumer demands. On the surface, Britain's consumer policymaking system may now appear more democratic than that of the

[75] *NCC, GM Food—The Consumer Interest* (London: National Consumer Council, 2004).

[76] "Tim Lang: Eating His Words," *Guardian,* March 16, 2004.

[77] Grant Jordan and Jeremy Richardson, "The British Policy Style or the Logic of Negotiation?" In *Policy Styles in Western Europe,* ed. Jeremy Richardson (London: Allen and Unwin, 1982), 80–110.

United States or Japan, but when all is said and done, it is highly susceptible to manipulation by manufacturer and government interests. For as long as this political state of affairs continues, the story of consumer opposition to GM foods in Britain will be tied up with questions of governmental responsiveness and accountability.

Conclusion

The more consumers learn about GM products, the less inclined they are to purchase them. For many consumers, GM foods have come to symbolize the negative effects of free market economics and globalization, including the erosion of basic political, economic, ecological, and ethical principles, as well as the decline of consumer influence in national political economies.

In each of the three cases examined in this chapter, consumers and their representatives have, to varying degrees, called for the reassertion of democratic principles and state control over the production and marketing of GM foods. But the ability of consumers to wrest concessions from their governments differs markedly in response to national contexts. In the United States, where the consumer interest once had the upper hand vis-à-vis producer interests, ordinary consumers know comparatively little about agricultural biotechnology; meanwhile, those who are knowledgeable and would like to see GM foods regulated have generally been excluded from a policy process that now favors producer interests. Japanese consumers, by contrast, know considerably more about GM foods. They have also extracted some significant concessions from their government as the space for consumer politics widens. British consumers, finally, have failed to achieve their goals in the policy sphere even though the extent of their opposition to GM foods has been nearly enough to topple the Blair government. The reasons for their failures lie primarily in a political system that is structured to deliver little more than symbolic concessions to nonproducer interests.

Despite these discrepancies in national consumer power, the movement to oppose GM foods has recently scored some significant victories from an international perspective. First, with the prominent exception of the United States, many countries have introduced labeling standards for GM foods that at least partially fulfill the consumer's rights to safety, to know, and to choose. Second, as the EU prepares to lift its moratorium on GM foods, more and more retail shops throughout Europe are responding directly to consumer preferences by refusing to sell food products containing GMOs. These and related developments have had a profound effect on the industry. Once hailed as a rising star, the biotech industry is now under siege as investment levels decline and firms like Monsanto cut their workforces.[78] Even some American farmers have raised their voices in protest, refusing to go along with Monsanto's plans to produce genetically modified wheat for fear of losing key export markets like Japan.[79] Consumers may not always be able to exercise influence over the industry via the political system, but they can still do so through the basic market mechanisms of supply and demand.

In response to these trends, the U.S. government has taken drastic steps to shore up the industry's international standing. In May 2003, the Bush administration made good its longstanding threat to file suit at the WTO against the EU's moratorium on imports of GM products. The case, which is based on the scientific finding that GM foods pose no known threat to human health, stands on sound legal grounds. Europe is, after all, violating international free trade rules.[80] From the political and ethical perspectives, however, the case misses the point: consumers in Europe and many other regions of the world do not want to be force-fed foods that they did not ask for and cannot control.

[78] "Monsanto Posts Loss, to Cut Jobs," *Fox News,* October 15, 2003. http://www.foxnews.com/story/0,2933,100172,00.html.

[79] "Japan Hurdle to U.S. Foothold in China Biotech Wheat Market," *Japan Times,* March 9, 2004.

[80] Clyde Prestowitz, "Don't Make Europe Gag," *International Herald Tribune,* January 27, 2003.

11

HOUSEHOLD DEBT AND CONSUMER EDUCATION IN POSTWAR JAPAN

TAKAO NISHIMURA

Consumer credit has become widely available to the Japanese over the past four decades. As household incomes increase, consumers have sought more affluent lifestyles by taking out not only home mortgages but also loans and lines of credit for the purchase of high-end products and services such as cars and foreign vacation packages. For those searching for quick and easy ways to bridge the gap between their material aspirations and their income streams, consumer finance companies offering small-scale loans with no collateral have become extremely popular, even though the interest rates tend to be extremely high. Recently, much to the surprise of those who view Japan as a nation of savers, Japanese consumers have overtaken Americans in their use of credit. More problematically, Japan has been struggling with mounting household indebtedness and personal bankruptcies.

As the scope of consumer debt expands, consumer education has become an increasingly important component of Japan's consumer protection regime. Government authorities at both the national and local levels are stepping up their efforts to arm consumers with the knowledge and skills they need to make rational decisions in the marketplace. More and more private consumer organizations, meanwhile, are prioritizing consumer education after decades of focusing on savings promotion, and several new organizations have been set up to promote financial education. Even a few firms are jumping on the bandwagon. This movement toward consumer education in the financial sphere is predicated on an emerging consensus that *informed* consumers are *safe* consumers and that education is essential to economic growth in the era of deregulation and globalization.

The purpose of this chapter is twofold. First, I chronicle the development of and changing attitudes toward consumer debt in Japan, paying particular attention to the bubble years and their aftermath. I then trace the history of consumer education programs in Japan, including recent educational developments in the realm of consumer finance. In so doing, I show that consumer education has developed in response to specific economic and political trends, most notably the economic and financial crises of the immediate postwar period, the rise of consumer spending during the 1960s and 1970s, and the subsequent expansion of consumer indebtedness. More recently, educational programs have received renewed attention from government, business, and private organizations in the wake of governmental efforts to deregulate; as government sheds many of its regulatory controls over the economy and encourages both business and individual consumers to conduct themselves in a "self-responsible" fashion, consumer education has become an essential resource for ordinary consumers who lack comprehensive governmental or legal protections against unscrupulous business behavior.

One would expect that introducing or expanding consumer education programs would be a straightforward and uncontroversial affair. But for Japan, this transition has not been easy. In a country that is markedly ambivalent about consumption and that values producer over consumer interests, consumer education has the potential to strengthen the political and economic hand of consumers vis-à-vis business. Consequently, the state was relatively slow to introduce comprehensive consumer education programs after World War II and to accord consumers with the rights needed to act assertively on their knowledge. As the pages to follow will illustrate, it was in the unprecedented context of deregulation and rising consumer debt that consumer education was finally prioritized and that resistance to education and consumer rights more broadly began to subside.

The Expansion of Household Debt and Consumer Credit in Japan

Japanese Attitudes toward Saving and Debt

With the introduction of a British-style postal savings system in 1875 and the subsequent establishment of a commercial banking system, the Meiji state poured its energies into encouraging ordinary Japanese to be frugal and to save. As Sheldon Garon notes in this volume, Japan's official savings campaigns eventually transformed saving into a moral virtue and produced one of the highest saving rates in the world. The primary target of these campaigns was the ordinary housewife (*shufu*)—the family member who, as manager of household finances, was best poised to "cut back on spending and prudently increase one's income" (*deru o seishite hairu o hakaru*). After the Great Kantō Earthquake of 1923, governmental officials intensified their exhortations to save by organizing a large-scale campaign to increase deposits in the postal savings system. To that end, they established the Central Council to Encourage Diligence and Thrift (Kinken shōrei chūō iinkai), the precursor to today's Central Council for Financial Services Information (Kinyū kōhō chūō iinkai), a leading government player in the financial education of consumers.

The fundamental objective of this savings campaign was to acquire the capital necessary to strengthen Japan's industrial base and military infrastructure as the country struggled to catch up with the West. The government was also determined to service the debt resulting from decades of massive military and other expenditures. During the postwar period, the postal savings system provided the government with much-needed capital for economic reconstruction and, later, rapid growth. Throughout its history, the state-backed system—which is now slated for privatization—has enjoyed the trust of consumers.[1]

In light of this penchant for saving, it should come as no surprise that many Japanese consumers regarded debt as shameful. As Andrew Gordon notes in his chapter in this volume, when the American-style installment plan (*geppu*) was introduced into Japan as a way to boost retail sales, many Japanese viewed it as improper. It certainly did not help that the word *geppu* was pronounced the same way as the Japanese word for "burp."[2] All this began to change as installment plans multiplied (see Gordon), the more neutral-sounding terms "credit" and "loan" entered the popular lexicon, and consumption levels rose. Thus, long before credit cards were introduced, the idea of "credit" had lost much of its moral stigma.

By the rapid growth period, consumers were facing a barrage of conflicting signals about the virtues of spending and saving. On the one hand, government policy—combined with an emerging national consensus over the economic goal of catching up with the West—lent new meaning to preexisting tendencies to sacrifice and save for the sake of the nation. The lack of a comprehensive social security system, moreover, gave consumers personal incentives to salt money away. On the other hand, many Japanese embarked on a spending spree as the economy entered a period of unprecedented expansion that peaked around the time of the 1964 Tokyo Olympics.

One of the driving forces behind the rising consumption levels during the 1960s and beyond was the emergence of department stores like Midoriya and Marui that specialized in installment buying. These stores helped transform the spending habits of consumers, who until then had

[1] Chochiku zōkyō undō iinkai, *Chochiku undōshi* [History of savings campaigns] (Tokyo: Chochiku zōkyō undō iinkai, 1983), 7–10. Consumer confidence in the postal savings system was especially high following the commercial bank failures of the mid- to late 1990s.

[2] Sanwa ginkō, *Shōhisha shinyō no chishiki* [Consumer credit and knowledge] (Tokyo: Nihon keizai shinbunsha, 1970), 95–96.

relied on cash as their primary means of payment. Starting in the late 1970s, when the vast majority of Japanese had come to regard themselves as members of the middle class, Marui implemented a highly successful marketing strategy that focused on the Baby Boom generation. The retailer appealed to its prized consumers' sense of uniqueness by referring to them as the "New Thirties" and, during the 1980s, the "New Forties." In later years, Marui continued to attract new customers by keeping up with fashion trends and selling its products on the installment plan. This strategy helps explain Marui's remarkable expansion over the years. It also suggests that consumers had come to embrace credit as an acceptable form of payment despite Japan's longstanding valorization of saving.

The Current State of Household Debt

Japan's consumer credit market has roughly tripled in size over the past twenty years. As the economy mushroomed during the bubble years of the 1980s, capital gains—on stocks and real estate—reached abnormally high levels, and consumer spending expanded accordingly. With the collapse of the economic bubble, however, the economy contracted rapidly and has been in a state of protracted recession. Despite these trends, the consumer credit market has continued to grow.

Table 11.1 illustrates the growth of the consumer credit market (these figures exclude home mortgages and other forms of collateralized financing). Measured in terms of the total amount of credit repayments, the market increased from almost 21 trillion yen in 1981 to nearly 76 trillion yen in 2002. During the early 1980s, debt repayments as a percentage of household disposable income averaged roughly 12 percent. Today, that figure has increased to 25.5 percent, which means that a quarter of disposable income is currently being allocated for credit repayment. For households with mortgages, the burden of consumer debt is even more onerous.

The stable growth of the consumer lending market is an ironic feature of the post-bubble years. As corporations restructure and reduce both overtime pay and bonus payments, household incomes are declining. But consumers who do not wish to adjust their lifestyles to harder times are compensating for their declining incomes by increasing their debt burden. To that end, many consumers are turning to consumer finance companies that promote easy financing but at high interest rates.

Japanese consumers are also increasing their reliance on credit cards. The credit card, one of the most widely used forms of consumer credit in Japan and elsewhere, has become so popular that Japanese adults now possess two to three cards on average.[3] Credit card usage since 1981 is illus-

[3] The number of credit cards in circulation totaled 250 million in 2002. Because there are approximately 100 million adults over the age of 20 in Japan (out of a total population of

TABLE 11.1.
Consumer credit growth and repayments as percentage of household disposable income

Year	Consumer credit repayment (trillion ¥)	Credit repayment as a percentage of household disposable income
1981	20.83	11.5
1982	24.20	12.8
1983	26.39	13.2
1984	29.75	14.2
1985	32.42	14.7
1986	34.85	15.1
1987	39.46	16.7
1988	24.61	17.2
1989	47.38	18.0
1990	55.39	19.7
1991	62.65	22.2
1992	65.33	22.5
1993	66.01	22.3
1994	69.93	23.2
1995	72.97	23.9
1996	75.18	24.6
1997	77.43	24.9
1998	79.43	25.3
1999	72.28	24.7
2000	75.19	24.5
2001	75.73	25.4
2002	75.64	25.5

Source: Nihon kurejitto sangyō kyōkai, *Nihon no shōhisha shinyō tōkei, 2004 nenpan* [Japanese consumer credit statistics: 2004] (Tokyo: Nihon kurejitto sangyō kyōkai, 2004), 77; *Nihon no shōhisha shinyō tōkei, 1997 nenpan,* 78; *Nihon no shōhisha shinyō tōkei, 1992 nenpan,* 66

trated in table 11.2. The numbers are astounding: although Japan has yet to match the United States—the world's credit card "superpower"—in terms of the scope of credit card usage, credit card shopping has increased eightfold over the past two decades.

While the number of department store credit cards has increased steadily over the years, the use of bank-affiliated credit cards that must be paid off every month—like the JCB and Diners Club cards—has expanded even more rapidly. These credit cards are popular for a number of reasons, not least of which is the simplicity of the application procedure. And even though many consumers have lost confidence in the commercial banks as a result of the bank failures of the 1990s, they tend to trust bank-affiliated

127.5 million), this means that on average, each adult possesses 2.5 credit cards. Statistics collected from Nihon kurejitto sangyō kyōkai, *Nihon no shōhisha shinyō tōkei, 2004 nenpan,* 66; and Sōmuchō tōkeikyoku, *Sekai no tōkei 2004 nen* [World statistics: 2004] (Tokyo: Sōmuchō tōkeikyoku, March 2004), 14.

TABLE 11.2.
Growth of credit card shopping

Year	Amount (trillion ¥)
1981	2.79
1982	3.28
1983	3.82
1984	4.20
1985	5.09
1986	5.75
1987	6.59
1988	7.86
1989	9.46
1990	11.53
1991	12.49
1992	13.10
1993	13.10
1994	13.63
1995	14.69
1996	16.75
1997	18.12
1998	19.01
1999	20.15
2000	21.79
2001	23.27
2002	24.68

Source: Nihon kurejitto sangyō kyōkai, *Nihon no shōhisha shinyō tōkei, 2004 nenpan* 66; *Nihon no shōhisha shinyō tōkei, 1997 nenpan,* 68; *Nihon no shōhisha shinyō tōkei, 1992 nenpan,* 69

credit cards far more than those of nonbank institutions. Most consumers seem to prefer paying their debts in full each month, as is required by many of these credit cards.

For many years, the government denied the commercial banks the right to offer revolving terms of credit in an effort to protect retailers and credit card companies that did offer such terms to their customers. This changed after the 1990 Structural Impediments Initiative (SII) talks, during which American trade negotiators persuaded the Japanese government to introduce a more flexible system for the commercial banks. The rationale behind this move was that access to bank-issued revolving credit cards would help stimulate consumer demand and, therefore, help correct the long-standing trade imbalance between the two countries. In an important but underappreciated step toward financial deregulation, the government lifted the ban on bank revolving credit in 1992; the types of payment plans offered by bank-issued credit cards have rapidly diversified since then.[4]

[4] For more on this subject, see Nishimura Takao, "Taryō saimu mondai to shōhisha kyōiku

The growth of the Internet since the early 1990s has also contributed to the expansion of consumer credit. Today, the most common form of payment in Internet shopping and auctions is the credit card, while the personal computer is becoming an increasingly acceptable means for paying bills. Together, these trends have spurred the growth of consumer financial services in Japan.

Although credit card usage has exploded in recent years, that most card holders still prefer plans requiring full repayment every month suggests that credit cards have yet to become the primary source of Japan's consumer debt problem. As the next section illustrates, consumer finance (*shōhisha kinyū*) companies have assumed this dubious distinction. Also known as *sarakin* (short for *sarariman kinyū*, "salaryman financing"), these firms, which cater to individual consumers, are legitimate credit companies that first appeared approximately four decades ago. It is possible, however, that credit cards will eventually overtake *sarakin* loans as the number one source of consumer debt now that the commercial banks are offering a wider variety of credit cards, including those with revolving payment plans.

The Growth of Consumer Financial Services and the Sarakin *Problem*

Japanese consumers struggling with the adverse effects of the prolonged economic slowdown have access to an expanding range of financial products. Many consumers are increasing their use of credit card cash advances, which can be obtained at ATMs located in banks and supermarkets. More desperate consumers have resorted to borrowing from illegal loan sharks at astronomically high interest rates. Loan sharks routinely mail fliers to potential customers and post advertisements on lampposts promising instant approval for cash loans; some even promise to deliver the loans directly to the customers' homes. As might be expected, the interest rates for these loans are exorbitant, not to mention illegal. More commonly, consumers have been taking advantage of the services offered by the *sarakin* firms. These firms operate a rapidly expanding network of unmanned lending machines located on street corners and along national highways. The interest rates for *sarakin* loans are high and, in some cases, in excess of legal ceilings. Small in scale and with no collateral requirements attached, *sarakin* loans have surpassed the pawnshop as a popular means for both blue- and white-collar households to supplement their paychecks. According to one estimate, the number of Japanese consumers who have resorted to such loans recently passed 12 million.[5] But as competition in this

---

[Debt issue and consumer education], *Kokumin seikatsu kenkyū* 32, no. 3 (December 1992): 26.

[5] *Gekkan shōhisha shinyō* [Consumer credit monthly] (September 2003): 27.

sphere intensified in the 1970s, it became all too apparent that these companies were lending excessively, charging inordinately high interest rates, and, like illegal loan sharks, practicing coercive collection techniques (*sarakin san aku,* the "three vices of *sarakin*").

The government tried to address the *sarakin* problem during the early 1980s in response to the demands of both ordinary consumers and the mainstream banking industry. In 1983, the National Diet passed the Money Lending Control Law (Shikingyō kisei hō), which imposed strict regulatory controls over the activities of moneylenders, and later amended the Capital Subscription Law (Shusshi hō) to include an interest rate ceiling of 40 percent for lending institutions.[6] In an effort to control the money-lending industry as a whole, furthermore, the government recognized industry associations in this sphere and made membership compulsory for all money-lending businesses.[7]

Unfortunately, these regulatory measures failed to solve the problems of this rapidly growing sector of the financial industry. In 1999, a scandal broke out involving a lending corporation that serviced small and medium-sized businesses. This well-known firm, which was large enough to advertise on prime-time television, allegedly told some of its customers who could not repay their loans to raise the money by selling their kidneys and other internal organs. The scandal triggered a parliamentary debate that culminated in further amendments to the Capital Subscription Law to lower the ceiling on interest rates from 40 percent to 29.2 percent and to establish a supervisory system for registered money-lending businesses. In 2003, the industry was rocked by another scandal involving a major consumer credit company. The chairperson of the company had apparently ordered subordinates to wiretap the telephone conversations of employees who had been critical of his management policies. The chairperson eventually resigned in disgrace.

These incidents helped fuel a further decline in the reputation of *sarakin* firms. And yet, the number of borrowers continues to rise. As of March 2004, the sum total of outstanding loans at Japan's top four *sarakin* companies was almost six trillion yen (roughly 60 billion dollars).[8] To the industry's credit, many of these firms have been trying to gain consumers' trust by improving their management practices and, since the mid-1990s, getting listed on the Tokyo Stock Exchange.

Meanwhile, the expansion of the consumer finance industry more gen-

[6] The Law Concerning the Regulation of Receiving of Capital Subscription, Deposits and Interest on Deposits, often called the Capital Subscription Law (Shusshi hō), was enacted in 1954.

[7] Nishimura Takao, *Kurejitto kaunseringu* [Credit counseling] (Tokyo: Tōyō keizei shinpōsha, 1997), 3.

[8] This figure is based on statistics posted on the websites of the four largest consumer finance companies (Takefuji, Akomu, Puromisu, and Aifuru) in March 2004.

TABLE 11.3
Consumer bankruptcy cases

Year	# of cases filed
1985	14,625
1986	11,432
1987	9,774
1988	9,415
1989	9,190
1990	11,273
1991	23,288
1992	43,144
1993	43,545
1994	40,385
1995	43,414
1996	56,494
1997	71,299
1998	103,803
1999	122,741
2000	139,280
2001	160,457
2002	214,638
2003	242,377

Source: Saikō saibansho jimusōkyoku, *Shihō tōkei nenpō 1, minji, gyōsei hen, Heisei 14nen* [Annual judicial statistics 1, civil and administrative affairs edition, 2002], 67. The data for 2003 was taken from the Supreme Court's recently issued preliminary report.

erally has had some serious repercussions for ordinary consumers and their families. As illustrated by table 11.3, the number of consumers filing for personal bankruptcy exceeded 240,000 in 2003—over twenty-five times the level of just fifteen years earlier. Although this is much lower than the U.S. personal bankruptcy rate—now approximately 1.5 million for a population that is only a little more than twice the size of Japan's—that it is steadily rising is cause for concern.[9]

The social repercussions of excessive or unethical lending practices are also troubling. Some borrowers, most of them unemployed men, have chosen to leave their families and live on the streets rather than face the shame of reneging on their financial obligations. And in a desperate attempt to escape the harassment of illegal moneylenders, many consumers—and, in a few cases, their families as well—have committed suicide. According to official estimates, at least 3,437 individuals who committed suicide in 2000 did so for reasons of indebtedness.[10]

[9] Statistics provided by the American Bankruptcy Institute, http://www.abiworld/org.

[10] Utsunomiya Kenji, *Shōhisha kinyū* [Consumer finance] (Tokyo: Iwanami shoten, 2002), 27.

The police are trying to prevent these ultimate expressions of consumer discontent by increasing their surveillance of illegal lenders. Since these individuals usually lack formal addresses, however, the police have been largely unsuccessful in apprehending the perpetrators of such abuses.

The Causes and Management of Consumer Debt

In 2002, the Japan Federation of Bar Associations (Nichibenren) conducted a poll of 1,027 consumers filing for bankruptcy to determine some of the root causes of consumer debt. Approximately 26.5 percent of the respondents stated that they had taken out loans in response to "low income and the strains of everyday life." Other reasons included "guaranteeing a debt or taking over the debt of third persons" (18.6 percent), "purchasing a home" (18.11 percent), "repaying preexisting loans" (16.55 percent), and "financing businesses" (15.68 percent).[11]

When a Japanese consumer decides to borrow money, he or she will look for lenders with comparatively low interest rates. For collateral-free loans, the top choices in descending order would be employer-financed loans, ATM card loans,[12] cash advances on credit cards,[13] and, finally, loans from *sarakin* and loan sharks. Although credit limits depend on income levels, interest rates commonly vary from less than 10 percent for a legal lender to more than 3,000 percent per annum for an illegal lender.[14] These dramatic variations in interest rate are a distinctive characteristic of the Japanese consumer finance industry.

High interest rates have contributed to the growing phenomena of multiple borrowing—a phenomenon that was facilitated during the 1980s by lax lending requirements for financial institutions. All new borrowers must adhere to strict repayment schedules. When those schedules are interrupted, however, borrowers invite pressure from money collectors. Consequently, many will take out new loans in order to pay off the old ones—even if this means paying higher interest rates. For some consumers, these steps can trigger a never-ending cycle of borrowing that puts intolerable pressure on their daily lives and ultimately leads to bankruptcy.

The following is a typical example of an indebted Japanese consumer. Mr. A made a 200,000–yen down payment on a condominium worth 23 million yen and arranged to pay off the rest with loans. Using credit cards,

[11] Nichibenren, *2002 nen hasan jiken oyobi kojin saisei jiken kiroku chōsa* [2002 survey of bankruptcies and personal recovery cases] (Tokyo: Nichibenren, 2003), 15.

[12] ATM card loans, or "bank card loans" (*ginkō kâdo rōn*), of up to 500,000 yen and at a rate of 7–8 percent are issued to bank customers with savings accounts. Borrowers can withdraw the funds from their accounts using ATM cards.

[13] Known in Japanese as "credit card cashing" (*kurejitto kâdo kyasshingu*), the interest rates for such loans are high, ranging from 14 to 27 percent.

[14] For more statistics on the consumer credit industry, see Utsunomiya, *Shōhisha kinyū.*

he paid 2 million yen in taxes, registration fees, and the commission for his real estate agent, and an additional million for furniture. He was then obligated to pay roughly 100,000 yen each month in loan payments and other fees, including 35,000 yen in maintenance fees and contributions to a reserve fund for renovations administered by the condo complex. Finally, he paid an additional 20,000 yen per month to service his credit card loans.

A year after he purchased his home, Mr. A had to take a 10 percent cut in his paycheck following the onset of the recession. But his personal expenses continued to rise, prompting him to take cash advances on his credit cards and purchase loans from vending machines operated by *sarakin* firms. He was so desperate by this point that he no longer paid any attention to interest rates. Although his wife tried to help out by taking on a part-time job, Mr. A was heading into a downward spiral of debt.[15]

Mr. A eventually sought the advice of a lawyer. He was given an opportunity to pay off his debts under civil rehabilitation procedures introduced in 2000 and based on the Chapter 13 bankruptcy model of the United States. Under these procedures, which enabled Mr. A to keep his home, his debts were reduced and the schedule for repaying his mortgage extended. The number of Japanese consumers seeking assistance under this new system has been growing in recent years.

Although Mr. A managed to solve his debt-related problems fairly effectively, other consumers have been less successful, in part because of the paucity of comprehensive consumer-counseling services. In addition to lawyers—who can be very costly—consumers can contact the Japan Federation of Bar Associations, local semigovernmental consumer centers, the Japan Credit Counseling Association (Nihon kurejitto kaunseringu kyōkai), or the Monetary Management Counseling Service (Kinsen kanri kaunseringu jimusho). Unfortunately, services operated by nonlawyers are severely restricted in terms of the kinds of services they provide. The Monetary Management Counseling Service (MMCS), created in 1997, is a good case in point. Based on the Credit Counseling Services (CCS) of the United States, which has been in existence for approximately four decades, this private organization depends on funds provided by the consumer finance industry. Also, like the CCS, it is able to provide indebted consumers with psychological counseling and advice on managing household finances. Since it has yet to establish offices outside of Tokyo and Osaka, however, its services are not as widely used as those of the CCS. More significantly, and unlike the CCS, the MMCS is not authorized to provide assistance with debt reduction or consolidation, both of which, under Japanese law, can only be carried out by licensed lawyers. The consumer centers face similar restrictions. Since they are not lawyers, the centers'

[15] Nihon shōhisha kinyū kyōkai, *Kinsen kanri kaunseringu keesu sutadishū* [Case studies in financial management] (Osaka: Nihon shōhisha kinyū kyōkai, 2002), 17.

"consumer lifestyle consultants" (*shōhi seikatsu sōdan'in*) offer no advice on debt consolidation. They are also handicapped by the requirement that they refer inquiries relating to *sarakin* practices to lawyers' associations.[16] Since its counselors work closely with lawyers, the Japan Credit Counseling Association *is* permitted to venture into these realms, but the high costs and red tape surrounding this service have prevented many Japanese from taking advantage of it.

These private and public counseling services are woefully inadequate given the rising level of household indebtedness of Japan. Clearly, more needs to be done in this regard. In addition, government and private organizations need to do more to prevent consumers from becoming indebted in the first place—something that after-the-fact counseling services cannot achieve. Tightening regulatory controls over lenders to prevent aggressive or lax lending practices is certainly one way to achieve this goal. In the context of the government's ongoing movement to deregulate, however, this option is no longer very attractive. The more viable option in this context is to expand national consumer educational programs.

Consumer Education in Japan

The immediate postwar period was one of near economic chaos caused by raging inflation, a devastated industrial base, widespread unemployment, and an increasingly militant workers' union. Rapidly rising prices and product shortages, meanwhile, forced many consumers into starvation. To cope with these crises, the government prioritized three economic objectives: (1) restoring confidence in the Japanese yen; (2) preventing inflation; and (3) stabilizing consumer prices. Among the measures introduced to meet these goals were the 1946 Emergency Financial Measures Ordinance (Kinyū kinkyū sotchirei), the Diet's Joint Resolution on Currency Stability (Tsūka antei ni tsuite no kyōdō ketsugi an), and, last but not least, a cabinet resolution to boost savings. The government reasoned that a higher savings rate would help avert an economic disaster by accumulating the capital required for currency stabilization and industrial recovery.

Shortly thereafter, the government established the Center for Currency Stabilization Policy (Tsūka antei taisaku honbu) in the headquarters and branches of the Bank of Japan. The center's organizational setup enabled the government, the Ministry of Finance, the Bank of Japan, and the Japanese parliament to work together in a nationwide campaign to "save the

[16] Consumer centers fielded 47,852 and 97,120 inquiries about *sarakin* firms in 2001 and 2002, respectively. Only inquiries pertaining to telephone information services surpassed these figures. *Shōhiseikatsu nenpō 2003* [Annual report on consumer lifestyles] (Tokyo: Kokumin seikatsu sentaa, October 2003), 23.

nation through saving" (*Kyūkoku chochiku undō*). Even children were targeted by the campaign, which sought to establish "children's banks" (*kodomo no ginkō*) in schools throughout Japan. The first children's bank appeared in January 1948 as part of the social studies program of an Osaka elementary school.[17] The government also set out to increase the number of "national savings associations" (*kokumin chochiku kumiai*), which had first appeared during the war, and to link the savings campaign with other national campaigns, including the Daily Life Improvement Campaign (Seikatsu kaizen undō) or, as it was known after 1955, the New Life Movement (Shin seikatsu undō).

In many ways, these early postwar savings campaigns continued the longstanding tradition of state interference in the private decisions of ordinary consumers. But as the postwar economy began to grow and consumers found themselves with more disposable income in their pockets, state policy gradually shifted away from directly controlling the financial behavior of individuals toward disseminating information that would enable more independent consumers to survive in an increasingly complex financial marketplace.

Fueling this shift were fundamental changes in consumer behavior. In 1956, the government released a widely publicized economic white paper that announced the official end of postwar economic reconstruction and marked the beginning of an extended period of rapid growth. As personal incomes rose in tandem with growth rates, lifestyles changed accordingly. Consumers scrambled to acquire large consumer durables like television sets and vacuum cleaners; meanwhile, they spent less time on household tasks and more time and money on leisure. This newfound acquisitiveness on the part of consumers was facilitated by rapidly expanding credit card and installment sale services. These and related changes marked a veritable "revolution" in the lives of ordinary consumers.[18]

An important milestone in the development of consumer education in the midst of these changes was the 1955 establishment of the Japan Productivity Center (Nihon seisansei honbu), a government-affiliated organization designed to enhance economic productivity with the cooperation of politicians, bureaucrats, businessmen, and even representatives from the labor unions. Although primarily geared toward the promotion of industry, the center also sought to help consumers. During the first few years of its existence, the center sent scores of Japanese—including private consumer advocates—to the United States on various kinds of study tours. One such tour included a visit to Consumers Union, which impressed the delegates in terms of its size, sophisticated product-testing facilities, and

[17] Chochiku zōkyō chūō iinkai, *Chochiku undōshi,* 17–18.

[18] Takeuchi Hiroshi, *Shōwa keizaishi* [A history of Shōwa economics] (Tokyo: Chikuma shobō 1988), 151–53.

educational programs.[19] Upon returning to Japan, center members joined forces with representatives of domestic consumer organizations to research consumer education in the United States and plan for comparable programs in Japan. Soon afterward, the Japan Productivity Center established a special committee to explore and promote consumer education in Japan. In 1961, this committee split from the center to become, with governmental assistance, the Japan Consumers Association (Nihon shōhisha kyōkai), a leading organization for consumer education affiliated with the Ministry of the Economy, Trade, and Industry (METI, formerly the Ministry of International Trade and Industry, or MITI).[20]

As defined by the government's Social Policy Council (Kokumin seikatsu shingikai) in 1966 and carried out in the Japan Consumers Association's magazine, *Kaimono jōzu* (Smart Shopping), the primary aim of consumer education during the 1960s was to train consumers to make rational purchasing decisions. This objective was embodied in the term "wise consumer" (*kashikoi shōhisha*), which apparently originated within the government as part of its broader program of consumer protection. From the government's perspective, providing citizens with the information they needed to become "wise consumers" complemented the formal regulations governing the conduct of producers and the quality of their products. (This policy is still partially in effect today, as the government attempts to nurture "self-reliant" consumers in the context of deregulation.) It did not, however, mean encouraging consumers to act assertively in the marketplace.

The notion of the "wise consumer" meshed well with the underlying principles of the 1968 Consumer Protection Basic Law (Shōhisha hogo kihon hō). The law, which was the first in Japanese history to uphold consumer protection as a governmental objective, outlined the obligations of various interests in the consumer protection realm. It specified the regulatory responsibilities of all levels of government toward consumers, the responsibilities of firms to improve the quality of their products and services and to respond to consumer claims, and the obligations of consumers themselves to acquire the knowledge for making rational purchasing decisions. Much to the disappointment of consumer advocates, however, the law made no mention of the consumer rights to safety, to know, to choose, and to be heard—rights that had first been articulated in the industrialized world in a 1962 message to Congress delivered by President John F. Kennedy.[21]

[19] Nishimura Takao, *Nihon no shōhisha kyōiku* [Japanese consumer education] (Tokyo: Yūhikaku, 1999), 50–51.

[20] Nihon shōhisha kyōkai, *Nihon shōhisha kyōkai 5 nen no ayumi* [A five-year history of the Japan consumer association] (Tokyo: Nihon shōhisha kyōkai, 1966), 17–20.

[21] John F. Kennedy, *Public Papers of the Presidents of the United States—John F. Kennedy* (Washington, D.C.: U.S. Government Printing Office, 1963), 235–36.

Since consumer rights have the potential to empower consumers legally and politically relative to producers, this omission reflected the prioritization of business interests in the political economy. It also magnified the importance of consumer information as the consumer's primary defense in the marketplace. But to the extent that individual rights encourage consumers to act more assertively in the political economy, the absence of an official consumer rights discourse limited the efficacy of information flows to consumers. Needless to say, this state of affairs benefited businesses, many of which were decidedly paternal in their dealings with consumers, believing that they were more capable of acting in consumers' best interests than consumers themselves.

These handicaps notwithstanding, the government took a number of significant steps designed to improve consumer access to information. A year after the enactment of the Consumer Protection Basic Law, it amended the 1947 Local Autonomy Law to make consumer protection an administrative priority for local governments. And in 1970, the government established the Consumer Information Center (Kokumin seikatsu sentaa) under the auspices of the former Economic Planning Agency. Now known in English as the National Consumer Affairs Center, the center carries out product testing, consumer research and opinion surveys, complaint processing, mediation services between consumers and producers, and consumer education. At the same time, semi-independent consumer centers (*shōhisha sentaa*) administered by prefectural and city governments were established around the country to perform similar functions at the local level. Information collected by both the centers and the NCAC is channeled into a national computer network administered by the NCAC, thereby enabling the centers to coordinate their responses to specific consumer problems.

By 1999, the total number of consumer centers in Japan reached 359.[22] Staffed by both full-time government employees and highly trained consumer lifestyle consultants, the centers have become adept at fielding inquiries from disgruntled consumers about defective products, improper sales practices, and, more recently, problems pertaining to consumer finance. Of particular note are the consumer lifestyle consultants, an administrative role that exists only in Japan. Consultants, the majority of whom are women, are private citizens who have received comprehensive training from organizations like the Japan Consumers Association in financial affairs, public relations, and legal issues pertaining to consumers. It is these individuals who stand at the interface of local government and ordinary consumers and who solve consumer-related problems on a case-by-case basis. As such, they form an integral part of the expanding consumer education infrastructure.

[22] Keizai kikakuchō kokumin seikatsukyoku, ed., *Handobukku shōhisha* [Consumer handbook] (Tokyo: Keizai kikakuchō kokumin seikatsukyoku, 1999), 17.

The government's positive efforts notwithstanding, the consultants and the centers they represent have inadvertently weakened the contributions of many private organizations to consumer education. During the early postwar period, housewives' organizations, consumer cooperatives, and other private citizens' groups were the first to address postwar consumer problems and inform consumers of their alleged rights. Many of them, for instance, published informative pamphlets and other literature on specific consumer issues, sponsored public lectures, and fielded inquiries from aggrieved consumers. Over time, however, private consumer advocates realized that they could not keep up with well-endowed government organizations in terms of providing these services to consumers. This is a marked contrast to the United States, where organizations like Consumers Union continue to play a leading role in a host of consumer-related services, including education. Today, private consumer organizations disseminate valuable information about consumer finance to ordinary consumers and frequently lobby the government for stronger laws and regulations in the financial realm. But, for better or worse, these organizations tend to take a back seat to governmental and semigovernmental entities in meeting the specific educational needs of the consuming public.[23]

Scholars have recently come to play a very important role in the sphere of consumer education. For much of the postwar era, academic research pertaining to the consumer was the almost exclusive domain of legal scholars, most of whom cooperated with government to develop more effective consumer protection policies. Few scholars addressed the subject of consumer education per se. In 1981, however, the field of consumer education was finally formalized in Japanese academe with the establishment of the Japan Academy of Consumer Education (Nihon shōhisha kyōiku gakkai). In its prospectus, the academy stated:

> The consumer's capacity to formulate precise preferences or to achieve self-actualization is lowered because information about goods and services is not forthcoming, is offered too late, or because the consumer is simply not aware that such information exists. In terms of enabling individuals to protect their values and enhance their quality of life, consumer education is highly significant and very necessary. Consequently, the Japan Academy of Consumer Education was established to research the ideas, methods, and effectiveness of consumer education.[24]

Led by home economics scholars, the academy includes academicians from the fields of marketing, business, and education; consumer move-

[23] For more in English on the functions of consumer organizations in Japan, see Patricia L. Maclachlan, *Consumer Politics in Postwar Japan: The Institutional Boundaries of Citizen Activism* (New York: Columbia University Press, 2002).

[24] Nihon shōhisha kyōiku gakkai, *Nihon shōhisha kyōiku gakkai* [Bulletin of the Japan Academy of Consumer Education], no. 1 (1982): 52.

ment representatives; consumer consultants who work in consumer centers; and even company employees who deal directly with consumers. The purpose of the academy is to facilitate the exchange of opinions and information among this diverse array of participants and to promote research on topics pertaining to consumer education. As evidenced by its 1985 sponsorship of the Kyoto International Symposium on Consumer Education and numerous study tours to the United States, the academy has also established international links that serve as important sources of information. The academy has been strongly influenced by the American system of consumer education, which emphasizes the development of critical thinking skills among consumers.

During the mid-1980s, another scandal erupted in Japan that further underscored the consumer's vulnerability to companies in the financial services sector. The incident involved the Toyoda Trading Company, an outfit that engaged in the door-to-door sale of gold to consumers, many of whom were worried about the effects of declining interest rates on their personal assets. The firm collected deposits from its clients in return for promissory notes and a commitment to provide a return of 10 percent interest on investments. The deal was a sham, of course, and many Japanese—including elderly consumers—were seriously hurt by it. The incident, which highlighted problems pertaining to consumer contracts in the financial sector, attracted a great deal of attention from the general public. It was even a topic of discussion in the Diet, where the Minister of Education acknowledged the need for more consumer education about financial services and contracts.

The Toyoda scandal eventually led to a deepening of financial education programs for consumers. In 1986, a prominent government advisory council released a report recommending the establishment of such a program—one that included instruction on consumer contracts—within the public school system.[25] Accordingly, the Ministry of Education established a curriculum for social sciences and home economics programs in schools around the country.[26]

In 1990, the Ministry of Education and the Economic Planning Agency, the latter of which, until its abolition in 2001, was responsible for coordinating governmental consumer policy at the national level, established the National Institute for Consumer Education (NICE, or Shōhisha kyōiku shien sentaa). Run by five full-time staff members, NICE is now an independent organization that performs functions similar to those of the National Council on Economic Education (NCEE), the Jump Start Coalition,

[25] Kokumin seikatsu shingikai, *Gakkō ni okeru shōhisha kyōiku ni tsuite* [School-based consumer education] (Tokyo: Keizai kikakuchō, 1986).

[26] Monbushō, *Kōtō gakkō gakushū shidō yōryō* [Educational leadership in high schools] (Tokyo: Okurashō iinsatsukyoku, 1989).

and the National Endowment on Financial Education in the United States. Working closely with private consumer organizations and local consumer centers, NICE takes consumer education in new directions by emphasizing more interactive educational techniques in the classroom like role-playing and case studies—techniques that have proven highly effective in the United States. Specifically, the institute conducts research on consumer education, sponsors workshops and seminars for public school teachers, creates educational materials, and develops domestic and international communication networks relating to consumer education. More recently, it has been cooperating with other organizations to develop educational seminars for universities.

Together, these programs marked the introduction of formalized consumer finance education to Japan. That said, Japan still lacked a system of consumer education in the full sense of the term. Cooperation among these programs was sporadic, and the problem of the duplication of functions remained unresolved. Meanwhile, very few citizens seemed to know about the services that these organizations provided. I estimate that only about 1 percent of Japanese schoolteachers are aware of NICE's existence even today. Needless to say, these problems hindered the overall effectiveness of consumer education in Japan, not to mention the public's consciousness of their rights as consumers.

Governmental deregulation has led to some significant improvements in this regard. Since the early to mid-1980s, the government has overseen the liberalization not only of telecommunications and transportation but also of the financial, insurance, and corporate securities industries. Deregulation, including the "Big Bang," a series of financial liberalization measures introduced between 1998 and 2001, benefited consumers in terms of lower prices and a broader range of product choice. But it also triggered widespread anxiety, particularly during the mid- to late 1990s as the lingering recession drove a number of major banks and insurance companies to bankruptcy and the debt load of consumers increased as they struggled to shore up their lifestyles. In response to these concerns, in June 2000 the Advisory Council for Financial Affairs (Kinyū shingikai) pressured the government to expand its system of consumer education.

One step toward that end was the establishment in 2001 of the independent Financial Supervisory Agency (FSA), an entity that used to be a part of the Ministry of Finance. Recognizing the accomplishments of the Central Council for Savings Information, the FSA renamed it the Central Council for Financial Services Information and authorized it to play the leading role in financial education for consumers. Accordingly, and in conjunction with relevant ministries and many of the educational programs mentioned above, the council has conducted research on European and American financial education systems, developed teaching materials, sponsored workshops for teachers, and, in 2002, announced guidelines for a system of financial education that would appeal to consumers of all ages. In 2003, the council introduced a system for promoting research in financial education within the public school system, designating the Kōfu Municipal Commercial High School as the nation's first such research center.[27] Although it is too soon to tell whether these recent developments will significantly improve Japan's haphazard system of consumer education in the financial sphere, they are undoubtedly a step in the right direction.

The substantive objectives of the council's financial education programs are fairly typical of consumer education more generally in Japan. Predictably, the council's predecessor focused on savings in order to promote capital accumulation for Japan's increasingly export-oriented economy. As the economy entered an extended period of rapid growth, it shifted its focus to the dissemination of information necessary for "daily life" and to the development of a "healthy economy." Today, the council emphasizes the economic and financial education of individual consumers and households. To that end, it provides consumers with basic financial and economic information, teaches them the "value of money" and the skills needed to distinguish the relative merits of different financial products (including loans), and instructs them on how to avoid excessive consumer debt and other financial problems. Finally, the council encourages "rational household accounts" (see Garon, chap. 7)—an objective that harks back to the early days of government-led savings campaigns but that is now geared toward the development of more self-responsible consumers in a freer marketplace.[28]

Deregulation and Consumer Law

As the government pursues its long-term policy of economic (including financial) deregulation and encourages consumers to become more "self-reliant" in the marketplace, consumer organizations, concerned scholars, some lawmakers, and the attentive public have put increased pressure on the government to do more to recognize and protect the rights of consumers. The reasoning behind this movement is simple: as the government slowly retreats from the marketplace, new steps must be taken to protect consumers—most of whom are accustomed to relying on government bodies for regulatory protections—from the effects of unfair business practices and to expand their menu of remedies when damages do occur.

The government has taken a few significant steps in this direction. Of particular note was the 2000 enactment of the Consumer Contract Law. This law establishes consumers' right to cancel contracts in the event that

[27] Interview with Kōfu Municipal Commercial High School officials, September 30, 2003.

[28] For an account of the council's aims and activities in English, see http://www.saveinfo.or.jp.

they receive faulty information—or no information at all—about their contents, and to unilaterally nullify clauses that may prove disadvantageous to them. Consumers had pressed for this law for years, only to face considerable resistance from business interests reluctant to give their customers more information about the goods and services they consumed—information that stood to weaken the upper hand of businesses in the political economy. Although consumer advocates have criticized the law for not doing enough to protect consumers, the legislation is a step toward the strengthening of consumer rights. It also enhances the efficacy of education programs in the financial sphere.

More recently, the government has introduced consumer protection measures in response to consumer concerns about food safety following a number of food-related scandals—measures that will have beneficial effects on consumer education programs in the financial sphere. In May 2004, for example, the Consumer Protection Basic Law was revised for the first time since its enactment in 1968. Renamed the Consumer Basic Law (Shōhisha kihon hō), the law has been welcomed by scholars and consumer groups for openly recognizing basic consumer rights, including the right to receive consumer education.[29] The government has also drafted bills to protect those who blow the whistle on corporate misconduct and to give consumer organizations the legal right to engage in group action.[30] In keeping with our earlier observations, these measures should enhance the efficacy of consumer education by strengthening the autonomy and powers of consumers in the political economy.

Although consumer advocates and legal specialists have been quick to praise these recent developments, they insist that more needs to be done. They point out, for example, that the new Consumer Basic Law may actually *increase* the risks confronted by consumers in the marketplace by emphasizing the responsibilities of consumers, as opposed to producers, regarding consumer protection. Furthermore, some critics argue that many of the recent laws and measures designed to help "self-responsible" consumers navigate the market are deeply flawed. The likelihood that consumer organizations will take advantage of the new group action provisions, for example, is decreased not only by the fact that consumer leaders are aging but also by the very time-consuming administrative procedures of the court system and the prohibitive costs of filing lawsuits and

[29] Article 2 of the revised Basic Law recognizes the following five rights: the right to safety; the right to choose; the right to information and consumer-related education; the right to have one's opinion reflected (in business and government); and the right to redress. The insertion of these rights into Japan's "consumer constitution" is a major milestone in the history of consumer protection in Japan.

[30] The Japanese courts recognize group action, but only by consumers whose rights or interests have been directly affected by certain corporate activities. If passed, the new law would permit consumer advocates to act on behalf of aggrieved consumers.

bringing them to completion—costs that are unlikely to be met by government pledges to increase public subsidies for such lawsuits. (Despite these restraints, a number of lawyers with an interest in consumer affairs are taking advantage of the 1998 Law to Promote Specified Nonprofit Activities, or NPO Law, to establish nonprofit groups that will focus on consumer-related group action.)[31] How, critics wonder, are self-responsible consumers to protect their rights in an increasingly complex and deregulated market without the state or adequate legal measures to fall back on?

The weaknesses of Japan's evolving consumer protection regime can be attributed to politics. Clearly, deregulation, the dramatic slow-down in growth rates since 1990, and the need of the Liberal Democratic Party (LDP) to expand its base of support enabled the introduction of these recent legal measures. Note, however, that much of the recent consumer protection legislation was initiated and drafted by the LDP-controlled government as opposed to specific elected legislators who may be more attuned to the demands of consumers. Not surprisingly, most of the new legal measures—actual and proposed—are highly sensitive to the demands of business. A proposed law for protecting whistle-blowers, for instance, defines very narrowly the circumstances under which whistle-blowers are to be shielded by law, a stipulation that may protect businesses from public and legal censure in all but the most egregious of cases.

Once again, education may help compensate for these legal shortcomings. In the financial realm, acquiring necessary information may prove difficult since financial products are invisible and their quality is difficult to assess. Unlike tangible products, moreover, financial products cannot be "returned" to a retailer if consumers are unhappy with them. These caveats aside, Japanese consumers can certainly enhance their knowledge about such products in a more rights-based consumer protection environment by becoming more conscious of their rights and responsibilities as consumers; actively seeking information about financial products and learning how to compare them to one another; learning how to withstand aggressive sales tactics; and acquiring the wherewithal to boycott companies with unfair business practices. But when all is said and done, consumers must be aware that for products like consumer loans that are constantly changing in response to corporate innovation and consumer demand, the law cannot be expected to anticipate and correct consumer-related problems before they arise. The primary responsibility of "self-responsible" consumers in such a market, then, must be to obtain the information necessary for circumventing these legal shortcomings.

[31] *Shōhishahō nyūzu* [Consumer law news], no. 57 (October 2003): 7–9.

12

URBAN CHINESE HOMEOWNERS AS CITIZEN-CONSUMERS

DEBORAH S. DAVIS

Contemporary China's attitudes toward consumer culture present us with an irony. As the sole Communist polity profiled in this volume, it might be presumed that the Chinese party-state would be the most ambivalent about surging consumer spending. Yet in the last two decades party leaders have promoted rapid increases in consumer spending with little of the ambivalence seen in its capitalist neighbors South Korea and Japan. Where the Chinese state remains wary of consumer culture, as this chapter illustrates, is in its potential to empower the consumer as citizen.

In the years immediately after the founding of the People's Republic of China in 1949, the Chinese Communist Party (CCP) drew on a rhetoric of modernization that lionized the industrial proletariat, stigmatized private property, and celebrated the state's ability to meet the material needs of a growing population. However, citizenship did not justify equal claims to the nation's resources, and the first constitution differentiated among citizens so that only a subset could enjoy the full benefits of the socialist transformation.[1] Improving the country's standard of living was a central goal of the revolutionary government, but the party-state would dictate the terms of improvement.

The author wishes to thank Peng Chen, Jean Hung, Jianying Li, Danni Wong, Shuping Wang, and the members of the 2002 CUHK-Yale summer workshop for their help with data collection as well as the Cheng-Lee Endowment at Yale University for financial support. James Farrer, Belinda Liu, Kevin O'Brien, Florence Padovani, Dorothy Solinger, and the editors provided valuable criticism for revision.

[1] Xingdong Yu, "Citizenship, Ideology, and the PRC Constitution," in *Changing Meanings of Citizenship in Modern China,* ed. Merle Goldman and Elizabeth J. Perry (Cambridge: Harvard University Press, 2002), 293.

For urban residents, these early CCP definitions of modernity and citizenship not only defined authority relations between urban residents and local state agents, they also created distinctively bureaucratized patterns of consumption that distinguished the Chinese experience from those East Asian societies (Japan, South Korea, and Taiwan) modernizing within capitalist economies. The post-1949 CCP blueprint for development radically de-commercialized city life and contained consumption within locations of production.[2] Employers issued ration tickets, originally designed to reduce wartime hardship, to control the peacetime sale of basic food items as well as of a wide range of household furnishings and items in daily use.[3] City dwellings were distributed as a de-commodified welfare benefit to the most deserving "supplicants" in a public housing queue.[4] Through the late 1970s, urban families routinely purchased rationed staples from state-controlled warehouses and even depended on government or enterprise bureaus for leisure travel, entertainment, and recreation.[5] The state renounced any role for consumer demand in their blueprint for economic development.

To some extent, the Soviet experience guided the CCP leaders' decision to de-commercialize the urban economy and subordinate individual consumption to state-directed production quotas. However, Chinese leaders also built directly on their own civil war practices in the Yan'an base camps, and they ultimately went further than the Russians in erasing consumers as economic actors and encapsulating urban life within production-focused enclaves.[6] Furthermore, because lifetime job assignments and police control over residential mobility intensified the dependence of urban residents on the bureaucratic allocation of necessities, urban China took a path to modernization after 1949 that was particularly hostile to consumerism.[7]

[2] Piper Gaubatz, "China's Urban Transformation," *Urban Studies* 36, no. 9 (August 1999): 1495–1521; and Deborah Davis, "Social Transformations of Metropolitan China since 1949," in *Cities in the Developing World,* ed. Joseph Guggler (Oxford: Oxford University Press, 1997), 248–58.

[3] Martin Whyte and William Parish, *Urban Life in Contemporary China* (Chicago: University of Chicago Press, 1984), 85–90.

[4] Deborah Davis, "Urban Household: Supplicants to a Socialist State," in *Chinese Families in the Post-Mao Era,* ed. Deborah Davis and Stevan Harrell (Berkeley: University of California Press, 1993), 50–76.

[5] Hanlong Lu, "To Be Relatively Comfortable in an Egalitarian Society," in *The Consumer Revolution in Urban China,* ed. Deborah Davis (Berkeley: University of California Press, 2000), 124–44; Shaoguang Wang, "The Politics of Private Time," in *Urban Spaces,* ed. Deborah Davis, Richard Kraus, Barry Naughton, Elizabeth Perry (Cambridge: Cambridge University Press, 1995), 149–72; and Whyte and Parish, *Urban Life in Contemporary China,* 57–106.

[6] Xiaobo Lu, "Minor Public Economy: The Revolutionary Origins of the *Danwei,*" in *Danwei: The Changing Chinese Workplace,* ed. Xiaobo Lu and Elizabeth Perry (Armonk: M. E. Sharpe, 1997), 21–41.

[7] Kamwing Chan and Li Zhang, "The Hukou System and Rural-Urban Migration in

Then, between 1979 and 1983, Deng Xiaoping broke decisively with these ideological preferences for de-commodified modernity and collective consumption.[8] The central leadership channeled investment into the production of consumer goods, discontinued rationing for consumer durables, and advocated a substantial role for consumer markets as drivers of economic growth. For urban residents, the government's enthusiasm for personal consumption dramatically improved the average standard of living. At the outset of Deng's market reforms, only a small minority of urban households had owned a television, a washing machine, or a refrigerator. Home telephones and air conditioners were unknown outside the compounds of high officials. Twenty years later, all of these consumer items had become routine purchases (see table 12.1 below). Most remarkably, by the turn of the century urban home ownership exceeded that of the United States, rising from 15 percent in 1992 to over 80 percent in 2002.[9]

In terms of material living standards and reliance on commercial transactions, re-legitimating markets produced a consumer revolution for urban households.[10] It also reshaped a political system that for decades had relied on controlled access to necessities—what Dorothy Solinger has termed "organized solicitude"—to discipline and motivate urban citizens.[11] Deng's embrace of consumer demand, private ownership, and global markets, however, did not include loosening the political monopolies of the Leninist party-state. As one would expect, the decision to expand consumer—but not political—choice created tensions that are not unique to contemporary China but are fundamental to understanding the Chinese experience.

After 1979, officials increasingly defined national success in terms of consumer gains, and citizens in turn calibrated the legitimacy of the party-state in terms of an improved standard of living. These trends do not mean that China by the twenty-first century had become a middle-class society where consumer demands drove national politics or that all households had reaped equal consumer gains.[12] Rather, I argue, Deng's reforms so

---

China," *China Quarterly*, no. 160 (December 1999): 818–55; and Xiangming Chen, "China's City Hierarchy, Urban Policy, and Spatial Development in the 1980s," *Urban Studies* 28, no. 3 (June 1991): 341–67.

[8] Barry Naughton, *Growing out of the Plan* (Cambridge: Cambridge University Press, 1995), 59–94.

[9] Xinhua News Agency, August 9, 2002, and www.calvert-henderson.com/shelter2.

[10] Deborah Davis, "Introduction," in *Consumer Revolution in Urban China*, ed. Davis, 1–24.

[11] Dorothy Solinger, *Contesting Citizenship in Urban China* (Berkeley: University of California Press, 1999), 2.

[12] Azizur Khan and Carl Riskin, *Inequality and Poverty in China in the Age of Globalization* (Oxford: Oxford University Press, 2001); and Xueguang Zhou, "Economic Transformation and Income Inequality in Urban China," *American Journal of Sociology* 105, no. 4 (January 2000): 1135–74.

TABLE 12.1.
Ownership of consumer durables in urban households, December 2001 (across 7 income levels)

	Lowest 10%	Next 10%	Next 20%	Middle 20%	Next 20%	Next 10%	Highest 10%
Color TV	103%	109%	115%	121%	126%	132%	138%
VCR	26	31	37	43	50	54	56
Computer	4	6	8	12	17	22	26
Camera	21	26	32	40	47	54	61
Air conditioner	14	20	25	35	43	53	63
Washing machine	79	85	90	93	96	99	101
Refrigerator	63	71	77	84	88	93	95
Electric rice cooker	79	86	97	108	120	126	137
Shower	31	39	45	52	59	67	71
Stove with smoke hood	34	41	49	58	64	68	72
Mobile phone	10	15	22	32	45	53	62

Source: Zhongguo tongji nianjian 2002 [China statistical yearbook] (Beijing: Zhongguo tongji chubanshe, 2002), 330.

dramatically reduced the dependency of households on bureaucratic allocation that urban residents experienced a heightened sense of autonomy in their personal relationships. At the same time, state agents, while not endorsing formal political democracy, became increasingly tolerant of unofficial forms of sociability centered on personal consumption.[13] In the case of new urban homeowners, control over a valuable financial asset liberated them from the "organized solicitude" of the Mao years (1949–76), and the new tolerance for unofficial sociability and associational life in private realms unleashed citizen energies in directions with which the party-state became increasingly uncomfortable and conflicted. To place the experience of these new homeowners in a larger institutional and cross-national perspective, I first review the policies of the 1950s that de-commercialized urban life and turned consumers into supplicants. I then describe how the contemporary political economy opened up social and political spaces for consumer-based activism that discomforted the architects of the economic reforms.

Creating and Dismantling a Socialist Property Regime

After their 1949 victory in the Civil War, the CCP prioritized heavy industry and socialist transformation. Their development blueprint marginalized—and later obliterated—individual property rights, and the party leaders envisioned an urban property regime built on the superiority of

[13] Davis, "Introduction."

collective ownership and bureaucratic management. In 1950, all urban land became the property of the state. Current homeowners could retain the title to their homes, but they could not transfer their property rights to anyone other than a state agent or an immediate family member. Real estate development moved from the productive to the nonproductive side of accounting ledgers, and urban shelter became a welfare benefit that employers allocated according to need and seniority. The result was a socialist property regime that guaranteed the social right to shelter while dissolving the civil rights of ownership.

Over time, however, the material consequences of collectivizing real estate and erasing consumer choice became increasingly problematic. As the baby boomers of the early 1950s came of marriage age, crowding increased and building quality and maintenance deteriorated. By 1978 average per capita living space was less than it had been in 1952.[14] Partially in response to these hardships, Deng Xiaoping announced the first experiments to privatize home ownership and thereby ignited the housing reforms that dismantled the institutions of the socialist property regime by the end of the 1990s.[15] In 1988, the National People's Congress (NPC) amended the constitution to allow the transfer of land use rights. In 1990, the NPC passed an ordinance allowing cities to sell long-term leaseholds on state land and retain the profits.[16] In 1991, Shanghai adopted the Singapore model of provident funds that required both employees and employers to contribute to savings accounts dedicated to home purchase (see Garon, chap. 7). Subsequently, state banks developed a range of financial instruments for individual loans and long-term mortgages.[17] Large coastal cities aggressively courted overseas real estate developers, and a national housing reform group worked with central and local governments to clarify ownership rights for those who bought apartments that had previously been collective rentals. The most decisive break with past practice came in July 1998, when State Council Circular No. 23 announced that as of year's end employers would be out of the housing business and "welfare housing" would be restricted to a small minority of low-income households.[18]

Over the next twelve months, the central and local governments fully

[14] Whyte and Parish, *Urban Life in Contemporary China,* 79.

[15] Zhongyi Tong and R. Allen Hays, "The Transformation of the Urban Housing System in China," *Urban Affairs Review* 31, no. 5 (May 1996): 625–58; Peter Nan-shong Lee, "Housing Privatization with Chinese Characteristics," in *Social Change and Social Policy in Contemporary China,* ed. Linda Wong and Stewart MacPherson (Aldershot, England: Avebury, 1995), 126; and Yaping Wang and Alan Murie, *Housing Policy and Practice in China* (London: Macmillan, 1999), 137.

[16] Tong and Hays, "The Transformation of the Urban Housing System in China," 636–40.

[17] Deborah Davis, "From Welfare Benefit to Capitalized Asset," in *Housing and Social Change,* ed. Ray Forrest and James Lee (London: Routledge, 2003), 187–88.

[18] *Guowuyuan Gongbao* [Gazette of the State Council], 1998, 679–82.

capitalized urban housing stock by legitimating the resale of public apartments and expanding the role of commercial banks in underwriting individual loans.[19] Most critical to this final stage toward full privatization were regulations issued by the Ministry of Construction on the resale of the collectively owned apartments that had been sold to sitting tenants at highly subsidized prices. These regulations went into effect May 1, 1999.[20] Henceforth all those who held full rights to their homes, regardless if they had purchased the home privately or through a subsidized sale of their original rental units, had the right to sell the property and retain all after-tax profits.[21] Three years later, the government announced that 80 percent of previously collectively owned housing stock was in private hands.[22] For all practical purposes, the socialist system of welfare housing had vanished, and the bulk of urban housing stock had become capitalized, privately owned assets.

Did this revolution of homeownership create consumers willing to take action in defense of their new property rights, or did it simply extend the existing social rights to shelter without eroding party-state monopolies of power? Because the privatization of property rights and the expansion of consumer choice in China did not occur simultaneously with political reforms, as they had in the former Soviet Union, nor in the context of a developed capitalist economy, as in South Korea or Singapore, high levels of home ownership could have simply left urban residents politically inert within the new hybrid system of communist-capitalism.

Five years after the demise of "welfare housing," it is too soon to assess the long-term political consequences of the rapid privatization on consumer activism. But close reading of the contemporary press and recent fieldwork in the major coastal cities has led me to conclude that the homeowner revolution has unleashed social and economic forces whose autonomy the CCP had not anticipated and against which they are now imposing new constraints. Nevertheless, the rhetorical enthusiasm of the official media for consumers indicates that the leadership harbors a lower degree of ambivalence towards surging consumer spending than Sheldon Garon, Andrew Gordon, Patricia L. Maclachlan, and Laura C. Nelson in this volume have observed in Japan or South Korea during comparable years of rapid economic growth. Rather, the Chinese government's discontents are primarily with the associational autonomy and grass-roots activism that pro-market, pro-consumer economic reforms implicitly support—not with the diversion of savings to increased levels of personal consumption.

[19] Document No. 43 (1999) of the Construction Ministry, Banking Bill No. 73 (1999), State Council Decree No. 262 (1999), Banking Bill No. 129 (1999), *Guowuyuan Gongbao 1999,* 268–71, 310–11, 852–54.

[20] *Guowuyuan Gongbao,* 1999, 1005–8.

[21] *Zhongguo fang dichan bao* [Chinese real estate news], March 1, 2000, 1.

[22] Xinhua News Agency, August 9, 2003.

The Party-State's Rhetorical Embrace of Consumers

Over the decade of the 1990s, Chinese official media diversified and direct CCP control weakened. The number of officially registered newspapers and television stations grew tenfold, and the Internet created an entirely new terrain for the exchange of commercial information.[23] In 1997, Ding Lei created Netease, the first commercial Internet provider, and approximately 600,000 people logged on. By 2003, Ding was the wealthiest man in China; 68 million people per week were logging on; 48 percent of the 470,000 sites in China were commercial enterprises.[24] Nevertheless, the party-state remained vigilant against criticism of national leaders and continued to view the state-owned media as the primary tool to disseminate party-state orthodoxy throughout the country.[25] Therefore, even in the midst of heightened media commercialization, articles in the state-owned newspapers and magazines provided a template of official policy on consumers and consumer rights. To capture the positions of the party-state, I summarize results from an overview of articles published between 1995 and 2002 in the party's premier newspaper *People's Daily* [Renmin Ribao] and in *Chinese Civil Affairs* [Zhongguo minzheng], a monthly magazine sent to local officials in residential neighborhoods throughout China.[26] Because China's first Consumer Protection Law went into effect in January 1994 and China entered the WTO in 2002, one could hypothesize that between these years the official media might increase their attention to the roles of consumer rights and consumer purchases. I then situate this contemporary discourse historically by examining coverage of consumers over the past half-century.

Between January 1995 and 2002, *People's Daily* ran 6,154 stories containing the word *consumer.* At the same time, there were only 117 articles that mentioned both consumers and excessive luxury, and only 181 that discussed consumers and waste. Moreover, over these eight years this pairing of consumption and excess declined, while those including both consumers and waste remained steady at about 3 percent.[27]

[23] In 1978, there were 186 newspapers, 32 television stations, and about 15,000 new book titles. In 2001, there were over 2,000 newspapers, 350 television stations, and 154,000 new book titles. *Zhongguo tongji nianjian 2002,* 758–60.

[24] Yi Hu, "Internet Users on Mainland," *South China Morning Post,* online edition, July 22, 2003; and Andrew Collier, "Netease Chief Tops Forbes," *South China Morning Post,* online edition, October 31, 2003.

[25] Bu Wei, "Shehui xingbie shijiaozhong de zhuanbo xin jishu yu nuxing" [New communications technology and women], *FunuYanjiu* [Women's studies], no. 3 (2003): 13–18. Guobin Yang, "The Co-evolution of the Internet in Civil Society in China," *Asian Survey* 43, no. 3 (May/June 2003): 405–22; and Jonathan Zittrain and Benjamin Edleman, "Empirical Analysis of Internet Filtering in China," 2002, http://cyber.law.harvard.edu/filtering/china.

[26] Practical considerations also necessitated this time interval. In 2004 when the research for this essay was completed, electronic archives for *Chinese Civil Affairs* did not go back further than 1994.

[27] Between 1994 and 2002, 117 articles contained the words *consumer* and *luxury* (*haohua*),

The decline of negative stories on consumption in *People's Daily* did not translate into explicit support for consumer rights. Only 18 percent of the selected articles included any mention of consumer rights or interests, and the specific phrase "consumer rights" appeared only seven times between 1995 and 2002. Nevertheless, it was noticeable that the first two articles in *People's Daily* to describe homeowners as activist consumers presented the government as standing on the side of the consumer.[28] In both cases, residents initiated complaints of shoddy construction by approaching the local government and party leaders and then seeking monetary compensation from the private contractors through the courts.

Overall, between 1995 and 2002, *People's Daily* presented consumers as economic actors who improved the functioning of the macro-economy. Reporters explained that because consumers shop for the best quality at the lowest price, they send signals to producers that increase overall efficiency and eliminate damaging monopolies.[29] In one March 1995 editorial, the writer went so far as to praise the perfect virtue of consumers who in their purchasing decisions are free of all selfishness.[30] More startling, reporters invoked the very icons of orthodox Leninism when writing about the need for officials to be responsive to consumer complaints. One such citation appeared in a January 4, 1995, article that favorably identified consumers not only as "gods" but also as those whom party organizations should serve in the spirit of Lei Feng.[31]

For a political party committed to the superiority of atheism, praise for such deities is remarkable, but drawing on the iconic Maoist hero Lei Feng is even more striking. Lei Feng was a People's Liberation Army soldier lionized during the Cultural Revolution for his life of ascetic simplicity. So the reporter's exhortation for government officials to serve consumers in the spirit of Lei Feng represents a conspicuously positive endorsement of consumers in the official discourse of post-Mao modernity.

With a narrower readership of government employees, *Chinese Civil Affairs* might be expected to have departed from broad messages in support of consumer gains and to have exhorted local administrators to eliminate specific consumer behaviors that degraded neighborhood life or impeded local governance. Yet in contrast to the South Korean and Japanese gov-

---

and 181 contained the words *consumer* and *waste* (*liangfei*). In 1995, in 4.4 percent of all articles in which consumers were mentioned, there was also discussion of luxury. After 2000 the percentage never went above 1.5 percent. For *waste*, the percentages remained steady at approximately 3 percent.

[28] *Renmin ribao* [People's daily], March 1, 1998, 4, provided an account of a dispute over quality of construction in a government-subsidized building in Qinghai that had been subcontracted to a private construction company. *Renmin ribao,* March 4, 1998, 10, described the grievances of a group of homeowners in a privately built commercial estate in Zhejiang.

[29] *Renmin ribao,* October 12, 1998, 4; December 3, 1998, 3; and May 12, 1999, 2.

[30] *Renmin ribao,* March 16, 1995, 6.

[31] *Renmin ribao,* January 4, 1995, 10.

ernments' emphasis on frugality and savings campaigns, the editorials of *Chinese Civil Affairs* never once charged officials to mount anti-consumption campaigns or to cast consumers as unpatriotic.[32] If anything, the editors rather consistently adopted a consumerist language and in particular focused on the economic benefits of creating fee-paying "consumers" for traditional welfare programs.[33]

The Party-State's Rhetoric in Historical Perspective

During the run-up to their entry into the WTO, it is not surprising that Chinese leaders moved quickly to speak in a pro-consumer discourse compatible with the expansion of global commodity chains and international trade. But to understand why a firmly established Communist leadership made the transition from plan to market with so little ideological trauma, it is helpful to place the party-state's rhetoric in a longer historical perspective. Figure 12.1 charts both the number of *People's Daily* articles that contained the word *consumer* (*xiaofeizhe*) at least once and, among those articles, all those in which the word *waste* (*langfei*) also appeared. During the 1950s, *People's Daily* published 1,297 articles with the word *consumer* and 203 articles with both *consumer* and *waste*. During the decade of the Cultural Revolution (1966–76), consumers virtually disappeared from the pages of *People's Daily*. But after market reforms took off in 1978, references to the consumer rose steadily and after 1991 never fell below 500 in any given year. Not only did consumers appear ever more frequently on the pages of *People's Daily*, but between 1995 and 2003 consumers became even more visible than either workers or university students.[34] Such enumerations capture only the grossest distinctions, but they do demonstrate that the party's premier daily erased consumers from its pages only in the years of the Cultural Revolution. Even in the heady days of the Great Leap Forward (1958–60) to accelerate the realization of communism, the party rarely linked consumers and waste. Instead, in accordance with Marxist orthodoxy, the CCP has used consumer gains as a material metric of the party's wisdom.

32 Based on electronic search of all issues, 1994–2002, http://online.eastview.com/cnki.

33 See, for example, Civil Affairs Social Investigation Group, "Yindi zhiyi" [Seek gain according to local conditions], *Zhongguo minzheng* (June 2000): 26–28; and Sun Taojun, "Tansu shequ fuli jujia yanglaomoshi" [Investigate thoroughly a model of district welfare home care], *Zhongguo minzheng* (November 2000): 15–16.

34 *Renmin ribao,* accessible at http://willard.library.yale.edu, reported 681 articles that included at least one reference to consumers, 504 to university students, 1,231 to workers, 3,450 to peasants, and 4,074 to the masses in 1995. For 2003, the comparable frequencies were 1,126 to consumers, 814 to students, 1,058 to workers, 3,768 to peasants, and 6,621 to the masses.

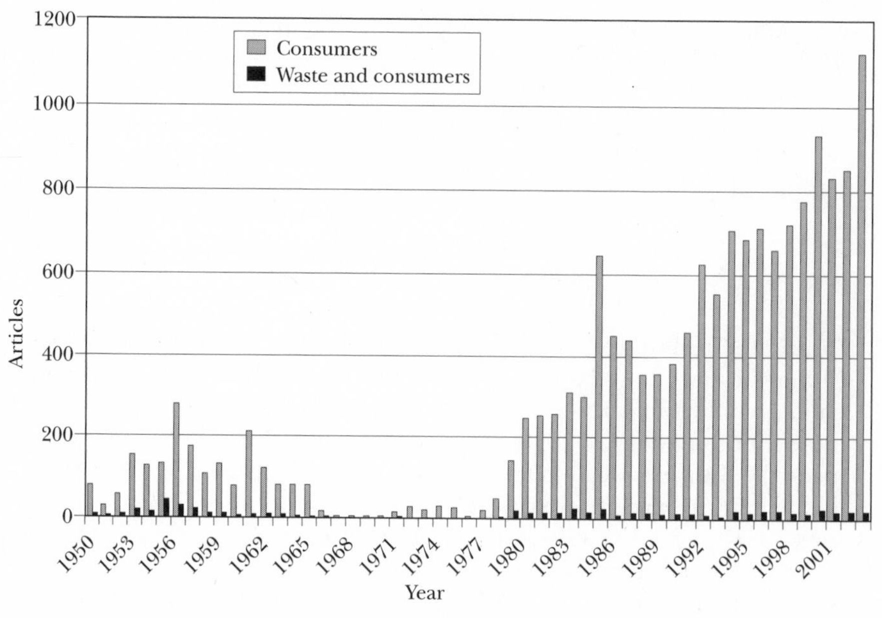

Source: http://willard.library.yale.edu

Figure 12.1. Coverage of consumers and waste in *People's Daily*, 1950–2003

The Consumer Protection Law

In October 1993, the National People's Congress passed China's first Consumer Protection Law.[35] In September of the same year, the NPC had passed the Law Against Unfair Trade and, a year later, the Advertising Law and the Compensation Law.[36] Together these four pieces of legislation established the legal framework that articulated individual rights in the consumer marketplace. Most relevant to urban homeowners, the Consumer Protection Law guaranteed consumers the right to correct information (Articles 8 and 13), the right to choose and exercise supervision over commodities and services (Articles 9 and 15), the right to fair trade including fair measurement (Article 10), the right to receive compensation for damages (Articles 11, 35, 36, 37, 38, 39, and 49), and the right to form social groups to safeguard legitimate rights and interests (Articles 12, 31, and 32). In addition, the law required the state to listen to consumer opinions

[35] For English translations, see http://www.qis.net/chinalaw/prclaw26.htm.

[36] Copies of these laws can be found on the website of the China Consumers' Association, www.cca.org.cn, and www.lawbase.com.cn.

when formulating laws (Article 26) and the courts to simplify the procedures for consumers to file lawsuits (Article 30).

Since 1994, the Consumer Protection Law has also gained prominence in official publications directed at professionals. In 2003, the weekly magazine of the China Law Society identified the Consumer Protection Law as one of the ten most influential laws enacted since the beginning of market reform.[37] To illustrate the significance of the law's impact on Chinese society, the Law Society cited surveys that showed an increase of more than 50 percent in the number of consumers filing for damages between 1994 and 1999; by 1999, it reported, even those whose losses were less than 2,000 yuan (approximately $240) were routinely seeking compensation.[38]

In the same year, one also finds official support for applying the law's consumer protections to homeowners. Previously, a major obstacle for homeowners seeking to invoke the law's provisions had been sellers' arguments that the Consumer Protection Law did not apply to the purchase of housing. In particular, sellers argued that homebuyers had no right to invoke the law's Article 49, which guaranteed compensation of double the sale price whenever consumers could prove that merchants had sold a fraudulent product or shoddy service. During the late 1990s, consumer activist Wang Hai popularized this principle of "double compensation," tirelessly publicizing his success via television appearances and his own website.[39] News of his success reached even the pages of *Chinese Civil Affairs,* motivating one local official to publish an article explaining why the "hero" Wang Hai didn't have to pay income tax on the refunds he got from merchants who had sold him faulty merchandise.[40] Whenever homeowners tried to follow Wang Hai's example and invoke Article 49, however, developers argued that Article 49 applied only to moveable items for daily use, and the courts generally agreed.[41] Then, in 2003, the official government organ of the real estate industry wrote that the Consumer Protection Law *did* cover homebuyers because consumer protection laws in other countries extend to home purchases and the original law placed no restrictions on the protection of purchases.[42] When the house organ of the

[37] "Gaozao zhongguo de shida jingdian li" [Majors laws during ten years of Chinese reforms], *Minzu yu fazhi shibao,* March 12, 2002, 12–15.

[38] "Gaozao zhongguo de shida jingdian li," 14.

[39] See http://www.wanghai.com/business.

[40] Chengning Ren, "'Dajia' yingxiong gaibugai nashui?" [For destroying fakes, must a hero pay taxes?], *Zhongguo minzheng* (September 1996): 6.

[41] In 2002, the muckraking weekly of Guangzhou, *Nanfang zhoumo,* gave extensive coverage to homeowners who had been swindled and could find no legal redress. See *Nanfang zhoumo,* January 24, 2002, 5; for stories on home owners in Wuhan, see March 7, 2002, 15; in Guiyang, Beijing, Guangzhou, and Shanghai, April 11, 2002, 8; in Beijing, April 18, 2002, 7; in Shanxi and Tianjin, April 25, 2002, 25–28; in Chongqing, Guangzhou, Pan Yu, and Shanghai, September 12, 2002, 14; in Shanghai, September 26, 2002, 9.

[42] Huidong Chen and Zhao Li, "Goumaizhe shi xiaofeizhe" [Home buyers are consumers], *Zhongguo fangdi chan,* no. 3 (March 2003): 41–45.

state real estate industry speaks unambiguously in support of consumers and explicitly against past court rulings, millions of homeowners interested in suing and hiring consultants to defend their claims gain principled support from the agents of the party-state.

By legally defining consumer rights and repeatedly endorsing the civil rights of citizens, recent party-state discourse may be distinguished from that of the first four decades of CCP rule. However, throughout its existence, the Communist party-state has disregarded the letter of the law whenever individual entitlements threatened its monopolies of power, and courts have rarely enforced claims of individuals against those of the party-state.[43] Therefore, it would be naive to read the new Consumer Protection Law as either a consistently enforceable contract between citizens and the government or as an unambiguous endorsement of consumer activism. On the other hand, because the passage of the Consumer Protection Law occurred within an expansion of legal rights that empowered citizens and weakened their dependence on local state agents, the law has provided a rights-based "road map" to guide aggrieved consumers in their struggles for compensation. Between 1982 and 2004, China revised its constitution four times to provide more legal protection to market institutions, and Chinese citizens gained substantial new rights and protections, particularly in civil disputes.[44] While Chinese citizens remain constrained by the politicization of the courts and the monopoly power of the CCP, top-down legal reforms have opened up a social and legal space in which consumers could mobilize.[45] Legal scholar Benjamin Liebman recently demonstrated how consumer demands for compensation, as stipulated in the several consumer protection laws, created important precedents for future consumer plaintiffs by strengthening the more general application of the Civil Procedure Law to class action suits.[46] Precedents do not, of course, guarantee enforcement. Given the difficult history of consumer activism in democratic capitalist societies, we would be prudent to interpret the recent legal gains of Chinese consumers not as a clear victory but rather as improved terms of engagement.

As fieldwork done in several of China's largest cities documents, even when buyers fail in court, they become ever more aware of their rights as consumers and more sophisticated in how they will subsequently protect their interests.[47] In response, local leaders find themselves forced to con-

[43] Kevin O'Brien and Lianjiang Li, "Suing the Local State," *China Journal*, no. 51 (January 2004): 75–96.

[44] Stanley Lubman, *Bird in a Cage* (Stanford: Stanford University Press, 1999), 250–319.

[45] Lubman, *Bird in a Cage*, 318–19.

[46] Benjamin Liebman, "Class Action Litigation in China," *Harvard Law Review* 111, no. 6 (April 1998): 1523–41.

[47] Benjamin Read, "Democratizing the Neighborhood," *China Journal*, no. 49 (January 2003): 31–60; Luigi Tomba, "Creating an Urban Middle Class," *China Journal*, no. 51 (Janu-

sider new associational forms to cope with more rights-conscious reside
who cannot be easily dismissed or ignored.

I next draw on my own observations of one Shanghai estate betwe
2002 and 2004 to illustrate how officials—committed to providing co
sumer services and rhetorically endorsing the rights of consumers—r
mained vigilant in curtailing organized consumer activism.

The Limits of Consumer Power in a Communist Party–State

Throughout the Mao years, a nested honeycomb of party-state control extended into every urban neighborhood through a system of residents' committees that were tightly linked and subordinated to the next higher level of city government.[48] The committees oversaw sanitation, maintained the household registries, and, after 1978, monitored compliance with the one-child campaign and the re-employment of laid-off workers. On average, a committee of five to eight residents supervised four hundred to six hundred families living in adjacent buildings.

During the early 1990s, city governments seeking to professionalize municipal services appointed nonresident administrative staff to the residents' committees.[49] However, by the end of the decade party leaders reversed course and again looked to local residents to "strengthen the connections and emotions between the party and the masses."[50] Despite their desire to reinsert party power into the neighborhood fabric, home ownership and the new consumer freedoms that had destroyed the "organized solicitude" of the Mao years challenged an easy return to past practice. Two specific market-based innovations of the commercial residential estates—management companies and owners' committees—assumed key obligations that had previously fallen under the jurisdiction of the residents' committees. Management companies and owners' committees first appeared after 1994 in estates built by Hong Kong and Singaporean developers.[51] Both organizations subsequently appeared in commercial estates throughout China. The management companies were fee-charging busi-

---

ary 2004): 1–26; and Tomba, "To Rebel is Justified," paper presented at the conference "Globalization, the State and Urban Transformation in China," Hong Kong Baptist University, December 15–17, 2003.

[48] Benjamin L. Read, "State, Social Networks, and Citizens in China's Urban Neighborhoods," Ph.D. dissertation, Harvard University, 2003; and Benjamin Read, "Revitalizing the State's Urban 'Nerve Tips,'" *China Quarterly*, no. 163 (September 2000): 806–20.

[49] Read, "Revitalizing the State's Urban 'Nerve Tips.'"

[50] *Renmin ribao*, June 24, 2001, 1.

[51] There is some disagreement if the first owners' committees were established in 1994 or 1997, and if they were proactive or reactive experiments by the state. See Read, "Democratizing the Neighborhood"; and Tomba, "Creating an Urban Middle Class" and "To Rebel is Justified."

sanitation services, routine building maintenance, ds. Owners' committees, on the other hand, were vol- ciations that represented the consumer interests of gotiations with the management company, the devel- , and the local government.

ther scholars between 1999 and 2002 indicated that al- e party-state supported consumer empowerment through committees, in practice officials opposed the associational nised in Articles 12, 31, and 32 of the Consumer Protection interviews in one Shanghai estate—which I will call West- illustrate how one local government responded when newly consumers attempted to act upon their new consumer rights. Garden is a commercial estate selling two- and three-bedroom at prices that are average for new neighborhoods outside the . The first buyers moved in during 1994, and by July 2002 there e than nine thousand residents. In April 2004, the estate had its planned capacity of 4,300 units with more than twelve thousand s. Like most new commercial estates in urban China, Western Gar- gated community that the developer has marketed as much for its n lifestyle as its location or price. The developer maintains an elabo- vebsite with multiple chatrooms where residents can register com- ts or link up with other residents for a wide range of recreational vities.[53] The website also has multiple links to real estate listings in ad- ning estates and in other cities of China. Pop-up advertisements and short deo clips constantly move across the screen promoting a wide variety of onsumer services as well as new real estate offerings of the developer.

Western Garden is not exclusively a residential neighborhood. Within the estate there are many private businesses. Stores, beauty salons, and restaurants occupy the ground floor in the oldest buildings, facing parking spaces and interior roads. In the latest phase of construction, retailers cluster in a two-story mini-mall across the street from the central administration building and tennis courts. It was in this mall during a visit in April 2004.that I observed a striking documentation of the explicit link between homeownership and consumers. On more than fifty light posts the developer had installed multicolored banners promoting his newest logo. There were similar promotional decorations along residential sidewalks in other developments I had visited. But only in Western Garden did I find a logo that so explicitly defined residential areas as neighborhoods built around

[52] Read, "Democratizing the Neighborhood"; Tomba, "Creating an Urban Middle Class" and "To Rebel Is Justified"; and conversations at the Chinese University of Hong Kong with doctoral candidate Belinda Liu, who conducted fieldwork in 2003 and 2004 in one estate in Shenzhen.

[53] To guarantee confidentially I cannot give the exact web address, but comparable websites can be found through the main portal, http://www.house.focus.cn.

consumers and consumption. At Western Garden, the banners read, "consumers make neighbors."

When I first visited Western Garden, the residents' committee occupied a five-room suite in one of the oldest residential blocks; by 2004 the committee had moved to new quarters in a building that also housed a rental agency and the offices of the management company. When I asked in 2002 why the residents' committee had such large accommodations within a private estate, the party secretary of the committee explained that government regulations require developers to provide space for a residents' committee in proportion to building construction.

In her briefing, the party secretary read directly from a promotional script of the developer. She stressed that the estate was a "closed community" that since 1995 had been recognized as a city-level "civilized district," a designation the city government grants to residential neighborhoods that have had no sanitation violations, no reports of crime, and no members of the heterodox religious group Falun Gong. In 2004, a rental agent told me that the designation of "civilized district" also increased real estate values.

When the first tenants moved to Western Garden in 1994, the developer sponsored a directly elected owners' committee. However, in 1998, after the leaders of the owners' committee had tried to mobilize other owners to seek compensation for shoddy building materials, the district government installed a residents' committee and greatly restricted the powers of future owners' committees. The party secretary explained that because the owners' committee included many non-owners, the local government deemed the original organization illegal. Subsequently, the residents' committee asked each household to nominate one member to vote for seven representatives whose main duties were to operate a nightly telephone hotline. Nevertheless, the party secretary told me that she found it difficult to control non–party members, unfavorably comparing the activism among the members of the owners' committee to that of residents who had volunteered to host informational sessions for perspective buyers.

In Western Garden, we observe a situation in which the government has withdrawn support for a consumerist organization that it had once endorsed as an ideal form of community governance for new commercial estates. We also see a merging of state and market authority over private residential space as well as the marked commercialization of the official obligations of local government staff. In Western Garden, the Chinese party-state has become deeply implicated in—if not comfortable with—consumer politics. It speaks in the language of individual consumer rights when it encourages citizens to rely on their own initiative and entrepreneurship but becomes ambivalent or hostile when consumers use their autonomy to challenge party-state political monopolies or business partnerships with private developers. In Western Garden the party-state still holds the balance of power, and it is not obvious when the provisions of the Consumer Protection Law will live up to its high praise by the China Law Society as one of the most influential legal reforms since 1980. However, the difficulties of Chinese consumers in realizing legal promises are attributable not only to an authoritarian Communist polity. As suggested by historical work on the ebb and flow of consumer power in America, the struggles of the Japanese consumer movement, and the changing political influence of British consumers, consumerism is not a consistently robust and powerful political force.[54]

Consumer identity rarely provides a focus for broad-based citizen activism. In contrast to business associations or large corporations, consumer organizations are weak because they cannot easily tax members or redirect profits to fund lengthy legal battles. In China, the CCP's hostility to any form of pluralist politics, the legal constraints on all NGOs, and the weakness of civil society further challenge consumer activism.[55] The defeat of the owners in Western Garden is a case in point. To readers familiar with the Maoist assault on all forms of material pleasures and the criminalization of private entrepreneurship during the Cultural Revolution, the possibility of citizen-consumers wresting legal protection from a still-strong Communist Party may seem rather fanciful.[56] Nevertheless, the party-state offers rhetorical support for consumers in the official media as well as explicit legislative protection for consumer rights; the consumer activist Wang Hai has become a celebrity; and consumerist organizations like the owners' committees continue to exist, even if they have not always realized their initially envisioned autonomy. These developments have made consumer activism and struggles over consumer rights part of the contemporary political landscape. The Consumer Protection Law continues to spawn court cases and facilitate out-of-court compensation. Each new estate must have an owners' committee comprised of elected members and possessing the right to meet with and canvas residents. Moreover, because several structural trends in the macro-economy support a central role for consumer spending and consumer satisfaction, the role of citizen-consumer in urban China is likely to become increasingly salient during the first decade of the twenty-first century despite the persistent ambivalence of the current leadership.

[54] Lizabeth Cohen, *A Consumers' Republic: The Politics of Mass Consumption in Postwar America* (New York: Knopf, 2003); Patricia L. Maclachlan, *Consumer Politics in Postwar Japan: The Institutional Boundaries of Citizen Activism* (New York: Columbia University Press, 2002); and Frank Trentmann in this volume.

[55] Stanley Lubman, *Bird in a Cage,* 298–319; O'Brien and Li, "Suing the Local State"; Read, "Democratizing the Neighborhood"; and Tomba, "Creating an Urban Middle Class."

[56] Anita Chan, *Children of Mao* (London: Macmillan, 1985); Nian Cheng, *Life and Death in Shanghai* (New York: Grove Press, 1986); B. Michael Frolic, *Mao's People* (Cambridge: Harvard University Press, 1980); and Heng Liang and Judith Shapiro, *Son of the Revolution* (New York: Knopf, 1983).

Conclusion

During the 1990s, Chinese city dwellers became a population of homeowners who defined themselves—and were defined by the official media—as consumers and proprietors with the rights to seek compensation and to organize to protect their property interests. Private ownership empowered citizens as consumers, and in the Consumer Protection Law, the party-state provided national legislation that extended civil rights to citizens as consumers. These gains for urban homeowners occurred because the CCP leadership had fundamentally abandoned the Maoist developmental plan of ascetic autarky that had previously constrained consumer spending and consumer autonomy. By the early 1990s, the leadership had adopted growth strategies that prioritized investment in light industry and consumer goods (conforming to GATT and later WTO regulations for nations with huge reservoirs of semi-skilled labor). Within this global division of labor, the Chinese economy grew steadily, disposable per capita income rose dramatically, and rising Chinese consumption became an engine of growth.[57]

The size of China's huge domestic market and the enormous pent-up demand after decades of sacrifice for public investment played a crucial role in the consumer revolution of the 1990s. These factors will continue to be consequential in the near future. By 2002, China had both the world's largest population and, according to Nicholas Lardy, "the highest saving rate of any major nation."[58] As a result, Chinese leaders look for future growth in domestic consumer markets as much as in increased exports to Japan, North America, and the European Union. High levels of ownership of consumer durables across all income levels, as seen in table 12.1, indicate the substantial gains in living standards, and high rates of household saving and sustained growth in per capita income suggest even greater consumer spending through the first decades of the twenty-first century. Figure 12.2 below summarizes the steady increase in cumulative and annual saving rates between 1978 and 2002. Following a period when both rural and urban households experienced a nearly fourfold increase in the real value of their consumption, household accumulated savings exceeded 80 percent of 2002 GDP; household savings in that one year approached 14 percent of GDP.[59]

It may appear paradoxical that the leadership of one of the few remaining Communist nations so unambiguously embraces consumer spending as an engine for national prosperity. But when one examines the

[57] Nicholas Lardy, *Integrating China into the Global Economy* (Washington D.C.: Brookings Institute Press, 2002), 1–22; and Naughton, *Growing out of the Plan,* 309–25.

[58] Lardy, *Integrating China into the Global Economy,* 3.

[59] *Zhongguo tongji nianjian 2002,* 68.

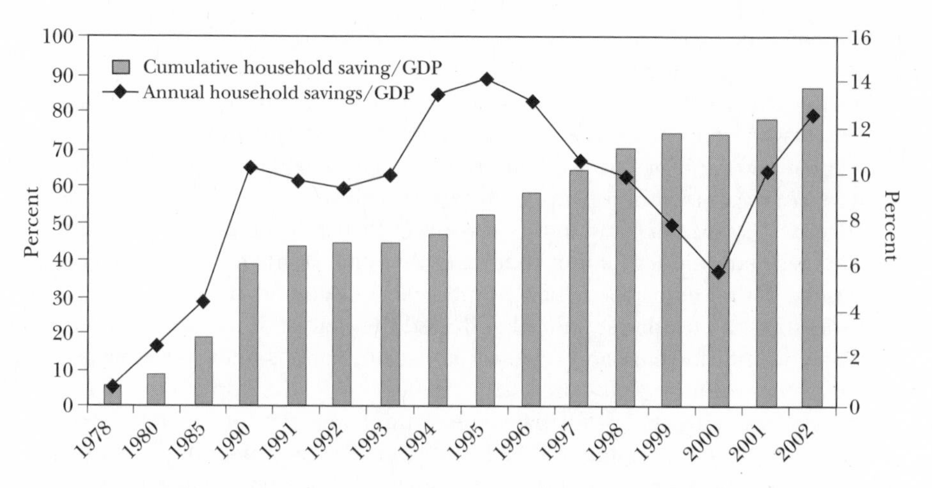

Source: Compiled from data in the online version of *Zhongguo tongji nianjian 2003*. Table created by Professor Shaoguang Wang at the Chinese University of Hong Kong, May 2004.

Figure 12.2. Cumulative and annual household savings rates, 1978–2002

unfolding of the Chinese consumer revolution within the context of China's recent past, the Communist leadership's enthusiasm is more understandable. China has enjoyed the most sustained economic growth in its history because of investment policies geared to world consumer markets. Yet the long-term future for the world's sixth-largest economy lies as much in its huge domestic market as in exporting to consumers in the industrialized world. Therefore, unlike the small city-state of Singapore, or even medium-sized Malaysia and South Korea, China can look inward to its 1.3 billion consumers as the key to becoming the world's second-largest economy by 2030. Unlike their orthodox Maoist predecessors, moreover, recent political leaders have chosen not to view personal consumption as a zero-sum threat to investment and saving.

Misgivings about consumers occur among Chinese leaders not when officials see ordinary people spending more of their incomes on cars, leisure travel, or restaurant meals, but when consumers demand legal rights and associational autonomy. Thus, as we observe at Western Garden, challenges to political authority, as opposed to ideological ambivalence about increased consumer spending, constitute the primary source of the government's discomfort with consumer culture.

To date, the weakness of the courts and the extensive police powers of the local state have severely limited consumer activism. Other actions of the party-state, however, serve to legitimate and encourage consumer activism, even shifting power toward consumers. For example, the rhetorical support for consumer autonomy in the official media as well as such consumer-friendly laws as the Consumer Protection Law (1993), the Advertising Law (1994), and the Compensation Law (1994) provide well-publicized justification for consumer activism. Praise for Wang Hai in the pages of *Chinese Civil Affairs* and the invocation of Lei Feng as a model for consumers in *People's Daily* place the party-state publicly on the side of consumers. Among scholars who have studied growing activism among rural residents and industrial workers, there is substantial evidence that ordinary Chinese citizens have succeeded in defending their interests when they have been able to "talk back" to state agents in the language of the state's own discourse. Thus, as Kevin O'Brien discovered in his analysis of the successes of rural protestors during the 1990s, when ordinary people become informed of their legal rights they "exploit the symbolic and material capital made available by the communist party-state itself" and force the Chinese state to compromise with their "rightful resistance."[60]

The commodification of public goods has reduced the dependence of urban residents on state provisions and enlarged the space for consumers to be decision-makers. In Western Garden, we observed how old modes of governance continue to limit consumer activism and civic autonomy. However, at the level of the macro-economy, the environment has decisively shifted away from government control and supervision. Even residents' committees share responsibility for serving the neighborhood with market and voluntary associations—the management company and the owners' committees. Because the law clearly protects consumer rights, the party-state itself has legitimated the economic and political institutions that could support active citizen-consumers.

Successful institutionalization of the formal promises to Chinese consumers will require at least as much struggle as consumer movements have confronted in democratic capitalist nations such as the United States, Britain, and Japan. The government's opposition to free-ranging owners' committees and the inability of consumers to receive compensation even when the courts decide in their favor are just some of the barriers to consumer-citizenship in contemporary China. At the same time, the party-state has so thoroughly valorized free markets and consumers as essential agents in the national project of modernization that it can neither easily refute the validity of consumer autonomy nor maintain a firewall between the rights of Chinese consumers and the civic rights of citizens.

[60] Kevin O'Brien, "Rightful Resistance," *World Politics* 49, no. 1 (October 1996): 34.

INDEX

Numbers in italics refer to figures and tables.